JUSTICE AND THE POOR

PATTERSON SMITH REPRINT SERIES IN
CRIMINOLOGY, LAW ENFORCEMENT, AND SOCIAL PROBLEMS

A listing of publications in the SERIES *will be found at rear of volume*

PUBLICATION NO. 139: PATTERSON SMITH REPRINT SERIES IN CRIMINOLOGY, LAW ENFORCEMENT, AND SOCIAL PROBLEMS

JUSTICE AND THE POOR

A STUDY OF THE PRESENT DENIAL OF JUSTICE TO THE POOR
AND OF THE AGENCIES MAKING MORE EQUAL
THEIR POSITION BEFORE THE LAW
WITH PARTICULAR REFERENCE TO LEGAL AID WORK
IN THE UNITED STATES

BY

REGINALD HEBER SMITH

OF THE BOSTON BAR

*Reprinted from the Third Edition
with the addition of an introductory essay
"Legal Aid and Elitism in the American Legal Profession"
by Ronald M. Pipkin*

MONTCLAIR, N.J.

PATTERSON SMITH

1972

First edition published 1919 by
the Carnegie Foundation for the Advancement of Teaching

Third and last edition published 1924

Third edition republished 1972 by
Patterson Smith Publishing Corporation
Montclair, New Jersey 07042

New material copyright © 1972 by
Patterson Smith Publishing Corporation

Library of Congress Cataloging in Publication Data

Smith, Reginald Heber, 1889–1966.
Justice and the poor.

(Patterson Smith reprint series in criminology, law
enforcement, and social problems. Publication no.
139)

Reprint, with a new introductory essay, of the
1924 ed., which was issued as Bulletin no. 13 of the
Carnegie Foundation for the Advancement of
Teaching.

Includes bibliographical references.

1. Legal assistance to the poor—United States.
I. Title. II. Series: Carnegie Foundation for the
Advancement of Teaching. Bulletin no. 13.

KF390.5.P6S55   1972   347'.73'1   79-129316
ISBN 0-87585-139-8

This book is printed on
permanent/durable paper

ANALYSIS OF CONTENTS

CONTENTS

LEGAL AID AND ELITISM
IN THE AMERICAN LEGAL PROFESSION

BY RONALD M. PIPKIN

REGINALD HEBER SMITH's treatise *Justice and the Poor*, first published in 1919, is now a landmark in legal aid literature and the legal aid movement. It was the first major attempt to argue on behalf of the interests of the poor in the legal system of newly industrialized America. It was the first systematic survey of existing efforts to reduce inequities in the administration of justice, meager though these efforts were. It was a reformer's tract which spoke to and influenced not only the bench and the bar but the public as well. Smith, and those who supported his work, intended this book to mobilize public opinion and the bar on behalf of the nascent legal aid movement.

At the time of Smith's writing, with fifty years of lucrative practice in the "Age of Enterprise" behind it, the bar had no interest in the small man with the small claim, especially the alien immigrant living in the urban slums. Yet lawyers, partly to insure their own indispensability to developing capitalism, had created a legal process so complicated that few laymen, let alone the ignorant and unresourceful, could pursue their own legal remedies. Perhaps more importantly in Smith's view, the indifference of the legal system and the bar to the problems of the poor had not only created an injustice but had directly contributed to the corruption of society itself. The inability of poor persons to enforce the rights afforded them by law had promoted their own exploitation; it had perverted the promise of the American Dream.

Smith stated his case with the fervor of a revolutionist:

> The system not only robs the poor of their only protection, but it places in the hands of their oppressors the most powerful and ruthless weapon ever invented. The law itself becomes the means of extortion. [p. 9]

> The poor come to think of American justice as containing only laws that punish and never laws that help. They are against the law because they consider the law against them. A persuasion spreads that there is one law for the rich and another for the poor. [p. 10]

The language was meant to provoke, but Smith was not a radical or revolutionary. He saw no class bias in the law: "The substantive law, with minor exceptions, is eminently fair and impartial" (p. 15). He did not see the rules of law as reinforcing the unequal distribution of wealth and power in the country or as fostering rather than inhibiting the exploitation of the poor and the working classes.[1] No injustice lay in the doctrine of freedom of contract when applied to the markedly unequal relationship between worker and capitalist employer. No injustice lay in the legal exploitation of tenant by landlord, debtor by creditor, where the laws favored one class over the other, nor in the large-scale violation of personal rights by legal officials. "The existing denial of justice to the poor," said Smith, "is not attributable to any injustice in the heart of the law itself" (p. 15). The injustice, Smith held, occurred in the misadministration of a basically just system—court delay, complex legal procedures, high court costs, the lack of inexpensive legal counsel. The system needed reforming, but what it needed was procedural reforms—legal aid, smallclaims courts, conciliation and arbitration procedures, administrative agencies, etc.—not a substantive reallocation of power.

In Smith's view, the state provided to all citizens, rich and poor alike, all components of justice,[2] except one. The legal system—the state's forum of justice—was unexcelled in its provision of just rules, just procedures, and just judges. But it did not provide lawyers. There a laissez-faire model prevailed. If legal counsel were readily available, no person who felt wronged would need to look outside the law and the state for more radical means of obtaining justice. If the bar were to make legal services accessible to the poor, a denial of justice would not exist. Such accessibility once prevailed, Smith said, but after the commencement of the American industrial revolution (circa 1870) "the largest and best [law] offices gave up general practice and engaged exclusively in business and corporation law. The charity work which had always been a part of the older type of office was discarded under the pressure of the new era" (p. 85). The elite law firms no longer willingly took on the burden of the poor. The lower-class members of the bar could not be relied on to do it. To Smith the answer was clear: a program of legal aid.

Smith believed that legal aid could avert injustice by merely making lawyers available to the poor. The need for an attorney arose from technical aspects of the law. Once the problems of "pleadings, procedure, and evidence have been eliminated, there is nothing left for the lawyer to do" (p. 72). But the value of the legal-aid attorney to society went beyond giving legal services to the poor. Clients were not only poor people with legal problems—they were often themselves problems for the legal system and society. A large part of the legal-aid lawyer's role was to adjust clients' expectations to the justice of the American

---

[1] It is important to realize that in the late nineteenth and early twentieth centuries the poor and the working class were basically the same societal subsection—one which corresponded, furthermore, very largely with the foreign born. See Herman P. Miller (ed.), *Poverty American Style* (Wadsworth Publishing Co., Belmont, California, 1968), pp. 6, 18; Don D. Lescohier, "Working Conditions," in John R. Commons (ed.), *History of Labor in the United States 1896-1932*, Vol. III (Macmillan Co., New York, 1935), pp. 41, 62.

[2] It is a basic tenet of the legal profession that law has a monopoly on justice. The slogan WHERE LAW ENDS TYRANNY BEGINS is engraved on the Department of Justice Building in Washington, D.C.

system[3] and, where necessary, to divert their clients' hostilities away from the system itself (a process which has come to be called "cooling out"). Smith wrote approvingly of legal aid societies who placed "their duty to the court before their duty to the client."[4] The poor were "served," but more often society and its dominant interests were the client.

If the reforming programs outlined in *Justice and the Poor* were widely accepted, Smith believed, then tremendous benefits would accrue to society. Class hostilities would diminish, the turbulent marketplace would return to stability, and the poor's disposition toward righteous conflict would be diverted. Society would be cleansed of its anarchistic elements, and the confidence of poor people in lawyers and the legal system would be re-established.

CONTROLLING ACCESS TO THE PROFESSION

Justice and the Poor was one report in a series of professional studies commissioned and published by the Carnegie Corporation. In 1905, Andrew Carnegie had established the Carnegie Foundation for the Advancement of Teaching. Henry S. Pritchett, former president of the Massachusetts Institute of Technology, was appointed its first president. The foundation was one of five major endowments embodying Carnegie's *noblesse oblige* "gospel of wealth." (Elihu Root, a man prominent in the legal profession and politics during this period, was made president of the Carnegie Endowment for International Peace. He played an important role in providing liaison between the Carnegie organizations and the national bar.) The endowment gave Pritchett the opportunity to develop his interest in the expansion of university-based professional education. He approached both the American Medical Association and the American Bar Association for authorization to study the educational and pre-professional training programs in their professions. The American Medical Association was immediately responsive. Since 1901 the organization had been using political pressure, with limited success, to try to eliminate all non-university-based medical schools and to gain control of educational and licensure requirements for physicians. The medical association was swayed by Pritchett's assurance that the proposed study would contribute substantially to

---

[3] For example, in 1902 a lawyer at the East Side Branch (facetiously called the Hebrew legal aid society) of the Legal Aid Society (New York City) reported two major difficulties with his clients. One was compelling clients to accept out-of-court settlements. "It is undoubtedly true that our clients are naturally litigious. The Hebrew . . . does not know any other redress than that offered by a court of law." The other problem was convincing religious Jews that the common practice of Ghet—summary divorce by a rabbi—was not lawful in America though it may have been acceptable in "the old country." (John MacArthur Maguire, *The Lance of Justice: A Semi-Centennial History of the Legal Aid Society, 1876–1926* (Harvard University Press, Cambridge, Mass., 1928) pp. 162, 171.)

[4] *Infra*, p. 165. Smith reported that the percentage of legal aid cases terminated by litigation was very small—in 1915 it was between 4 and 9 per cent. He justified this by saying: "The societies institute or defend cases in court only when they are reasonably convinced that the truth is on their side" (p. 164). Unless we are to assume that truth was seldom on the side of the poor this standard is much higher than that required of the private bar. More importantly, it is antithetical to the concept of partisan legal advocacy on which the adversary system is based.

their political purpose and that the obvious taint of self-interest would be minimized by the survey's purported impartiality. The lawyers' organization, on the
other hand, expressed no interest in any study of legal education.[5]

Abraham Flexner, a respected educator and a member of Pritchett's staff,
published in 1910 his comprehensive survey, *Medical Education in the United
States and Canada*, in which he documented the abominable state of professional medical education under the laissez-faire system. The report suggested
a series of reforms which through increased professionalization (occupational
autonomy) and increased self-regulation (i.e., decreased state regulation)
would create higher teaching and practice standards for medicine and medical
schools. The widespread publicity given to the report and the shock at Flexner's
findings generated the necessary support for his reforms. The public's usual
antipathy toward granting occupational monopolies was overcome, and many
previously reluctant legislatures began to impose the desired strict and pro-
fessionally regulated licensure requirements for medical schools and physicians.
In a short time nearly all marginal medical schools were out of business or
absorbed by universities,[6] and a monopoly of medical education and practice was
constructed under the effective control of the American Medical Association.

The influence of the "Flexner Report" did not go unnoticed in the American
Bar Association. Two factions in the association were locked in a struggle
for control of professional admission standards. On one side were the intel-
lectual, law-school-based, non-practicing, more reform-oriented lawyers (known
as the "schoolmen") and their friends in the practicing bar. On the other side
were loosely federated, conservative corporate lawyers. The self-interest of
each faction led them to agree that control of the gates to the profession
should be wrested from the bench and the state, but disagreement remained
over who should be the gatekeepers—law schools (Harvard and its idolaters)
or the practicing bar and its leadership.[7]

In 1913 the bar association's Committee on Legal Education and Admission
to the Bar (then functioning unofficially as an adjunct of the Association of
American Law Schools) sent a formal request to the Carnegie Foundation for
a study of legal education. The committee members represented the schoolmen. They reasoned that their arguments for stricter educational requirements would be advanced if, as was probable, the Carnegie Foundation's support were to result in a report on the legal profession that was comparable to

[5] Preble Stolz, "Training for the Public Profession of the Law (1921): A Contemporary Review" (mimeo), Appendix to a Report for a Conference on Legal Education, Association of American Law Schools (May 31, 1971).
[6] The number of medical schools in the country fell from 131 in 1910 to 85 in 1920. Admission standards were also
upgraded: in 1914 a high-school diploma was required, and in 1918 the prerequisite was changed to two years of
college in a pre-medical curriculum. (Stolz, *ibid.*, p. 134.)
[7] Between 1840 and 1921 the organized bar had no direct control over the standards for admission to practice law.
Licensure was haphazardly administered by legislatures and courts. Preparatory requirements were minimal or
non-existant, and almost anyone who desired to be licensed as a lawyer could be. See James Willard Hurst, *The
Growth of American Law: The Law Makers* (Little, Brown & Co., Boston, 1950), pp. 276-285.

the Flexner Report on medicine. After all, law and medicine were parallel professions.[8]

Pritchett agreed to fund the survey and Alfred Z. Reed, also an educator and non-lawyer, was commissioned to write the report. However, before the study was published, Reed, to the dismay of the schoolmen, made it known that he was his own man and, worse, unsympathetic to the interests of either faction of the bar association. He did not see lawyers and doctors sharing the same kind of public responsibility. In medicine the "unitary" model of the profession was supportable in a way that did not apply to law. He argued that medicine is a scientific profession where the requirement of uniform technical skills is not in dispute and is consistent with the societal value placed on health. However, law is a totally different enterprise. Contrary to the persuasions of some jurisprudes, law is not a science. Its preoccupation is with the allocation of power in society, where values are not generally agreed upon. The imposition of a unitary model on the legal profession (requiring all lawyers to be trained in schools all conforming to some elite model) would not only limit the usefully wide variation that existed in law practice but would also foster an upper-class monopoly totally incompatible with the ideals of a democratic society. Reed believed that legal education should have a contrary effect: values in the profession should be democratically represented and differentiation in the bar on social and political bases should be encouraged. Any restrictions, whether educational, social, political, or economic, which effectively worked to exclude lower-class aspirants from power and the profession were to be condemned. Had Reed's idea of the differentiated bar been accepted, the American bar would probably have a very different character today. However, the schoolmen rejected Reed's philosophy and instead institutionalized the unitary view of the legal profession.

In his report, published in 1921 under the title *Training for the Public Profession of Law*, Reed suggested a number of reforms (largely ignored by the bar) which would assist the profession in excluding incompetent practitioners without introducing class bias. He did side with the schoolmen by denouncing the prevailing easy access to a lawyer's license. But as far as the national bar association was concerned, Reed's support for a politically responsive, democratically representative bar put him in the same camp as an older enemy—the Populists.[9]

A century earlier Jacksonian democracy had brought to an end the era of self-

---

[8] Jerold S. Auerbach describes in detail the struggle between the teachers of law and its practitioners in "Enmity and Amity: Law Teachers and Practitioners, 1900–1922," in Donald Fleming and Bernard Bailyn (eds.), *Law in American History* (Little, Brown & Co., Boston, 1971), pp. 551–604.

[9] "In the nineteenth century . . . [the practice of law] was second only to the role of captain of industry as the road to success for the poor boy of the Horatio Alger legend." Hurst, *op. cit.*, p. 250. It was this myth that Reed's work supported and the schoolmen were trying to control.

regulation that lawyers fondly called the "golden age" of the profession. A similar egalitarianism was blamed for causing the present struggle. The contemporary threat to the profession and society from agrarian Populists, progressives, domestic socialists and communists was felt serious enough by the American Bar Association to justify the establishment of a special antiradical propaganda and lobby group called the Committee Against Judicial Recall, which sought (unnecessarily) to protect the tenure of appointed judges from the caprices of popular dissatisfaction. The committee annually warned of the need for constant vigil to prevent revolution.[10]

But egalitarianism was a troublesome argument that could not be simply disposed of as radical. It was, after all, no more than American for any citizen to regard himself the equal of any other. For the national bar association the issue was how, in the face of a long history of popular anti-elitist sentiment in America, it could generate the support necessary to create an elite-controlled occupational monopoly,[11] and at the same time support an image of lawyers as publicly responsible and committed to democratic values. A number of reforms were eventually undertaken with which to win the favor of public opinion, including the raising of ethical standards, the prevention of unauthorized practice, the creation of integrated bars (which made bar membership a condition of practice), the strengthening of legal education, and the introduction of uniform statutory codes. It is another reform in this category—legal aid —which concerns us here.

A criticism, reinforced by Reed, which had earlier been leveled at the bar association's plans to stiffen the professional licensure requirements was that if lower-class lawyers were as a result excluded from practice the poor would inevitably be hurt. Increased professionalization would remove the source of low-fee counsel from which the poor were benefiting in the market system then prevailing.

A rebuttal was offered which characterized the lower-status bar as being largely unethical and exploitive of the poor. The poor would be better off without them. Still, some positive alternative had to be proposed. What was needed was a reform program which illuminated the concern of the wealthy, socially

---

[10] As one example, in 1918, the committee filed a report to the A.B.A. entitled "The Socialist Menace to Constitutional Government." The following excerpt is typical: "We have ultimately little to fear from the effects of any menace by a foreign enemy, whether such enemy shall at any time appear in the form of Mexican banditti, or of the yellow peril of the Orient, or of Spanish tyranny, or of the yet barbarous and inhuman militarism of the Hun. The threat of any such invasion from without makes all true American hearts throb in a unison of response to the call to arms. . . . The most serious menace now threatening our free institutions is that of disruption and revolution from within." *The American Bar Association Journal*, IV:1 (January, 1918), p. 55.

[11] This issue was discussed at the 1919 meetings of the A.B.A. Committee on Legal Education. Franklin Danaher, of New York, capsulized the criticism: "It is an old saying that nobody loves a fat man, and it is equally true that nobody loves a lawyer. If we go before the legislature united and ask the enactment of some measure, along will come some lawyer member of the legislature and say, 'Oh, you want to fix it so that no one but an aristocrat . . . can be admitted to the Bar'; . . . members of the legislature have said to me, 'Nothing doing, you are asking too much, you are trying to keep the poor man out.' " *A.B.A.J.*, IV:1 (January, 1920), pp. 76–78.

conscious, but busy, segment of the bar for the problems of the less fortunate. On the other hand, and more quietly, corporate lawyers felt a need to assure their regular clientele that their allegiance had not been altered. It was at this point, and with this concern, that legal aid, which had existed for forty years, was "discovered." And, just as importantly, legal aid had an enthusiastic and articulate spokesman, young, to be sure, but most acceptable.

Reginald Heber Smith

In 1916 Reginald Heber Smith was twenty-seven, a recent graduate of Harvard Law School, and staff counsel for the Boston Legal Aid Society. He was brilliant, well indoctrinated in the Harvard perspective on needed legal reforms (mainly administrative), and experienced in legal aid through his work in a legal aid office established by the elite segment of the Boston bar. He was ripe to be picked for bar leadership and to conduct the survey of legal aid which was undertaken that year with Carnegie funds.

The American Bar Association first expressed its official interest in legal aid in September of the following year at the Special Conference of Members of the American Bar Association (the legislative section of the association) held in Saratoga Springs, New York. The declared purpose of the conference was indicative of the organization's approach to legal aid. The conference was called "to find the mechanism that will enable the organized Bar of the country better and more effectively to co-operate in the maintenance, the extension and the observance of the standards set by the American Bar Association."[12]

How was legal aid considered a device to control other lawyers? Smith, in his book, suggested one possible way:

Discipline is a primary concern of all bar associations. In this unpleasant and difficult work the legal aid societies have proved themselves valuable allies. They serve to supplement the jurisdiction of the bar associations by bringing to light abuses which would not otherwise be known. In the great cities, where the bar is so large that the members do not know one another, where personal acquaintance is limited to one's own circle of practice, the legal aid societies deal with a class of attorneys who are unknown to the leaders of the bar, they negotiate with them, try cases against them, and come into contact with them in daily practice, so that they are in a position to detect improper and unlawful conduct. [p. 227]

Just as they have served to extend the administration of justice into this great field at the bottom of society, so they have extended the watchfulness and discipline of the bar association. [p. 228]

---

[12] *A.B.A.J.*, III:4 (October, 1917), p. 581. Membership in the American Bar Association had always been voluntary. At this time only about 10 per cent of the nation's bar were members. The association's influence over local bar organizations and non-member attorneys was solely through persuasion.

At the conference, however, the idea of the legal-aid lawyer as policeman was not formally raised. The concern was rather for the ethical image of the profession. Smith, asked by Chairman Root to address the meeting because of his participation in the Carnegie study, said, "I think the most tragical thing about being counsel for a legal aid society is that such a counsel is generally a man who has the highest ideals of the profession and yet day after day he has to sit at his desk and have people pass in review before him, all of whom sincerely believe that lawyers are necessarily dishonest."[13] Legal aid, as an ethical legal ambassador to the slums, could dispel this pervasive antipathy.

After hearing Smith's speech, Charles Boston, a delegate attuned to the importance and presumed persuasive power of the new field of advertising, quickly introduced a motion which urged all state and local bar associations "to foster the formation and efficient administration in their respective jurisdictions of legal aid societies for legal relief work for the worthy poor."[14] (A little more quietly, Boston saw to it that young Smith was given his first appointment in the association: to the Standing Committee on Publicity. Smith served on that committee until his study was published two years later.) The resolution passed unanimously. The American Bar Association formally announced its alignment with legal aid, a term which was defined as "relief work for the worthy poor," but otherwise left vague. What it was that legal-aid lawyers were supposed to do was not discussed. The delegate from Georgia expressed his particular approval of the concept because to him it meant providing "a public officer to defend divorce suits, and prevent divorces being granted."[15] No one suggested otherwise.

Smith's completed report was first published in 1919 under the title *Justice and the Poor*. As he later summarized it:

> The book argued for these basic principles: (1) the Constitution of the United States and the constitutions of the several states guarantee to every person the equal protection of the laws; (2) in a democracy it is intolerable that any person should be denied the equal protection of the laws simply because he is poor; (3) the best solution of the problem is that afforded by the legal aid organizations of the Nation; and (4) the responsibility for the proper conduct of legal aid work and its development rests squarely on the shoulders of the organized bar.[16]

Many of the nation's newspapers gave the study front-page coverage. To meet the demand for copies of the report, three editions had to be printed be-

---

[13] *Ibid.* p. 590.

[14] *Ibid.* p. 592.

[15] *Ibid.* p. 595.

[16] Reginald Heber Smith, "Interest of the American Bar Association in Legal Aid Work," *Annals of the American Academy of Political and Social Science*, 205 (September, 1939), p. 108.

tween 1919 and 1924. In several cities it was reportedly used as a handbook
to set up some of the services commended by Smith as providing justice for
the poor.[17] The sense of reform was so strong that Pritchett stated in the introduction to the 1924 edition, "The Carnegie Foundation has deemed it unwise
at this time to undertake any revision of the original report because the current still runs so swiftly that any revision published to-day would itself be
antiquated in a year or two" (p. xiii).

The enthusiasm generated by the initial publication of Smith's report carried into the 1920 meetings of the American Bar Association. A large audience
attended the association's first symposium on legal aid. The principal attrac-
tion was Charles Evans Hughes, the previous Republican presidential candi-
date, former governor of New York, and president of the New York Legal Aid
Society. Other members of the panel were Judge Ben B. Lindsey of Denver,
a controversial judicial reformer, Ernest L. Tustin, connected with Philadelphia's municipal legal aid program, and Reginald Heber Smith, who was now
a partner in the prestigious Boston firm of Hale and Dorr and, since the
publication of his popular survey, the association's legal expert on legal aid.[18]

At the conclusion of the panel discussion a "spontaneous" motion was introduced from the floor and approved: that a special committee on legal aid
be immediately established to be chaired by the bar's most august figure, Charles
Evans Hughes.

The following year, the special committee, by its own recommendation and
the unanimous consent of the 1921 convention, became the Standing Committee
on Legal Aid of the American Bar Association. With Hughes having resigned
to join President Harding's cabinet, Reginald Heber Smith was made chairman, a position he retained for fifteen years. The committee's first appropriation was only $250: but it signified investiture by the national bar of the con-
cept of legal aid, whose previous forty-year existence had been tenuous and
parochial.

ORIGINS OF LEGAL AID

Organized legal aid in the United States began in 1876 with the establishment
of the Deutscher Rechtsschutz-Verein (German Legal Protection Society), a
specialized spin-off of the German Society. The mother organization, founded
in 1784, had become active and influential with the massive German immigration to America of the 1840s. Its manifest purpose was to help confused
and ignorant German immigrants adjust to the new country. In some cases
this meant merely providing a cultural refuge for German-speaking people in

---

17 While Smith saw the purpose of the book as encouraging the growth of legal aid societies, its greatest success
was in the propagation of small-claims courts (infra, p. xxvii).
18 A.B.A.J., VI:5 (October, 1920), pp. 83–87.

an English-speaking society. In others, it meant protecting immigrants from being cheated by the swindlers who swarmed the docks and from being exploited by petit-bourgeois shopkeepers and employers. In still others, it was to assuage the frustration and anger that inevitably came from disillusionment with the American Dream. But like most early ethnic self-improvement organizations, the German Society and the Rechtsschutz-Verein felt their essential, overall, unstated responsibility to be to the group's elite. The low-status German-American immigrant was to be prevented from jeopardizing in any way the social and economic position of the group's affluent members who had "made it" in the new world.

In 1890, Arthur von Briesen was appointed second president of the Rechtsschutz-Verein. By this time the great German immigration had passed. The German-American elite was relatively secure in American society and no longer feared being displaced. Other ethnic immigrations were bringing in floods of people more threatening to Anglo-Saxon dominance than Germans. The easing of pressures on the German-Americans had left the Rechtsschutz-Verein in bad financial condition. Donations from wealthy German-Americans were sporadic and declining. The men who had appointed von Briesen assumed that he would merely supervise the organization's demise.

But von Briesen knew that the organization would survive if he could convince the elite of the dominant society that they could make use of the service legal aid had performed for the German-American community. He cut off ties with the German Society and went to the capitalists for patronage. What he had realized was that among the Anglo-Saxon elite there was a strong fear that the masses would rise up and seize the wealth which many had gained through ruthless means.

In the nineties, laissez-faire economics was in crisis. The system so passionately supported by the capitalists no longer seemed to work. Society was being shaken by economic chaos and social violence. A financial crisis beginning in 1893 gave way to a double-cycle depression lasting until 1898. The violence of the Haymarket Riot in 1886 had been followed by the bloody Carnegie Homestead Strike in 1892, and the even more extensive and brutal Pullman Strike in 1894. Many of the corporate elite believed a revolution was imminent.

According to one historian of the period, the capitalists became Marxists: "The proponents of the system . . . accepted, on the evidence of their own experience as well as their casual and distorted knowledge of his ideas, the analysis made by Karl Marx, and set about to prevent his prophecy of socialism and communism being fulfilled."[19] It was directly to this phobia and this program that Arthur von Briesen appealed.

---

[19] William Appleton Williams, *The Contours of American History* (World Publishing Co., Cleveland, 1961), p. 351.

His argument was simple. Legal aid is counter-revolutionary. It could help protect the ruling class from Marx's dire predictions. From 1890 to 1900, von Briesen's annual reports of the legal aid society included the following paean:

> The work done by us comes home to every citizen; *it keeps the poor satisfied*, because it establishes and protects their rights; it produces better workingmen and better workingwomen, better house servants; *it antagonizes the tendency toward communism*; it is the best argument against the socialist who cries that the poor have no rights which the rich are bound to respect. *Communism and socialism have, it seems, lost their grip upon our New York population since our Society has done its effective work in behalf of the poor.*[20]

Von Briesen's appeal was successful. The Rechtsschutz-Verein had not been expected to survive much longer but at the end of 1893 it had more cash on hand than the year previous.[21] In 1896 it changed its name to "The Legal Aid Society."

While the society took credit for undercutting "the proletariat in the class struggle," on occasion it performed a less abstract service for New York's upper classes. An early historian of the society recounted that:

> One of the Society's long-standing rules is that an applicant to have his case accepted must present a claim sound not merely in the technical sense but also in the moral sense. Many miscellaneous illustrations of this doctrine might be adduced, but its largest and most striking application provides the very best example. It is law, at least in New York, that a person employed for an indefinite period is subject to discharge without notice and, correspondingly, may throw over his position without notice and without forfeiting his right to unpaid compensation for time actually worked. In the field of domestic service this principle may originally have operated favorably for employers, but of late years, with an increasing demand for and a decreasing supply of competent servants, it has had quite the reverse effect. The New York cook not infrequently walked out at six P.M. with a dinner party coming on, the New York coachman or chauffeur sometimes abandoned his box or steering-wheel in the very midst of a shopping trip. And on top of such annoying action the departed servant could and would make a legally enforceable demand for back pay. . . .
>
> The word went forth that, where a domestic servant abandoned his or her employment without reasonable notice, the Society would refuse to further recovery of back wages. New York gasped. Mere man had dared to tackle the servant problem![22]

Most cases brought to the society did not involve relationships between the upper and lower classes. The elite's interests benefited by the society's refusal

[20] Quoted in Maguire, *op. cit.*, p. 55. Emphasis added.
[21] *Ibid.*, p. 65.
[22] *Ibid.*, pp. 83–84.

to assist workers injured in industrial accidents, or defendants charged with crimes, or victims of official violence, or organizations such as unions whose purpose was to organize the poor. Nor did it defend those individual liberties we have come to call civil rights.

What the society did do was attempt to rationalize the economic relationships of the urban working class, chiefly by handling wage claims against small employers.[23] By representing workers in disputes with dishonest employers (those who cut their labor costs by refusing to pay wages), a blow was struck against unionism, labor strife, radicalism, and revolution. In many ways this policy paralleled the attempt of big business to rationalize its operations through federal regulation. Gabriel Kolko has persuasively argued that during this period business interests, in order to create their mammoth trusts free from local and state control, promoted the "progressive era" legislation which supposedly was for their own regulation.[24] Legal aid's efforts were obviously on a smaller scale. But it is significant that two men who were closely aligned with the interests and the promotion of the Legal Aid Society were also major figures in the development of a philosophy for "anti-trust" regulation—Elihu Root, the capitalists' legal spokesman, and Theodore Roosevelt, known as the "trust-buster."

Of the latter, the historian Eric Goldman wrote, "Roosevelt had a patrician's disdain for greedy businessmen, a patrician's sense of *noblesse oblige* toward the downtrodden, and a patrician's fear of socialism or some other 'riotous wicked' surge from the bottom groups."[25] "Roosevelt," according to Kolko, "was consciously using government regulation to save the capitalist system, perhaps even from itself, for the greatest friend of socialism was the unscrupulous businessman who did not recognize that moderate regulation could save him from a more drastic fate in the hands of the masses."[26]

In New York City the same Rooseveltian philosophy lay behind Arthur von Briesen's extension of business regulation into the lower reaches of society through legal aid. It was this concept of legal aid that was the prototype for other cities. Smith was right when he wrote that "it is this fact which makes the development of ideas about the work in New York of such great importance, for those conceptions were largely copied, often for no other reason than that New York did its work in that particular way" (p. 140).

Although the legal aid movement's first effort dated from 1876, when Smith began his survey most programs were recent ventures. Only fifteen societies

---

[23] The wage claim disappeared as a staple of the legal aid diet and as a source of legal fees in the twenties: improper withholding of pay was changed from a civil offense to a crime.

[24] Gabriel Kolko, *The Triumph of Conservatism: A Reinterpretation of American History, 1900-1916* (Free Press of Glencoe, New York, 1963).

[25] Eric F. Goldman, *Rendezvous with Destiny* (Alfred A. Knopf, New York, 1952), p. 126.

[26] Kolko, *op. cit.*, p. 130.

were operating in the country by 1910, eleven of which were less than ten years old. But within six years of that threshold year, the total number of organizations which could be identified as providing legal aid increased to forty-one. Part of the reason was that the provision of a free lawyer had become one aspect of the relief work adopted by many "progressive" charities. However, none of these were particularly large efforts. The typical legal aid society consisted of one full-time lawyer and, if he were fortunate, some secretarial assistance and perhaps the occasional part-time services of another attorney. The legal aid effort was intimately related to the success of the charitable fundraising abilities of the supporting agencies.

These pre-war years in which legal aid flourished were in terms of labor strife the bloodiest in American history.[27] The violent suppression of unions and strikes intensified and expanded labor–management conflicts. The widespread appeal of domestic socialism and the increasing threats of the nihilistic International Workers of the World began to terrify the business community. Rampant and ruthless political, economic and legal exploitation of the working class provoked bloody reaction. As in the nineties, the country again seemed to be on the brink of chaos.

LEGAL AID IN THE WAR

The legal aid organizations remained outside this mainstream of social strife, quietly doing their work of transforming the collective political and economic grievances of the urban working class into individualized legal categories. Justice for the poor meant fragmenting the nascent class-consciousness of the exploited, the immigrant poor, and those whose impoverished condition might lead them to support radical movements.[28]

In April, 1917, the country went to war. In many cities legal aid work was immediately suspended. Contributions had dried up and the country was being drained of young attorneys—the ranks from which legal aid staffs were drawn. Older lawyers were not available for service to take their place. In the best circumstances salaries paid by charities could not compete with those from private practice, and in wartime the private sector was in a scramble for the lucrative practices left behind by the "brothers at the front."

What threatened legal aid as a movement even more than its sudden shortage

[27] Philip Taft and Philip Ross, "American Labor Violence: Its Causes, Character, and Outcome," in Hugh Graham and Ted Gurr (eds.), *Violence in America: Historical and Comparative Perspectives* (Bantam Books, New York, 1969), p. 320.

[28] It was this work that William Guthrie, ex-president of the Bar of the City of New York and of the New York State Bar Association, credited in 1928 with saving the country from revolution. Without the work of legal aid societies "a drift toward communism, revolution, and anarchy would have been inevitable. In a word, failure of the legal aid movement might have spelled ultimate national disaster." (William D. Guthrie, Introduction to Maguire, *op. cit.*, p. viii.)

of funds and staff was the immense vacuum in national leadership created by the resignation, in February, 1916, of von Briesen as president of the New York Legal Aid Society. Smith detailed many of von Briesen's specific contributions (see pp. 134–149), but of his resignation after twenty-six years as president, Smith said only that he resigned "so that, in his own words, 'younger and stronger hands might take the helm' " (p. 136). Smith did not record that in fact von Briesen had been driven from office because of his ethnic loyalties.

Shortly after the war had begun in Europe in 1914, von Briesen, like many prominent German-Americans, had expressed his view that Germany was not solely at fault in the conflict. Though the United States had declared itself neutral, in the sphere of influence of the pro-British New York *Times* such talk was traitorous and labeled as such, even when it was voiced by a veteran of the Union Army. Von Briesen knew he would have to resign from office if his legal aid society were not to lose its benefactors. Rather than see his organization destroyed, he relinquished his presidency in 1916. With active life ended and his loyalty impugned, his health began to fail. He died in 1920, one of the more prominent victims of the anti-German hysteria which plagued the German-American community during the war.[29]

Ironically, the injustice which von Briesen had suffered kept him from the Saratoga Springs conference where the leaders of the legal profession discussed "justice for the poor." (The conference chairman, Elihu Root, was a member of the board of directors of the New York Legal Aid Society and a former friend of von Briesen, but during the war he became passionately anti-German, viewing the war as one which pitted the forces of Christ against those of Odin.[30]) Perhaps the greater irony in the destruction of von Briesen's career, however, was that it was caused by what others, including Smith, have called his greatest achievement—the Americanization of legal aid. In his effort to build a little-known ethnic self-improvement society, the Deutscher Rechtsschutz-Verein, into the New York Legal Aid Society, he had made himself dependent on and vulnerable to the caprice of the dominant classes. Although the society had Carnegie and Rockefeller as its patrons, lesser capitalists as its regular supporters, and Elihu Root and Theodore Roosevelt as directors, none of these influential men defended von Briesen's right to speak.

After America's entry into the war, chauvinism exploded into a national mania, and an open season was declared not only on German-Americans but on labor radicals, the I.W.W., socialists, and civil-libertarians. The flag-waving fervor of a quarter of a million members of the American Protective League (Attorney General Gregory's unofficial "secret service"), the racial hatred of

---

[29] Maguire, *op. cit.*, pp. 220-222.

[30] Philip C. Jessup, *Elihu Root*, Vol. I (Dodd, Mead & Co., New York, 1938), p. 236.

the newly revived Ku Klux Klan, and the nativists's campaign to "Americanize" the foreigner, by violence if necessary, spread throughout the land.[31]

It was during this period of stridency and strife that Smith wrote the tempered pages of a book on justice and the poor. He pleaded for legal aid and court reform to end the *unintentional injustice* which unequal accessibility to the legal system produced. He raised the specter of anarchy should these reforms not be affected. But it was not in Smith's brief to deal with anarchy's root causes or current manifestations: vigilante violence, race riots, private and governmental racial discrimination, exploitive labor contracts, foul working conditions, corrupt courts, and the many forms of lawful injustice inflicted on members of society. In his lawyer's philosophy, the concept of lawful injustice was excluded as self-contradictory.

Throughout his life, Reginald Heber Smith remained, through the A.B.A., close to the legal aid movement. After his death in 1966, the Office of Economic Opportunity memorialized his contributions by naming after him the prestigious fellowship awarded to meritorious Legal Services attorneys. The Reginald Heber Smith Fellowships (called "Reggies") have since become prized awards in legal service for the poor.

EFFECTS OF SMITH'S WORK

What contributions did Smith and his co-workers make to American society? Although individual persons were certainly aided, the poor as a class seem not to have been much affected, so restricted was the legal aid movement in the range of service it offered its clients and in its efforts in seeking them out. Little was done to broaden the program. In a survey of legal aid conducted in 1947, thirty years after Smith's publication, Emery A. Brownell concluded that legal aid—even on its own terms—had made practically no progress since 1916.[32]

The movement itself was totally unaware of the inadequacy of its effort. In one of his last attempts to cajole the bar into financing legal aid, Smith said in 1951, "The cost of Legal Aid is so modest that there is not the slightest excuse for running hat in hand to Washington."[33] Authorities outside the movement knew differently. The director of the Legal Services Program, operating as part of the federal government's War on Poverty in the 1960s, estimated that $300,000,000 to $500,000,000 would be required to provide adequate civil legal services to the poor.[34] And when the Legal Services Program was intro-

[31] See Joan M. Jensen, *The Price of Vigilance* (Rand McNally, Chicago, 1968); Nathaniel Weyl, *The Battle Against Disloyalty* (Thomas Y. Crowell Co., New York, 1951); and John P. Roche, *The Quest for the Dream* (Quadrangle Books, Chicago, 1963).
[32] Emery A. Brownell, *Legal Aid in the United States* (Lawyers Co-operative Publishing Co., Rochester, 1951), especially pp. 246-248.
[33] Reginald Heber Smith, Introduction to Brownell, *op. cit.*, p. xix.
[34] O.E.O. press release 67-51, "Law Reform Should Be Top Goal of Legal Services" (March 18, 1967), cited in Sar A. Levitan, *The Great Society's Poor Law: A New Approach to Poverty* (Johns Hopkins Press, Baltimore, 1969), p. 178.

duced, it was immediately smothered in an avalanche of clients—despite the tremendous increase in the number of legal aid lawyers which it provided. The legal aid movement had been operating on such a narrow base during its ninety-year history that the legal profession had failed to anticipate the vast latent demand for legal assistance.

Justice and the Poor, on the other hand, did serve the interests of the elite bar by providing a popular basis on which to formalize a conjunction between legal aid and the bar association. Even token legal aid served to vent anti-elitist pressures directed at the bar's leadership. The profession's concern for the poor could not be doubted if "justice for the poor" were a part of the bar's platform.

Ironically, the pressures on the bar's elite which encouraged the preparation of *Justice and the Poor* had already begun to ease by the time the work was published. The pre-war demands for a profession responsive to the lower as well as the upper classes had been defused by nativist wartime sentiment. The anti-radical, anti-foreign, chauvinist elements which rose to the surface during the war did not disappear with the Armistice. The Palmer Raids and the Red Scares of the 1920s, Sacco and Vanzetti's trial, Henry Ford's anti-Zionist tirades, the immigration restriction acts, and the anti-Catholicism of the 1928 election, were among the nativist triumphs which created a climate sympathetic to the elite bar's effort to form a closed profession. Another war was to pass before the issue of justice for the poor once again began to stir the American social conscience.

To Reginald Heber Smith and other pioneers of the legal aid movement we are in great debt. Their vision of justice for the poor may have been constrained by a patrician *Weltanschauung.*[35] It may have been manipulated by elitist interests. It may have suffered the slow death of bureaucratization. But it did inspire great personal dedication to the righting of one of society's wrongs; and, as a legacy of that vision, *Justice and the Poor* presents the modern scholar with a valuable social document on how this particular social ill was conceptualized, measured, and treated.

University of Massachusetts
Amherst
May, 1972.

---

[35] See *Americanization Studies* (William S. Bernard, ed.), Vol. 9: Kate Holladay Claghorn, *The Immigrant's Day in Court* (Patterson Smith, Montclair, N.J., 1971), chap. 11.

PREFACE TO THE THIRD EDITION

AS all the copies of the first and second editions of this Bulletin have been exhausted, it has been necessary to publish a third edition, which is simply a reprinting and not a revision of the earlier editions.

The reader will understand that, while the substance of the book remains true, much of its detail is obsolete and many of the defects it pointed out in our administration of justice have been remedied. Only five years have passed since the Foundation published *Justice and the Poor*, but during this short interval significant progress has been made in the entire field of legal aid.

It is only possible here to point out the major changes that have taken place.

From the outset, the Bulletin was successful in arousing a genuine public interest in this subject. It secured the attention of newspapers and periodicals throughout the country; it caused a widespread discussion, and it drew some criticism. In the judgment of competent legal scholars, as evidenced by the reviews in leading law journals, it was accorded the position, which it still maintains, of being the most authoritative treatise in this special field of law reform. The first six chapters, which state and define the problem of adjusting our administration of justice to the imperative needs of the poorer people, particularly in the large cities, have been generally accepted as a sound and trustworthy analysis of the difficulties that must be overcome. When one considers how slowly the cause of law reform in general makes headway against the obstacles of inertia and indifference it is distinctly encouraging to realize what legislatures, judicature commissions, bar associations, and laymen, aided by a favorable public opinion, have already accomplished in making justice more accessible to the poor.

In 1919 there were only seven small claims courts in the United States: to-day there are approximately one hundred. This new type of court, specially adapted to dispose of small cases with maximum speed and at minimum expense, has demonstrated its value. It has been made an integral part of the judicial system of California, Massachusetts, Minnesota, and most recently Idaho. Our first experiments with conciliation tribunals have been undertaken by acts of the legislature in Iowa and in North Dakota, where the constitutionality of conciliation tribunals has been upheld by decision of the state supreme court. The possibility of adjusting certain types of litigation through the method of conciliation was the main topic for discussion at the Conference of Bar Association Delegates in 1923. Arbitration, as an al-

ternative method, remains in the foreground because of its increasing use by business men in composing their disputes. New York in 1920 enacted a statute sanc-
tioning arbitration as a method of settling disputes by providing that an agreement
to arbitrate cannot be revoked but must be complied with by the parties to it, and
this law in 1924 was upheld, even as to agreements to arbitrate maritime disputes,
by the Supreme Court of the United States. Arbitration has not been given any
special application to the cases of the poor because, where small claims courts exist,
it is unnecessary.

There has been less progress in the extension of domestic relations courts. The
ancient cleavage in our law between civil and criminal jurisdictions continues to make
difficult the practical working out of a unified domestic relations court having jurisdiction over all family matters, irrespective of whether the relief sought calls for civil
or criminal procedure.

Our administrative tribunals, as exemplified by the industrial accident commissions, continue to be popular and useful. The administrative plan of doing justice,
with its machinery for direct investigation of the facts by the tribunal itself and its
facilities for substantial legal aid to the parties that come before it, is a challenge to
the *laissez-faire* conception of our traditional common law judicial system, and the
movement toward administrative, judicial agencies has by no means spent its force.
More workmen's compensation statutes have been enacted; and in Arizona, Minnesota, and New Jersey original jurisdiction over compensation claims has been taken
away from the courts and vested in administrative commissions. There is a growing
tendency to entrust the collection of wages to labor commissioners who are by law
empowered to act as attorneys for unpaid laborers. There may be a question as to
whether this departure from our traditional court system is dangerous, but there is
no question as to the fact that these administrative tribunals have given a more satisfactory effort at justice to indigent claimants, whose cases were within their jurisdiction, than the courts have been able to render in the past. It seems unlikely, therefore,
that the administrative method will be given up at least until the courts generally
are equipped and empowered to render an equally satisfactory service.

The Voluntary Defenders' Committee in New York and the two offices of Public
Defender in Los Angeles (one for the county and one for the city), whose work was
reported in *Justice and the Poor*, continue to provide counsel to indigent persons
in criminal cases, and if their experience be taken as the test, the public defender
plan is entitled to be regarded as a success. There has always been a division of

opinion as to whether agencies furnishing lawyers' services to poor persons should
be public offices under public control or whether, for an experimental period at least,
they should have the greater freedom and flexibility enjoyed by private societies
supported by private subscriptions. The argument for public control is clear; the
danger is equally clear, and has been illustrated by the abolition of the office of
Public Defender in Portland, Oregon, following a partisan change in the municipal
administration. Nevertheless, the whole tendency is to make the defender in criminal cases a public official. Public defenders have been established in San Francisco,
Omaha, and Minneapolis. The most interesting development has been in Connecticut
where, by virtue of a statute enacted in 1921, the judges of the Superior Court
appoint for each county a public defender who serves for compensation determined
by the court and paid out of the county treasury. Here, for the first time, we find a
form of legal aid work maintained as a public undertaking but operated under judicial, as distinguished from municipal, control.

The legal aid organizations, whose primary service is to render legal assistance in
civil cases, continue to flourish and to expand. The latest figures given in *Justice
and the Poor* showed that in 1916 there were 41 legal aid organizations, and that
their clients in the same year totaled 117,201. The statistics published in the 1923
Year Book of the American Bar Association reveal that in 1922 there were 47 organizations and their clients numbered 125,205. New legal aid offices have been
opened in such important centres as Philadelphia, Indianapolis, Providence, Louisville, Bridgeport, and Grand Rapids. Here, curiously enough, the type of agency
that is most successfully established is the private society, although one must note
that the Philadelphia Municipal Legal Aid Bureau, operated under the Department
of Public Welfare, has to date rendered a greater service than the private agency
which preceded it. In June, 1923, at a convention held in Cleveland, there was formed
the National Association of Legal Aid Organizations, whose membership embraces
nearly every legal aid office in the United States. This new Association at once gave
proof of its value by securing the adoption of a uniform system for classifying and
recording the nature, source, and disposition of all legal aid cases.

Because of our large immigrant population innumerable cases arise where one interested party is in this country and another party is in Europe. To provide for the
better handling of such international cases the Association has been instrumental
in securing action by the League of Nations looking toward the convening of an international legal aid conference.

In the Introduction to the first edition of *Justice and the Poor*, I ventured to say:

> "This report, prepared with great care and stated in moderate terms, deserves at the hands of the members of the bar serious and sympathetic attention. If those who officially represent the law do not bend their energies and give their best thought to make the administration of justice fair, prompt, and accessible to the humblest citizen, to what group in the body politic may we turn with any hope that this matter will be dealt with wisely and justly?"

The response of the organized bar, once this problem was squarely presented to it, has been altogether admirable. At its annual meeting in 1920 the American Bar Association held a symposium on legal aid work, and in 1921 by amendment to its constitution added the Committee on Legal Aid Work to its other standing committees. In all, more than 36 bar associations have taken direct action for the furtherance of legal aid work. It is believed that in the smaller cities and towns where no legal aid organization is necessary the work may best be entrusted to the local bar associations, and this plan is now in operation in Illinois under the auspices of the State Bar Association.

The success of legal aid work and the maintenance of its efficiency at its present level must in the long run depend mainly on the sustaining interest of the organized bar. The watchful guardianship of the bar will be assured when it is established that legal aid work is one of its traditional responsibilities, one of its regular and continuing activities. Sufficient time has not elapsed for such a tradition to become firmly rooted, but it is not too soon to record the fact that already an excellent beginning has been made.

The problem of devising ways and means and machinery whereby justice may be better secured to the poorer people is common to every industrial, urban society in the world. Every civilized nation is confronted by it. It is a problem in Tokio, Copenhagen, and London, as well as in New York, Chicago, and San Francisco. In the effort to reach a solution each nation has naturally worked along its own traditional lines. Our knowledge of the legal aid agencies of other countries is extremely limited. What information we have indicates that England, for example, has made marked progress in eliminating the difficulty of court costs, that in Paris the system of assigned counsel has been made to operate far more efficiently than it has ever done in our country, and that in Denmark the method of conciliation has been given a much wider application than we have yet considered to be feasible here. There is reason, therefore, to believe that a study of comparative legal aid systems in various countries might produce much material of direct benefit and help to us in further carrying out our plans in America.

The Carnegie Foundation has deemed it unwise at this time to undertake any revision of the original report because the current still runs so swiftly that any revision published to-day would itself be antiquated in a year or two. At some future date the Foundation hopes to issue another report on this subject, including some study of the European systems in so far as they may be found to have instructive value to us, and bringing down to date the record of our own accomplishment.

HENRY S. PRITCHETT,
President of the Carnegie Foundation.

April 15, 1924.

FOREWORD

THIS book began in a study of Legal Aid Societies designed to secure thorough information and a just estimate of value for the benefit of those who are called upon from time to time to contribute to their support.

The work has grown into a systematic treatise and practical handbook upon the Administration of Justice in the United States in the direction which is at this time of the most critical importance. It is full of trustworthy information and suggestion, and should be of great value to the multitude of Americans who are interested in the Americanization of the millions of foreigners who have immigrated to this country, and who fail to understand or who misunderstand American institutions. It should be useful to the members of the American Bar, who during the past few years have been gradually awakening to a sense of their responsibility for the administration of law in general, beyond the interests of the particular cases in which they are engaged. This subject was under consideration in the Conference of Bar Associations at Saratoga in September, 1917, and I commend this book to the attention of all the gentlemen who were interested in that discussion.

New projects are continually suggested for improving the condition of the poor by the aid of government, and as to many of them there is a debatable question whether they come within the proper province of government and whether official interference will not in the long run do more harm than good to the beneficiaries and to the community. No one, however, doubts that it is the proper function of government to secure justice. In a broad sense that is the chief thing for which government is organized. Nor can any one question that the highest obligation of government is to secure justice for those who, because they are poor and weak and friendless, find it hard to maintain their own rights. This book shows that we have not been performing that duty very satisfactorily, and that we ought to bestir ourselves to do better.

I do not think that we should be over-harsh in judging ourselves, however, for the shortcomings have been the result of changing conditions which the great body of our people have not fully appreciated. We have had in the main just laws and honest courts to which people—poor as well as rich—could repair to obtain justice. But the rapid growth of great cities, the enormous masses of immigrants (many of them ignorant of our language), and the greatly increased complications of life have created conditions under which the provisions for obtaining justice which were formerly sufficient are sufficient no longer. I think the true criticism which we should make upon our own conduct is that we have been so busy about our individual affairs that we have been slow to appreciate the changes of conditions which to so great an extent have put justice beyond the reach of the poor. But we cannot confine ourselves to that criticism much longer; it is time to set our own house in order. And as we do so we should recognize with gratitude the noble and unselfish men and women whom this book shows to have been devoting themselves to the task which most of us have been neglecting.

ELIHU ROOT.

July, 1919.

INTRODUCTION

THE present Bulletin constitutes the second in a series of studies of legal education and cognate matters that is in course of publication by the Carnegie Foundation, under the general charge of Mr. Alfred Z. Reed. The first number, published before the war, was the report of Professor Redlich upon the Case Method. The present volume will be followed by a detailed study of law schools and examinations for the bar. A large number of persons have coöperated in the general undertaking, and the mass of material is not only enormous, but complex.

It was inevitable that any such comprehensive study should touch at many points the administration of the law itself and the effects of this administration upon the people for whose protection and contentment law and courts exist. The presentation of the present report as a special bulletin in this series was suggested in the first instance by the application of certain legal aid societies to the Carnegie Corporation for grants of funds. The trustees of the Corporation, while disposed to look upon the work of these bodies as important, felt that a thoroughgoing report on the whole question of legal aid should precede any such action on their part. They agreed, therefore, to defray the expense of such a report if prepared with the coöperation of the Carnegie Foundation in conjunction with its already partially completed enquiry. The work, including the visitation of all legal aid societies in the United States, and the reduction of the material into its present form, has been accomplished in a most careful and discriminating fashion by Mr. Reginald Heber Smith, of the Boston bar. Although primarily designed to deal only with legal aid work, the scope of the study inevitably broadened. It proved impossible to consider existing legal aid societies without taking into account at the same time other agencies which experience has suggested in the effort to make the administration of justice direct, simple, and accessible alike to rich and poor. The present report deals, therefore, with the whole question of administration of the law as it affects members of the body politic who by reason of poverty, ignorance, or lack of knowledge of the language are at a disadvantage in the effort to secure justice as between man and man in the various disputes that arise in our present complicated industrial and social relations.

The study touches so closely the source of much current discontent and points the way to constructive action so important and yet so feasible, that its publication now is especially timely. There never was a time when it was more important to provide machinery that shall be adequate to accomplish in fact that justice at which the law aims and for whose attainment amongst men it was established. It is not enough for the law to intend justice. It must be so administered that for the great body of citizens justice is actually attained. Be the law never so good in theory, uncertain or dilatory administration, through the present cumbersome or defective machinery, goes far to defeat its aims. The widespread suspicion that our law fails to secure justice has only too much basis in fact. If this suspicion is allowed to grow unchecked, it will end by poisoning the faith of the people in their own government and in law itself, the very bulwark of justice.

That justice can be attained only through the law is made clear at the outset of this report. Human experience in all ages and in all countries proves that our only hope to attain a fair equality of justice for every member of society, wise or ignorant, good or bad, rich or poor, lies in a system of law based on principles long tried and administered by those removed from the pull of personal interest. A citizen of any state may have a reasonable confidence in justice for himself only so long as his rights and privileges are defined by the rules of law and not by the whim of any individual. Freedom and justice for the individual member of the body politic can be hoped for only through the reign of law, and not through the favoritism of any ruler or class or faction. No lesson of human society can be more clear than this, that law is nothing other than the crystallized experience of mankind, embodied in principles that aim at the attainment of justice as between man and man and as between society and the individual.

It follows directly from this conception of law, however, that in the process of social development some readjustment of the law, in the light of altered conditions and widened experience, is from time to time required. Otherwise our inherited body of legal principles and our ideals of abstract justice are in danger of growing apart. If the task of bringing them together again should by any chance be deferred until a large element of our population suffer long continued grievances under the existing law, a temper of mind is created that does not make for sane reform by orderly methods.

The conclusion to which the author of this study is led is that in so far as concerns what is technically known as the substantive law, the poor are at no special disadvantage as compared with the rich. If no more were required for the even-handed distribution of justice than this, that the rights of all men, rich or poor, strong or weak, should be impartially and equally defined under the law, then democracy has come near to realizing its ideal. No special procedure for enforcing this substantive law needs to be invoked when it is well settled, and is well known, and no dispute exists in regard to the facts and all parties affected are strictly law abiding. Fortunately the great number of our activities are conducted in this manner.

There is, however, a class of activities, exceptional yet enormous in the aggregate, where these conditions do not obtain — where the substantive law, determining the point at issue, is not settled, or if settled, is not known to the individual; or where the parties affected disagree, in good faith, as to the facts upon which their relative rights depend; or where one or the other of them does not respect the law, whether from impatient desire to remedy what he conceives to be its defects, or more frequently from naked self-interest. These are the cases where justice has to be actually administered with the aid of lawyers and of courts. If for any reason this necessary machinery of justice cannot be employed, then the theoretical protection that the individual possesses under the law is of no practical use to him.

It is on this side that the author shows the danger to lie. In the law that fixes and prescribes the machinery through which rights are enforced or defended—that is to say, in what is technically known as procedural or adjective, as distinguished from substantive law—he finds grave defects. He shows how, not because any one has deliberately intended to do wrong, but because no one has squarely faced the needs of our new immigrant citizens, our increasing class of wage-earners, and of our vast urban populations, the expense and delay needed to obtain legal relief are frequently such that the poor cannot afford it. Many are actually deprived of their rights. Still others believe that they are so deprived and cherish grievances that a less expensive and more prompt administration of the machinery of justice might serve to dispel. Even if they are not quite sure that they are in the right, the mere fact that they cannot have their claims quickly passed upon by an impartial tribunal under simple procedure seems to them an unjust discrimination, devised by the rich to oppress the poor. Under these conditions the claim of the demagogue or of the sincere but mistaken doctrinaire that justice can be made to order by some new form of social machinery falls upon ready ears. The long lesson of human experience in the effort to attain justice is easily forgot, and those who are discontented by reason of real or fancied ills and who are more directly interested than any other members of the body politic in a freedom defined by law are ready to have their civil liberty defined in terms of personal influence or of class prejudice.

How much the present weaknesses in the administration of the law work against the interest of the poor as such it is of course impossible to say. It would be a mistake to assume that the cost of litigation and the law's delay benefit the rich exclusively. In a great number of cases they work to the advantage of the dishonest poor. The deserving poor man is helpless to obtain speedy justice from any one, poor or rich. The question is not primarily one as between rich and poor, but concerns rather the fundamental necessity in a free country to place justice, so far as it is humanly possible to do so, within the reach of those who occupy any station in life. Our civilization rests upon an honest and sincere attempt to realize this ideal.

While the poor, like the rich, come to serious disputes with their fellow-men and with the agencies in the social order with which they have relations in many ways, the great proportion of questions which they desire to bring to settlement lie in a few fields—questions concerning wages, those resulting from injury while in employment, and those which originate in the family relations and affect directly the happiness of wives and children and the integrity of the home. The very natural failure of the administration of the law to keep pace with the rapid industrial transformation of the country is the source of much of the complaint of the poor and particularly of the poor man who is also an alien, touching all the matters relating to his employment, his citizenship, and the disputes which arise in his domestic relations.

The study here presented sets forth in simple and non-technical language, first the defects in the administration of the law which work in effect a denial of justice to the poor or to the ignorant; and secondly, the agencies, supplementary to the existing machinery, whose object is to remedy these defects.

The important defects are three—delay, court costs and fees, and the expense of counsel. The agencies suggested to remedy these defects fall into two groups according as the nature of the case admits of settlement without legal counsel or, on the other hand, requires counsel for the full protection of the disputants.

In the first group of remedial agencies are placed the small claims court, the agencies for conciliation and arbitration, the domestic relations courts and administrative tribunals, and all officials authorized to deal promptly with disputants. For the other group of cases—those for whom legal counsel is necessary—the present report discusses the defender in criminal cases, the assignment of counsel, and finally and most exhaustively the legal aid organizations.

The outcome and the object of the report is the effort to prove that these various agencies, if properly articulated with the existing system of the administration of justice, can be made to secure, so far as human means can do, the practical equality of all men before the law and to afford to all citizens without regard to wealth or rank or race the means for a prompt, inexpensive, and fair adjudication of their complaints.

For no group in the citizenship of the country is this more needed than in the case of the great mass of citizens of foreign birth, ignorant of the language, and helpless to secure their rights unless met by an administration of the machinery of justice that shall be simple, sympathetic, and patient. To such the apparent denial of justice forms the path to disloyalty and bitterness.

This report, prepared with great care and stated in moderate terms, deserves at the hands of the members of the bar serious and sympathetic attention. If those who officially represent the law do not bend their energies and give their best thought to make the administration of justice fair, prompt, and accessible to the humblest citizen, to what group in the body politic may we turn with any hope that this matter will be dealt with wisely and justly?

The world is to-day filled with the word "democracy." Sometimes it is used to denote a government in which the civil rights of the individual rest upon a constitutional guarantee, sometimes to describe a class rule more autocratic than that of the Czar. An autocracy can exist without law, but a free democracy cannot. The very existence of free government depends upon making the machinery of justice so effective that the citizens of the democracy shall believe in its impartiality and fairness.

HENRY S. PRITCHETT,
President of the Carnegie Foundation.

June, 1919.

PART I

THE EXISTING DENIAL OF JUSTICE TO THE POOR

CHAPTER I

FREEDOM AND EQUALITY OF JUSTICE—THE IDEAL

To no one will we sell, to no one will we refuse or delay, right or justice.
MAGNA CARTA, cap. 40.

FREEDOM and equality of justice are twin fundamental conceptions of American jurisprudence. Together they form the basic principle on which our entire plan for the administration of justice is built. They are so deep-rooted in the body and spirit of our laws that the very meaning which we ascribe to the word justice embraces them. A system which created class distinctions, having one law for the rich and another for the poor, which was a respecter of persons, granting its protection to one citizen and denying it to his fellow, we would unhesitatingly condemn as unjust, as devoid of those essentials without which there can be no justice.

From the dawn of Anglo-Saxon legal history, this idea has been manifest. The earliest laws continually directed that justice be done alike to rich and poor.[1] The equal right to law was asserted in the Charter of Liberties of Henry II.[2] The idea received its classic embodiment and statement in the fortieth paragraph of Magna Carta, where was inscribed "*nulli vendemus, nulli negabimus, aut differemus, rectum aut justiciam.*" As a purely historical fact this did not signify, or inaugurate, an era of absolute freedom of justice, but it was a first step in that direction. Its supreme importance, however, lies in the tradition[3] which gradually attached to it, and which glorified the idea into an ideal—an ideal which steadily persisted in men's minds throughout five centuries, and which was brought by the colonists to the New World.[4]

In the constitutional conventions which followed the American Revolution the ideal was given concrete expression in the various state Bills and Declarations of Rights.[5] The Massachusetts Constitution, adopted in 1780, declared:[6]

"Every subject of the Commonwealth ought to find a certain remedy, by having recourse to the laws, for all injuries or wrongs which he may receive in his person, property, or character. He ought to obtain right and justice freely, and without being obliged to purchase it; completely, and without any denial; promptly, and without delay; conformably to the laws."

As state after state has been added to the Union, its people, in constitutional assembly, have written the same declaration into their fundamental law. In New York the

[1] Pound: *Causes of Popular Dissatisfaction with the Administration of Justice,* 29 Am. Bar Ass'n R. (1906) 395; citing *Secular Ordinance of Edgar,* cap. I; *Secular Ordinance of Cnut,* 2; *Laws of Ethelred,* VI, 1; *Laws of Edward,* Preface.

[2] Stimson: *Federal and State Constitutions* (1908), page 16.

[3] McKechnie: *Magna Carta* (1914), pages 127, 395-398.

[4] For a general discussion of the influence of Magna Carta on American institutions see H. D. Hazeltine: *Influence of Magna Carta on American Constitutional Development,* 17 Columbia L. Rev. (1917) 1.

[5] Our American Bills of Rights bear a direct relation to Magna Carta. See James Q. Dealey: *Growth of American State Constitutions—1776 to 1914,* page 35. Bryce aptly called them "the legitimate children of Magna Carta." 1 American Commonwealth, 422.

[6] Part I: Declaration of Rights, Article XI.

declaration is contained in a statute,[1] but this is exceptional. To-day, the constitution of nearly every state, by express provision of the Bill of Rights, guarantees the freedom and equality of justice.[2] The Fourteenth Amendment to the Constitution of the United States adds to the state guaranty the authority of the supreme law of the land.[3]

As a matter of law, the right stands inviolable. It is recognized and established by the highest possible authority. But that is not all. Its incorporation into the Bills of Rights transformed the principle from merely a legal or juristic conception to a political consideration of supreme importance. Not only was the right to freedom and equality of justice set apart with those other cardinal rights of liberty and of conscience which were deemed sacred and inalienable, but it was made the most important of all because on it all the other rights, even the rights to life, liberty, and the pursuit of happiness, were made to depend.[4] In a word, it became the cornerstone of the Republic.

Ours was designed to be, and is, a government of laws and not of men. Under a government so constituted the right of the individual to life, to freedom of motion, of thought, of conscience, to his children, to his home, and the social interest in securing these things to human beings all depend, in last resort, entirely and absolutely on law. This is recognized by our constitutions, and has been repeatedly emphasized by decisions of courts, in the speeches of statesmen, and in treatises on government.[5] The New Hampshire constitution,[6] which is typical, thus expresses it:

> "It is essential to the preservation of the rights of every individual, his life, liberty, property, and character, that there be an impartial interpretation of the laws and administration of justice."

To secure impartial laws and an equal administration of justice, and thereby to make possible the enjoyment of the rights and opportunities contemplated by a democracy, the State itself exists.[7] The best welfare and the greatest possible happiness of the men, women, and children of the nation is the ultimate goal. The State is their servant and its government the means by which the desired end can best be obtained.

Concerning these fundamentals there is no dispute, at least within America. Their extended statement here would be superfluous but for the fact that, although the dependency of every right and interest on law is recognized, the consequences which in-

---

[1] *Civil Rights Law,* § 10 ; I. Birdseye's Cumming and Gilbert: *Consolidated Laws of New York,* page 620.

[2] For citations to each state constitution see Stimson: *Federal and State Constitutions,* pages 148, 149.

[3] Root: *Addresses on Government and Citizenship* (1916), page 460.

[4] "These cardinal rights may be divided into the four great realms of Rights to Liberty, to Property, to Law, and Rights of the People as against the Government. Logically and historically the first is the right to law, for there can be no property, no government, and no real liberty without law." Stimson: *Federal and State Constitutions,* page 10.

[5] See Cotting *v.* Kansas City Stock Yards Co. 183 U. S. 79, 84. Wheeler: *American Liberty Protected and Ruled by Law,* 48 Am. L. Rev. (1914) 1. Root: *Addresses on Government and Citizenship,* pages 98, 106, 540. 73 Annals of the American Academy of Political and Social Science (1917), 137. Lyman Abbott: *Report of Speeches at New York Legal Aid Society Banquet* (1901), page 31.

[6] *Constitution of New Hampshire* (1792), Part I, Bill of Rights, § 35.

[7] "That to secure these rights governments are instituted among men." *Declaration of Independence.*

evitably flow from such a form of government seem not to be generally appreciated.

These consequences, summarily stated, are:—First, there can be no political, social, or economic equality, no democracy, unless the substantive law by fair and equitable rules gives reality to equality by making it a living thing. Second, the substantive law, however fair and equitable itself, is impotent to provide the necessary safeguards unless the administration of justice, which alone gives effect and force to substantive law, is in the highest sense impartial. It must be possible for the humblest to invoke the protection of law, through proper proceedings in the courts, for any invasion of his rights by whomsoever attempted, or freedom and equality vanish into nothingness.

To withhold the equal protection of the laws, or to fail to carry out their intent by reason of inadequate machinery, is to undermine the entire structure and threaten it with collapse. For the State to erect an uneven, partial administration of justice is to abnegate the very responsibility for which it exists, and is to accomplish by indirection an abridgment of the fundamental rights which the State is directly forbidden to infringe. To deny law or justice to any persons is, in actual effect, to outlaw them by stripping them of their only protection.

It is for such reasons that freedom and equality of justice are essential to a democracy and that denial of justice is the short cut to anarchy.

CHAPTER II

DENIAL OF JUSTICE—THE FACT

> Of all the questions which are before the American people, I regard no
> one as more important than the improvement of the administration of jus-
> tice. We must make it so that the poor man will have as nearly as possible
> an equal opportunity in litigating as the rich man, and under present condi-
> tions, ashamed as we may be of it, this is not the fact. Ex-President Taft
> *in an Address before the Virginia Bar Association.*

THE inhabitants of the American colonies learned from the tyrannies and arbitrary conduct of George III and the Royal Governors what denial of justice
meant, and it incited them to rebellion.[1] In their first law-making, after attaining
independence, they declared that justice must be equal and accessible to all. This
principle they regarded, not as an utopian ideal, but as the indispensable safeguard of
their hard won liberties, and they proceeded to give it immediate effect. Their determination is still evidenced by our constitutional provisions[2] protecting persons accused
of crime, which were originally written by the framers to eliminate from our institutions the most glaring inequality of the English law.[3]

By contrast with the complexity of the present task, their problem was relatively
simple. They were a vigorous, self-reliant, homogeneous people, possessed of average
intelligence and shrewd common sense, living mostly in small towns and agricultural
communities, so that there was not much litigation. As only the simplest sort of judicial machinery was required, mechanical defects, with their attendant delays, were at
a minimum. Inexpensive justice was demanded and was secured—sometimes by the
doubtful economy of providing cheap judges.[4] In the lower courts where the smaller
cases were heard the poor could plead their own causes. This seemed natural because
it had been done very largely during the colonial era,[5] and it was possible because
there was little law and few precedents; in fact, many of the judges were laymen.[6]
This early administration of justice was in many respects inferior to our present system, but whatever its shortcomings it at least made some provision for the smaller
cases and there was no insuperable barrier of expense fixed between the poor and
the courts.

The forces, in short, which have caused our administration of justice to break
down as to the small causes and the claims of the poor, are not inevitable, or inex-

---

[1] *Declaration of Independence*, Paragraphs 3, 4, 11, 17, 20, 21, and particularly Paragraph 10 — "He has obstructed
the administration of justice by refusing his assent to laws establishing judiciary powers."

[2] *United States Constitution*, Amendments V, VI, and VIII. For citations to the state provisions, and for a complete discussion, see Stimson: *Federal and State Constitutions*, pages 164 *et seq.*

[3] The English criminal law of the eighteenth century not only inflicted extreme punishments but deprived prisoners of a fair trial, as by forbidding them counsel for their defence. This injustice was ameliorated in 1836 and
abolished by the Prisoners' Defence Act of 1903.

[4] American Judicature Society, *Bulletin VIII* (1915), page 26.

[5] Lawyers had repeatedly been excluded by assembly enactments from appearing in the courts. Warren: *History
of the American Bar* (1913), pages 4, 106.

[6] *Ibid.*, page 16.

tricably interwoven in the development of our institutions, or even of long duration, but are rather the result of the tremendous changes which have taken place in every phase of the nation's life.

These changed conditions, to which our rigid court organization with inflexible machinery was unable to adapt itself, are mainly due to immigration, the rise of the wage-earning class, and above all, to the startling growth of urban population with all that it entails. With the great cities came the infinite complexity of modern life, of business, and of affairs in general which breeds litigation.[1] The law itself became highly complicated. With thirteen thousand decisions of courts of last resort being made each year and twelve thousand laws annually enacted by the legislatures, no man could determine his rights without employing attorneys.[2] The legislative attempt to fix the machinery of justice in all its details made of procedure a maze which precluded litigation unless the suitor could engage counsel to guide his case through all the technicalities. The first attempt to meet the enormous pressure of litigation was by multiplication of courts, which served only to confound the confusion[3] by injecting additional questions of jurisdiction, venue, and procedure[4] into a system already enmeshed in its own superabundant technicalities. The situation is summarized by Dean Pound in these words:[5]

"Our judicial organization and the great body of our American common law are the work of the last quarter of the eighteenth century and the first half of the nineteenth century. On the other hand our great cities and the legal and social problems to which they give rise are of the last half of the nineteenth century,[6] and indeed the pressing problems do not become acute until the last quarter of that century."[7]

One of these problems was "to make adequate provision for petty litigation in communities where there is a huge volume of such litigation which must be dealt with adequately on pain of grievous denial of justice; to provide for disposing quickly, inexpensively, and justly of the litigation of the poor, for the collection of debts in a shifting population, and for the great volume of small controversies which a busy, crowded population, diversified in race and language, necessarily engenders."

The realization that there are grave defects in the administration of justice came but slowly. Had not enough laws been passed, enough courts organized, court houses built, judges, clerks, and officers provided and paid salaries—what more was necessary? When Roscoe Pound delivered his epoch-making address on "The Causes of Popular Dissatisfaction with the Administration of Justice" before the American

---

[1] *Preliminary Report on Efficiency in the Administration of Justice*, for the National Economic League, page 29; American Judicature Society, *Bulletin I* (1914), page 1; represented in 52 Ann. Am. Ac. Pol. & Soc. Science (1914), 208.

[2] Root: *Addresses on Government and Citizenship*, page 159.

[3] American Judicature Society, *Bulletin VI* (1915), page 18; Pound: *Administration of Justice in the Modern City*, 26 Harvard L. Rev. (1913) 308, 313.

[4] 73 Ann. Am. Ac. Pol. & Soc. Science (1917), 15.   [5] Pound: *op. cit.*, pages 303, 310, 315.

[6] New York did not have a population of one million until 1880.

[7] It is interesting to note that organized legal aid was first considered in 1875.

Bar Association in 1906,[1] his was like a voice crying in the wilderness. From the reported discussion,[2] one would judge that most of the lawyers present were incredulous, and that not a few were indignant at the intimation that our justice was not closely akin to perfection itself.

In the twelve years that have followed, the evidence has become overwhelming. The facts, though not the causes which underlie them, are well known. The administration of American justice is not impartial, the rich and the poor do not stand on an equality before the law, the traditional method of providing justice has operated to close the doors of the courts to the poor, and has caused a gross denial of justice in all parts of the country to millions of persons.

Sweeping as this indictment may appear, it is substantiated by ample authority.[3] A few statements deserve to be presented here.

"If there is one sad anomaly that should stand out in our present days of conscientious self-searching, it is the harsh fact that, with all our prating about justice, we deliberately withhold it from the thousands who are too poor to pay for it."[4]

"The sources from which industrial unrest springs are: . . . 3. Denial of justice in the creation, in the adjudication and in the administration of law."[5]

"The equal administration of the laws is a right guaranteed by the fundamental law of the land; and yet no person will deny that this privilege is more honored in the breach than in the observance; for there are very many people in every American community who, through ignorance of their rights or their inability to pay the imposts levied by the state as a condition precedent to the pursuit of justice in the courts, are constantly being denied that equal administration of the laws and the justice that is supposed, logically, to follow it."[6]

"Taking the country as a whole it is so obvious that we have almost ceased to remark it, that in petty causes, that is, with respect to the every day rights and wrongs of the great majority of an urban community, the machinery whereby rights are secured practically defeats rights by making it impracticable to assert them when they are infringed. Indeed in a measure this is so in all causes. But what is merely exasperating in large causes is downright prohibitive in small causes. While in theory we have a perfect equality, in result, unless one can afford expensive and time-consuming litigation, he must constantly forego undoubted rights, to which in form the rules of law give full security but for which, except where large sums are involved, the actual conduct of litigation affords no practicable remedy."

---

[1] 29 Am. Bar Ass'n R. (1906) 395.   [2] *Ibid.*, beginning page 55.

[3] Hyde: *Reorganization of the Bar*, 8 Illinois L. Rev. (1913) 241; San Francisco *Recorder* of July 13, 1914 (editorial); *Proceedings of Virginia Conference of Charities and Correction* (1916), 78; *Report of Proceedings of Third Conference of National Alliance of Legal Aid Societies* (1914), 36; Wood: *Position of the Public Defender in the Administration of Justice* (1914), 23 ; 15 Boston Legal Aid Rep. (1915) 8; 1 San Francisco L. A. R. (1916) 3; 106 Outlook (1914), 660, 661; 26 World's Work (1913), 663; Commercial Club of Nashville *Tattler* of July, 1916, page 21; 73 Ann. Am. Ac. Pol. & Soc. Science (1917), 5, 106, 140.

[4] American Judicature Society, *Bulletin VIII* (1915), page 24.

[5] Summary of the *Manly Report of the United States Commission on Industrial Relations* (1915), 5; see also page 9.

[6] San Francisco *Recorder* of November 6, 1916, page 1.

"Many causes have contributed to this neglect which disgraces American justice."[1]

The majority of our judges and lawyers view this situation with indifference. They fail to see behind this denial of justice the suffering and tragedy which it causes, the havoc it plays in individual lives, and its influence in retarding our Americanization program. "The judicial department," said Chief Justice Marshall,[2] "comes home in its effects to every man's fireside. It passes on his property, his reputation, his life, his all." Because law is all-embracing, the denial of its protection means the destruction of homes through illegal foreclosures, the loss through trick or chicanery of a lifetime's savings, the taking away of children from their parents by fraudulent guardianship proceedings.[3] Hundreds of thousands of men, many of them immigrants, have been unable to collect their wages honestly earned.[4]

Denial of justice is not merely negative in effect; it actively encourages fraud and dishonesty. Unscrupulous employers, seeing the inability of wage-earners to enforce payments, have deliberately hired men without the slightest intention of paying them.[5] Some of these employers are themselves poor men, who strive in this way to gain an advantage. The evil is not one of class in the sense that it gives the poor over to the mercies of only the rich. It enables the poor to rob one another; it permits the shrewd immigrant of a few years' residence to defraud his more recently arrived countrymen. The line of cleavage which it follows and accentuates is that between the dishonest and the honest. Everywhere it abets the unscrupulous, the crafty, and the vicious in their ceaseless plans for exploiting their less intelligent and less fortunate fellows. The system not only robs the poor of their only protection, but it places in the hands of their oppressors the most powerful and ruthless weapon ever invented.

The law itself becomes the means of extortion. As Lord Brougham said of the English administration of justice in 1800, it puts "a two-edged sword in the hands of craft and oppression." From the cradle to the grave the poor man is the prey of a host of petty swindlers,[6] who find it easy, through such devices as fraudulent assignments, trustee process, or garnishment of wages for fictitious debts,[7] to rob and

[1] Pound: *Administration of Justice in the Modern City*, 26 Harvard L. Rev. (1913) 316.

[2] *John Marshall*, 10 American Statesmen Series, 249.

[3] For such cases see 1 Kansas City L. A. R. 7; 7 Detroit L. A. R. 9, case 9; 14 Boston L. A. R. 19; 3 Buffalo L. A. R. cover.

[4] 2 Kansas City L. A. R. 5; 3 Detroit L. A. R. 11, case 9; 4 Detroit L. A. R. 8, case 5; 32 Minneapolis L. A. R. 26; Newark L. A. R. for 1916, 4; 15 Louisiana Bar Ass'n R. 331; 2 Hartford L. A. R. 6; 19 New York Educational Alliance R. 32.

[5] 40 N. Y. L. A. R. 16, 32.

[6] St. Louis Bar Ass'n L. A. R. 1–3.

[7] For a complete discussion of such abuses in Missouri see 1 Kansas City L. A. R. 14–20; numerous other instances are found in 2 Boston L. A. R. 7; Boston L. A. S. case 9262, case 6750 of 1918; Pittsburgh L. A. S. Prospectus (1909), Purpose Clause of Constitution; 4 Pittsburgh L. A. R. 12, 13; 1 Philadelphia L. A. R. 2; Portland (Oregon) Social Service Bureau *Report* (1913), 47; St. Louis Bar Ass'n L. A. R. 2.
    An investigation in Omaha disclosed a case in which the defendant's summons had been left in his woodpile. By the time he discovered it, a default judgment had been entered.

despoil. There exist to-day businesses established, conducted, and flourishing on the principle that as against the poor the law can be violated with impunity because redress is beyond their reach. It is this situation which allowed such unrestrained abuse of the laws regulating the assignment of future wages that a sort of quasi-slavery resulted, which brought the loan shark into being, and permitted flagrant usury to grow into a monstrous thing.[1]

The effects of this denial of justice are far reaching. Nothing rankles more in the human heart than the feeling of injustice. It produces a sense of helplessness, then bitterness.[2] It is brooded over. It leads directly to contempt for law, disloyalty to the government, and plants the seeds of anarchy.[3] The conviction grows that law is not justice[4] and challenges the belief that justice is best secured when administered according to law. The poor come to think of American justice as containing only laws that punish and never laws that help.[5] They are against the law because they consider the law against them.[6] A persuasion spreads that there is one law for the rich and another for the poor.[7]

How this comes about can be simply told. One afternoon, Arthur v. Briesen, President of the New York Legal Aid Society, took Theodore Roosevelt, then Police Commissioner of New York, to the Society's office to see what went on. They sat at the interviewing desk. A glazier came in and related that he had set twenty-two panes of glass in a barn and that the owner of the barn had refused to pay him $6.60, the agreed price.[8] He had been out of work and needed this money to buy bread and milk for his family's supper. On his way home from the West Side, where he had worked, to the East Side, where he lived, he crossed Fifth Avenue at Forty-fourth Street and passed the luxurious restaurants on either corner. His own children went to bed supperless. The next morning he sought out a lawyer, who told him that to bring suit the costs and the fee would be ten dollars. This he could not pay. From there he went to the Municipal Court, originally known as "The Poor Man's Court," where he saw a judge, who was obliged to explain that he had neither the time, nor the money, nor the right to undertake the necessary proceedings; that as the man had no money, he could not prosecute the case; and that, inasmuch as the expenses would exceed the amount in dispute, he had better drop it. As the man told

[1] For a graphic description of the extent of the loan business see an article in the New York *Times* for March 25, 1917, Magazine Section, page 4, quoting from Arthur H. Ham, Director of Division of Remedial Loans, of the Russell Sage Foundation; also *Business of Licensed Petty Loan Brokers in Baltimore*, a study made in 1916 by the Legal Aid Bureau of the Federated Charities of Baltimore.

[2] Cf. *United States Bureau of Labor Bulletin No.* 98 (1912), page 289.

[3] Theodore Roosevelt in the *Metropolitan Magazine* for May, 1917, page 66; Municipal Court of Philadelphia, *Report* for 1915, pages viii, 37.

[4] Root: *Addresses on Government and Citizenship*, page 480.

[5] St. Louis Department of Public Welfare, Legal Aid Bureau, *Report* to the Mayor (April 10, 1916), page 7. Cf. Pound: *Administration of Justice in the Modern City*, 26 Harvard L. Rev. (1913) 315.

[6] Catchings: *Work of the New York Legal Aid Society*, 15 Green Bag (1903), 313, 318.

[7] Wells: *The Man in Court* (1917), page 30.

[8] This is the case referred to by Mr. Roosevelt in his speech at the Twenty-fifth Anniversary Dinner of the New York Legal Aid Society. *Report of Speeches* (1901), page 12.

his story, sitting in the office of the legal aid society, he was an incipient anarchist.

The effect on the immigrant is peculiarly unfortunate. He comes to this country, often from lands of injustice and oppression, with high hopes, expecting to receive fair play and square dealing. It is essential that he be assimilated and taught respect for our institutions. Because of the strangeness of all his surroundings, his ignorance of our language and our customs, often because of his simple faith in the America of which he has heard, he becomes an easy prey. When he finds himself wronged or betrayed, keen disappointment is added to the sense of injustice. Through bitter disillusionment he becomes easily subject to the influences of sedition and disorder.[1]

The essentially conservative bench and bar will vehemently deny any suggestion that there is no law for the poor, but, as the legal aid societies know,[2] such is the belief to-day of a multitude of humble, entirely honest people, and in the light of their experience it appears as the simple truth. Consider, for example, this actual case.[3] A woman borrowed ten dollars in 1914, and for two years paid interest at 180 per cent. In 1916 a law was enacted fixing 36 per cent as the maximum rate.[4] The lender, by a device contrary to the statute, compelled her to continue paying 156 per cent interest. The law also provided that if excess interest were charged, the loan would be declared void by a suit in equity.[5] The law was on the books. The court house was open, the equity court in session with its judge on the bench and its officers in attendance. All that was of no avail to her, for the law could not bring its redress until five dollars was paid for service of process and entry fee, and ten dollars to an attorney to draw, file, and present the necessary bill of complaint. Fifteen dollars she did not have and, because of her condition, could not earn. For her there was no law.

Repeated warnings have come from sources entitled to respect that such a condition of affairs is capable of producing incalculable harm.

"When litigation is too costly, the result for many persons is a denial of justice. Such denial or partial denial of justice engenders social and commercial friction. The sense of helplessness thus caused incites citizens to take the law into their own hands. It causes crimes of violence. It saps patriotism and destroys civic pride. It arouses class jealousies and breeds contempt for law and government."[6]

"The problem is fundamental. It strikes at the very root of our economic, social

---

[1] See *The Immigrants in America Review*, vol. i, No. 4 (January, 1916), pages 31, 32; *Second Report*, California Commission of Immigration (1916), 101, 103; Prospectus of New Jersey Legal Aid Society: *A Legal Clinic* (1906), 2; 17 Ann. Am. Ac. Pol. & Soc. Science (1901), 165; *Report* of Massachusetts Commission on Immigration for 1914, House Document No. 2300 of 1914, page 111.

[2] 1 Buffalo L. A. R. 3; 5 Buffalo L. A. R. 6; 6 Cleveland L. A. R. 7; Cleveland L. A. S.: *Justice for the Poor*, page 1; Nashville Commercial Club: *The Legal Aid Society* (1915); 1 Pittsburgh L. A. R. 3; 8 Philadelphia L. A. R. 15; 16 Jewish Charities of Chicago R. (Bureau of Personal Service) 70, 72, 73; 26 N. Y. L. A. R. 5; Wood: *Office of Public Defender* (Los Angeles), page 3; 2 L. A. Rev. No. 2, p. 1; 8 L. A. Rev. No. 3, p. 2; *Report of Proceedings*, Third Convention National Alliance L. A. S., page 22; *Ibid.*, Fourth, page 123.

[3] Mary —— v. Star Finance Co., reported in full in 16 Boston L. A. R. 12–14.

[4] Mass. Acts of 1916, chap. 224.

[5] Mass. Acts of 1911, chap. 727, §§ 10, 13.

[6] Chief Justice Olson in the *Eighth and Ninth Annual Report* of the Chicago Municipal Court (1915), page 128.

and political structure. The man or woman who has honestly toiled and cannot obtain the wages earned, loses faith in humanity and the efficacy of our laws and courts; is often turned out a beggar, vagrant, or criminal, or seeks redress by forcible means."[1]

"If ever a time shall come when in this city only the rich man can enjoy law as a doubtful luxury, when the poor who need it most cannot have it, when only a golden key will unlock the door to the court room, the seeds of revolution will be sown, the firebrand of revolution will be lighted and put into the hands of men, and they will almost be justified in the revolution which will follow."[2]

In that direction we have imperceptibly, unconsciously, and unintentionally drifted. The end of such a course is disclosed by history.[3] Differences in the ability of classes to use the machinery of the law, if permitted to remain, lead inevitably to disparity between the rights of classes in the law itself. And when the law recognizes and enforces a distinction between classes, revolution ensues or democracy is at an end.

[1] *Sixteenth Biennial Report* of the California Bureau of Labor Statistics (1914), page 15. Cf. Harley : *Ultimate Types of Inferior Courts and Judges*, 22 Case and Comment (1915), 6.

[2] From a speech by Lyman Abbott at the Twenty-fifth Anniversary Dinner of the New York Legal Aid Society. *Report of Speeches* (1901), page 32.

[3] By the third century A.D. class distinction had been set up by the Roman law. For an excellent statement, see Davis: *The Influence of Wealth in Imperial Rome* (1910), page 323.

CHAPTER III

THE DEFECTS IN THE ADMINISTRATION OF JUSTICE

> The profession and the courts must take up vigorously and fear-
> lessly the problem of to-day — how to *administer* the law to meet
> the demands of the world that is. ROSCOE POUND *in Justice Ac-*
> *cording to Law.*[1]

§ 1

THE end of all our legal institutions is to secure justice. What is the just decision in any controversy we determine, not by the arbitrary will or opinion
of any individual, but in accordance with definite rules of law. This is the method
Preliminary   of justice according to law, and because it so far surpasses all other
Definitions   attempts at human justice it stands as a basic principle from which we
             cannot safely depart.

Our system of justice according to law has clear defects which exist first, because
law is not omnipotent but has limits beyond which its action is ineffective,[2] and second, because the system, like all finite projects, has its own particular weak points.[3]
From the ensuing discussion, defects traceable to these limitations and disadvantages
must be eliminated, for so long as we desire to retain the manifold benefits of justice according to law, it is profitless to quarrel about its concomitant and inherent
shortcomings.

§ 2

Freedom and equality of justice for the poor depend first on an impartial substantive law and second on an even-handed administration of that law. The substantive
Substantive   law is primary, for through it are created, stated, and defined all the
Law   rights, obligations, and relationships between individuals, between in-
              dividuals and the State, and through it are secured the social interests
in the health, safety, security, and general well-being of the individual and the community. It is an absolute condition precedent, for if it acknowledged differences in
rights between rich and poor, a perfected machinery of enforcement would serve only
to accentuate the distinctions and make them the more intolerable.

The body of the substantive law, as a whole, is remarkably free from any taint
of partiality. It is democratic to the core. Its rights are conferred and its liabilities
imposed without respect of persons. While, in this age of transition, it is confronted
with tremendous problems as yet unsolved, while it is slow to employ the more liberal premises demanded by a new era,[4] it deserves to be recognized as a remarkably
satisfactory human achievement. This is the opinion of our greatest legal scholars and

---

[1] 13 Columbia L. Rev. 696; 14 Columbia L. Rev. 1, 103 (1913-14). In the reprint in separate form see page 39.

[2] Pound: *Limits of Effective Legal Action*, 3 Am. Bar Ass'n Journal, No. 1 (January, 1917), 55, particularly pages 65-70.

[3] Pound: *Justice According to Law*, particularly pages 17, 18.

[4] Cf. Pound: *Ibid.*, page 60.

of the most searching critics of our judicial institutions; of such men as Roscoe Pound, John H. Wigmore, and the group who comprise the membership of the American Judicature Society.[1] A careful examination of the fairness of the substantive law from the point of view of the poor has recently been made by Judge Parry of the English County Courts,[2] from which it is instantly apparent that the legal disabilities of the poor in nearly every instance result from defects in the machinery of the law and are not created by any discriminations of the substantive law against them.

Three branches of substantive law, it is true, have been much criticized. With regard to public service law it has been popular to claim that the railroads, traction companies, gas and electric light corporations were imposing on the public without let or hindrance from the law. The better opinion is that the provisions of substantive law were entirely fair and adequate, but that the courts, without administrative machinery, were unable to cope with the problems of enforcement and supervision.[3]

Again, much of our landlord and tenant law is still feudal in its conceptions. The rule that most of our city dwellers, because they occupy without written leases, are only tenants " at will" and so liable to immediate dispossession does not accord with modern conditions and often causes extreme hardship. Legislative attempts, as in Massachusetts,[4] to invest such tenants with a measure of security by requiring notice to quit two weeks in advance have been frustrated by the courts' adherence to the common law rule that the landlord may give a written lease for a year to a third person, who then has a higher legal estate with right of possession after forty-eight hours' notice.[5] In practice this means that fictitious leases are delivered to ejectment companies,[6] which exercise their superior title by removing the tenant's household furniture to a warehouse to be interned till all charges are paid. This anachronism could easily be remedied, however, by giving to proper courts discretionary power to control the time which tenants, for cause shown, may continue in possession after the landlord's notice to vacate.[7]

Finally, the redress afforded injured employees by the law has called forth the bitterest attacks, and here the impartiality of the substantive law has most justly been challenged. The workman who sought to recover for injuries sustained at work, due to the negligence of his employer, was placed at an enormous disadvantage by the rules defining the master's liability. The fellow servant rule and the doctrine of assumption of risk, growing out of two cases which are now severely condemned[8] and

---

[1] See also, Pound: *Administration of Justice in the Modern City*, 26 Harvard L. Rev. (1913) 302 ; 73 Ann. Am. Ac. Pol. & Soc. Science (September, 1917), pages 133, 134, 136 ; *Report of Proceedings* of Missouri Bar Association in 1914, page 146. Cf. Bentwick : *Legal Aid for the Poor*, 105 Contemporary Review (1914), 559.

[2] Edward Abbott Parry : *The Law and the Poor* (1914). A limited examination is made by Frances M. Burdick in an article entitled, " Is Law the Expression of Class Selfishness ? " 25 Harvard L. Rev. (1912) 349. Professor Burdick's conclusion is in favor of the fairness of the substantive law.

[3] American Judicature Society, *Bulletin VI*, page 7.   [4] *Mass. Revised Laws of* 1902, chap. 129, § 12.

[5] Pratt *v.* Farrar, 92 Mass. (1865) 519 ; for a statement of the general doctrine see Swift *v.* Boyd, 202 Mass. (1909) 26.

[6] See Lewis : *Leasing out the Tenant at Will*, 2 Mass. L. Quarterly, No. 6 (August, 1917), 640.

[7] This is stated more fully in Chapter VIII, Small Claims Courts, § 7–4, page 59.

[8] As to Farwell *v.* Boston & Worcester Ry. (the first American case) 4 Metcalf (1842), 49, see Abbott: *Justice and*

elaborated by a process which can only be called judicial legislation,[1] came perilously near to constituting an actual class distinction in the law. Happily this stigma no longer attaches, because within the last seven years workmen's compensation statutes, which supplant the outworn doctrines of liability with the principle of insurance, have been enacted in nearly every jurisdiction.

On examination and on authority, the statement is warranted that the substantive law, with minor exceptions, is eminently fair and impartial. In other words, the existing denial of justice to the poor is not attributable to any injustice in the heart of the law itself. The necessary foundation for freedom and equality of justice exists. The immemorial struggle is half won.

§ 3

In sharp contrast, there are grave defects in the administration of the law. It is the wide disparity between the ability of the richer and poorer classes to utilize the machinery of the law which is, at bottom, the cause of the present unrest and dissatisfaction. Denial of justice to the poor is due to the *Defects in Administration* conditions, imposed by our traditional system, upon which alone can suits be brought and conducted. There is something tragic in the fact that a plan and method of administering justice, honestly designed to make efficient and certain that litigation on which at last all rights depend, should result in rearing insuperable obstacles in the path of those who most need protection, so that litigation becomes impossible, rights are lost, and wrongs go unredressed.

The present inequalities and defects in the administration of justice are not the result of any deliberate intention. No dominating group or class has consciously set out to foreclose the rights of the poor. The procedural laws have been passed by the legislatures in good faith. The courts have interpreted and applied the adjective law without bias or favor. Corruption has played no part.[2]

The fact is that no one clearly perceived the general trend of affairs. A Bureau of Justice of the type advocated by Dean Pound before the Conference of Delegates of State and Local Bar Associations,[3] in 1917, could have detected and prevented the breakdown before it became serious, but as yet our judicial administration lacks that necessary adjunct. Complaints gradually became audible that whereas all other business was pointed toward efficiency, reduction of costs, and a general speeding-up, judicial machinery remained cumbersome, wasteful, time-consuming, and very expensive.

the Modern Law (1913), page 264. As to Priestly v. Fowler (the first English case), 3 Meeson & Welsby (1837), 1, see Parry: The Law and the Poor, pages 76 et seq.

[1] Judicial treatment of this particular class of cases incurred such strong public disapproval that such cases have now been taken out of the courts and entrusted to administrative tribunals. See post, Chapter XII, Administrative Tribunals, page 83.

[2] There are, of course, specific instances of bribery and judicial corruption. Most conspicuous is the old justice of the peace system, cf. post, page 42. On a broad view, however, corruption has played such a trivial part in breaking down our administration that it can be dismissed.

[3] This is mentioned in 24 Case and Comment (October, 1917), 423.

These complaints sounded in terms of delay and annoyance, not prohibition. Even to-day it is only dimly understood that this faulty organization and procedure,[1] which is exasperating in large suits between persons of means, in all small suits and in all litigation to which the poor are party causes an absolute denial of justice.

The conditions, under which our customary system requires litigation to be conducted, impair rights guaranteed by the substantive law because law is not self-enforcing; only through application in the courts does the law have life and force.[2] The most fundamental rights remain idle abstractions unless the courts are able to give them efficacy through enforcement. The Mexican Constitution exceeds any of our bills of rights in its solicitude for life, liberty, and property, and yet in no country have these rights been more steadily violated with impunity.[3] For this reason the mechanics of the law occupy a place of great importance. The vital problem of to-day in the administration of justice is to repair the breakdowns and to overhaul parts of the machinery so that it may work more smoothly and may be workable by all.

§ 4

The defects in the administration of the law fall into three distinct divisions. In the language of Piers Plowman:

> "To the poor the Courts are a maze,
> If he plead there all his life,
> Law is so lordly
> And loath to end his case;
> Without money paid in presents
> Law listeneth to few."

These three difficulties are not yet overcome. They still weigh heavily on the poor.

The Particular Defects   Delay plays its unfair part. Money must be paid in fees and costs or else the courts are closed. The law is necessarily an intricate and complicated science, which may not be understood or utilized without the assistance of a trained counsellor and advocate who must be paid.[4]

These are the conditions of modern litigation. The following three chapters consider their precise nature and their results.

---

[1] "Our system of courts is archaic and our procedure behind the times." Pound: *Causes of Popular Dissatisfaction with the Administration of Justice*, 29 Am. Bar Ass'n R. (1906) Part I, 395, 408. See also *Report* of the Committee on Judicial Procedure of the Massachusetts Constitutional Convention (July 16, 1917), *Convention Report No.* 314.

[2] "Applicatio est vita regulae," 2 Bulstrode, 79. "The law as a practical force always receives its final effect through the pronouncement of the judge." Wigmore: *The Qualities of Current Judicial Decisions*, 9 Illinois L. Rev. (1915) 529.

[3] Ezra R. Thayer: *Judicial Administration* (1915), page 1.

[4] All that can be done within the scope of this work is to examine these cardinal defects which have brought about a denial of justice to the poor. Many other factors, such as the frailties in human nature, maladjustments in our social order, ignorance, unfairnesses in our economic system, contribute to this deplorable result.

One further cause is so closely linked to the administration of justice that it must be stated, although it cannot be discussed in detail. There are to-day many members of the Bar so ill-trained in law and so poorly equipped to practise law that the cases entrusted to them are mishandled and ruined and the rights of their clients lost. Unquestionably too large a proportion of the existing denial of justice is traceable to this source.

CHAPTER IV

THE FIRST DEFECT—DELAY

While the law is enforced, justice waits. The possibilities of delay and of forcing a compromise to avoid expense and annoyance induce litigation by those who wish to escape the faithful performance of their contracts. The calendars are crowded with such cases. In such a game the poor stand little chance against the rich, or the honest against the unscrupulous. ELIHU ROOT.[1]

§ 1

Denial of Justice through Delay

ALTHOUGH the days of Jarndyce *v.* Jarndyce are over, the course of American justice still amply provides the opportunity for delay " which gives to monied might the means abundantly of wearying out the right." Delay is not entirely bad. In cases where it serves to cool hasty tempers and stay spiteful litigation it is desirable. But when it becomes so prolonged that the issue ceases to be that of the merits of the case and becomes one as to the respective length of the parties' pocketbooks, it is altogether intolerable.

This evil of delay is established and the injustice which it causes is universally recognized.[2] It works to defeat justice in two ways: first, by making the time required to reduce a case to final judgment so long that persons, unable to wait, do not start the case at all but give it up; and second, by forcing unfair settlements and compromises on persons so situated either before suit is brought or in discount of a verdict after trial in exchange for a waiver of appeal. In a wage claim speed is the essence of justice, for the suit is brought to obtain the means of livelihood. A judgment years or even months later is little better than no judgment.[3] In negotiations between counsel for the settlement of personal injury cases it is customary to deduct something from the amount agreed on as fair damages on the theory that less is better now than more three years hence in the due course of the law. The evil tends to aggravate itself by encouraging parties without meritorious defences to make a sham contest so that they may avail themselves of delay and perhaps beat down the claim against them.[4] The natural delay of the system is thus increased by this artificial burden; it is like throwing sand in unoiled gears.

---

[1] Root: *Addresses on Government and Citizenship* (1916), page 493; and see *Ending the Scandal of the Law's Delay, Ibid.*, page 177.

[2] Taft: *The Administration of Justice — Its Speeding and Cheapening*, 72 Central L. Journal (1911), 191, 193, 194; (same article) 18 Yale L. Journal, 28; Pound: *Administration of Justice in the Modern City*, 26 Harvard L. Rev. 302, 312, 313; Chicago Bar Association *Annual Report* for 1912, page 12; Storey: *Reform of Legal Procedure* (1911), page 3; Harley: *A Unified State Court System* (n.d.), page 10; Root: *Addresses on Government and Citizenship*, pages 125, 177, 179, 440, 493; *Report* of Special Section of the California Bar Association, Exhibit 3, printed in the San Francisco *Recorder* for July 14, 1916, page 6; *The Mediator*, vol. iv, No. 6 (June, 1912), p. 11; 6 Legal Aid Review, No. 4, p. 25; 7 L. A. R. No. 4, p. 25.

[3] In recognition of this fact, special industrial courts have been created in European countries, *United States Bureau of Labor Bulletin No.* 98 (January, 1912), p. 281.

[4] See Chicago Bar Association *Annual Report* for 1917, page 32.

§ 2

Delays are mainly of two sorts: those encountered in getting a case, after its entry in court, actually heard and determined, and those occasioned by the taking of ap-

The Nature of Delay

peals on points of law to the highest courts. The following case illustrates the delays in securing a final judgment in Philadelphia before the creation of the municipal court in 1913, and is typical of a condition which has existed in every large city:[1] A wage-earner had a claim for ten dollars, which represented a week's work. On January 19, 1911, the Legal Aid Society tried his case in the Magistrate's Court and secured judgment. On February 8, 1911, the defendant appealed to the Court of Common Pleas, which gave him the right to have the entire case tried all over again. On March 11, 1911, the plaintiff's claim was filed in the Court of Common Pleas and the case marked for the trial list. Owing to congested dockets the case did not actually appear on a trial list until February 7, 1912.

Here entered a rule of procedure which would be incredible if it did not exist.[2] A case marked for trial Monday must be tried Monday or Tuesday or else go off the list entirely. That is, if any prior case or cases marked on Monday's calendar should occupy the time of the court during Monday and Tuesday, then all other cases assigned on that list are cancelled and the parties must begin at the bottom again, re-marking the case for trial and awaiting the assignment. While this is going on in one session, another session of, the same court may have no cases and so be obliged to suspend, for, under the legal procedure, it was forbidden to do the common-sense thing of transferring cases from a congested to an empty session of court.

The wage-earner's case, assigned for February 7, 1912, was not reached on that day or the next, and so went off the list. It was re-marked and assigned for April 3, 1912. Not being reached on April 3 or 4, it again went off and did not reappear until October 10, 1912. Fortunately, it was reached and tried on October 11, 1912, and judgment entered for the plaintiff. It took one year and nine months, and required eleven days in court for both attorney and client, to collect the original ten dollars.[3]

In the criminal law, delays while awaiting trial are even more serious, for, where the defendant is too poor to furnish bail, delay is equivalent to a sentence of imprisonment for poverty.[4]

In appeals taken to the courts of last resort on points of law, a reasonable delay is to be expected. The right of appeal cannot be cut off, and a certain deliberation

---

[1] See *Eighth and Ninth Annual Report*, Municipal Court of Chicago (1915), page 11.

[2] Compare the similar rule in the Suffolk County (Mass.) Probate Court referred to *post*, page 77.

[3] *Report of the Proceedings* of Second Conference of Legal Aid Societies (1912), page 22 ; *Address* of Charles L. Brown, President Judge of the Municipal Court of Philadelphia (December 8, 1914), page 9. Before the creation of the Cleveland Municipal Court the Common Pleas Court was two years behind in its docket. *Report of Proceedings* of Second Conference of Legal Aid Societies, page 70.

[4] See *Justice for the Poor*, a report of the Committee on Criminal Courts of the (New York) Charity Organization Society.

of the points raised is desirable. Such appeals are relatively few in number and are not objectionable. But when the highest courts get years behind in their cases, as has happened in California and New York, and parties appeal not to secure rights but to secure delay, to get the benefit of the old adage that "time fights for the defendant," with hopes that the opposing party will die, or run out of funds, or become discouraged and give up, then delay becomes an outrage.

§ 3

The delays which mar the existing administration of justice originate in, and are made possible by,[1] our faulty court organization and our "thoroughly antiquated civil and criminal procedure." [2] With unification of court organization and simplification of procedure unconscionable delay will be swept away.

The Elimination of Delay

The outlook for a speedy reformation is promising. Already great strides have been taken.[3] On this score the public conscience is aroused. The elimination of intermediate appeals permitting two trials on the facts has accompanied the creation of modern municipal courts and has done away with one of the most flagrant abuses.[4] The municipal courts, despite their vast number of cases, are keeping abreast of their dockets.[5] The intelligent propaganda of the American Judicature Society is clearly pointing to the methods whereby judicial administration can be lifted out of the muddle into which it has fallen, and there is an increasing disposition on the part of the courts, the bar, and the legislatures to make the needed changes. With the passing of delay one great cause of denial of justice to the poor will be at an end.

Tedious proceedings and long delays are not necessary. They are not inevitable or inherent in the nature of our judicial institutions. They can be abolished whenever we so will it.

---

[1] Philadelphia Municipal Court *Report* for 1915, page vii; American Judicature Society, *Bulletin VI*, page 8; *Preliminary Report* for the National Economic League on *Efficiency in the Administration of Justice*, pages 20–26.

[2] Redlich: *The Common Law and the Case Method*, Carnegie Foundation for the Advancement of Teaching, *Bulletin No.* 8 (1914), page 49.

[3] 73 Ann. Am. Ac. Pol. & Soc. Science (1917), 3, 211.

[4] *Report* of the Boston Municipal Court for 1916, pages 5–7.

[5] In February, 1917, the New York Municipal Court rendered judgment in a tort claim for an accident which happened in February. It is not unusual for judgment in breach of contract cases to be entered the same month in which the breach occurred.

CHAPTER V

THE SECOND DEFECT—COURT COSTS AND FEES

> Believing that courts as governmental agencies are operated as a part of our so-
> cial system for the benefit of all, we are unwilling to subscribe to the view that
> the litigant should pay all expenses of maintaining the court. Inasmuch as
> the law of the state requires that fees and costs be taxed and charged to the
> litigants and has conferred no power upon this court to abolish them entirely,
> we could not consider doing away with all fees however desirable that might
> seem. COMMITTEE ON COSTS *of the Cleveland Municipal Court.*[1]

THE entire question of the costs and fees paid to courts and court officers is one
that has been neglected in discussions concerning the betterment of the administration of justice. While the total expense of litigation and the injustice which it
causes is a common topic, the precise part played by the system of imposts fixed and
levied by the State on persons who are compelled to resort to the courts for protection or redress has never received any general or extended consideration.[2] The American Bar Association's "Special Committee to Suggest Remedies and Formulate Proposed Laws to Prevent Delay and Unnecessary Cost in Litigation," which has been
in existence since 1907 and has submitted annual reports, has laid almost all of its
emphasis on procedure and has done but little with the subject of costs.[3]

This is perhaps natural, for the present system and tariff of fees is so curious that,
with the exception of the taxing clerk and those attorneys who live by costs, few
lawyers understand its details or why many of the items exist. And yet, inasmuch
as these costs form no inconsiderable item and are a prolific source of denial of justice
to the poor, they require careful statement and examination.

§ 1

Costs have existed so long that there is a general disposition to regard them as

*Nature and
History of
Costs and Fees*
fundamental, as immutably bound up with our legal institutions.
This is a mistake; costs are not established by our constitutions, they
are not the product of common law, they exist solely and entirely as
creatures of statute.[4]

The early English law had no system of costs. An unsuccessful plaintiff or defend-

---

[1] From the second page of the *Report* of the Committee on Costs of the Cleveland Municipal Court, submitted September 26, 1913. This report was adopted by unanimous vote of the judges, and its reduced schedule of costs went into effect October 1, 1913.

[2] The Cleveland *Report* is possibly an exception to this. While the judges on the Committee examined into the subject thoroughly, the report itself is brief and local in application.

[3] In three reports there is some consideration of fees. In 34 Am. Bar Ass'n R. (1909) 600 there is a short discussion; in 35 A. B. A. R. (1910) 622 a bill to diminish costs on appeal is submitted; in 38 A. B. A. R. (1913) 552, 572, it is proposed to eliminate travel expenses in certain cases by permitting marshals to mail processes to deputies in outly-
ing districts. In the summary of the work of this Committee set out in 42 A. B. A. R. (1917) 336-339, costs are not mentioned.

[4] 11 Cyclopedia of Law and Procedure, 24; cases cited.

ant might be amerced *pro clamore falso*, that is, the court might impose a fine for setting up a false claim or defence, but it is doubtful if this was done to any extent.[1] So far as costs played any part, they were included in the damages or, on occasion, assessed in the arbitrary discretion of the judge.[2] It is true that it was the royal prerogative of the earlier kings to charge suitors for writs to the King's Court, but it was an accepted maxim that the poor should have their writs for nothing.[3] "Before the Statute of Gloucester (6 Edward I, cap. 1) no person was entitled to recover any costs of suit either in plea, real, personal, or mixed."[4]

With this statute of Edward I the system of fixed costs begins. The motivating causes which led to the establishment of court fees are not clear. They seem to have been a survival of the idea of revenue, a carrying over of the conception of fines for a false claim (for in theory only the wrongdoer bears costs), and a desire to impose a deterrent to litigation. At the same time, there was a clear idea that, while revenue and a deterrent were desirable, costs ought never to operate as a prohibition, and by the time of Henry VIII ample provision had been made to safeguard the rights of the poor.

The Statute of 11 Henry VII, cap. 12, permitting poor persons to sue without payment of costs merits quotation, for the centuries which have intervened between its enactment in 1495 and the establishment of the small claims court in Cleveland in 1913 bear witness to no more comprehensive attempt to secure freedom of justice to the poor. The tendency has, in fact, until recently been entirely in an opposite direction. It was provided—

"That every poor person or persons which have or hereafter shall have causes of action against any person within this realm shall have by the discretion of the Chancellor of this realm, for the time being, writs or writs original, and subpoenas according to the nature of their causes, therefore nothing paying to your Highness for the seals of the same, nor to any person for the writing of the said writs to be hereafter sued; and that the said Chancellor shall assign clerks to write the same writs ready to be sealed; and also learned counsel and attornies for the same, without any reward taken therefor; and if the said writ or writs be returned before the king in his bench, the justices shall assign to the same poor person or persons, counsel learned, by their discretions, which shall give their counsels, nothing taking for the same; and the justices shall likewise appoint attorney for such poor person or persons and all other officers requisite and necessary to be had for the speed of the said suits, which shall do their duties without any reward for their counsels, help and business in the same; and the same law shall be observed of all such suits to be made before the King's justices of his Common place, and barons of his Exchequer, and all other justices in the courts of record where any such suit shall be."

This was the origin of the in forma pauperis proceeding.[5] It is an important landmark which has been too much forgotten. Because it gives effect to the spirit of Magna

---

[1] 11 Cyclopedia of Law and Procedure, 24; 17 Fed. 2; 4 Blackstone, 379.
[2] John Hullock: *Law of Costs* (London, 1796), 2-4.   [3] Pollock and Maitland: 1 History of English Law, 174.
[4] Hullock: *op. cit.*, 2-4; *Society for Comparative Legislation*, vol. i (1st Series), 241.
[5] 16 Encyclopedia of Pleading and Practice, 675 ; Roy *v*. Louisville & Nashville Ry. Co., 34 Fed. 276.

Carta it has been regarded as establishing a constitutional principle.[1] This enactment was carried to its logical completion by 23 Henry VIII, cap. 15, which freed
a pauper plaintiff from imposition of costs if he failed to obtain a verdict or was nonsuited. The statute left the defeated poor suitor to be subjected to such other punish-
ment as the judges deemed reasonable. The old books state that if a pauper abused the
proceeding or was nonsuited, he might be taken to the market-place and whipped;[2] but
the general spirit of the law was such that when a motion came before Lord Chief
Justice Holt to order a nonsuited pauper to be whipped, he denied the motion, observ-
ing that there was no officer for the purpose and that he had never known it done.[3]

These statutes remained in force in England until 1883, when by the Statute Law
and Civil Procedure Act (46 & 47 Victoria, c. 49) they were repealed and, with them,
these rights and privileges swept away.[4] The English law remained inhospitable to
poor suitors until the great changes inaugurated in 1913.[5]

The American states carried over into their judicial systems the plan of costs and
fees, but many neglected to include the necessary corollary of the proceeding in forma
pauperis. In Pennsylvania it has been held that the statute of 11 Henry VII, c. 12, is
part of the common law of the state,[6] but in practice the statute is ignored. To-day,
the permission to sue without costs is granted by statute in about half the states.
Even in such states the right is a good deal hedged about, by limiting it to specified
types of cases, as wage claims, by confining it to proceedings in certain courts,[7] and by
holding it inapplicable to cases on appeal.[8] In several states it has fallen into disuse.

§ 2

It is extremely difficult to present with any conciseness the existing costs and fees
in the United States. The items are innumerable, they vary from state to state, and
within a state they differ in different courts, in different proceedings,
The Present and a line of cleavage runs through law and equity. In the Boston
Situation Municipal Court service of process must be made by a sheriff or constable whose fees are paid by the plaintiff; in the Cincinnati court the constable must
serve processes, but he is paid a salary by the city; in Cleveland the mail is used; in
New York any disinterested person may serve the summons. In some states fees are

---

[1] Frederick J. Stimson in *Federal and State Constitutions* (1908) lists this statute in his historical digest of constitutional principles, Book II, chap. ii, p. 100.

[2] *Bacon's Abridgment*, vol. ii, tit. Costs, § 4, p. 51.   [3] Salk. 506; Bacon, *op. cit.*; Hullock : *Law of Costs*, page 213.

[4] Bisschop: *Legal Aid for the Poor*, 48 Law Journal (1913), 242; Bentwick: *Legal Aid for the Poor*, 47 Law Journal
(1912), 48.

[5] These are discussed *post* in Chapter XIV, Assigned Counsel, page 102; and in Chapter XXV, A More Equal Administration of Justice, page 248.

[6] Cowan *v.* City of Chester, 2 Delaware County R. 234; 7 Weekly Notes of Cases, 31; *Roberts' Digest* (second edition,
Philadelphia, 1847), 116; 1 Johnson on Practice in Pennsylvania, 71.

[7] In Maryland the in forma pauperis act does not apply to the People's Court in Baltimore; in New Jersey it does
not apply to the District Courts.

[8] 16 Encyc. Pleading and Practice, 693. It seems to apply to appeals only in the Federal Courts and in Georgia.
Fite *v.* Black, 85 Ga. 413; in North Carolina, Mason *v.* Osgood, 71 N. Car. 212; and in Tennessee, Lynn *v.* Mfg. Co.
8 Lea, 29.

charged for marking cases on the calendar, for entering judgment, for issuance of execution; in others such costs are unknown. If a cook, suing for wages earned on land in Boston, takes an appeal from the Municipal Court to the Supreme Judicial Court, the entry fee is three dollars; but if a cook, suing for wages earned on a vessel which comes into the port of Boston, takes an appeal from the District Court to the Circuit Court of Appeals, the entry fee is thirty-five dollars. In Oregon, to the regular filing fee in the county court there has been added a one dollar fee for the benefit of the Multnomah County law library.[1] In many states jury fees varying greatly in amounts are charged — California $24 per day, Connecticut one payment of $6, Minnesota $3, Pennsylvania $4, Virginia $1.50, Oregon $6 (jury of six); in Ohio a law prescribing a jury fee of $5 was declared unconstitutional.[2] In California, until changed in 1915 at the instance of the Public Defender,[3] the cost of entering and marking a case on appeal was borne by the plaintiff, although the judgment in the lower court was in his favor and he had not taken the appeal. In some jurisdictions a defendant must pay a fee before he can appear and file an answer. In Illinois the respondent in a divorce case has been obliged to pay three dollars for the privilege of contesting, while in Missouri the court was doing its utmost to prevent divorces by default, and thereby to safeguard the interest of the state.[4]

It is impossible to find any principle by which costs are determined and regulated. They are too low to deter the rich, but high enough to prohibit the poor. They bear little relation to the actual disbursements of the parties.[5] "Term fees" which are taxed in favor of the successful party represent no cash expenditure by anybody. The bill of costs includes one dollar for a writ that can be purchased at any law stationer's for five cents. It allows to the prevailing party two or three dollars as an attorney's fee, while the actual charge made by the attorney to his client is probably ten times that amount.

The fees paid by the litigants bear no closer relation to the state's expense in maintaining the judicial organization. The average daily cost to the state for a trial with jury is variously estimated to be from fifty to one hundred and fifty dollars.[6] The total fees paid by litigants for such a trial range from three to thirty-two dollars.

If the existing system were brought forward de novo, it would be ridiculed as absurd. Considering it as a part of our traditional method of working out justice, it is fairer to call it an anachronism. The Cleveland report[7] accurately summarizes the situation:

[1] Lord's *Oregon Laws*, § 1125.
[2] Second Cleveland Municipal Court R. (1913) page 16; L. A. Griffin Co. *v.* R. & F. Co., *Common Pleas Court Journal*, 189, page 1079; Aff. Court of Appeals, vol. i, p. 91 (1913).
[3] California Code of Civil Procedure, § 981.
[4] For a statement of the divorce proctor and his work in Missouri, see *post*, Chapter XIV, Assigned Counsel, page 102.
[5] Storey: *Reform of Legal Procedure*, page 34.
[6] The expense of litigation to the state is presented more fully in Chapter XIX, Types of Legal Aid Organizations, page 183.
[7] *Report of Committee on Costs* of the Cleveland Municipal Court, filed September 26, 1913.

"The old standards worked serious inequalities and frequently discriminated against the smaller cases. Charges are made in smaller cases for services which are not charged in larger. For example, in the justice code fees are charged for services of the judge in trying the case and in entering judgment, while for similar services rendered by judges of common pleas no charge is made. There are also instances of greater charges for purely clerical or ministerial work, for example, taking affidavits, bonds, undertakings, issuing process, orders of attachment, poundage, etc. The committee was of opinion that like services should be charged for equally.

"In making the revision we have endeavored to adapt the charges to modern conditions. The present schedule is a relic of stage coach days and in many respects has come down to us unchanged from the laws of the Northwest Territory and from the first enactments of Ohio after achieving statehood, passed in February, 1805. These schedules of fees were enacted under different conditions, when communication was difficult, facilities of transportation were scarce and labor-saving devices unknown.

"An inspection of the old schedule under modern conditions shows also disproportionate charges and absurdities; for instance, the charge of twenty-five cents for copies which are now made by using carbon paper and not by long hand as was necessary before the day of the typewriter. So is the method of charging mileage or travelling expenses inexcusable. For these reasons your committee deemed revision of many fees necessary."

By eliminating all fictitious costs and leaving the worry over that puzzle to the taxing clerk, and so narrowing the inquiry to the actual cash expenses for costs which must be met by persons desiring to use the courts, it is possible to make a more concrete presentation. Because of radical differences, it is convenient to separate costs into three groups: first, costs in the trial court paid to the court or its officers; second, costs on appeal; third, costs for witnesses, transcripts of evidence, and briefs. As to the first, there being several trial courts, each with its own costs, it is advisable to study only the inferior courts, where the cases of the poor are generally heard, except where the inferior court's limit of jurisdiction is so low that cases are necessarily brought in the superior courts.

§ 3

The actual expenses in a trial court, exclusive of witness fees, may be reduced to the writ or summons, the service of process, entry fee, calendar fee, trial fee, entry of judgment, and issuance of execution. It is proper to eliminate the jury fee,

Costs in the Trial Court for so long as a trial by a judge is possible, no denial of justice can fairly be alleged. For a similar reason fees for attachment or garnishment are excluded. Each court uses a different combination of these items. In some one or two payments cover everything, in others the charges are made separately. Since our inquiry is only to determine the actual expense, all the various items may be rolled into one total. The figures given below are not absolute; they may be varied by the distance traveled for service, by the number of motions or interlocutory proceedings, and by other factors; but they fairly represent the minimum cost in an ordinary case.

City	Court	Minimum Cost
Baltimore	People's Court	$2.40
Boston	Municipal Court	2.65
Chicago	Municipal Court	3.50
Cincinnati	Municipal Court	2.00
Cleveland	Small Claims Court	.52
Dayton	Municipal Court	2.00
Hartford	City Court	5.76
	Superior Court	15.51
Jersey City	District Court	4.00
Los Angeles	Justice's Court	5.00
	Superior Court	8.00
Minneapolis	Municipal Court	3.50
New York	Municipal Court	2.00
Philadelphia	Municipal Court	11.00
Pittsburgh	County Court	5.50
Richmond	Justice's Court	1.30
	Law Court	3.50
Portland	Small Claims Court	1.75
Saint Paul	Justice's Court	3.00

These figures would be much higher were it not for the advent of municipal courts, which have done much to reduce costs. In Cincinnati, Columbus, and Dayton, for example, it is provided by the court act that costs, exclusive of witness fees, shall not exceed two dollars. While these actual expenses may seem small in substantial causes, they loom large in the troubles of the poor. In claims under fifty dollars, an immediate expenditure of four or five dollars may well be disproportionate; in any event it is often more than the needy litigant can afford, particularly where additional outlays for witnesses and attachments are necessary.

Before considering how the general situation as to costs in the trial court may be improved, it is necessary to make passing mention of two plans by which costs are charged. In some jurisdictions, as Ohio and Maryland, costs are not prepaid; they are charged only at the end of the proceedings, with the result that often they are uncollectable. Such a plan assists the unscrupulous more than the poor and unnecessarily deprives the State of revenue in cases which could bear costs.[1] In other places, as in Virginia and Texas, costs are not prepaid but a bond to cover them is filed. This might occasionally assist a destitute suitor whose character enabled him to procure sureties.

The two immediate and practicable remedies are to scale down all costs to a mini-

[1] In its survey of Columbus, the New York Bureau of Municipal Research found in the Municipal Court in one year 400 cases where the fees had never been paid. In its report, dated January 31, 1917, and filed with the City Council, it recommended "that all fees be payable in advance." Also reported in Ohio *State Journal*, February 7, 1917.

mum and to vest in the judges discretionary power to permit in forma pauperis proceedings in all cases in all courts. A general reduction of costs is desirable,[1] and it can be accomplished without materially impairing the state's revenue. The expense of service of process, which in many inferior courts is the largest item,[2] can be eliminated by permitting citizen's service as in New York and Minnesota, or by the simple expedient of using the mails.[3] All proceedings in the Cleveland Municipal Court may now be served by mail.[4] The California Industrial Accident Board sends its notices by mail.[5] Probate citations in Massachusetts may, on the court's order, be served by mail.[6] This has proved successful; it is the opinion of Cleveland judges that fewer motions to remove defaults are brought in cases of service by mail than by constables; and it effectuates a reduction of this item from $1.75 to $.12 or $.02, without depriving the state of any revenue.

Where reduction of court costs is accompanied by efficient court organization no loss to the state results. In 1914 the tariff of costs in the Cleveland Municipal Court was radically lower than in 1913, and yet the cost of the court to the tax-payers was less in 1914 than in 1913.[7] In the Municipal Court of the District of Columbia, where the cost of suit is $1.85, the court's accounts for the year ending June 30, 1913, showed a profit over and above all expenses including rent of more than $12,000.[8]

If costs are lowered in this manner, the number of persons who cannot secure a trial will be reduced to a minimum. Provision should be made for such persons by a comprehensive in forma pauperis statute, similar to that in the federal courts under which it is possible for a poor person to carry a case through the Supreme Court of the United States without payment of costs to the court. Proceedings in forma pauperis, where properly guarded, as in Scotland and in France under "l'assistance judiciaire,"[9] cause but slight loss to the state, for such suits are permitted only when a good cause of action is disclosed, so that in the majority of cases a judgment follows and the costs paid by the defendant may be used to reimburse the state.

Such steps would not swamp the courts with specious litigation. In Cleveland no abuse has resulted from the radical reduction of costs. While from the nature of the proposition statistics are impossible, it is the general opinion that fewer, and certainly no more, fraudulent claims for personal injuries are presented to Industrial Accident Boards where there are no costs than were formerly brought to the courts where fees obtained.

[1] Taft: *Administration of Justice*, 72 Central L. Journ. 191, 196.

[2] In the Boston Municipal Court, 60 per cent.

[3] See 73 Ann. Am. Ac. Pol. & Soc. Science (1917), 164; 2 Philadelphia Municipal Court R. 19; 2 Cleveland Municipal Court R. 9, 11, 20; 3 *Ibid.*, 84.

[4] 4 Cleveland Municipal Court R. 11, 20, 71, 73 insert.

[5] 1 Southwestern L. Rev. (January, 1917), 81.

[6] Massachusetts *Acts of* 1915, c. 24.

[7] 3 Cleveland Municipal Court R. 8, 57.

[8] Baer: *Justice for the Small Man*, 90 Century Magazine (1915), 144, 147.

[9] These systems are discussed in detail in Chapter XXV, A More Equal Administration of Justice, page 247.

§ 4

Costs on Appeal Costs paid to the court on appeal consist of the entry fee and the expense of making up and printing the record of the case on appeal, or on exceptions, or on writ of error. Such costs in the aggregate are seldom less than twenty-five and often run over a hundred dollars. While appellate costs affect the poor only in a proportionately small number of cases, it is highly desirable in the interests of justice,[1] and for the sake of a well-rounded development of our common law, that it be possible for poor persons to obtain decisions on questions of law which arise in their cases. The condition which has been too common under the compensation acts, of having cases appealed, briefed, and argued only by the insurer, the employee being unable to meet the expense, is not healthy. One-sided argument inevitably tends to produce a one-sided construction of the law.[2]

These expenses represent a waste and are unnecessary. With proper organization of courts they will automatically disappear. In a unified court, as in England, there is no entry fee, for the appeal is effected merely by transfer from the trial to the appellate division. There is no necessity for printing of records, transcripts, bills of exceptions, certificates of evidence, and the like, for, since the appellate and trial tribunals are simply branches or divisions of one court, each judicially knows the records of the other, and uses all the original files, papers, and documents.[3]

§ 5

Witnesses, Briefs, and Transcripts Expenses incurred in litigation for witness fees, briefs, and transcripts of evidence, which counsel invariably needs for his own preparation, raise an entirely different problem. Their amount varies indefinitely according to the number of witnesses summoned, the complexity of the points to be argued, and the length of the trial. The peculiar difficulty which they present is that they are not payments which the state can waive. Persons who are compelled to leave their work to testify in court, printers, and stenographers are unquestionably entitled to be paid. Such expenses cannot be scaled down, nor can they be eliminated by any reorganization of courts or procedure.

There is no solution except for the state to provide a fund to be disbursed by, and under the supervision of, its judicial department or legal aid bureau.[4] Such a propo-

---

[1] Root: *Addresses on Citizenship and Government*, page 133. See a pamphlet by Hiram T. Gilbert (the author of the Chicago Municipal Court Act), dated May 25, 1910, and entitled "A Synopsis of a Bill for an Act in Relation to Courts to be Introduced in the 47th General Assembly," at page 14.

[2] See an article entitled "Preventive Law" in 15 N. Y. Legal Aid Rev., No. 2 (April, 1917), p. 3.

[3] Pound: *Organization of Courts*, American Judicature Society, *Bulletin VI*, page 25; Pound: *Causes of Popular Dissatisfaction with the Administration of Justice*, 29 Am. Bar Ass'n R. 395, 410. The same thing holds true in the Boston Municipal Court as between the trial and appellate divisions.

[4] Cf. the suggestions made by Hiram T. Gilbert in his book, *Practice in the Municipal Court of Chicago* (1908), at page 546, and in his pamphlet, *A Synopsis of a Bill for an Act in Relation to Courts to be Introduced in the 47th General Assembly*, at page 114, § 2036.

39611

sition is not wholly without precedent. It is a general rule that the state will reimburse for expenses incurred in disbarment proceedings.[1] In the municipal legal aid bureaus provision is made for the expenses incurred in the litigation of the bureau's clients. The Duluth Legal Aid Bureau has expended out of the public treasury the following amounts: in 1914, $150; in 1915, $126.01; in 1916, $108.18. In Los Angeles the Public Defender is authorized[2] to apply to the county treasury for litigation expenses, although he has never done so, fearing that such a course might be unconstitutional.[3] The 1913 Rules of the English High Court of Judicature, in making provision for poor litigants, call for the defraying of their expenses by a Treasury grant.[4] Mr. Taft, in speaking before the Virginia Bar Association in 1908, after arguing for "a mandatory reduction of court costs and fees," said:[5]

"I believe that it is sufficiently in the interest of the public at large to promote equality between litigants, to take upon the government much more than has already been done, the burden of private litigation."

§ 6

Certain it is that until thoroughgoing changes are made, denial of justice to the poor because of inability to pay the required court costs and fees will continue. That the present system of costs works daily to close the doors of the courts

Denial of Justice through Costs

to the poor is proved by ample evidence.[6] In Boston the Legal Aid Society has kept precise figures since April 1, 1916. During the seventeen months ending August 31, 1917, there were 551 cases which could not be settled out of court, which were meritorious and required court action; 386 were taken to court and won, 36 were taken and lost, and 129 could not be brought before the courts because of the client's inability to pay the costs. In other words, the fees required by the state caused a total failure of justice to twenty-three per cent of the persons who needed to invoke the aid of the machinery of justice.

How the existing system of costs literally forbids resort to the courts by the poor is illustrated by the laws requiring security for costs. A plaintiff must not only pay the costs for summons, service, entry, trial, judgment, and the like, but in addition he

---

[1] See Connecticut *Practice Book* of 1908, page 206. This includes the expense for attorney's services, Burrage v. County of Bristol, 210 Mass. (1911) 299.

[2] Section 23 of the Charter of Los Angeles County provides, "The costs in all actions in which the Public Defender shall appear under this section, whether for plaintiff or for defendants, shall be paid out of the County Treasury."

[3] This question arises from the decisions holding unconstitutional statutes giving to laborers, who obtain judgments under mechanic's liens, a special attorney's fee to be paid by the defendant on the ground of denial of equal protection of the laws. See Atkinson v. Woodman, 74 Pac. 640; note in 17 Harvard L. Rev. 355, citing cases.

[4] See 48 Law Journal, 243, 468.

[5] Taft: *Administration of Justice*, 72 Central L. Journal, 191, 196; 4 National Municipal Review, 454.

[6] San Francisco Legal Aid R. for 1916, 9; 8 Pittsburgh L. A. R. 14, 17; *Office of the Public Defender* (Los Angeles), pages 14, 24; *Place of the Public Defender in the Administration of Justice*, pages 23, 24; 5 Boston L. A. R. 6; *Bulletin of Legal Aid Society of Chicago*, 1916-17, No. 2, pp. vii, viii; 31 Chicago L. A. R. 29; 33 Am. Bar Ass'n R. 81; 4 United Charities of Rochester R. 12; 6 Cincinnati L. A. R. 3; 2 Philadelphia Municipal Court R. 34, 35; 1 Milwaukee L. A. R. 8. The legal aid societies in Cincinnati, Newark, New Orleans, Omaha, and Philadelphia state that proper litigation is often rendered impossible because of the inability of clients to pay the required court costs.

must, on motion, furnish a bond to guarantee that the defendant, if successful, shall not be out of pocket. In the Connecticut law, for example, the bond is in the sum of fifteen dollars in the City Court of Hartford and seventy-five dollars in the Superior Court.[1] The defendant may bring such a motion on the ground that the plaintiff is a poor person. The net result is that a poor person who is unable to give or secure such a bond may be thrown out of court altogether. In Campbell v. Chicago, etc., R. Co.[2] a defendant moved that the plaintiff, a poor person, be required to furnish a bond. The judge continued the case for a week to give the plaintiff time to file such a bond and, on his inability to do so, dismissed his case. On appeal the court said:

> "We have no statute which permits a person to sue in forma pauperis. It seems almost like a hardship that a poor person should not be able to litigate. But this is a matter for the legislature to regulate and not the justice."

Laws requiring security for costs, despite their patent harshness to the poor, have uniformly been upheld.[3] In striking contrast are the early English decisions which, perceiving the injustice of a rule of exclusion, and without hiding behind the absence of a legislative mandate, gave to the common law the proceeding in forma pauperis. If, as excellent authority has stated,[4] this was done as "an indulgence arising out of the humanity of the judges," what can be said for our nineteenth century judges who, acting in a democratic country, were not even willing to follow the fair provisions of the common law?

The result is no different than it would be if our bills of rights read, — "Every subject who can furnish a bond for fifteen or seventy-five dollars ought to obtain justice freely, completely, and without delay; to all others the courts are closed." In a democratic government of laws, where the state exists to guarantee through its administration of justice the security of fundamental rights, it is a sad perversion for the state, by its law, to cut off any class of citizens from the protection of the courts. On the one hand, the state through its criminal statutes respecting breach of the peace and larceny forbids persons to redress their own wrongs or collect their debts by self-help and remits them to the courts, and on the other it imposes conditions as to the use of the courts which the poor cannot satisfy.

An epoch-making decision by the Supreme Court of California, rendered in 1917,[5] lends judicial sanction to the ideas expressed in this chapter. The case is striking. It will be recalled that jury fees in California are twenty-four dollars a day, to be paid in advance. A day laborer, the father of ten minor children all wholly dependent on him for support, desired to bring suit in the Superior Court for the wrongful killing of his daughter and claimed his right to a jury trial. He filed an affidavit that he did not have more than twenty-five dollars and asked leave to sue in forma pauperis. There is a local

---

[1] Connecticut *General Statutes of* 1902, §§ 714, 716.   [2] 23 Wisconsin, 490.

[3] Gesford v. Critzer, 7 Ill. 698; Grover's Succession, 49 La. Ann. 1050; Haney v. Marshall, 9 Md. 194; Akling v. St. Louis Packet Co., 46 S. W. 24; Miller v. Norfolk, etc., Ry. Co., 47 Fed. 264.

[4] 31 Harvard L. Rev. (January, 1918) 486.

[5] Martin v. Superior Court of Alameda County, 54 California Decisions, No. 2874 (October 19, 1917), p. 422.

statute permitting such a proceeding before a justice of the peace, but none making provision for suits in the courts of record. The Superior Court refused the application.

The attorney for the San Francisco Legal Aid Society intervened as amicus curiae, and the case was appealed.[1] The Supreme Court held that the in forma pauperis proceeding was a part of the English common law, which had become part of the American common law, and that the court had inherent power to grant leave to sue without costs so that justice might not be denied to the poor.

Parts of this decision, which is the first ever to translate into action the fundamental constitutional principles of freedom and equality of justice, express the situation so clearly that it is difficult to understand why the majority of courts have always been blind to it.[2]

> "Imperfect as was the ancient common law system, harsh as it was in many of its methods and measures, it would strike one with surprise to be credibly informed that the common law courts of England shut their doors upon all poor suitors who could not pay fees, until Parliament came to their relief. Even greater would be the reproach to the system of jurisprudence of the state of California if it could be truly declared that in this twentieth century, by its codes and statutes, it had said the same thing. . . ."

> "Again we say that it would be an unmerited reproach cast upon the legislative branch of our state government to hold that it . . . designed to forbid such a poor suitor from prosecuting his action according to the laws of the land in a court of record, when rights might and could be all-important and his recovery of the utmost consequences."

Costs have their place as a deterrent, but they should serve to discourage, not all litigation, but false litigation, specious pleas, vexatious proceedings taken for delay, and to insure prompt compliance with court orders. The system of costs in equity approaches this plan, and in England the use of costs for such purposes is established.[3]

<h1 style="text-align:center">§ 7</h1>

Summary   Costs, like delay, present in the main no fundamental or inherent difficulty. A reduction of costs and provision for in forma pauperis proceedings can easily be effected. It is a question of the will to do it. The proposal for direct state aid as to the expenses which cannot be eliminated goes somewhat farther. It will depend very largely on the development of state controlled legal aid bureaus, for in nature and result the embarrassment caused by these unavoidable expenses of litigation is precisely like that caused by the necessity of retaining and paying an attorney.

---

[1] Cf. 1 San Francisco L. A. R. 9.

[2] See the excellent note in 31 Harvard L. Rev. (January, 1918), 485–487. For a recent decision holding that the requirement of costs is not in contravention of equal protection of the laws, see *In re* Lee, 168 Pac. 63. In a comment on this case it is well pointed out that the rule would be tenable if the costs statute provided for in forma pauperis proceedings. 16 Michigan L. Rev. 192.

[3] See American Judicature Society, *Bulletin XI*, pages 102–107; *Ibid.*, *Bulletin VI*, page 67.

CHAPTER VI

THE THIRD DEFECT—EXPENSE OF COUNSEL

The office of the attorney is indispensable to the administration of justice,
and vital to the well-being of the court. JUSTICE KILLITS *in In re Thatcher*.[1]

THE lawyer is indispensable to the conduct of proceedings before the courts, and
yet the fees which he must charge for his services are more than millions of persons can pay. Simple as these propositions are, they are too often forgotten in the
discussions concerning the administration of justice. The emphasis has been on simplification of procedure and reorganization of courts; but even the best procedure in
the most orderly courts will require the presence of the trained advocate. When those
highly desirable ends are accomplished, the problem of the attorney will still remain
the great stumbling-block in the path toward freedom and equality of justice.

§ 1

The expense of counsel is a fundamental difficulty because the attorney is an integral part of the administration of justice. While the precise origin of the attorney

*The Essential
Nature of the
Lawyer's
Function*

is veiled in some obscurity,[2] it is clear that when courts are regularly
constituted and a method of administering justice is established, the
attorney soon makes his appearance. The real beginnings of court
organization and of a definite procedure were made in the reign of
Henry II, and by the time of Henry III the need of retaining good
lawyers was everywhere appreciated.[3] In one of the first year books the reporter makes
the chief justice say,—"B loses his money because he hadn't a good lawyer."[3] In our
colonial era repeated attempts to do without lawyers were made, but soon proved
impracticable. With the development of American law and the establishment of
courts the lawyer rapidly assumed the important position in the administration of
justice which he has ever since maintained.[4]

With a vast body of ever changing law, which a man after a lifetime of devotion
is only beginning to master, it is apparent that the layman, in order to understand
his rights, what he can and cannot do, must have the assistance of counsel.[5] We do
not, as in Nero's time, write our laws in small letters at the top of high columns,
but the multitudinous laws in our voluminous case books and statute books are as
hard to learn.[6] Similarly, the procedural law, in accordance with which litigation

---

[1] 190 Fed. 969; aff. 212 Fed. 801.

[2] See Brunner: *Early History of the Attorney*, 3 Illinois L. Rev. (1908) 257.

[3] Zane: *Bench and Bar in the Golden Age of the Common Law*, 2 Illinois L. Rev. (1907) 18.

[4] Warren: *History of the American Bar;* see particularly the introductory chapter called "Law Without Lawyers."

[5] Cf. Root: *Addresses on Government and Citizenship*, page 159; *Proceedings* of Virginia Conference of Charities and Correction in 1916, page 79.

[6] The volumes of the reports of our cases number 1300 and include more than 1,113,000 cases. 12 Illinois L. Rev. 349, 350.

must be conducted, is a maze to the uninitiated; it is a science in itself. The law permits every man to try his own case, but "the lay vision of every man his own lawyer has been shown by all experience to be an illusion."[1] It is a virtual impossibility for a man to conduct even the simplest sort of a case under the existing rules of procedure, and this fact robs the in forma pauperis proceeding of much of its value to the poor unless supplemented by the providing of counsel.[2]

It is not easy to convey in few words a true impression of the enormous importance of the attorney in our system of achieving justice, but the mention of the broad outlines of his work is suggestive. He must start the case properly by satisfying all the requirements of venue, jurisdiction, service, entry, and the law of pleadings. When the case is before the court, our system contemplates the doing of justice by applying general laws to the facts of the particular case. In many cases the attorney must be ready to assist the court in determining the law applicable, and in every case he must have ascertained the facts by investigation, must have selected the material facts admissible according to the law of evidence, must have the witnesses and documents at hand, and must present the case in accordance with the rules governing trials. When judgment is rendered, he must transform that into an execution, and finally undertake to satisfy such execution by levy on the defendant's property. At every stage the attorney supplies the motive power; without him the judicial machinery would never move.[3] It is estimated that, on an average, all property passes through the hands of lawyers as often as once in each twenty-five years.[4]

The lawyer is as necessary as the engineer or the doctor; each is a specialist who applies the laws he knows for the benefit of the civilized community. Without uprooting our entire administration of law it would be as impossible to abolish the lawyer as it would be the judge. Justice Miller in *Ex parte* Garland [5] stated:

> "It is believed that no civilized nation of modern times has been without a class of men intimately connected with the court, and with the administration of justice, called variously attorneys, counsellors, solicitors, proctors, and other terms of similar import. They are as essential to the successful workings of the court as the clerks, sheriffs, and marshals, and perhaps as the judges themselves, since no instance is known of a court of law without a bar."

In similar vein, Dean Wigmore has said of the lawyer,[6]

> "He is a necessary part of the State's function of doing justice. In the part he plays, he is as essential as the judge."

---

[1] Pound: *Administration of Justice in the Modern City*, 26 Harvard L. Rev. 319. Cf. 1 Kent's Commentaries, 307; Honestus (Benjamin Austin): *Observations on the Pernicious Practice of the Law* (1819), page 29.

[2] 20 N. Y. L. A. R. 10; 23 N. Y. L. A. R. 11.

[3] "All men at all times and in all places do stand in need of Justice and of Law, which is the rule of Justice, and of the interpreters and Ministers of the Law, which give life and motion unto Justice." Preface Dedicatory to Sir John Davies' *Reports* (1615).

[4] Illinois State Bar Ass'n R. for 1903, Part II, p. 102; Carter: *Ethics of the Legal Profession* (1915), page 36.

[5] 4 Wall. 333, 384.

[6] Carter: *op. cit.*, Introduction, page xxii; see also, page 31; and 6 Cleveland L. A. R. 6.

§ 2

The inability of the poor to pay for the services of counsel has often been stated,[1] and the general fact is known. The vast number of persons who are thus debarred from legal advice and the essential services of the lawyer in court, however, is not realized. It is possible to form an estimate of what this number must be. It is known that in 1913 the average wage of the clients of the Cincinnati Legal Aid Society was $10 per week,[2] and that in the year 1916 out of 1981 cases analyzed by the Legal Aid Society in Newark, 1579 or 80 per cent of the applicants earned less than $20 each week.[3] It is safe to say that single persons earning less than $500 yearly and that married persons, with dependent families, earning less than $800 each year are never in a financial position where they can afford to pay any substantial sum for attorneys' services.[4] Within these classes, according to Dr. King,[5] there are 3,758,000 single persons and 7,040,000 families. Inasmuch as each member of a family, the wife and children as well as the husband, may need legal advice and assistance, it is proper to multiply the families[6] out to their number of constituent individuals.

Inability of the Poor to Pay for Counsel

From this calculation it appears that there are in the United States over 35,000,000 men, women, and children whose financial condition renders them unable to pay any appreciable sum for attorneys' services. It is true that in country districts and in the smaller towns such people generally are able to secure assistance from lawyers[7] as a matter of kindness or charity; consequently it is primarily in the larger cities that inability to pay fees results in a denial of justice. Even if we were to eliminate, however, the seventy-eight per cent[8] of our population living in cities and towns containing less than one hundred thousand inhabitants, there would still remain nearly 8,000,000 persons who do not know where to turn for legal advice and assistance when the need arises. These figures are only approximations. Cut them in two and it is still perfectly apparent that a thoroughgoing, equal administration of justice must take cognizance of, and provide for, a class of citizens, numbering millions, who cannot secure for themselves the legal services without which the machinery of justice is unworkable.

§ 3

This is the great difficulty. Part of the need for attorneys' services is undoubtedly artificial. There is no reason why a court summons should read, "We command you

---

[1] Hyde: *Reorganization of the Legal Profession*, 8 Illinois L. Rev. (1913) 243; Doerfler: *Duty of the Lawyer as an Officer of the Court*, 24 Green Bag (1912), 74; *Summary* of the Manly *Report* of the United States Commission on Industrial Relations, page 9 ; *Office of the Public Defender* (Los Angeles), page 22; 23 N. Y. Legal Aid R. 10.

[2] 6 Cincinnati L. A. R. 10.   [3] New Jersey L. A. R. for 1916, Table 6, page 11.   [4] Cf. 3 Cleveland L. A. R. 5.

[5] King: *The Wealth and Income of the People of the United States* (1915), page 224.

[6] *Ibid.*, page 129. The average family is 4.5 persons.

[7] See Chapter XX, The Present Position of Legal Aid Work, page 188.   [8] King: *op. cit.*, page 16.

to appear before our Justices of the Municipal Court on Saturday the twenty-first day

Cost of
Counsel the
Fundamental
Difficulty

of December, A.D. 1918, at nine o'clock in the forenoon. Fail not of appearance at your peril;"[1] so that it is necessary to employ counsel to explain that the plain English words do not mean what they say, but in law mean that you are not required to appear before the court at all, but must file an answer with the clerk any time on Tuesday, December the twenty-fourth.[2] A little modernizing will eliminate such purely parasitic services.

But with all reformation of procedure and reorganization of courts the true and essential functions of the attorney will remain and the need for his services will, as to the vast proportion of advice work, consultation, negotiation, and litigation, be the same. This great underlying problem cannot be summarily disposed of or dismissed with few words. The remainder of the report is essentially a presentation and examination of the various methods and agencies, both those within and those without the judicial system, which have come into existence and are being utilized in the endeavor to remove this inequality and thereby to promote the ideal of freedom and equality of justice.

---

[1] Form of summons in use by the Municipal Court of the City of Boston.

[2] Compare the need of employing attorneys to interpret the complicated New York Codes. Root: *Addresses on Government and Citizenship*, pages 435, 469.

PART II
AGENCIES SECURING A MORE EQUAL ADMINISTRATION OF THE LAWS

CHAPTER VII

THE NATURE AND POSITION OF THE REMEDIAL AGENCIES

The fundamental difference between the law of the nineteenth century and the law of the period of legal development on which we have entered is not in the least due to the dominance of sinister interests over courts or lawyers or jurists. It is not a conflict between good men and bad. It is a clash between old ideas and new ideas, a contest between the conceptions of our traditional law and modern juristic conceptions born of a new movement in all the social sciences. ROSCOE POUND *in Justice According to Law.*

§ 1

THERE are in the United States to-day a number of agencies and methods which are attacking and to an extent remedying the inequalities caused by our customary and traditional method of administering justice. Most of these agencies are the creations and developments of recent years, some having been brought into being for the direct purpose of securing more adequately the rights of the poor, others having this only as a collateral object, and not a few being forced, by the enormous pressure which has made itself felt, to provide and furnish some assistance to poor persons in matters within their jurisdiction.

Introductory

In general, and with only a rare exception here and there, it must be said that these agencies and their developments have not been brought about by judges acting as a body in charge of the administration of justice, or by lawyers acting as a group through their recognized Bar Associations. In addition to the rigidity of court organization which has made progress difficult, there has seemingly been an ignorance of, or indifference to, the disadvantages under which the poor have struggled. The Constitution of Illinois required the judges of the Supreme Court to report annually to the Governor such defects in the laws as they might find, together with suggestions for improvement, but under this general power nothing [1] was done. The Michigan courts neglected for years their wide rule-making powers, with the result that the legislature was forced to pass several thousand sections relating to practice and procedure.[2] The Bar, likewise, has been slow to take up the task, with which it may fairly be charged, of working for the steady betterment of justice.[3] In an effort to arouse the Bar from its conservatism and inertia to a more lively sense of the splendid possibilities of its concerted action, Dean Vance of the University of Minnesota Law School said:[4]

"Bluntly put, the American lawyer has proved a failure. In no other free and civilized country are the laws so ill-administered as in these United States. We lead the world in most of the great struggles mankind is making, but in the

[1] Cf. Gilbert: *A Synopsis of a Bill for an Act in Relation to Courts to be Introduced in the 47th General Assembly* (1910), page 5.
[2] Harley: *A Unified State Court System*, page 3.
[3] Cf. Gilbert: *op. cit.*, page 19; Carter: *Ethics of the Legal Profession*, Introduction by Dean Wigmore, page xxiii; 73 Ann. Am. Ac. Pol. & Soc. Science, 5.
[4] Storey: *Reform of Legal Procedure*, page 5.

administration of the law America lags two generations behind the rest of the civilized world. No constructive reforms of a comprehensive kind have been seriously attempted since the days of David Dudley Field, now passed a half century and more."

When the propriety of contingent fees has been discussed, lawyers have not been wanting to proclaim the necessity of giving the poor an equal chance, but one may read the proceedings of all the bar associations and find no mention made of taking care of those cases—the vast proportion of the cases of the poor—which cannot pay even a contingent fee.

These things are said simply because they explain, in large measure, the present situation of the remedial agencies and their peculiar relation to the regular administration of justice. It is due to the zeal and enthusiasm of small and isolated groups of judges, lawyers, and laymen, working independently in different places, that the path of reform has been blazed. The natural result has been that agencies designed to meet the same need are, in different localities, entirely dissimilar, and that they lack any semblance of uniformity or coöperation. Each is virtually a law to itself. And the further inevitable result has been that the agencies have developed as patches on, and additions to, our judicial machinery instead of as integral parts of it. Although they are administering justice as much as the courts themselves, many of them exist to-day outside of our traditional legal machinery, as extra-legal institutions, some in the eyes of the law having no relationship whatever to the administration of justice and others standing in an ill-defined relationship.

Further, if duplication of tribunals, wasted effort, and unnecessary friction is to be avoided, and unless history is to reverse itself, these agencies must ultimately become incorporated as integral parts of our judicial institutions. This process of assimilation, which indeed has already begun, must be kept steadily in mind, for some of the advantages claimed for the remedial agencies are those of an extra-legal organization, of justice without law, which in all probability will be thoroughly changed, if not reversed, as the process of assimilation goes on.

§ 2

Any attempt to reduce to a hard and fast classification the various agencies which are playing a part in equalizing the administration of the law is somewhat arbitrary

Classification of the Agencies
because the newer agencies and methods for disposing of controversies, having grown up locally and independently, do not readily conform to type. Each has a different jurisdiction and organization; even those bearing similar names and designed to meet the same purpose differ so much in degree as to constitute a difference in kind. Nevertheless, some grouping is necessary so that an orderly presentation may be made. The following classification will be used:

1. Small Claims Courts.
2. Conciliation Courts and Conciliation in General.
3. Arbitration by Courts and Other Organizations.
4. Domestic Relations Courts.
5. Administrative Tribunals.
6. Administrative Officials.
7. Assigned Counsel.
8. Defenders in Criminal Cases.
9. Legal Aid Organizations.

§ 3

It is the purpose of the following chapters to examine these various agencies, study their history, set out the work they have done, and from that background to try to ascertain how far they now are, or may be developed into, sound methods for more nearly equalizing the administration of justice.

Tests applied to the Agencies

One simple line of approach which is helpful is made possible by the fact that the legal difficulties of the poor, though legion in number, fall as to a high percentage of the total into these four well-defined groups:

1. Claims for wages.
2. Domestic difficulties.
3. Personal injuries.
4. A vast number of miscellaneous small debts and claims, as for rent, groceries, loans, and arising out of chattel mortgages and assignments of wages, in which the poor may appear either as plaintiffs or defendants.

Many of the agencies deal specifically with these problems. Their proper solution means a vast improvement in the legal position of the poor, so that this is in the nature of a test which can be applied to the agencies in appraising them.

The real test of their success, however, will steadily be their effect on delays, costs, and above all on the great stumbling-block of the expense of employing attorneys. The one connecting thread which runs through them all is this attack, often disguised and sometimes unconscious, on the fundamental difficulty of the expense of counsel. There are conceivably three solutions: the first, to abolish the expense by abolishing the attorney; the second, to eliminate the expense by making the attorney's services unnecessary; and the third, to avoid the expense to the poor by supplying them with attorneys gratuitously.

All three methods, singly or in combination, are being tried. Before passing to a consideration of each group of agencies in detail, it may be helpful to visualize the general situation by means of the following simple diagram:

CHART SHOWING THE THREE METHODS USED BY THE NINE AGENCIES IN
ATTACKING THE PROBLEM OF THE EXPENSE OF COUNSEL[1]

1	2	3
PROHIBITING THE ATTORNEY	MAKING THE ATTORNEY UNNECESSARY	SUPPLYING THE ATTORNEY OR SOME ONE TO PERFORM HIS FUNCTIONS

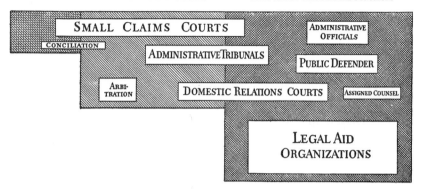

[1] The proportions are not based on mathematical computations. Sufficient figures do not exist. The chart gives a correct impression of: 1. The total extent to which each method is used. 2. The present relative importance of the different agencies. 3. The proportionate extent to which each agency uses each method.

CHAPTER VIII

SMALL CLAIMS COURTS

The splendid thing about Judge Levine's court [the Cleveland court for small causes] is that, for the mass of cases, it does justice where before now there was no court justice at all. It fills a vacant space. JOHN H. WIGMORE.[1]

§ 1

THE inability to provide justice in small causes has always been one of the weakest points in our system of administering justice. From the days of ordeal by battle, the method provided by the common law for proving and reducing to judgment any type of small claim has been cumbersome, slow, and expensive out of all proportion to the matter involved.[2] Our legal system has taken too literally the ancient maxim, "de minimis non curat lex."[3] A complicated procedure requires the attorney, but the expense for his services is more than the traffic can bear. It was once asked at a meeting of the American Bar Association whether a lawyer in suing for seven dollars wages due his client, a blacksmith, was justified in charging a fee of half that amount.[4] The question reveals the common dilemma—the services were worth the amount charged and yet, to the blacksmith, it would hardly be satisfactory to collect seven dollars at a cost of three dollars and a half. As Dean Pound puts it:[5]

Inadequacy of the Common Law Machinery

"For ordinary causes our contentious system has great merit as a means of getting at the truth. But it is a denial of justice in small causes to drive litigants to employ lawyers and it is a shame to drive them to legal aid societies to get as charity what the state should give as a right."

Similarly, court costs constitute an expense prohibitory to small litigation. The man hired at fifteen dollars a week who is put off the first week and not paid the second has a valid claim for thirty dollars but often not a dollar in his pocket. In addition to an attorney's fee, he cannot pay court costs because he has not been paid, and yet because he has not been paid court action is imperative. It is indeed a vicious circle, but within that circle thousands of unpaid wage-earners have been caught.

Delay plays its part by permitting a debtor, who has no real defence, to file an appearance and answer and interlocutory motions, to have the case continued once or twice, and then, when it is finally called for trial, to default.[6] This serves to hold

---

[1] American Judicature Society, *Bulletin VIII*, page 23.

[2] Justice Strasburger (of the Municipal Court for the District of Columbia): *A Plea for the Reform of the Inferior Court*, 22 Case and Comment (1915), 20; Grinnell: *Constitutional History of the Supreme Judicial Court of Massachusetts*, 2 Mass. L. Quarterly (1917), 472, note; *Preliminary Report on Efficiency in the Administration of Justice*, page 29.

[3] Cf. 1 Hartford L. A. R. 6.   [4] 33 Am. Bar Ass'n R. 79.

[5] Pound: *Administration of Justice in the Modern City*, 26 Harvard L. Rev. 318.

[6] In the Boston Municipal Court the number of defendants who defaulted when the case was finally called for trial numbered 2165 in 1913, 2388 in 1914, 2385 in 1915 (eleven months). See *Report* for 1916, page 54. For a statement as to appeals taken solely for delay see *Ibid.*, page 7.

the plaintiff off for months, to cause him loss of time in court attendance, and to rob the ultimate judgment of much of its worth.[1]

Small tradespeople to-day are forced to the practice either of wiping all small claims off their books or of selling them at a ridiculous discount to professional collection agencies. They have the possible relief of increasing the price of the necessities they sell, thereby adding the waste of the judicial system to the cost of living. The wage-earner and the small lodging-housekeeper, under conditions of modern competition, have not even that relief; they have been obliged to stand their losses.

Claims of this sort are often contemptuously spoken of as "petty litigation." But it is in this very field that the courts have their greatest political effect. In every urban community these are the cases of the large majority of citizens. As they are treated well or ill, so they form their opinion of American judicial institutions.[2] The vast number of such cases demanding attention cannot be told from our court dockets, for, as Dean Wigmore says,[3] "this class of cases simply does not ordinarily appear in the regular courts." An idea may be gained from the English County Courts, where provision is made for "petty litigation." Of 1,224,000 cases entered in 1913, 1,207,000, or 98½ per cent, were for claims under £20, and the average claim was about £3.[4] For such matters, Mr. Root has said,[5] " Our procedure ought to be based upon the common intelligence of the farmer, the merchant, and the laborer. And there is no reason why it should not be. I say it not without experience in legal procedure. There is no reason why a plain, honest man should not be permitted to go into court and tell his story[6] and have the judge before whom he comes permitted to do justice in that particular case, unhampered by a great variety of statutory rules." Instead of that, "we have got our procedure regulated according to the trained, refined, subtle, ingenious intellect of the best practiced lawyers, and it is all wrong."

This deplorable condition is not the result of the evil machinations of any group or class; it is the consequence of the failure of the judicial system to keep pace with the changing conditions of life. In our judicial history small cases were first entrusted to justices of the peace. This plan for a while gave simplicity and despatch, but when applied to cities it failed utterly. The justices, being subject to no supervision, and depending so much on their fees that J. P. came to mean "Judgment for the Plaintiff," formed unholy alliances with collection agencies, instalment houses, and the like, and very generally became actually corrupt.[7] They were so strongly

[1] Strasburger: *A Plea for the Reform of the Inferior Court*, 22 Case and Comment (1915), 23; Pound: *Administration of Justice in the Modern City*, 26 Harvard L. Rev. 319; Alger: *Swift and Cheap Justice*, 27 World's Work (1913), 167; 11 N. Y. Legal Aid Rev. No. 4, p. 8.

[2] Julius Henry Cohen: *The Municipal Court Bill*, 5 N. Y. Legal Aid Rev., No. 2, p. 9; Root: *Addresses on Government and Citizenship*, pages 135, 136, 185.

[3] American Judicature Society, *Bulletin VIII*, page 23.

[4] Rosenbaum: *Studies in English Court Procedure* (1916), vol. ii, *The County Courts*, pages, 1, 2. Cf. 1 Cleveland Municipal Court R. (1912), 51.

[5] Root: *Addresses on Government and Citizenship*, page 231.

[6] This is the system in the English County Courts. See Parry: *The Law and the Poor*, page 102.

[7] See *Proceedings of the First Conference for Better County Government in New York State* (1914), pages 47, 48;

entrenched in local politics that the process of ousting them, which is not yet completed, has been long and difficult. They have aptly been called "those barnacles of jurisprudence"[1] because they have clung on long after their usefulness expired.

In the cities, the justice of the peace was first supplanted by specially created magistrates who, as the cities continued to grow, became just as inefficient and even more corrupt.[2] Finally, they were succeeded by the organized modern municipal court of the type that is now familiar. With the municipal court came honest, trained, and capable judges, but also there came the rules of pleading, of procedure, and of evidence. Honesty and certainty were secured at the sacrifice of simplicity and speed. There has been a steady tendency to increase the jurisdictions of the municipal courts so that they have lost sight of the little cases; expense and delay have been allowed to creep in, with the result that small claims have not been cared for satisfactorily.[3]

In a few communities the last and logical step has been taken of combining the simplicity, speed, and cheapness which were sought in the justice of the peace plan[4] with the honesty and efficiency of the municipal court by a new type of court termed variously "small claims court," "small debtors' court," "conciliation court," and "court for small causes." The name of "small claims court" is the most descriptive and, to avoid confusion, will hereafter be applied to all such courts. Small claims courts exist in Cleveland, Chicago, Minneapolis, Portland (Oregon), and in three cities in Kansas.[5] They present so many differences, some being fundamental, that before any generalizations as to the nature, the success, and the future of this type of court are warranted, they must each be described.

§ 2

The Kansas small claims courts, which are to be found in Topeka, Leavenworth, and Kansas City under the name of "Small Debtors' Courts," were made possible by a 1913 act of the legislature.[6] The law was drawn by the attorney-general, who, so the story goes, had the inadequacy of our regular courts brought vividly to his attention

1 Kansas City L. A. R. 13; Nashville L. A. R. for 1915-16, page 2; Baer: *Justice for the Small Man*, 90; The Century (1915), 144, 145; Harley: *Ultimate Types of Inferior Courts and Judges*, 22 Case and Comment, 3; American Judicature Society, *Bulletin VIII*, page 26; *Ibid.*, *Bulletin VII-A*, page 57; Fuessle: *Making Americans by Justice*, 55 Collier's (July 3, 1915), 27.

[1] Olson: *Proper Organization and Procedure of a Municipal Court*, in 7 Proceedings of the American Political Science Association (1910), 80.

[2] Harley: *Ultimate Types of Inferior Courts and Judges*, 22 Case and Comment, 4; *The Forgotten Army, Report of Six Years' Work of the Committee on Criminal Courts of the New York Charity Organization Society* (1918), page 11.

[3] The best illustration of this is afforded by the New York Municipal Court which, when created, was called "The Poor Man's Court." See Root: *Addresses on Government and Citizenship*, pages 135, 185; Frederick De Witt Wells (a Justice of the New York Municipal Court): *The Man in Court* (1917), page 101. The District Court in Jersey City has undergone a similar evolution.

[4] See American Judicature Society, *Bulletin VII-A*, pages 56, 57, and also pages 71, 72.

[5] The New York Municipal Court with its 1917 Rules for Arbitration has in effect provided a small claims court. This is considered in detail in Chapter X, Arbitration, page 71.

[6] Kansas *Session Laws of 1913*, c. 170, p. 291; *General Statutes* of Kansas (1915), c. 27, art. 19, §§ 3316-3327.

by the fact that a washerwoman, in whom he was interested, was owed three dollars
The Kansas by a well-to-do man, who refused to pay her and whom she was un-
Small Claims able to sue because she could not pay the necessary counsel fees and
Courts costs.[1] Having in mind the informality of some of the Canadian courts
in hearing small matters,[2] he wrote a bill, which was passed and became law on March 15, 1913. This law merits partial quotation because it represents the violent reaction that is taking place against our traditional procedure which
has become so formal, costly, and inefficient.[3]

"Section 2. It shall be the duty of the appointing power—the board of county
commissioners or the mayor—to select as judge of such small debtors' court
some reputable resident citizen of approved integrity who is sympathetically inclined to consider the situation of the poor, friendless and misfortunate, . . . "

"Section 3. The judge of the small debtors' court may hold his court in his own
home, or in his own office or place of business, or at some place provided by the
power appointing him."

"Section 6. Before entertaining any suit in such small debtors' court, the plaintiff must appear before the judge of the court personally, . . . and state his case
orally, and if the judge believes the plaintiff has a cause of action he shall docket
the same by an entry in his docket, and shall summon the defendant orally,
or by United States mail, or by telephone, and try the cause considerately and
summarily and give judgment thereon. But no costs shall be assessed or charged
to either party."

"Section 10. The judge of the small debtors' court shall serve without pay, fee,
or award; and no attorney at law or any other person than the plaintiff and
defendant shall concern himself or intermeddle in any manner whatsoever with
the litigation in the small debtors' court, nor shall it be necessary to summon
witnesses, but the judge may informally consult witnesses or otherwise investigate the controversy between the parties, and in every case give judgment according to the very right of the cause."

The act restricts the courts to small debts and accounts (thereby excluding all
matters sounding in tort) not exceeding twenty dollars in amount, owed by defendants who reside in the county or city of which the court has jurisdiction.[4] Further,
the plaintiff must satisfy the judge not only that he has a good cause of action, but
that he cannot afford to employ counsel or use the regular courts.[5]

In the Topeka court from May 18, 1913, to May 18, 1914, 378 cases were filed
and in addition about 50 were settled at once before any docket entry was required.[6]
The claims ran from the twenty dollar maximum down to a claim for forty-five cents
brought by a newsboy. The average judgment rendered was $4.65. In the Leaven-
worth court, 100 cases were docketed and heard during its first year, and another

[1] Appo: *Justice Tempered with Mercy,* 112 Outlook (1916), 153.
[2] For a brief statement of the informal procedure in Toronto see American Judicature Society, *Bulletin VIII,* page 35.
[3] *Ibid.,* page 48.   [4] Kansas *Session Laws of* 1913, c. 170, § 4.   [5] *Ibid.,* §§ 5, 11.
[6] 22 Case and Comment, 30.

100 matters were disposed of without entry.[1] The Kansas City court tried its first case on August 25, 1913, and from that date until October 17, 1916, has been called upon in about 400 matters. Wage claims furnish the greatest number of cases. Most of the judgments rendered are paid[2] and very few appeals are taken.[3]

How these courts meet the three defects of the customary administration of justice is expressed in the law and carried out in practice. Costs are abolished. Delays in obtaining a trial are eliminated, for the judge can hold his court day or night and at any place, so that when he telephones the defendant to appear he can always fix a reasonable time for appearance within a day or two. It is sought to prevent delays through appeal by denying any appeal to the plaintiff and by making it burdensome to the defendant.[4] The fundamental difficulty of the attorney's expense is met by the legislative fiat forbidding attorneys from "intermeddling" in cases before these courts. This prohibition would not, of itself, be successful; the problem is really solved by the procedure of the court and the functions of the judge. The judge himself makes out the simple forms which start the case, he summons the defendant and any necessary witnesses, he is authorized to investigate the facts in any manner he chooses, and at the hearing the parties tell their own stories under the direction of the judge without regard to rules of evidence or trial procedure. It is therefore more accurate to say that these courts avoid the expense of counsel by making the presence of counsel unnecessary in their proceedings. The act further attempts to equalize the situation on appeal by providing that no pleadings shall be required in the District Court and that the defendant, if he loses, must pay fifteen dollars to the plaintiff for his attorney's fees.

Aside from their extremely narrow jurisdictional limits, these courts are unsound in two particulars. They represent a recurrence of the old unfortunate tendency of creating new courts for new needs, which inevitably causes duplication and confusion. More serious, they indicate a renewed attempt to secure justice without trained judges and without law. Any reputable layman may be the judge, and his duty is declared to be to give his decision not according to the law but according "to the very right of the cause." This means justice according to individual conscience after the manner of an Eastern Cadi.[5] One may doubt whether in the long run this plan can succeed when like plans throughout our legal history have always ended in failure. At the present time the courts are superior to the act which formed them. Judge Lee of the Kansas City court is a capable, trained lawyer of integrity, whose notion of right generally conforms with the rule of law. But in a system without supervision or re-

---

[1] American Judicature Society, *Bulletin VIII*, page 48.

[2] Where the defendant fails to pay, the judge certifies his judgment to the District Court so that execution may issue. In Topeka, out of 326 judgments, only 30 were so certified, and in Leavenworth only 2 per cent were certified.

[3] In three years only 15 appeals have been taken from the Kansas City Court; 6 being taken by one firm.

[4] Kansas *Session Laws of* 1913, c. 170, § 8.

[5] Cf. American Judicature Society, *Bulletin VIII*, page 48.

sponsibility, lacking in all the safeguards demonstrated by history to be necessary, there is no guarantee for the future.

In fact, these courts are less like courts and more like legalized legal aid societies.[1] The provision that they are to assist only such persons as cannot afford to employ attorneys is directly analogous to the legal aid rule, the judge must be satisfied as to the merit of the case as must the legal aid attorney, and in his decision the judge is only slightly more judicial than the legal aid attorney who always is desirous of hearing both sides and of acting accordingly. The only difference is that the judge of the small claims court has the sanction of the state behind him, and his decision when made becomes a legal judgment.

The great accomplishment of these courts is that they have concretely demonstrated that justice administered without regard to procedural and evidential rules of law not only meets with popular approval[2] but is entirely feasible; in other words, that as to small civil causes the three defects in the traditional administration of justice can be readily overcome.

§ 3

The small claims court of Portland, Oregon, technically known as the Small Claims Department of the District Court for Multnomah County, was created by act of legislature in 1915.[3] Judge Dayton, and the persons interested in the proposal,[4] had the Kansas courts in mind, so that the law in many of its sections follows its Kansas prototype. Jurisdiction is limited to money claims not exceeding twenty dollars,[5] there are no pleadings, the hearings are informal "with the sole object of dispensing speedy justice,"[6] and the judge may consult the witnesses informally and otherwise investigate the case.[7] Costs are not abolished, but are limited to seventy-five cents,[8] so that the provision requiring process to be served by court officers[9] does not cause excessive expense. The plaintiff cannot appeal, and if the defendant does, he is liable to the fifteen dollars attorney's fee and must give a bond to secure all costs.[10] On this appeal in the Circuit Court, no pleadings are necessary.[10] Attorneys are forbidden to appear in the court, with a saving clause that the court may in its discretion admit them.[11]

The procedure differs in that there are no restrictions concerning the poverty of the plaintiff or as to the merit of his cause. He is entitled, as of right, to go before

The Portland Small Claims Court

---

[1] Walton Wood recommended that in his civil legal aid work in Los Angeles he be given power to arbitrate disputes and to render judgment. See *The Place of the Public Defender in the Administration of Justice*, page 26. If this had been done, his office would have become exactly like a Kansas small claims court.

[2] These courts have attracted wide attention and elicited much comment. In addition to the articles already cited see *The Docket* (1915), page 1280; *La Follette's Magazine* for October, 1915; Boston *Evening Transcript* for February 6, 1915.

[3] Oregon *General Laws of* 1915, c. 327.   [4] Cf. *Report of the Portland Associated Charities* for 1913, page 47.

[5] *General Laws of* 1915, c. 327, § 1.   [6] *Ibid.*, § 9.   [7] *Ibid.*, § 8.   [8] *Ibid.*, § 3.

[9] *Ibid.*, § 4.   [10] *Ibid.*, § 12.

[11] *Ibid.*, § 8. In practice attorneys seldom ask and seldom are allowed to appear.

the clerk of the District Court, who thereupon fills out the appropriate form of claim, has it signed and sworn to by the plaintiff,[1] makes out a summons to the defendant, and assigns the date for hearing,[2] which must be at least five days, but not more than ten days, after service of the summons.[3]

This court is a great improvement over its Kansas model in that it secures the advantages of simplicity, cheapness, and speed, without sacrificing any fundamentals. It is justice by trained judges who, although given wide discretion by the statute,[4] in fact decide cases according to substantive law and not their own arbitrary opinion of right and wrong. It is an entire breaking away from our traditional justice conducted according to procedural and evidential law, but its justice is nevertheless ascertained and administered according to substantive law. It thus reëmphasizes the lesson afforded by the Kansas courts, that justice in small causes can be secured without reliance on technical procedure and without the assistance of counsel. Further, the court has the advantage of not being a separate court, but a department of the District Court (which corresponds to a municipal court). There is a curious and wholly unnecessary taking over of the Kansas idea of a distinct court in the provision that a judgment of a judge sitting in the small claims department is not automatically given full legal effect, but must first be certified to the clerk who enters it in the District Court docket, whereupon it acquires validity and execution may issue.[5]

The court has been eminently successful. Its procedure appeals so strongly to the average person that in known instances plaintiffs with valid claims over twenty dollars have deliberately scaled them down in order to be able to avail themselves of the speed and inexpensiveness of the small claims department. The court has published no report, but from an examination of its docket made November 6, 1917, the volume of its business was ascertained to be:

From May 24, 1915, to May 24, 1916	705 cases
From May 24, 1916, to November 6, 1916	1123 cases.

When one considers how defendants in the regular courts use the technicalities of procedure and evidence to delay and to defeat valid claims, it would seem inevitable that under the Portland plan defendants would appeal to the Circuit Court where, by having attorneys, they could interpose technical objections. The docket, however, shows that out of the total 1828 cases in seventeen months there have been only two appeals. It seems a fair conclusion that the spirit and procedure of the court command such respect that its judgments are accepted.

There was some indication in Portland of the existence of a factor that must be reckoned with because it is the greatest menace to the success of this kind of court. There was evidence that not all of the judges were by temperament and training qualified to conduct the court. A weak, or incapable, or narrow-minded judge can do more harm in a court of wide discretion, as a small claims, a juvenile, or a domestic

[1] *General Laws of* 1915, c. 327, § 2.   [2] *Ibid.*, § 3.   [3] *Ibid.*, § 6.   [4] *Ibid.*, § 8.   [5] *Ibid.*, § 13.

relations court, than anywhere else. The greatest latent flaw in the otherwise admirable conception of this type of court is the demand that it makes for superlative judges, without whom it cannot succeed.

§ 4

The Cleveland small claims court, technically known as the Conciliation Branch of the Municipal Court, has had a most interesting development. Though still lacking in certain important attributes, it stands to-day as the most nearly per-
The Cleveland Small Claims Court
fect type of a court for small causes to be found in the United States.
The Municipal Court of Cleveland was established[1] in 1912 to rid the city of the intolerable abuses of the justice of the peace system. The public opinion which secured the legislative enactments demanded not only an honest administration of justice, but likewise a simple and easy judicial procedure.[2] As a first attempt to realize this, the court passed two rules,[3] one providing for assistance by the clerk to parties having small cases and the other for arbitration by a judge. The latter was not acted upon, but under the former a clerk was designated, beginning February 24, 1912, to help parties draw and file the necessary papers required by the municipal court procedure and also to endeavor to adjust claims between parties where opportunity offered.[4] William F. Burke, chief clerk of the civil branch of the court, was assigned to this novel post, and with rare insight and great courage he began in all claims involving small amounts of money and the detention of personal property to try to bring the parties together and secure a settlement without litigation. His method was simply to write a letter—which had no legal standing whatever—to the defendant, inviting him to call and talk the matter over. Thus far the work was exactly like that of a legal aid society. In 1912, about twelve hundred cases were successfully disposed of in this way.[5] The judges were greatly impressed, and decided to expand the idea from a ministerial to a judicial function. Their deliberations were going on during the latter part of 1912 at precisely the time when a similar but independent line of thought was developing in Kansas. The amendment to the municipal court act permitting service by mail made the next step possible, and on March 15, 1913,—two months before the first Kansas Small Debtors' Court,—the Conciliation Branch was opened.[6]

The effect of the mail service law was to change the clerk's letter to the defendant from a mere request to a legal summons by the simple expedient of having the letter

---

[1] For the acts see 99 Ohio Laws, 362; as amended, 101 Ohio Laws, 155.
[2] 1 Cleveland Municipal Court R. 15; cf. White: *Conciliation Branch of the Municipal Court*, 13 N. Y. Legal Aid Rev., No. 4, p. 2.
[3] See Rule 24, "Clerk to assist Parties in Small Cases," and Rule 25, "Settlement Room," quoted in 1 C. M. C. R. 39.
[4] 1 C. M. C. R. 49; 2 *Ibid.* 38.
[5] 1 *Ibid.* 49 (table giving detailed statistics); Moley: *Justice through Common Sense*, 33 The Survey (1914), 101.
[6] 2 C. M. C. R. 38.

deposited in the mail box by the bailiff. Thereby the court acquired legal jurisdiction and could proceed to hear the case or enter an automatic default according as the defendant answered or neglected the letter summons.

The present course of procedure is as follows: A person goes to the clerk of the Conciliation Branch, who has a separate office, exactly like a legal aid society, where the person may feel at home and at liberty to talk the difficulty over with the clerk. If the dispute seems one that offers fair hope of immediate adjustment, the clerk, like a legal aid society attorney, telephones or writes the defendant and endeavors to secure an amicable settlement. If that fails, or if the case at once appears likely to demand judicial consideration, the clerk fills out in the court docket a very brief statement of claim, which the plaintiff signs. A date for the hearing—the defendant being entitled to three days' notice—is at once assigned, the plaintiff being given a little card bearing the date, the time, the court room, and the court address and telephone number. A summons is made out, and delivered to the bailiff, who deposits a copy in the mail box and certifies to that effect on the original summons. At first registered mail was used, but to-day ordinary mail is employed because in the event of a defective address it is returned more promptly. If the summons cannot be delivered, it is returned at once to the court and the bailiff amends his return of service. The summons states the precise time and the exact room for the hearing, and the case is tried at that time and place.

The small claims court room is like any other court except that attorneys are noticeably absent. They are not excluded by law, but the attitude of the court and the opinion of the bar is to discourage their attendance. Omitting the conciliation feature for the moment, the court tries the case by letting the parties tell their stories, and by questioning them and permitting them to question each other. The court is as dignified, its proceedings are as orderly, it commands as much respect as a supreme court. The judgment rendered by the court is final on the facts, and an appeal on law goes directly to the Court of Appeals.[1]

The court handles only matters involving less than thirty-five dollars. It is not limited to actions of contract or debt.[2] All kinds of small matters, including torts, have been heard and determined. While the court has had no difficulty with actions of tort for the detention of personal property (particularly the retention of trunks and furniture under claims of landlord's or lodging-housekeeper's liens), it has often found that its procedure is not adapted to torts for negligence, as in automobile collisions causing property damage. If parties appear with counsel, or with a large number of witnesses, or if the issues involve extended accounts or any problem not adapted to informal treatment, the case is transferred from the small claims court to the regular trial court, which is accomplished merely by the judge's direction to that effect, inasmuch as both courts are simply departments of the one municipal court.

---

[1] 4 C. M. C. R. 35. Originally there was an intermediate appeal to the Court of Common Pleas.
[2] Conciliation Branch, Rule 1; 2 C. M. C. R. 18.

The work of the small claims court may be summarily presented as follows:

Year	Cases disposed of	Amount of Judgments
1913[1]	2367	$10,410.53
1914[2]	4719	20,752.64
1915[3]	5106	32,872.14
1916[4]	5182	

These statistics show only the cases that reach the trial stage. A large number are disposed of through the advice, correspondence, and negotiation of the clerk's office. A statement of this work appears in each annual report;[5] that for 1916 gives an accurate idea of its extent. Two hundred and twelve money claims amounting to $1896.69 were settled without commencement of suit for $1736.24; 106 were found on investigation to be without merit; and in 28 the plaintiffs dropped the proceedings. In 197 claims for the detention of personal property, 107 were settled by a surrender of the property on receipt of a letter from the clerk's office, 37 had no merit, and 13 were dropped by the claimants. The clerk assisted parties to institute 38 actions of replevin. There was much further miscellaneous work done. This is an excellent illustration of legal aid work performed under judicial direction, and at public expense.[6]

The Cleveland small claims court is unquestionably a remarkable institution. Like the Portland court, it is a branch or session of the regular municipal court, so that no difficulties of jurisdiction are created. It exists not under statutory regulation but under rules of the municipal court, which is a preferable plan because changes can be more readily made as needs arise or as experience may dictate; thus its limit of thirty-five dollars may at any time be raised. It is a court of election, not compulsion. The original rule requiring all cases involving amounts under thirty-five dollars to be entered on the small claims docket was given up in favor of a rule[7] requiring the clerk to place cases on the docket only when so requested by the plaintiff. The court may issue attachments, which the Portland court is forbidden to do,[8] but their use is discouraged except in cases where the defendant's home address is unknown, but his place of work is known, so that garnishment serves to give the court jurisdiction and bring the claim to the defendant's attention. Speed is secured, most cases being heard and determined within a week after their filing; and the cost is extremely low, the total fees and costs amounting only to fifty-seven cents.[9] The procedure is so simple that no pleadings at all are required.

[1] 2 C. M. C. R. 39.

[2] 3 Ibid. 51, insert. Note the increase of 81 per cent due largely to the reduced tariff of costs which went into effect October 1, 1913.

[3] 4 Ibid. 43.   [4] Report for 1916 not published at this writing. This figure was furnished by the clerk.

[5] For 1913, see 2 C. M. C. R. 38; for 1914, 3 Ibid. 54; for 1915, 4 Ibid. 41.

[6] See post, Chapter XXV, A More Equal Administration of Justice, page 246.

[7] The rule was changed in 1915. Cf. Conciliation Branch, Rule 1, as stated in 3 C. M. C. R. 29 with the same rule as stated in 4 Ibid. 17.

[8] Oregon General Laws of 1915, c. 327, § 9.

[9] The fees are five cents for filing, twenty-five cents for issuing summons, twenty cents for bailiff's copy and return of service, two cents postage for service by mail. Cf. American Judicature Society, Bulletin VIII, page 14.

This is clearly a court in which justice is not conducted according to the usual procedural or evidential rules of law; but it is none the less dispensing a justice that meets with universal approval. The number of cases disposed of is sufficient evidence of the opinions entertained by parties. From the state's point of view, the procedure permits a judge in two morning sessions a week to dispose of over five thousand cases a year, which is at the rate of about one hundred each full day. The local public opinion is reflected in an editorial of the Cleveland *Press* of January 16, 1915, which praises the court and calls it " a movement towards justice in spite of lawyers," and an indication of general public opinion is afforded by the fact that this editorial was copied verbatim in the Salt Lake City *Evening Telegram* for January 22, 1915.

There has been some discussion as to whether this court ascertained and administered its justice in accordance with the rules of substantive law. Judge Levine has been called a Haroun-al-Rashid,[1] the inference being that he dispensed a sort of Oriental justice without regard to rules of law. The court unquestionably exercises wide equity powers—wider, perhaps, than can be supported by adjudicated cases. In a suit for the conversion of shoes it has ordered the shoes returned instead of giving a judgment for damages. Where a defendant admitted that he owed four dollars but had refused to pay it because the plaintiff had insulted his wife, and the plaintiff denied that he personally had insulted her but admitted that one of his employees had used improper language, the court ordered him to telephone to the wife apologizing for anything that had been said, which he gladly did, using the telephone in the judge's room; he was then given a judgment for the four dollars.

Fundamentally, however, the court is a court of law. Its judges are trained judges, who render their judgments by applying to the proved facts the rules of substantive law. In the now famous mattress case,[2] where a boarder set fire to the mattress by smoking in bed, for which the landlady demanded twenty-five dollars, and the judge by telephoning a department store ascertained that an identical mattress could be had for eight dollars, which the boarder was quite willing to pay and for which judgment was entered,—it would never occur to the judge to dismiss the case because he personally approved of smoking in bed and considered landladies amply paid to insure against such risks, or to give the landlady the desired twenty-five dollars on the ground that he thoroughly disapproved of smoking in bed and desired to give the community an object lesson.

§ 5

The Chicago small claims court is a branch of the Municipal Court, created by and operating under rules of that court. It was brought into existence on February 26, 1916, the purpose being as much to secure to the state the advantage and economy

---

[1] See Fuessle: *The People's Court,* 55 Collier's (July 3, 1915), 27.

[2] See Moley: *Justice through Common Sense,* 33 The Survey (1914), 101.

of disposing of a vast number of cases quickly and at small overhead cost as to assist poor persons. All money claims within the small claims jurisdiction are, therefore, automatically entered by the clerk on the small claims docket. Costs were not lowered and remain the same for the small claims branch as for the regular branches. Speed is secured, the case being defaulted or tried on the return day. An early attempt to break down the plan and secure delay by claiming jury trial was defeated by having two jury sessions in readiness to hear such cases at once. The pleadings are simple, the plaintiff files an informal statement of claim, but the defendant need only appear in court on the day set for hearing; it is unnecessary for him to file either an appearance or an answer.[1]

The Chicago Small Claims Court

The outstanding feature of the court is the simplicity and despatch of the proceedings at the trial, with the added fact that this informal procedure has been successfully applied in cases involving larger amounts of money than has been attempted in any other small claims court. Technicalities are not countenanced. Attorneys are not forbidden by law, but they seldom appear and their conduct of cases in the small claims branch has been discouraged by resolution of the Chicago Bar Association.[2]

Like its prototypes, the court has been popular and is considered successful.[3] An expert in judicial administration calls it "undoubtedly the solution of one of the most difficult questions which court reform has faced, to wit: the successful adjudication of small civil cases."[4] The Chicago Legal Aid Society finds it of great assistance.[5] That this movement is of national interest is again evidenced by the fact that when the establishment of such a court was first discussed, the plan received editorial endorsement from the Boston *Evening Traveler*,[6] and that shortly thereafter the editorial was reprinted in Los Angeles. The exact volume of the work is not yet known, but its first year's business is estimated at more than 25,000 cases.[7]

§ 6

These four types of small claims courts have amply demonstrated that as to small civil causes the defects of the traditional administration of justice can easily be eliminated. In these courts delay is entirely absent. Costs, either through reduction or abolition, cease to forbid access to the courts. The fundamental difficulty of the expense of lawyers is avoided by a simplicity of pleading and procedure in which there is no need for any attorney. The accruing advantage of having the parties brought

[1] There is no specific rule to this effect, but it is the practice followed. Cf. Olds: *The Small Claims Court*, 1 Southwestern L. Rev. (1917) 100.

[2] Chicago Bar Association *Report* for 1915, page 41; *Ibid.* for 1916, page 26.

[3] 1 Journal of the American Judicature Society, No. 5 (February, 1918), p. 145.

[4] Herbert Harley, Secretary of the American Judicature Society, in an address to the Louisiana State Bar Association on May 8, 1915, reprinted in pamphlet form under the title of "A Modern Experiment in Judicial Administration." See page 20.

[5] 11 Chicago L. A. R. 26.   [6] Boston *Evening Traveler* for January 2, 1915.

[7] 1 Journal of the American Judicature Society, No. 2 (August, 1917), p. 27. In a more recent number (No. 5, p. 145) in February, 1918, the estimate is increased to 35,000 cases, which is half of the entire civil business of the court.

into direct contact with the judge, of making justice seem a more real thing to the
average man with its resultant beneficial effects on good citizenship
and loyalty can only be mentioned here. The small claims courts are
a mighty force in revising the present day opinion of the humbler
classes as to law and courts.[1]

Future Extension of Small Claims Courts

There are three basic principles which must be adhered to by these
courts if their promised advantages are to be realized. First, the small claims court
must not be a distinct entity, as in Kansas, but a branch of the regular court organization, as in Cleveland and Chicago.[2]

Second, the proceedings must be conducted without lawyers. Only in this way can
the simplicity of procedure be maintained and the prohibitive expense of lawyers'
services be eliminated.[3] On all the evidence there seems to be no danger in informality of procedure in these small cases. The only test which can be applied to determine whether parties feel aggrieved or believe that injustice has been done is to examine the number of appeals.[4] Complete figures are lacking, but enough exist to be
illuminating. We may compare the appeals taken from the English County Courts,
the Kansas and Portland small claims courts, and the Municipal Court of the District of Columbia[5]—all courts where informal procedure obtains—with the appeals
taken from two Massachusetts inferior courts where all the traditional safeguards of
common law pleadings, rules of procedure, rules of evidence, and lawyers are to be
found. Judgments rendered after an informal hearing seem comparatively immune
from appeals in clear contrast to those reached after a technical trial.

Court	Period	Cases	Appeals	Per Cent Appealed
English County Courts[6]	1902	46,000	140	.3
English County Courts[7]	1913	802,600	788	.1
Kansas City Small Claims Court[8]	Aug. 25, 1913, to Oct. 17, 1916	400	15	3.8
Portland Small Claims Court[9]	May 24, 1915, to Nov. 6, 1916	1,828	2	.1
Municipal Court, District of Columbia[10]	March, 1909, to January, 1913	92,736	448	.5
Boston Municipal Court[11]	Several years prior to 1913	—	—	10.0
Southern Essex District Court[12]	1912–14	700	209	30.0

[1] See *National Municipal Review* for January, 1915, pages 455, 456; American Judicature Society, *Bulletin VIII*, page 43; Fuessle: *Making Americans by Justice*, 55 Collier's (July 3, 1915), 27.

[2] Cf. Harley: *A Modern Experiment in Judicial Administration*, page 41.

[3] American Judicature Society, *Bulletin VIII*, pages 21, 22.

[4] Cf. 1 Journal of the American Judicature Society, No. 5 (February, 1918), p. 145.

[5] The Municipal Court of the District of Columbia has not been discussed in this chapter because it is not a small claims court. But for the purposes of the test it is helpful because its procedure is entirely informal. Cf. Baer: *Justice for the Small Man*, 90 The Century (1915), 144.

[6] Storey: *Reform of Judicial Procedure*, page 190.

[7] Rosenbaum: *Studies in English Civil Procedure*, 2 The County Courts, p. 2, note 7.   [8] See *ante*, page 45, note 3.

[9] See *ante*, page 47.   [10] Baer: *Justice for the Small Man*, 90 The Century (1915), 144, 146.

[11] Before 1913, an appeal on facts lay from the Boston Municipal Court to the Superior Court. Absolute figures are unknown. The percentage figure is taken from the Boston Municipal Court *Report* for 1916, page 7.

[12] *Report No. 4* (March, 1915) of the Committee on Law and Procedure, Association of Justices of District, Police, and

The third principle is that while procedural law can be cast aside, rules of substantive law must be adhered to. This is the situation at present[1] and in future extensions of the idea it cannot safely be departed from. In other words, while the small claims courts clearly demonstrate that the doing of justice is not dependent on religious observance of our traditional rules of procedure and evidence, they do not at all invalidate or weaken the principle that justice is best done when it is ascertained and administered by a trained judge, according to the rules of substantive law.

As against the manifest advantages of this sort 'of court, only two objections have been urged. The first is that they will encourage litigation. They will increase litigation, for they make possible justice in cases where justice hitherto has not been done and they open the courts to persons who hitherto have found that the courts were not for them. To such an objection, Dean Pound makes this short answer:[2]

"When better provision for petty litigation is urged, many repeat the stock saying that litigation ought to be discouraged. It will not do to say to the population of modern cities that the practical cutting off of all petty litigation, by which theoretically the rights of the average men are to be maintained, is a good thing because litigation ought to be discouraged."

The other objection is that collection agencies will flood the courts with their business.[3] Judge Levine of Cleveland answers this by saying that collection agencies were not deterred by the former procedure and costs. In fact, it played into their hands by giving them, in addition to the judgment, a large bill of costs with which they could further harass their debtors. The result of the small claims court is to save a debtor anywhere from two to ten dollars. If any undesirable tendency manifests itself, it can readily be controlled by requiring the original claimants, and not their assignees, to sign the statement of claim and to present the case to the judge in person.[4]

How far can these courts be extended? There is no reason why they should not be created immediately in every large city as an indispensable department of a modern municipal court. Minneapolis secured such a court on April 17, 1917.[5] Judge Wheeler, who made an investigation for the Philadelphia Municipal Court, strongly recommends the addition of a small claims branch.[6] Legislation toward this end has

Municipal Courts of Massachusetts. Some latitude must be allowed in these figures, for they represent appeals after trials, whereas the other figures give the proportion of appeals out of all entries. But these figures as they stand may be compared with the English County Court record of 32,000 judgments made by judges in 1913 with only 167 appeals and 621 motions for new trials.

[1] This opinion has been expressed in foregoing pages. It is confirmed in American Judicature Society, *Bulletin VIII*, page 36 ; but see *Ibid.*, pages 18, 19.

[2] Pound: *Administration of Justice in the Modern City*, 26 Harvard L. Rev. 320.

[3] See American Judicature Society, *Bulletin VIII*, page 41 ; Philadelphia *Municipal Court R.* for 1915, page 40.

[4] This has been done in Portland by statute. Oregon *General Laws of* 1915, c. 327, § 7. In Cleveland the judges have, as occasion required, insisted that the creditor himself appear.

[5] Minnesota *Session Laws of* 1917, c. 263. Costs are abolished and attorneys are excluded, § 3. This court is discussed in 1 Minnesota Law Review, 107; 2 Journal of the American Judicature Society, No. 1, p. 16.

[6] Philadelphia *Municipal Court R.* for 1915, page 33; see also page 19; *Ibid.* for 1916, page 11.

been introduced in the Connecticut legislature but not yet acted on.[1] The Rochester Legal Aid Bureau expresses the need for some such court.[2] The modern municipal courts of Milwaukee, Pittsburgh, Buffalo, and Atlanta, under their rule-making powers, can establish small claims branches at short notice.[3] The New York Municipal Court with its 1917 rules for conciliation and arbitration has substantially established a small claims court.[4] A movement for such a court is clearly under way in Boston,[5] in Newark, and in Jersey City.[6] There is every reason to predict that the immediate future will see small claims courts established in all of the larger cities of the United States.[7] If this comes about, it will mean an enormous step forward toward freedom and equality of justice. Remembering that small claims courts are able to handle nearly all wage claims and miscellaneous small debt matters which together form a substantial part of the litigation of the poor, it is not too much to say that with a wide territorial expansion, these courts are capable of reducing by one quarter the existing denial of justice.

Not all claims of the poor, even in the fields of wages and miscellaneous debts, are below twenty or even thirty-five dollars. The question of how far the monetary limit of the small claims jurisdiction can be extended is not easy to answer. If claims up to two or five hundred dollars can be adjudicated properly without formal procedure and without attorneys, the serviceability of these courts to the poor will be proportionately increased. The precise question is not as to raising the jurisdiction of the whole court, but as to fixing the point at which it ceases to be practicable and wise to transfer cases to a special department where the proceedings are informal.

The Kansas limit of $20 was increased in Cleveland to $35. Chicago, beginning at $35, very quickly raised its jurisdiction to $50, then to $100, and finally to $200.[8] It is superficially said that informal procedure cannot be extended to larger claims because they are more complicated. Every lawyer knows that in contract and debt actions the size of the claim has little relation to the complexity of the issues or the difficulty of proof.[9] It is easier to prove a five thousand dollar claim on a note than a five dollar claim for wages where there is a defence of improper workmanship. To this problem no deductive answer can be made. The only sane course to pursue is gradually to mark the limit up, and to stop when signs appear that the plan is not workable. The answer must be inductive and therefore must rest on future experience.[10]

---

[1] House Bill 443 (1915), filed by Thomas Hewes, attorney for the Hartford Legal Aid Committee.

[2] 4 United Charities of Rochester R. 13.   [3] American Judicature Society, *Bulletin VIII*, page 44.

[4] This is discussed in detail in Chapter IX, Conciliation, and Chapter X, Arbitration, pages 63 and 71.

[5] See House Bill No. 590, filed in the Massachusetts Legislature by Richard W. Hale in 1918.

[6] 1 Journal of the American Judicature Society, No. 5 (February, 1918), p. 157.

[7] *Ibid.*, p. 149; 42 American Bar Ass'n R. (1917) 377.

[8] See 8 & 9 Chicago Municipal Court Reports (1913-15), 129; Chicago Bar Association *Report* for 1917, page 31.

[9] And see Parry: *The Law and the Poor*, page 145; *Docket* (West Publishing Co.) for 1915, page 1523.

[10] This is the conclusion arrived at by Dean Wigmore, who has addressed himself to the precise question. See American Judicature Society, *Bulletin VIII*, pages 20 et seq.

§ 7

The essential features of a small claims court are extremely low costs or none at all, no formal pleadings, no lawyers, and the direct examination of parties and witnesses without formality by a trained judge who knows and applies the substantive law. There are, in addition, five collateral functions which these courts ought to undertake. Varying combinations of the five are found in different courts. None as yet are empowered to perform them all.

Collateral Functions: 1. Assistance to Litigants by Clerks

The first is to provide some official who shall assist parties. While the lawyer is largely rendered unnecessary, certain bits of his traditional functions remain and must be performed by some one. It is highly desirable that all cases should not at once be docketed for trial. In many, a letter to the defendant will secure the desired result, and in such cases the court ought not to be bothered or the parties caused loss of time in attendance. The statement of claim, however simple, must be filled out under the supervision of a person who knows the law and procedure. Parties need advice as to their rights. A successful litigant needs instructions as to collecting his judgment. There will be, even in small disputes, cases presenting complicated states of fact or raising intricate questions of law wherein the judge needs the assistance of counsel and the parties require representation if justice is to be done. There must be some official to sort such cases and, especially where one side has retained counsel,[1] to advise consulting a lawyer or the legal aid society. There is always a danger that persons (as has been the case with injured workmen and industrial accident commissions) will rely too much on the court and expect from it more protection and safeguarding of rights or defences than it can legally, or in the nature of things, give.

In Kansas the judge affords this assistance and in Portland the clerk. In Cleveland more has been done than elsewhere through the creation of a special department of the clerk's office, which has already been described. In one case where the defendant had appealed, raising a jurisdictional question, the clerk prepared for the plaintiff a brief on the point and instructed him as to its filing. This illustrates the necessity of maintaining a watch over the small cases in order that when an attorney does become necessary, the party may be so advised. Under a proper coördination of work the legal aid society would be called in, or counsel assigned, in all such cases. Courts are more and more undertaking such work,[2] and unless rights and defences are to be sacrificed in a margin of cases, it is essential.

A second power which a small claims court should have is that of ordering the judgment paid by instalments. This is not only a fairness to the defendant who under modern conditions of the weekly wage seldom has enough at any one time to pay a

---

[1] See 8 Cleveland L. A. R. 6.

[2] In addition to Kansas, Portland, and Cleveland, see Rule 13 of the Cincinnati Municipal Court; Philadelphia *Municipal Court Report* for 1915, page xi.

judgment in full, but also it facilitates the court's disposition of cases. A defendant
often denies a debt simply because he cannot pay it. If he realizes
that he is not to be harassed, he is more willing to confess judgment
and try to obtain suitable terms. This power to order and accept
instalment payments is granted by law to the Kansas, Portland,
and Minneapolis courts.[1] In Cleveland it is done de facto.

2. Payment of Judgment by Instalments

Such a power might be attacked on constitutional grounds as impairing the obligation of contract, but it would probably be upheld because, under our law forbidding imprisonment for debt and giving liberal exemptions, it is in fact of great benefit to creditors. The present proceeding of examination after judgment or poor debtor process is designed only to discover existing property. The instalment payment order is a means whereby a judgment can be paid out of future earnings. It is only a slight extension of the Massachusetts equitable proceeding, permitted by statute[2] after a judgment founded on necessaries, whereby a judge may order a defendant to pay so much a week, and which has been held constitutional.[3] This plan is used in the English County Courts; in 1913 about £2,700,000 was so collected and paid over to suitors.[4] The sweeping provisions of the Soldiers' and Sailors' Civil Relief Act permit every court in entering or staying judgment against a man in military service to order that the judgment shall be paid in instalments.[5]

The small claims courts statutes do not specifically state what is to happen in case the debtor fails to pay the ordered instalments. The procedure should be, as in England and Massachusetts, for the issuance of a summons, promptly returnable, at which time the enquiry is not what the debtor has, but whether he has had the funds out of which to pay the ordered amount. If it appears that he has had money and has refused to apply it in payment, he is amenable to such orders as the court deems fair, for he then stands not only in default but in contempt of a court order.

A third function which every small claims court ought to exercise, and one which will speedily be thrust upon it if it employs the instalment plan to any extent, is that of acting as trustee for a debtor who owes numerous creditors. It is obviously an injustice for the court to lend its aid to one creditor, to the exclusion of others who have been more lenient and refrained from bringing suit, thereby causing a clear preference. It would automatically force all creditors to bring suit, and their proceedings, coupled with attachment and garnishment which they could legally use, would in turn make it impossible for the debtor to pay the ordered instalments. The court would be robbed of much of its power for good; instead of helping all parties, it would cause costs to all and bring relief to none. The needed procedure is like informal bankruptcy. In essence, it per-

3. The Function of Court Trustee

---

[1] Kansas *Session Laws of* 1913, c. 170, § 7; Oregon *General Laws of* 1915, c. 327, § 10; Minnesota *Session Laws of* 1917, c. 263, §§ 4, 5.

[2] Mass. *Revised Laws of* 1902, c. 168, §§ 80–86.   [3] Brown's Case, 178 Mass. (1899) 498.

[4] Rosenbaum: *Studies in English Civil Procedure*, 2 The County Courts, p. 10, note 18.

[5] *Public Act No.* 103 of the 65th Congress, § 204.

mits a debtor to come into court, disclose his assets, state his creditors, and then, after notice and hearing, to have the court fix the proportion of his income which is to be set aside for creditors, and to issue an order protecting him from garnishment and attachment.

The small man does not owe many creditors or much money. For such matters bankruptcy is too expensive and cumbersome, and where a debtor desires to pay, the law ought not to force an election between canceling all debts and perpetual harassing. One creditor of a man who owes five creditors one or two hundred dollars may, by garnishment, tie up all his wages or cause him to be discharged, so that he has difficulty in supporting his family and little opportunity of meeting his obligations.[1]

The trusteeship suggested has never been carefully tried in America. In Kansas the court can protect the debtor against further proceedings by the judgment creditor,[2] but not as against other creditors. In Cleveland the enterprising clerk's office established a trustee department which succeeded at first,[3] but failed, as it was doomed to fail, because the court had no power to restrain creditors or to protect the debtor. The legal aid societies have had as much success with the plan as their limited authority permitted,[4] particularly in Nashville, where the Legal Aid Bureau[5] through its close affiliation with the Commercial Club has a quasi-legal hold over the creditors and so can afford a genuine protection to the debtor, which is unquestionably the sine qua non of any such plan. The necessity for the establishment of such a court department has been repeatedly urged in various cities,[6] and a law giving such power to the Columbus Municipal Court was passed,[7] but nothing has as yet been accomplished.

In England, under the name of "administration orders," the plan of having the County Court act as trustee for a small debtor is in very general use. The plan differs slightly in that it is a part of the bankruptcy law, so that the courts may order partial payment in full satisfaction by way of composition or dividend. This would be both unnecessary and undesirable in America. In 1913 these courts made 5426 administration orders, of which 2884 were for payment in full. The average total indebtedness was ascertained to be £25, 16s., and the average creditor's claim to be £2, 7s. The court may refuse to issue a protecting order if the petition for the order or the incurring of the debts appears fraudulent, but in only 11 per cent of the total applications has a refusal been necessary. The effectiveness of the method has been vitiated in part by the excessive court costs which attend these orders. There seems to be no

---

[1] Cf. American Judicature Society, *Bulletin VIII*, page 15.

[2] Edholm: *The Small Debtors' Court*, 22 Case and Comment, 30.   [3] 3 Cleveland Municipal Court R. 55.

[4] A great deal of this work has been done in Chicago and Duluth. In both instances, the plan has had a measure of success only because of the moral hold which the legal aid society had on the creditors. See also 1 Milwaukee L. A. R. 10.

[5] Nashville Legal Aid Bureau *Report* for 1915-16, page 10; Commercial Club *Tattler* for July, 1916, page 29; *Proceedings of the Fourth Conference of Legal Aid Societies*, pages 111, 112.

[6] See 6 Cleveland L. A. R. 8; 7 *Ibid.* 16; 9 *Ibid.* 12; 6 Cincinnati L. A. R. 9; *Proceedings of the First Conference of Legal Aid Societies*, page 43. Cf. Rochester L. A. *Leaflet* for 1915, page 3.

[7] 1 Supplement to Page and Adams' Ohio General Code, §§ 1558-54 c (page 592). After its protecting order has been issued, the court may stop creditors' suits by writ of prohibition.

doubt that if this difficulty were removed, the plan, under proper supervision, would be an instrument of great service to creditors and debtors alike.[1]

A fourth power which could well be added to the small claims courts is a discretionary control over ejectment proceedings. Any authority to exercise discretion to

4. Control over Ejectment Proceedings

forbid the ejection of tenants either after expiration of the tenancy by notice or for non-payment of rent is unknown in the United States.[2] Our common law gives the landlord certain rights, and these the courts must enforce regardless of the circumstances of the case. A control over the right to occupy or eject from premises is as necessary as our homestead laws and our provisions exempting certain property from attachment and execution. Both are based on the theory that at a certain point the interest of the state supervenes and rises superior to the rights of the creditor.

The vast majority of the poorer people living in cities possess their homes without written leases, so that in law they are merely tenants at will. They are liable to eviction on summary notice whether they have paid their rent or not. Homes are of social as well as individual importance, but millions of homes are at the mercy of a law which has altered but little from feudal days when a tenant at will was only one grade better than a trespasser. Admittedly an economic problem is involved. Landlords are entitled to their just dues, but a more even balancing of rights and interests is desirable and this may best be secured by entrusting to the courts a discretionary control over ejectments. In England, if the judge finds the landlord entitled to use and occupancy, he has power, after considering the circumstances, to make an order for "possession in a week" or even "in six weeks." This discretionary power is vested in the court by statute.[3]

The final power which every small claims court should in unmistakable language be given is the authority to endeavor to conciliate the parties and to assist them in

5. Conciliation

reaching a satisfactory solution or adjustment by agreement. This matter of conciliation has such great possibilities and is so little understood that it deserves a careful presentation and consideration which is attempted in the next chapter.

---

[1] The English system is fully presented in Rosenbaum: *Studies in English Civil Procedure*, 2 The County Courts, 47–51. Cf. Parry: *The Law and the Poor*, pages 120–124.

[2] Since this was written, a very important beginning has been made. As to cases in which soldiers and sailors and their dependents are involved, this power has now virtually been given to every court in the United States by the Soldiers' and Sailors' Civil Relief Act. *Public Act No.* 103 of the 65th Congress, § 300. For a commentary see 12 Illinois L. Rev. (February, 1918) 449, 459.

[3] Rosenbaum: *op. cit.*, pages 46, 47.

CHAPTER IX

CONCILIATION

It is the duty of a good judge to remove causes of litigation. . . .
(1628.) 2 *Institutes*, 306.[1]
The conciliation system marks a new epoch in the administration
of justice in this State. . . . (1917.) *Statement of the Justices of the
New York Municipal Court.*[2]

THE idea of conciliation is not new, but it is to-day so little understood that attempts to employ it as a method of settling litigation are very generally viewed by the bench and bar with suspicion and distrust, if not hostility. It therefore becomes necessary to state what conciliation means and to explain that in its true form it is neither revolutionary nor destructive of cherished institutions.

§ 1

By reason of the fact that the Cleveland small claims court was given the name of "conciliation court" there is a mistaken idea abroad that conciliation is a particular court or that it pertains only to small matters.[3] Conciliation is a method *Definition* or principle for settling litigation, and as such can be used in every court and is applicable to all civil cases, and to certain types of criminal cases.

Conciliation is the process used by two lawyers who succeed in adjusting a dispute between their clients. The duty to conciliate in proper cases is enjoined by the Canons of Ethics.[4] Judicial conciliation means nothing more than giving to the court power to follow the advice of Abraham Lincoln, which has been deemed proper enough to be used as a preface to the American Bar Association Canons of Ethics:[5]

"Discourage litigation. Persuade your neighbors to compromise whenever you can. Point out to them how the nominal winner is often the real loser—in fees, expenses, and waste of time. As a peacemaker the lawyer has a superior opportunity of being a good man."

There is no set form for judicial conciliation. It is an entirely voluntary affair, an informal proceeding by which the two disputants are enabled to discuss the issue before a trained and impartial third person having the dignity of judicial office, who explains to them the rules of law applicable, informs them of the uncertainties and expense of litigation, tries to arouse their friendly feelings and suppress their fighting instincts, and if an adjustment agreeable to the parties is reached, draws up a

---

[1] The same maxim, in a more extended version, is contained in 4 Coke, 15 b; 5 Coke, 31 a; Bart. Max. 191.
[2] When the new conciliation rules of the Municipal Court of the City of New York were promulgated, a statement, prepared by Justice Spiegelberg, was issued to the press. See page 1.
[3] Cf. American Judicature Society, *Bulletin VIII*, pages 28, 29; 2 Journal of the American Judicature Society, No. 1. p. 3.
[4] See Canon 8, 33 Am. Bar Ass'n R. (1908) 578; see also Sharswood: *Legal Ethics* (5th ed. 1884), page 109.
[5] 33 A. B. A. R. 574.

proper agreement, has it executed, and gives it the sanction of a judgment. All of this is done without prejudice to the parties if adjustment fails and a trial is rendered necessary.[1]

§ 2

In the reform wave of 1846 to 1852, which accomplished certain improvements in the administration of justice, provisions respecting conciliation were inserted in six *History* of the new constitutions which were adopted during that period.[2] The New York provision read:

> " Tribunals of conciliation may be established, with such powers and duties as may be prescribed by law, but such tribunals shall have no power to render judgment to be obligatory on the parties, except they voluntarily submit their matters in difference and agree to abide the judgment, or assent thereto, in the presence of such tribunal, in such cases as shall be prescribed by law."

A bill to carry this clause into effect was prepared, but failed of passage. The constitutional provision became a dead letter and was eliminated in 1894.[3] In the other jurisdictions the plan met with like failure, for the time was not ripe. Meanwhile conciliation as a means of settling collective disputes was slowly coming to the fore in nearly all European countries and in America, and so clearly demonstrated its superiority over the litigious method of injunction, suits for damages, and the like that to-day, in the event of a strike or lockout, the first thought of the parties and of the general public is of the possibility of employing conciliation.[4]

Inasmuch as the use of conciliation by American courts to settle individual disputes is of extremely recent origin, it is necessary to examine briefly the plan of conciliation as employed in Europe in order to gain some concrete idea of what it is and how far it is successful.

§ 3

In Norway and Denmark courts of conciliation have existed since 1795.[5] The court has jurisdiction of every civil proceeding, and before any lawsuit can be instituted *Conciliation in Europe* the dispute must be submitted to the local conciliation commission, which consists of two members. Unless a suitor can present a certificate that this condition precedent of an attempt at judicial conciliation has been complied with, the law courts will refuse to hear the case. The costs are seventy-

---

[1] Charles A. Boston gives substantially the same definition in 73 Ann. Am. Ac. Pol. & Soc. Science, 112.

[2] New York Const. of 1846, Art. VI, § 23; Ohio Const. of 1851, Art. IV, § 19; Indiana Const. of 1851, Art. VII, § 19; Michigan Const. of 1850, Art. VI, § 23; Wisconsin Const. of 1848, Art. VII, § 16; California Const. of 1849, Art. VI, § 13.

[3] See New York Const. of 1894, Art. VI; 73 Ann. Am, Ac. Pol. & Soc. Science, 111.

[4] The use of conciliation in the United States, Canada, Great Britain, and in Europe is fully set forth in *United States Bureau of Labor Bulletin No.* 98 (1912). The serviceability of the method in the United States is well known. For the English experience see pages 123, 137.

[5] 2 Journal of the American Judicature Society, No. 1 (June, 1918), pp. 5, 9.

five cents, the hearings are in secret in order that no disclosures may prejudice subsequent litigation, and lawyers are rigidly excluded. Proceedings are most informal, the disputants tell their own stories, and the conciliation commissioners endeavor to guide them to a fair adjustment.

As conciliation has no validity except what it obtains from the voluntary consent of the litigants themselves, it would be wholly worthless unless it worked. But it appears that in Norway 75 per cent and in Denmark 90 per cent of all litigation is peaceably adjusted through judicial conciliation.[1] Precise figures for the Norwegian courts in 1888 are known. The total number of civil cases brought was 103,969, of which 2300 were dismissed by the Conciliation Commissioners. Of the remaining 101,669 conciliation produced adjustments agreeable to the litigants in 81,015 cases, and in addition 7886 were submitted to the Conciliation Court by the parties for decision. Thus only 12,768 cases went to the regular courts for formal litigation, this informal preliminary tribunal of conciliation having disposed of 87 per cent of all matters to the satisfaction of both parties. That the method of conciliation works no injustice is well attested by the fact that throughout a period of over a century during which constitutions have been liberalized and systems of law recast, the courts of conciliation have not only been left intact, but have steadily been strengthened and perfected.[2]

In the industrial courts of France, Switzerland, and Germany which have jurisdiction over disputes between employers and employees, conciliation plays a leading part. These courts, whose history began in France in 1806,[3] had no counterpart in American judicial institutions, with the exception of an isolated attempt made in Pennsylvania in 1883, which immediately failed,[4] until the creation of the small claims courts. The essential features of the system are the same as those already described. These courts accomplish their great volume of work by conciliation and not by trial and judgment.[5] Conciliation is frankly their primary object.[6] The statistics again show that conciliation fits in with human nature and that, when rightly conducted, it is very successful.

Court	Year	Settled by Conciliation	by Judgment
France [7]	1905	17,731	5,041
France	1906	19,064	6,637
Geneva [8]	1908	793	139
Geneva	1909	914	222

---

[1] American Judicature Society, *Bulletin VIII*, page 9.   [2] *Ibid.*
[3] *United States Bureau of Labor Bulletin No.* 98, p. 292.
[4] *Ibid.*, p. 290.   [5] *Ibid.*, p. 280.   [6] *Ibid.*, p. 278.   [7] *Ibid.*, p. 437.   [8] *Ibid.*, p. 452.

§ 4

The legal aid societies have always recognized the possibilities of conciliation and have steadily employed it.[1] In the words of the greatest figure in all legal aid work:[2]

Conciliation In the United States "The Legal Aid Society brings antagonists together, inculcates the spirit of compromise and adjustment, under authority of the searching legal mind, expert in resource, linked with reserve compulsory powers; yet in the persuasive and kindly attitude of a lover of humanity unselfishly seeking to render unto every one his own."

Judicial conciliation in the United States begins its history with the establishment of the Cleveland small claims court in 1913. The rules merely say that the judge shall endeavor to effect an amicable adjustment,[3] and leave the rest to his tact, discretion, and patience. In 1914 judgments were rendered in 1879 cases and 794 were settled by the parties;[4] in 1915 the judgments were 2754 and the settlements 634.[5] In this court, if conciliation fails, the court may proceed to hear the case and render judgment forthwith.[6]

In 1917 a small claims branch was added to the Minneapolis Municipal Court and the right to attempt conciliation conferred on the court.[7] It is provided that a person may bring a matter before the conciliation judge either by going directly to the judge or by filing a claim with the clerk. The defendant may be summoned orally, or by telephone, or by mail, or by the usual summons. There are no costs and no attorneys. At the hearing, if a settlement is reached, it becomes a judgment when countersigned by the judge. If conciliation fails, the court must dismiss the case if the claim or counter-claim exceeds fifty dollars; otherwise it may proceed to a hearing at once and render judgment.[8]

In these courts it is difficult, if not impossible, to determine where their function as a conciliation tribunal ends and their work as a small claims court begins. Fortunately it is not necessary. In the field of small claims the two merge and become indistinguishable because both are based on precisely the same informal procedure.

In April, 1917, the justices of the Municipal Court of the City of New York, acting under authority of the new municipal court act,[9] promulgated a series of rules

---

[1] McCook: *The Judicial Aspect of the Works of the Legal Aid Society*, 5 N. Y. Legal Aid Review, No. 3, p. 17; 6 *Ibid.*, No. 1, p. 3; 3 Cleveland L. A. R. 7; *Proceedings of Third Conference of Legal Aid Societies*, page 25; *Ibid.*, *Fourth Conference*, page 128.

[2] Arthur v. Briesen, long president of the New York Legal Aid Society. This quotation is taken from the program of a concert given on May 2, 1908, for the Society's benefit.

[3] Conciliation Branch, Rule 3.

[4] 3 Cleveland Municipal Court R. 56.   [5] *Ibid.* 43.

[6] Conciliation Branch, Rule 4.

[7] Minnesota *Session Laws of* 1917, c. 263.

[8] This court is discussed by Dean Vance of the University of Minnesota Law School in 1 Minnesota L. Rev. No. 2 (February, 1917), p. 107.

[9] Lauer: *Municipal Court Code in the City of New York* (1916); see Section 6, subdivision 6, and Section 8, subdivision 5, of the Code. See also Justice Lauer's article in 1 Journal of the American Judicature Society, No. 5 (February, 1918), p. 153.

establishing and regulating conciliation.[1] The important points in these rules are that attorneys shall play a part in the proceedings only in the court's discretion, there are no costs, service is by mail, and the court cannot render a judgment in any case. This last is overcautious; if the disputants have come to an agreement under circumstances which preclude coercion and overreaching, there is no reason why it should not be made a judgment and thereby given legal validity. The framers of the rules doubtless feared that any compulsion would jeopardize the plan. Compulsion exercised to force a settlement is, of course, not conciliation at all, but unless an agreement can be enforced, the door is left open for fraud by refusal to abide by the adjustment, so that the proceeding merely results in loss of time and disappointment. This detail should not be adopted elsewhere. It will do little mischief in New York because a parallel system of rules for arbitration was concurrently provided by the justices, under which a binding award may be secured.[2] The distinguishing feature of the New York conciliation rules is that no monetary limit is fixed. Therefore any claim under one thousand dollars, the maximum jurisdiction of the Municipal Court, may be submitted for conciliation. This should provide experience from which the conciliation plan may be further developed as a method of settling large as well as small causes.

In fields other than small claims there have been slight experiments with conciliation, but all informal in nature and without any clear legal sanction. In matters of divorce and domestic difficulties there are great possibilities for conciliation[3] with a view to reconciliation, and progress in this direction is quietly being made in the domestic relations courts of Philadelphia, Cincinnati, Cleveland, Kansas City, and elsewhere.[4] Industrial Accident Commissions have begun to employ it as a preliminary to a formal hearing. In Massachusetts, for example, in many cases the parties request a "conference"—a thing not to be found in the statute—at which they appear before a single member of the Industrial Accident Board, talk the matter over informally, have the benefit of his observation, and often come to an amicable understanding which is then validated as a binding agreement.[5]

Judge Levine, who was largely responsible for the development of conciliation in the Cleveland Municipal Court, has carried his faith in its efficacy to the Common Pleas Court, of which he is now a judge, and has used it more widely than any one else. Several notable triumphs stand to his credit. In a suit for repairs to a large "butterfly valve" with a defence of non-compliance with specifications, the type of case which bristles with the most technical engineering points, the parties arrived

[1] These rules are printed in New York *Law Journal* for April 26, 1917, and in 1 Journal of the American Judicature Society, No. 2, p. 13.

[2] This is discussed in the next chapter, page 71.

[3] The National Desertion Bureau of New York has had great success with conciliation. See *Family Desertion, Report of the Committee on Desertion* (1912), page 16. For further conciliation in general see Parry : *The Law and the Poor*, pages 127, 187, 298.

[4] This particular development is considered more in detail in Chapter XI, Domestic Relations Courts, § 4, page 80.

[5] This is later mentioned in Chapter XII, Administrative Tribunals, page 88.

armed with their lawyers, models, and experts. A trial in usual course would have consumed about ten days, and each side was paying about two hundred dollars a day in expenses. At the close of the first day's trial, the Judge called the parties into his room, reduced the issue, as he saw it, to its simplest terms, and asked if they were unable to come to any agreement. They asked for time, and returned the next morning having come to an agreement, and prepared to continue instead of break off their business relations. The model of the valve was given to the Judge as an expression of appreciation.

In a delicate case of slander where honor, not damages, was the issue, where one might expect conciliation to fail, the Judge, after conference with the plantiff and defendant, discovered that at bottom the difficulty was a misunderstanding. His suggestion that the defendant state in writing that he had never believed the plaintiff dishonest and that the plaintiff dismiss her case met with cordial approval by the parties and was done. The following statement to the jury is almost unparalleled in legal annals:[1]

> "Gentlemen of the Jury, in your absence I have conferred with both sides to this lawsuit. After hearing the evidence so far given, and after speaking to both sides, I felt it was the duty of the Court, in view of its conviction, to be of some substantial assistance to both sides, if possible. I was convinced that I was dealing with good people, who had a serious misunderstanding. I saw the futile loss, part of which you have heard; I saw the burden which each side would have to bear, by way of waste of time and court expenses, and after speaking to both plaintiff and defendant, I was convinced that neither bore any real feelings towards the other, but that it was purely a case of an unfortunate, serious misunderstanding.
>
> "The defendant in this case signed the following statement . . .
>
> "It has been agreed between the parties to call this legal strife to an end. . . . I hope that the end of this lawsuit upon which you both agree by common consent, will be the end of all controversy or feeling between you, for you have no cause to feel anything but the deepest friendship for one another.
>
> "Gentlemen of the Jury, I hope this meets with your approval. (*Applause by the Jury*.)"

The traditionally trained judge or lawyer unconsciously feels a certain distrust and aversion for such a proceeding. This is an illustration of the tendency to make law a thing apart, an end unto itself, forgetting that only as it squares with life and aids human beings has it any reason for existence. It is difficult to see how exception can properly be taken to a proceeding which has satisfied the litigants, saved them unnecessary expense, saved the state nearly a thousand dollars, enabled other cases to be reached sooner, and tended to heal rather than inflame a misunderstanding between honest people. Justice has various definitions, but this runs counter to none.

---

[1] From the stenographic record in Payne *v.* Henry, No. 145,594, Cuyahoga County, Court of Common Pleas.

§ 5

The significance of judicial conciliation for this study is that, of its very nature, it is a prompt proceeding, calling for minimum or no court costs,[1] and involving no expense to the parties, not even for attorneys' fees. The attorney is eliminated because conciliation depends for its effect on bringing the parties together, on smoothing out irrelevancies by confrontation, and then proceeding to a direct, business-like, personal adjustment of the real issue. It is the almost universal experience that conciliation is best worked without lawyers.[2]

The Signifi-cance of Conciliation

It results that as conciliation automatically obviates the three difficulties in the traditional administration of justice, it is capable of reducing denial of justice to the poor exactly in proportion as it makes headway in being used by the courts. When a poor person is able to go before a judge, have the defendant summoned at once or in a few days, obtain an informal hearing out of which an amicable adjustment becomes possible, and have a judgment rendered thereon, he has indeed partaken of free and equal justice.

§ 6

The most perplexing problem raised by conciliation is whether the court which attempts conciliation should have authority, if it fails, to proceed to a hearing and judgment. In New York the court cannot, in Cleveland it can, and in Minneapolis it depends on the amount involved. In Norway the judge can render a judgment only if both parties have consented; in the industrial courts the hearing for judgment is before a larger body, but of which the conciliation officials are members.

Future of Conciliation

There is a fear that if the same judge exercises both functions, it may result in forced compromises. When the case is one which is to be tried according to strict rules of evidence there may be a danger in permitting a judge to hear the stories with the fullness in which they are told at the conciliation stage. Yet this is no more than a judge, sitting without a jury, does every day. He passes on the admissibility of evidence which he actually hears and then determines his finding according to a state of facts from which such evidence in law is excluded. In small claims, where the trial itself is under informal procedure, it is difficult to see why the judge should not be empowered to pass judgment. It may be said that a judge would be biased or piqued by the refusal of one party to accept his suggestion, but if judges were not able to rise above such personal considerations, they would equally take offence at every exception and a thousand things that occur in any hard fought trial. If two hearings by two tri-

---

[1] The industrial courts in Europe have most successfully eliminated delay and expense. *United States Labor Bulletin No.* 98, p. 281.

[2] It has already been noted that they are excluded in Norway, Denmark, and Minneapolis; that in fact they seldom appear in Cleveland; that in New York their appearance is only by permission. In the European industrial courts they rarely appear. *United States Bureau of Labor Bulletin No.* 98, pp. 278, 320. See also, American Judicature Society, *Bulletin VI,* page 60.

bunals are to be required, much delay and waste of judicial time will be caused. The answer can only be worked out empirically. It will be safer to attempt it first in the simpler matters and then gradually to experiment with extensions. The line of cleavage between the two functions which cannot safely be departed from is that as conciliator the judge may suggest any solution likely to be acceptable to the parties, but as judge he must abide by the rules of substantive law.

How far conciliation may be counted on as a solution for the existing denial of justice is doubtful. As with the small claims courts, there is evidence of its general popularity.[1] The proposed New York Code planned to make provision for it.[2] The American Judicature Society in its draft for a model State-Wide Judicature Act includes a system of conciliation by local magistrates.[3] The New York State Bar Association in 1916 adopted resolutions calling for the appointment of a Commissioner in Conciliation.[4] A bill has been introduced in Wisconsin providing for the establishment of conciliation branches in the Civil Court of Milwaukee County.[5]

Despite these promises of development, it is well not to put too much reliance on conciliation as of great immediate value in securing more adequately the rights of the poor. Conciliation is compounded of common sense and psychology. The American people may take slowly to the idea. Judges are likely to be distrustful of the plan and of their ability to carry it through. It is a delicate adjustment, depending much on custom, drawing a large part of its moral suasion from a public opinion that parties ought to try to conciliate, and calling for judges experienced in its use. Such things can come but slowly.

---

[1] See editorials in the Cleveland *Press* for February 4, 1915, and Duluth *Evening Herald* for November 18, 1916.

[2] 1 Report of the Board of Statutory Consolidation (1915), 9, 25, 228.

[3] American Judicature Society, *Bulletin VII–A*, pages 57, 72.

[4] New York State Bar Ass'n R. for 1916, pages 291, 309; 3 Am. Bar Ass'n Journal, No. 1, p. 35. See also 1 Journal of the American Judicature Society, No. 5 (February, 1918), p. 157.

[5] 1 Journal of the American Judicature Society, No. 1, p. 25.

Chapter X

ARBITRATION

> It would be better for the people if more of their controversies
> should be settled by arbitration, and justice would be quite as likely
> to be done as when administered by the more formal methods of
> litigation in the courts. *Curtis* v. *Gokay*, 68 *N.Y.* 300, 305.

ARBITRATION, as a method of settling disputes, is more generally and better known than conciliation. It stands midway between conciliation and court litigation. Like the former, it is a method that can be used only by consent, and so differs from judicial procedure which rests on compulsion. But once the agreement is made, and the arbitration tribunal has entered its award, the enforceability of the decision rests not on consent as in conciliation, but on the compulsion of legal process by judgment and execution.

In its details, arbitration has meant different things at different times, so that its present form, and what is more important, the significance of its present tendency in relation to our problem of the administration of justice, may more easily be described after a brief preliminary review.

§ 1

Arbitration is an ancient practice at common law,[1] but it has had a checkered development. In earlier times the courts, having few cases and being jealous of their prerogatives, viewed it askance and accorded it little support;[2] later,
The Rise of Arbitration having crowded dockets and being overworked, the courts set the seal of their emphatic approval upon it. Again, arbitration has at times been in vogue and has then relapsed into disuse. It was frequently employed in an organized way by New York merchants as early as 1768,[3] and in Boston in 1819 a plea was made for its more extended development.[4] It underwent a process of statutory development, following the course in England,[5] but during the last quarter of the nineteenth century it existed as an unused appendage to the legal machinery for disposing of controversies.

Arbitration as provided for by statute[6] in effect permits disputants to create a tribunal of their own either by agreeing on the persons to arbitrate or by agreeing to use the arbitration machinery of some private organization, as a chamber of com-

---

[1] 5 Corpus Juris, 16.

[2] 1 Journal of the American Judicature Society, No. 2, p. 15.

[3] *Commercial Arbitration, Report of the Special Committee on Arbitration of the New York Chamber of Commerce* (1911), page 5.

[4] Honestus: *Observations on the Pernicious Practice of the Law* (1819), page 8.

[5] For a history of the English statutory development see American Judicature Society, *Bulletin XII*, page 12.

[6] Typical statutes are those of New York, *Code of Civil Procedure*, chap. 17, tit. VIII, §§ 2365–2386.

merce. This agreement is generally called a "submission," and if it contains a provision to that effect, the law permits the award to be entered as a court judgment and enforced in like manner. The great defect in the American statutes is that either party may, after the submission and any time before the final award, revoke his agreement and thereby annul all the proceedings.[1]

The arbitration proceeding is obviously one not conducted according to the legal rules of procedure and evidence. So long as the arbitrators give the disputants a fair chance to present their full case, they can conduct the hearings as they like and accept such evidence as seems to them helpful. More important, statutory arbitration need not at all be a determination of right and wrong according to rules of substantive law. An award may be revoked for fraud, corruption, or serious and prejudicial misconduct, just as the decisions of a court may be set aside on like grounds, but there is no authority for revoking a finding because it fails to accord with rules of law. In its *Handbook for Arbitrators* the New York Chamber of Commerce says:[2]

"If any law points are involved, they should disregard pure technicalities and go to the merits. If they believe that the legal proposition is based upon sound sense and the experience of mankind generally, they should follow it."

Arbitration has been coming more and more generally into use through the insistence of merchants acting through their trade groups or chambers of commerce. Under the energetic guidance of Charles L. Bernheimer a splendid organization has, since 1911, been built up under authority of the Chamber of Commerce of the State of New York,[3] which has been followed elsewhere, notably by the Chicago Association of Credit Men.[4] This revival has been forced by three considerations, — first, a desire for a decision by an expert having personal knowledge of trade conditions and customs, a thing which the courts have never been able to afford;[5] second, a hope of supplanting the enmity provoking litigious method with an amicable procedure which would not interrupt business relationships; and thirdly and chiefly, a determination to escape from the intolerable delays of the regular administration of justice.[6]

While business men have desired expert decisions, a more liberal attitude toward trade customs, and have preferred a prompt decision according to conscience, the arbitrium boni viri of the Roman law,[7] to a delayed judgment according to law, the rise and expansion of these organized but extra-legal arbitration tribunals does not at all reflect a dissatisfaction with a justice ascertained and administered according

[1] This has been remedied in England. American Judicature Society, *Bulletin XII*, page 19.
[2] *Commercial Arbitration, Report of the Special Committee on Arbitration of the New York Chamber of Commerce* (1911), page 52.
[3] See *Annual Reports* of the Committee on Arbitration of the New York Chamber of Commerce, 1911-16; also 3 Am. Bar Ass'n Journal, No. 1, p. 28.
[4] American Judicature Society, *Bulletin XII*, pages 3, 63.
[5] Warren: *History of the American Bar*, page 148; American Judicature Society, *Bulletin XII*, pages 4, 52.
[6] Taft: *Administration of Justice*, 72 Central L. Journal, 193; *Business Arbitration*, 99 Outlook (1911), 104; Werner: *Voluntary Tribunals*, Missouri Bar Ass'n *Proceedings* for 1914, pages 145, 150; *Commercial Arbitration, Report of the Special Committee on Arbitration of the New York Chamber of Commerce* (1911), page 3.
[7] Cf. 73 Ann. Am. Ac. Pol. & Soc. Science, 136.

to rules of substantive law.[1] This fact is of the highest importance, for it lays the solid foundation for judicial arbitration. Indeed, the chief difficulty with extra-legal arbitration has been the inability to combine with technical knowledge and prompt, informal proceedings the desire to have the controversy determined according to substantive law which calls for trained judges.[2]

Commercial arbitration has not solved expense[3] because it has not tried to. Costs and fees have not been prohibitive to business men. It has, however, served to eliminate delay, it has greatly reinforced the idea of conciliation, of which the New York Chamber of Commerce Arbitration Committee says,[4] "Perhaps the most important work of your Committee has been in the way of conciliation," and it has, through its informal procedure, occasionally been of direct assistance to poor persons.[5] For us, its great significance is that it has revived the idea, and delivered a body blow to that legal Cerberus of pleading, procedure, and evidence by proving that justice can be as faithfully, more satisfactorily to the parties, and more quickly administered, even as to claims as large as one hundred and fifty thousand dollars, through an informal tribunal which has found no necessity for technical pleadings, or for a predetermined detailed procedure, or for excluding the kind of logical evidence which all the world, except the courts, uses in making its decisions.

Through several other channels the arbitration idea has steadily been coming to the fore.[6] In the legal aid societies the principle of arbitration in conjunction with conciliation is daily employed.[7] In the workmen's compensation acts, in order to emphasize the informality of the hearings of disputed claims, such proceedings are given the name of arbitration instead of trial. The 1910 Protocol in the New York cloak, suit, and skirt industry provided a machinery whereby individual disputes of all sorts between employers and employees, including claims for wages, might be conciliated and arbitrated, and this proved one of the most successful features of the truce.[8]

---

[1] This point is very strongly made by William L. Ransom, former Justice of the City Court of New York and Chief Counsel of the New York State Public Service Commission for the First District, in an article entitled "The Layman's Demand for Improved Judicial Machinery," printed in 73 Ann. Am. Ac. Pol. & Soc. Science, 132, particularly pages 148, 149.

[2] Cf. American Judicature Society, *Bulletin XII*, page 3.

[3] The expense of an arbitration hearing under the New York Chamber of Commerce is about sixty dollars.

[4] New York Chamber of Commerce Committee on Arbitration, *Report* for 1914, page 3.

[5] A woman in Maine bought by mail order a corset cover for sixty-eight cents which she claimed was defective. The Chamber of Commerce adjusted the dispute with the mail order house.

[6] See 3 Am. Bar Ass'n Journal, No. 1, pp. 36, 49–51.

[7] 4 Buffalo L. A. R. 5; 5 Chicago L. A. R. 22; *Report of Jewish Charities of Chicago* for 1916, page 70; 4 Cleveland L. A. R. 7, 8 ; 6 Cincinnati L. A. R. 3; 21 Whittier House (Jersey City) R. 25; 22 Jersey City L. A. R. 17; *Louisville Associated Charities Report* for 1914, page 19; *Office of the Public Defender* (Los Angeles), page 3; *Place of the Public Defender in the Administration of Justice*, pages 25, 26; 10 Newark L. A. R. 5; Nashville Commercial Club *Tattler* for July, 1916, pages 28, 30 ; 2 Philadelphia L. A. R. 3; 3 *Ibid.* 4; 6 *Ibid.* 5; 1 Pittsburgh L. A. R. 4; 4 *Ibid.* 9 ; 30 N. Y. L. A. R. 51; 32 *Ibid.* 29; 10 N. Y. Educational Alliance R. 31; 7 N. Y. L. A. R., No. 3, p. 23; *Ibid.*, No. 4, p. 26; 11 *Ibid.*, No. 2, p. 3; *Ibid.*, No. 3, p. 14; 15 *Ibid.*, No. 3, p. 7 ; 1 Milwaukee L. A. R. 9; *Report of First Conference of Legal Aid Societies*, pages 8, 13 ; *Ibid., Fourth Conference*, page 8; *Proceedings of Virginia Conference of Charities and Correction* in 1916, page 80 ; *Report of the Attorney of the St. Louis Legal Aid Bureau to the Mayor*, page 3. In Germany several of the legal aid offices are empowered to act as official arbitrators. *Reichs-Arbeitsblatt* for July 27, 1911, page 526.

[8] *United States Bureau of Labor Bulletin No. 98*, pp. 203, 230, 247, 248; Brandeis: *Business a P ofession* (1914), page xxxviii.

An interesting manifestation of arbitration is to be found in New York's East Side, where the newly arrived immigrants, having learned by experience that if both parties to a lawsuit in a Russian court were Jews both would lose, have been in the habit of submitting all controversies to the Rabbi for his arbitration. The plan was entirely successful until it was attempted in the same informal manner to obtain divorces.[1]

§ 2

"There is a growing disposition on the part of our organized city courts to assist in this movement"[2] toward arbitration. There are signs that the courts are profit-

Judicial Arbitration ing from the object lesson and are preparing to do their share. In the Cleveland and Cincinnati Municipal Courts provision is made by rule for arbitration.[3] The Municipal Court of Chicago has established an Arbitration Branch as an auxiliary to commercial arbitration.[4]

In April, 1917, the Justices of the Municipal Court of the City of New York issued a series of rules by which it is now possible for parties, by agreement, to submit a dispute to an agreed arbitrator who may be the judge of the court.[5] Under these rules there are no costs or fees of any kind, the only pleadings are a brief recital of the nature of the controversy, rules of evidence do not apply, the parties may not withdraw after the first hearing, and an award becomes a judgment two days after filing. No statistics of work are yet available, but it is estimated that under these rules, together with the conciliation rules, half a million controversies will annually be settled.[6] As the Justices say in their statement accompanying the rules, "an opportunity is now given to have controversies settled impartially, quickly, and without expense."

A judicial arbitration of a small claim is exactly the same as a proceeding in a small claims court, for the keynote of both is an informal procedure which makes for despatch, saves expense, and generally renders the attorney unnecessary. And in both the judgment rendered is in accordance with substantive law. Arbitration, however, is not limited to small claims, but extends to all claims, irrespective of amount.

§ 3

The successful extension of judicial arbitration will be one more step toward free-dom and equality of justice. As to the cases which can come within its sphere, it

---

[1] 11 Educational Alliance R. 55; 22 N. Y. L. A. R. 11.

[2] 1 American Judicature Society Journal, No. 2, p. 15.

[3] Rule 23 of the Cincinnati Municipal Court; Rule 29 of the Cleveland Municipal Court.

[4] 1 American Judicature Society Journal, No. 2, p. 15; *Ibid.*, No. 5, p. 145.

[5] These rules are printed in the New York *Law Journal* for April 26, 1917, and in 1 American Judicature Society Journal, No. 2, p. 15. See also No. 5, p. 153.

[6] *Report of the Philadelphia Municipal Court* for 1915, page 37.

breaks down two of the defects of the traditional administration of justice, for where
it exists costs are minimized or abolished and delays are absent. The
Future of
Judicial
Arbitration
fundamental problem of the expense of counsel is solved because in
most cases it will be unnecessary for parties, in the absence of pleadings, technical procedure, and rules of evidence, to retain attorneys.
The clerk tells them how to file the submission, and for the rest they merely appear
and tell their stories.

Arbitration is, of course, always subject to the limitation that it can begin only
by agreement. How far it can go is to-day purely a matter of conjecture. When it
was sought to change the Athenian rule that if a plaintiff claimed a debt of twenty
minae and proved eighteen judgment must be for the defendant, Aristotle replied
that such a proposal would turn a judicial proceeding into a mere arbitration. The
modern world says if that be arbitration, then by all means let us have it. The temper of to-day is to pay scant regard to such theoretical logical perfection if by its
sacrifice a more practical, efficient, and serviceable judicial administration may be
secured.[1] While this disposition is calculated to secure for arbitration a definite place
in the machinery for administering justice, the development will not come in a day
or a year. As with conciliation, arbitration offers no immediate guarantee of a more
equal administration of the laws.

§ 4

In their effect on the problem of denial of justice and in the solution that they
afford, small claims courts, conciliation, and arbitration have much in common. In
all three, court costs cease to prohibit, for they have been minimized or
Summary
abolished. The proceedings, in their very nature, make despatch easy
and delay difficult. In parallel ways they avoid the fundamental difficulty of the
expense of counsel by making the employment of attorneys unnecessary. In all conciliation, in the large proportion of small claims, and generally in matters submitted
to arbitration, after rules of pleadings, procedure, and evidence have been eliminated,
there is nothing left for the lawyer to do.

We now pass to a different type of agency dealing with a different sort of case in
which the solution is not so easily obtained, wherein, even after simplification of procedure has done its best, a part of the function of the attorney and the need for his
services still remain.

---

[1] Cf. 73 Ann. Am. Ac. Pol. & Soc. Science, 19.

CHAPTER XI

DOMESTIC RELATIONS COURTS

In my judgment the present system of enforcing the payment of alimony by court proceedings should be supplemented by the power lodged in the same court to issue a warrant for non-support in proper cases. A technical contempt proceeding costs a destitute wife more than she is apt to get out of it if her lawyer receives what his services are worth. JUDGE LACEY *of the Detroit Court of Domestic Relations.*[1]

§ 1

OF the four great classes of cases which make up the larger proportion of the legal difficulties of the poor, the second is domestic troubles. In this unhappy and perplexing field are included all the difficulties between husband and wife, between *The Present Situation* parent and child, illegitimacy, juvenile and contributory delinquency, guardianship, custody, and adoption. Here the law, even at its best, labors under a heavy disadvantage in trying to work out justice because the controversies are peculiarly intimate in nature and because they are produced by causes as variable and elusive as human nature itself, further influenced and complicated by everything in our present day civilization from the economic structure of society to religion. Yet in precisely this field the law is increasingly being urged to put forth its supreme effort, its sphere is being widened, new complementary administrative agencies are being added to it,[2] because in all these controversies is involved the security of the home, on which the existing state is founded, and the welfare of children, on whom the future state depends. In the main the state must rely on individual complaint to discover wrongs in the home, and only through the proceeding instituted by the individual claimant can the state set in motion its protecting and guarding machinery. In affairs of such import denial of justice transcends individual or personal injustice and, like a cancer, eats into the health and moral well-being of the body politic.

For securing these interests the substantive law makes reasonable provision. There are to-day a multitude of rights, remedies, and punishments. As between husband and wife there is divorce, with or without alimony, to be paid in a lump sum or under a decree for periodic payments; separate maintenance (also called separate support, judicial separation, or limited divorce), with or without a decree ordering periodic payments for support; and the criminal proceedings for desertion, abandonment, and non-support, which do not separate the parties, but either order payments for support or punish the offender for the crime. In these proceedings, questions of custody and support of children may or may not be involved. As between parent and child

---

[1] 25 American Legal News, No. 9 (1914), p. 13. The word "alimony." in Michigan law, means payments under a separate support decree.

[2] Pound: *Limits of Effective Legal Action*, 3 Am. Bar Ass'n Journal, No. 1, p. 66.

there is guardianship, custody, and the criminal proceedings for desertion, abandonment, non-support, and contributory delinquency. Concerning children, there is adoption, truancy, and other juvenile delinquency. As to illegitimacy, some states give civil remedies, others criminal, and a few none. With all these proceedings the poor, and the children of the poor, are immediately concerned.

No one court as yet comprises within its jurisdiction all these matters. One disintegrating force is the sharp historical distinction between the civil and the criminal law. As courts are now organized, each has a slice of this whole jurisdiction. There is neither unification, nor specialization, nor even uniformity. In Boston divorces are granted by the Superior Court with an appeal to the full bench of the Supreme Judicial Court, separation suits are heard in the Probate Court with an appeal to the Superior Court on the civil side, complaints for non-support are heard in the Municipal Court with an appeal to the Superior Court on the criminal side, and juvenile matters are determined in the Juvenile Court with a like appeal. In Cleveland family cases may come before any one of eighteen judges.[1] The confusion that results from such multiplicity robs the law of much of its possible effectiveness.[2] Instances such as the following have happened in Boston. A wife, living apart from her husband because of his brutality, brings a proceeding in the criminal court of one district to compel the husband to support herself and the children. The court rules that until the Probate Court has passed on the question of her right to live apart and substantiated her position by giving her a decree legally permitting her to live apart, it cannot order the husband to support a wife not living with him. The wife then goes to the Probate Court, proves her case, and gets her decree. Meanwhile she has taken another position and moved her home, or the husband may have moved. She then brings her complaint in another district court which has jurisdiction and is told that inasmuch as a probate decree is outstanding, the criminal court has no jurisdiction and cannot hear the case.[3] Both decisions are honestly made by judges who are interpreting the law as they understand it; but the result is disastrous.

§ 2

It is the consensus of the best opinion that there must be unification of jurisdiction and specialization by judges.[4] These ends have been accomplished to an extent by the creation of special courts, or special sessions of courts, to which all cases of a given type are sent and where the same judge permanently presides. Such are the

[1] 8 Cleveland L. A. R. 7.
[2] Seventh Report of the Municipal Court of Chicago (1913), page 89.
[3] See Association of Justices of District, Police, and Municipal Courts of Massachusetts, Committee on Law and Procedure, Report No. 7 (1916), page 17.
[4] American Judicature Society, Bulletin VI, pages 21, 22; Address of Judge Brown of the Municipal Court of Philadelphia before the National Conference of Probation Officers (1917), page 6; Harley: Ultimate Types of Inferior Courts and Judges, 22 Case and Comment, 6.

domestic relations courts in Chicago, Cincinnati, New York, Philadelphia, and Boston. In the development toward unification, the interesting fact, and *Increasing* one which is of great immediate concern to our problem, is that the *Use of Criminal Remedies* criminal jurisdiction is absorbing the civil, instead of the civil the criminal. Although the domestic relations and juvenile courts which are to be found chiefly on the criminal side of the court are rapidly eliminating the traditional forbidding aspects of a criminal trial by informality of procedure, by using the summons instead of the arrest, by having the attending officers in plain clothes, and by having the parties sit around a table with the judge instead of standing in cages or behind bars, nevertheless the machinery of the criminal law is more and more being used.

This is entirely logical because the law has always claimed that the state has a direct interest in all marital and family questions, and the best way to enforce that interest in fact is through criminal proceedings to which the state is a party and over which it can keep a much closer watch. The accretion to criminal jurisdiction at the expense of civil jurisdiction, however, is less the result of logic and more of the fact that the domestic relations courts have proved more effective and more capable than their civil predecessors. Nearly all of these matters were originally civil; then followed a series of statutes, culminating in the comprehensive uniform desertion act, which afforded criminal remedies.[1] To care for the large volume of cases brought under the criminal statutes, the domestic relations courts[2] or sessions were established, and they went at their task so thoroughly and served so efficiently that inevitably a tendency set in to widen their jurisdiction.[3] The Philadelphia Domestic Relations Court, which has jurisdiction over all matters except full and limited divorce, now asks that divorce jurisdiction be added to it.[4] In addition to the criminal proceedings, the Cincinnati Court of Domestic Relations has jurisdiction over divorce, separate support, and annulment, and it administers the mothers' pension fund law.[5] Its jurisdiction is complete except as to matters of guardianship, adoption, and illegitimacy.

The most complete court was that in Detroit under a law passed unanimously by both houses of the legislature in 1913, establishing a domestic relations court and giving to it, in addition to the usual criminal jurisdiction, exclusive control over divorce, separate support, custody of children, illegitimacy, and violations of the compulsory education law. The court was organized September 1, 1913, and was declared illegal by the Michigan Supreme Court on the ground that the act which created it

[1] Cf. Association of Justices of the District, Police, and Municipal Courts of Massachusetts, Committee on Law and Procedure, *Report No. 7* (1916), page 6.
[2] The term "domestic relations courts" in its widest sense, which is here used, includes the juvenile courts.
[3] In 1910 the Pittsburgh Legal Aid Society argued along this line. 2 Pittsburgh L. A. R. 11, 12. See also *Family Desertion, Report of the Committee on Desertion of the National Conference of Jewish Charities* (1912), pages 37, 38.
[4] *Report of Philadelphia Municipal Court* for 1915, page 5.
[5] *First Annual Report, Court of Common Pleas, Division of Domestic Relations, Hamilton County* (1915), page 3.

was local, instead of general, as required by the constitution.[1] Of this broad jurisdiction, Judge Lacey writes:[2]

"In conclusion, let me emphasize the tremendous advantages of a court with combined jurisdiction over all family cases in that it prevents either spouse from shifting from one court to another and prevents the separation of the family in its litigation. The court should be able to deal with the family as a unit and given ample power to effectuate justice. The present system of non-support cases in one court, abandonment in another, divorce in a third, and children in a fourth tends to nullify the power of each court for good. . . .

"I believe the most essential and valuable feature of the Domestic Relations Court of Wayne County was the combination of jurisdiction which it had over all family cases, which aimed to enable one judge to hear and dispose of every phase of the whole controversy in a disturbed household."

§ 3

Desertion and refusal to support wives and children were made crimes in order to protect the state's interest in the family, but this change automatically worked a
Significance of Domestic Relations Courts
great improvement in the position of the poor before the law because it made available the processes of the criminal law.

There are no court costs to prohibit access to the criminal courts. There are no fees for writs, entry, trial, or judgment. Service of process is made by police officers without charge to the complainant. Witnesses are summoned in like manner and their fees for attendance paid out of public funds. Deserted wives, who formerly have found the path to relief through the civil courts blocked by the requirement of costs which, by hypothesis, they were in no position to pay, now are accorded unpriced relief.

Criminal process is summary. The return day is as soon as the accused can be found and taken into custody. If the defendant is not bailed, the case is tried at once; if he secures bail, there may be a continuance, but rarely for more than a week, and that often is granted only on condition that a payment be made to support the wife during that week. It is only natural that under these circumstances persons should prefer the criminal remedies.[3] The contrast between the two systems, and the denial of justice caused by the delays in the former administration of justice, is strikingly illustrated by the following case.[4] A narration of the facts renders comment superfluous.

A woman, who had suffered physical abuse from her husband and was not being supported by him, applied to the Legal Aid Society for relief. The attorney investi-

---

[1] 25 American Legal News, No. 9 (1914), p. 5. For the decision see 180 Mich. 329.
[2] *Ibid.*, p. 13.
[3] Association of Justices of the District, Police, and Municipal Courts of Massachusetts, Committee on Law and Procedure, *Report No. 7*, page 17.
[4] In the files of the Boston Legal Aid Society, number 1009; Probate Court for Suffolk County, number 162,928; Domestic Relations Session of the Boston Municipal Court, number 1914 D 161.

gated the case and filed a petition for separate support in the Probate Court on October 31, 1913. The next day he called for the citation and had it served by a constable at a cost of $1.60. He had affidavit of service made, filed it, and then awaited the elapse of fourteen days until return day, when the respondent filed an appearance. As the parties reached an agreement, a decree was entered on November 20, 1913, ordering the husband to pay ten dollars per week. Had there been no agreement, it would have been necessary to notify the respondent's attorney, see a judge, and have the case assigned for hearing; and if the case were not reached on the assigned date, it would go off the list, and in certain instances a new assignment would be necessary. The respondent disobeyed the order and paid nothing. The legal aid attorney then filed a petition for contempt proceedings, secured the citation, had it served, made affidavit of service and filed it, and again awaited the elapse of fourteen days till return day. Again the respondent filed an appearance. The procedure of notice to his attorney and seeing the judge was gone through and the case assigned for March 30, 1914. The respondent did not appear and was defaulted. A capias authorizing his arrest was issued. This was delivered to a sheriff, who arrested the husband after four o'clock when court had adjourned, so that he was taken to jail to be kept overnight at the wife's expense. The next morning the sheriff brought him before the court, the case was heard, and the judge released the respondent on his agreement to do better. The cost for the sheriff and the board at jail was $16. During April and May the husband still paid nothing.

On June 2, 1914, the wife again appealed to the Legal Aid Society. On the same morning the attorney had a criminal complaint sworn out, which was at once delivered to police officers for service. The husband was traced and found at midnight trying to get out of his room by means of the fire escape. He was put under arrest and brought into court the next morning. Trial was had at once, the husband was convicted, and sentenced to three months at hard labor, the state to pay fifty cents a day toward the wife's support. The civil proceeding took five months, cost $17.60, and resulted in nothing; the criminal proceeding required twenty-six hours, cost nothing, and resulted in punishment of the guilty husband and provision for assisting the wife.

Judges of domestic relations courts have been the first to sacrifice their own convenience for the sake of the persons coming before them, so that hearings might be prompt and no loss through absence from work be occasioned. In Kansas City the court opens at 7.30 A.M. and in Los Angeles it begins at 5 P.M. and sits as late as is necessary. These courts are respectively called "The Sunrise Court" and "The Twilight Court," and they deserve the prominence which their picturesque titles have given them because of their consideration for the parties who need their assistance and must earn their living at the same time.

Thus our first two defects in the traditional administration of justice are conspicuously absent from the modern domestic relations courts. As to cases within their jurisdiction, delays and court costs do not operate to defeat justice. These courts, likewise, squarely meet the third and greater difficulty of the attorney's expense and reduce it to a minimum by the double process of eliminating the attorney's function so far as it is dispensable and, as to the rest, of supplying the attorney or some one to perform his functions.[1] Complaints have been so standardized[2] and simplified that a wife, under the direction or with the assistance of the clerk, can make out the necessary papers to start proceedings. Under the general practice the complaint is passed on by the judge before the warrant issues. In this way the clerk and judge decide for her the questions of jurisdiction, venue, and the items of the complaint which on the civil side would require an attorney to draw the libel for divorce or the petition for separate support. While this plan is generally satisfactory, it is not always so. Errors in allegations, in material dates, or in jurisdiction are sometimes made because the court may not have in its possession the facts which an attorney would ascertain before drawing any petition. In some jurisdictions this danger is obviated by having a preliminary investigation by the probation staff, or by giving the wife the assistance of a deputy district attorney.

After proceedings are begun and the defendant is served with notice or arrested, the need for the attorney's function manifests itself in three places, — in investigating and preparing the case for trial, in conducting the trial, and in following up the case after judgment. This last is a peculiarity of domestic relations cases, but it is perhaps the most important of all because the decrees or orders for support are generally for weekly or other periodic payments, so that unless an order is kept track of, and supplemental proceedings are instituted where necessary, the judgment or order is of very little value.

The work of preparation for trial is now universally in the hands of the probation staff, which is an indispensable adjunct of every domestic relations court.[3] Thus far this plan of investigation by officers of the court has proved eminently successful. In addition to the facts of the dispute, the personal history of both parties is fully investigated, the coöperation of employers, churches, and charities is secured, and a typewritten report as accurate and as complete as any attorney would expect from his junior or his investigator is prepared.

At the trial, several plans are in use. In some courts the proceedings are quite informal, so that the complainant has little difficulty in telling her own story and in answering the judge's questions. In others, the probation officer acts as a sort of informal counsel. In yet others, the complaining witness has the benefit of the state's counsel, either an assistant district attorney, or an assistant city prosecutor. There is much complaint that these attorneys try the cases in a most perfunctory manner.

[1] In New York the Legal Aid Society reports: "The Domestic Relations Court, dealing with support, has gone a long way toward relieving us of the burden heretofore borne in non-support cases." 41 N. Y. L. A. R. 17.

[2] See Association of Justices of District, Police, and Municipal Courts of Massachusetts, Committee on Law and Procedure, *Report No. 7*, page 21.

[3] For a statement of this sort of probation work see *Annual Report* of Division No. 2 of the Kansas City (Mo.) Municipal Court (1912–13), page 14; Association of Justices of District, Police, and Municipal Courts of Massachusetts, Committee on Law and Procedure, *Report No. 7*, page 35. Cf. Wells: *The Man in Court*, page 269.

This objection is founded on fact, but it is a matter outside the scope of this report, its cure being political, not judicial reform. Any system that can be devised is necessarily predicated on the theory that the officers appointed by the state or elected by the people will perform their work to the best of their ability. Of the three plans, it is hard to say which is best. The first two, if the defendant has no counsel, secure an informality, an absence of interruption and technical objection, which greatly facilitates the court in dealing with cases of this sort. On the other hand, where the defendant's liberty is at stake, he has a constitutional right to counsel and a right to have his guilt clearly established in the manner prescribed by law. If he does appear with counsel, and if he raises questions of law or fact with which the probation officer cannot cope, the wife ought not to be left at a disadvantage. It is imperative that the judge, and highly desirable that the probation officer, should remain impartial, so that it is unwise to thrust on them the burden of conducting the wife's case. It would not be impossible to work out a combined procedure whereby the matter would be heard informally if the parties did not appear with counsel, and, if the defendant did appear with an attorney and the case was one where the wife's interests required similar protection, the court could order a short suspension or continuance and summon in an attorney from the district attorney's office or the legal aid society to conduct the prosecution.

In the work of following up orders the procedure in the domestic relations courts is unexcelled. Under a civil order for support the husband generally pays the alimony or allowance directly to the wife. It inevitably results that there are frequent disputes as to just what has been paid. The system breeds litigation. And further, as we have seen, if the husband fails to pay, the wife is obliged to start a new form of proceeding called " an order to show cause why the respondent should not be adjudged in contempt of court," which proceeding again involves delays, costs, and attorney's fees. These civil supplementary proceedings are a failure. Respondents who are advised as to how they can delay, and procrastinate, and finally escape altogether, worry not at all about their technical contempt, but feel a genuine contempt for the court and its weak proceedings.

On the criminal side, the order requires the husband to pay the weekly sum directly to the probation officer or to some like officer, as the Public Trustee in Los Angeles. Thereafter there can be no dispute about payments. If the man fails to pay, a probation officer checks up the case to see if the failure was occasioned by unemployment or illness. If it was wilful, the supplementary proceedings are summary. In law, the court order has put the husband on probation, therefore if he violates the terms of the probation, he must be surrendered to the court. This means that an officer is sent out to arrest the defaulting probationer and bring him before the court. The hearing is most summary. When these matters are originally heard the courts quite frequently make a finding of guilty, impose sentence, then suspend sentence, and put the man on probation. At the supplemental hearing, therefore, the court merely puts into effect the original sentence. The only facts in issue are whether the husband has failed to pay, and whether the refusal was wilful. All these facts are within the probation officer's possession. As to all proceedings after judgment in the domestic relations court the private attorney is obviously unnecessary, being entirely supplanted by the probation officer. The rights of the wife are perfectly protected.[1]

The following statistics, showing how much has been collected for wives and children through the machinery of the domestic relations courts which operate without any expense to the parties, afford striking evidence of the great progress made in recent years in this particular field of law toward a free and more equal administration of justice.

Domestic Relations Court or Probation Staff[2] in	Period	Actual Payments for Support
Chicago[3]	1911	$19,618.05
Chicago	1912	61,419.78
Chicago	1913	99,433.44
Chicago	1914	94,869.08
Chicago	1915	117,179.78
Philadelphia[4]	1913	320,989.08
Philadelphia	1914	345,490.94
Philadephia	1915	409,329.59
Philadelphia	1916	520,066.80
Cincinnati[5]	1914	10,157.34
Cincinnati	1915	17,343.19
Detroit[6]	Sept., 1913, to April, 1914	46,875.00
Boston[7]	1913	23,003.00
Boston	1914	36,500.00
Boston	1915	34,621.00
Massachusetts[8]	1916	303,009.01

§ 4

As the domestic relations courts have applied themselves to the fast growing problem of desertion and non-support they have more and more employed the method of conciliation. The interest of the state in these cases is that homes should not be broken up except for grave causes and that families should be reunited whenever possible A litigious proceeding is destructive, it is calculated to embitter the contestants, and after a trial in open court

Conciliation in Domestic Relations

[1] For a concrete illustration of how thorough the probation work is, see the forms used in Philadelphia, printed in Philadelphia *Municipal Court Report* for 1915, pages 235–243. Forms 5-9 relate to follow-up work. See also *Address of President Judge Brown before the Men's Club of Market Square Presbyterian Church* (1914), page 17.

[2] For a statement of the orders made in the New York Juvenile Court, see its *Report* for 1916, page 56.

[3] *Eighth and Ninth Reports* of the Chicago Municipal Court, page 60.

[4] Philadelphia *Municipal Court Report* for 1915, page 154; *Ibid.* for 1916, page 67.

[5] *First Annual Report*, Hamilton County Court of Common Pleas, Division of Domestic Relations (1915), page 18.

[6] 25 American Legal News, No. 9, p. 6.

[7] Association of Justices of District, Police, and Municipal Courts of Massachusetts, Committee on Law and Procedure, *Report No. 7*, page 27.

[8] *Eighth Report of the Massachusetts Commission on Probation* (1916), *Public Document No. 85*, page 9.

husband and wife feel a real grievance toward each other where before there may have been only a temporary discontent. A conciliation proceeding gives the court its only chance to repair, reunite, and construct.

A conciliation proceeding, as has earlier been pointed out, is simply a method and one that can be used in any case in any court. It can be employed in divorce as well as in non-support, in the criminal court as well as in the civil. To the extent that it is used, it automatically promotes equality before the law because in its nature it is a summary proceeding requiring no costs, and depending for success more on the absence than the presence of counsel. Conciliation is used very generally by the domestic relations courts as a sort of preliminary proceeding, particularly in Chicago,[1] Philadelphia,[2] and Kansas City.[3] In Cleveland a special division of the Court of Common Pleas, where divorce matters are heard, is in contemplation.[4] Where the domestic relations courts have been given civil jurisdiction, as in Cincinnati[5] and Detroit,[6] they have extended the use of conciliation to the civil proceedings of divorce and separate support.

§ 5

It is readily apparent that the domestic relations courts, as to the large majority of cases within their jurisdiction, secure freedom and equality of justice to a degree *Future Development* hitherto never attained. There is a margin where, owing to the complexity of the issues or the difficulty of legal points involved, the services of an attorney will be required, but such cases are the minority. This type of court is now clearly established, and will undoubtedly in a short time extend itself into every large city. It almost completely solves the problem of denial of justice in cases of desertion, abandonment, non-support, and also of illegitimacy, where such cases are within its jurisdiction.

For the greater part, divorce, separate maintenance, and questions of custody remain unaffected. But we have seen the steady drift toward incorporating these matters within the jurisdiction of the domestic relations courts, and further the tendency of such courts, wherever they have acquired civil jurisdiction, to apply to the civil matters the same processes as those originally developed through the summary criminal remedies. This movement is only at its inception, but signs of its development are clear. In Detroit the court carried over into divorce cases all the machinery for investigation by the probation staff.[7] The Philadelphia court urges legislation to

---

[1] *Seventh Report*, Chicago Municipal Court, page 88.

[2] Philadelphia *Municipal Court Report* for 1915, pages viii, 9, 159 ; Theodore Roosevelt: *The Brotherly Court of Philadelphia, Metropolitan Magazine* for May, 1917, page 66. As to the success of conciliation, see Philadelphia *Municipal Court Report* for 1916, page 65.

[3] *Annual Report*, Division No. 2, Municipal Court of Kansas City (1912–13), page 11.

[4] *Proceedings of Fourth Conference of Legal Aid Societies*, page 113 ; see also *The New Republic* for December 2, 1916. page 124.

[5] *First Annual Report*, Hamilton County Court of Common Pleas, Division of Domestic Relations, page 6.

[6] 25 American Legal News, No. 9, p. 7.   [7] *Ibid.*, pp. 10, 11.

permit it "to utilize the probation arm of the Court in divorce proceedings."[1] In Cincinnati, every divorce case is thoroughly investigated and reported on to the Court before the parties put in their evidence.[2] The report blanks require, in addition to the facts of the dispute, a complete personal history, including such matters as church membership, moral character, temperance, mentality, occupation, a statement as to the character of the home, its sanitation, cleanliness, and order, and detailed figures as to the earnings and joint holdings of the parties. The Detroit Court proposed to use the summary criminal processes for enforcing the payment of civil orders in divorce and separation cases.[3]

From our particular point of approach this means that delays are being reduced, and that part of the attorney's work of preparation and of following up court orders is being done by the administrative arm of the court. How far this may go is problematical. A complete development is justified in order to give the state an opportunity to protect its paramount interest. Denial of justice to the individual decreases in exact proportion as the administrative work done in the state's interest increases.

While the territorial expansion of domestic relations courts will be rapid, the increase in jurisdiction of each court to include all domestic disputes and all proceedings relating thereto will probably be slow. There is a gulf, fixed by history and tradition, between civil and criminal matters that will not easily be bridged. The individualistic conception in law revolts at the idea of a court deciding a divorce case on what it knows through its own agents instead of from such evidence as the parties choose to offer, and this idea will die only as the fact that the state is the supreme party in interest in all litigation, particularly domestic litigation, gradually becomes recognized.

---

[1] Philadelphia *Municipal Court Report* for 1915, page 5.

[2] In 1915 the probation staff made 359 interviews and ordered 14 medical examinations in divorce cases. *First Annual Report*, Hamilton County Court of Common Pleas, Division of Domestic Relations, page 18.

[3] See quotation at the head of this chapter.

CHAPTER XII

ADMINISTRATIVE TRIBUNALS

> So far for three generations our political life has been controlled by court decisions. But no court can alter on review the formal decision of our mightiest commission. While we cling to all the extraneous and adventitious elements of a mediaeval procedure, civilization pours its real judicial problems into new channels that are almost without a semblance of contentious procedure. HERBERT HARLEY in *A Modern Experiment in Judicial Administration.*[1]

IF one were compelled to state the most important experiment in the administration of justice made in the twentieth century, the answer would unhesitatingly be the attempt to secure justice through administrative tribunals. Such tribunals have sprung up with amazing rapidity, they have taken over an enormous amount of litigation formerly handled by the courts, and the law concerning administrative justice is the most rapidly growing branch of law in our entire jurisprudence.[2] Profound as has been the effect of this great movement, which has extended throughout the United States,[3] on our traditional method of judicial administration, its effect on our particular problem has been no less significant and important. For one of the chief causes which swept these tribunals into being on a wave of popular feeling was the general dissatisfaction with the inequalities of the old law,[4] not only in its substance but in its enforcement.

There are two great classes of administrative tribunals,—those which administer the workmen's compensation acts, generally named Industrial Accident Commissions, and those supervising and regulating the public service corporations, such as railway, gas, and electric lighting companies, of which the United States Interstate Commerce Commission is the most powerful and the chief exponent. Though having much in common, the two groups are sufficiently distinct to warrant separate consideration. The Industrial Accident Commissions will be dealt with first.

§ 1

In discussing the relation between denial of justice and the substantive law we have earlier seen that the one great charge which could properly be made against the

---

[1] *An Address before the Louisiana State Bar Association* in 1915, reprinted separately. See page 86.

[2] *Report of Dean Pound to the President of Harvard University* for 1915-16, at page 1.

[3] For example, the workmen's compensation acts began to be adopted in 1911. At the close of 1917 such acts were in force in thirty-seven states and three territories.

[4] This dissatisfaction has by no means subsided. The current of affairs still runs into the new channel. The war legislation which prescribes the allowances and allotments for soldiers and their dependents, awards compensation for injuries in line of duty, grants insurance to all fighting men, and protects their policies of insurance from lapse or forfeiture is giving rise to hundreds of thousands of claims which will in the near future run into the millions. No part of this work has been entrusted to the courts. Entire and exclusive authority is vested in what has already become the world's greatest administrative tribunal—The Bureau of War Risk Insurance.

equality of the substantive law was its treatment of injured workmen.[1] And we have
seen that around this inequality of substance grew up a monstrous inequality of administration and procedural enforcement which constitutes one of the blackest pages of our legal history.

Delays and Costs under the Compensation Acts

That delays were systematically used by defendants and by the liability insurance companies in particular to defeat or impair rights is
common knowledge. Costs were entirely beyond the reach of the average plaintiff,
for in addition to the usual fees paid to the court, there were always a number of
witnesses to be summoned, and the medical expert, charging his expert fee, was an
essential element in the proof of every case. As the workmen's compensation acts
remedied the substantive defect, by substituting the principle of insurance for that
of liability for fault, so they also dealt rigorously with the procedural defects of administration. Delays have been greatly lessened; so far as the Industrial Accident
Commissions and the proceedings before them are concerned, unconscionable and
unreasonable delay is entirely absent.[2] A member of the California Industrial Accident Commission has well expressed it:[3]

> " In industrial accident cases more than in any other form of legal controversy
> a delay of justice often amounts to a denial of justice. It is therefore incumbent
> upon the Commissioners charged with the administration of the act jealously
> to guard procedure against falling into the rut of procrastination. It is the pur-
> pose of the Commission to decide cases in as short a time and with as little for-
> mality as is consistent with correct decision. We do not regard as incompatible
> the prompt determination and just disposition of pending causes. Under the
> rules of practice and procedure adopted by the Commission the average case is
> brought to a final determination in a fraction of the time usually consumed in
> the trial of a personal injury case in a court of law."

Costs cease to act as a prohibition. No fees are paid to the commissions for their
services.[4] Such processes and notices as are required are sent by mail.[5] Witnesses must
still be summoned, but fewer are generally required because of the information which
the commission itself secures, and the great expense for expert medical fees is very
largely made unnecessary. The compensation acts provide for the appointment by the
commission of a physician who, acting in an impartial capacity, examines the injured
man and reports to the commission. The charge for his services is borne either by the
insurance company or by the state. In some states it is provided that the report itself
shall be admissible in evidence, so that there is not even the expense of an ordinary

---

[1] See *ante*, Chapter III, § 2, page 14.

[2] For typical statutory provisions see Connecticut *Public Acts of* 1913, c. 138, as amended by *Public Acts of* 1915, c. 288, Part B, §§ 24-27; Minnesota *General Laws of* 1913, c. 467, § 22 (2), as amended by *General Laws of* 1915, c. 209, § 10. Cf. *Report of New York Industrial Commission* for 1915, page 124; *Ibid.* for 1916, page 115.

[3] Hon. Meyer Lissner: *Procedure before the California Industrial Accident Commission*, 1 Southwestern L. Rev. 83.

[4] Fees are abolished by most compensation acts.

[5] 1 Southwestern L. Rev. 81; Massachusetts *Acts of* 1911, c. 751, Part II, § 17; Rule No. 4 of the Massachusetts Industrial Accident Board.

summons and attendance fee.[1] Costs on appeal still play their unfortunate part except under plans like that in Ohio, where in certain cases the commission itself undertakes the appeal.[2]

§ 2

The defect in the traditional method of administering justice, of making as an absolute condition precedent to all litigation the retaining of attorneys at prices which

Attorneys under the Compensation Acts

parties could not afford to pay, reached its most acute form in this field. Several factors combined to create a thoroughly bad situation. It was about 1880 that the great industrial expansion began, when all the accent of business was on production, on "speeding-up" output, and not on safety. Employment in many industries became more hazardous than military service even in time of war. Thousands of injured workmen, to secure the redress vouchsafed by law, faced long and difficult litigation calling for the expenditure of much money for expenses and lawyer's fees. This same commercial expansion left its mark on the practice of law. Many of the largest and best offices gave up general practice and engaged exclusively in business and corporation law. The charity work which had always been a part of the older type of office was discarded under the pressure of the new era.[3]

There was no place to which an injured workman could turn for assistance. To meet the general demand caused by these changed conditions, the legal aid society came into existence, but it was only a straw in a hurricane. It had little support, was hopelessly inadequate to meet the need, and lacked the vision even to do its utmost, for it actually declined to accept any personal injury cases. In fairness it must be added that at this time legal aid work had only lukewarm support and a good deal of hostility from the Bar, so that it feared to take accident cases lest it be accused of competing with lawyers and have its slender support withdrawn.

As justice was organized and as law practice was conducted, there was no one to help an injured workman. There was a void in the system. To fill the gap came the contingent fee. The system of charging fees depending on the success of the litigation was the necessary result of the conditions which were allowed to exist. Without doubt it was better than nothing. The man whose leg or arm had been cut off would prefer to accept half of the amount awarded him by a jury than to receive nothing through inability to get his day in court. Many honorable lawyers took cases on the contingent basis, conducted their cases honestly, and charged as small a percentage of the recovery as they could.

---

[1] Massachusetts *Acts of* 1911, c. 751, Part III, § 8, as amended by *Acts of* 1914, c. 708, § 10 and *Acts of* 1916, c. 72.
[2] See *post*, page 89.
[3] Rowe: *Joseph H. Choate and Right Training for the Bar*, 24 Case and Comment (September, 1917), 264, see particularly pages 266, 272; 12 N. Y. Legal Aid Review, No. 4, p. 1.

Nevertheless, the system as a whole has been, and is, the greatest blot on the history of the American Bar. There is little doubt that if a modern contingent fee agreement had been offered to any judge a hundred years ago, it would unhesitatingly have been declared illegal and void. The bar did not sanction it without a struggle,[1] and the courts resorted to fictions before they upheld it.[2] Stripped of verbiage, and in actual practice, the system is one whereby the lawyer gambles on the outcome of litigation. If he loses his investment in one case, he must recoup out of his winnings in the next. It is obviously inconsistent with any theory that the lawyer is a minister of justice; he is an interested party to the litigation because he is betting on its outcome. However much it might be glossed over, when the acid test was applied this truth was judicially admitted. Contingent fees have been justified on the ground that only by them could the poor obtain justice, but when a poor injured workman applied for permission to sue in forma pauperis the court refused the petition, saying, " the suit is carried on partially for the benefit of the counsel."[3]

The contingent fee system brought about a thousand abuses of its own. It attracted undesirable persons to become members of the profession. Because the stakes were high and the players essentially gamblers it induced the unholy triumvirate of lawyer-runner-doctor conspiring together to win fraudulent cases. It has degraded expert testimony and served as a cloak for robbery through extortionate fees. Unquestionably it has done more than anything else to bring the bar into deserved disrepute.[4] The late Joseph H. Choate, always an optimist concerning the bar, had this to say of contingent fees:[5]

> "But the chief cause of detraction from our absolute independence and disinterestedness as advocates is that fatal and pernicious change, made several generations ago by statute, by which lawyers and clients are permitted to make any agreements they please as to compensation—so that contingent fees, contracts for shares, even contracts for half the result of a litigation, are permissible, and I fear not unknown. How can we wonder, then, if the community implicates the lawyer who conducts a cause with the morale of the cause and of the client? If he has bargained for a share of the result, what answer can we make to such a criticism? And how can we blame the community when it suspects that such practices are frequent or common, and even sanctioned by eminent members of the profession, if they confound us all in one indistinguishable crowd and refuse to accord to any of us that strictly professional relation to the cause which the English barrister enjoys? And how can courts put full faith in the sincerity of

[1] The question of contingent fees came up when the Canons of Ethics were discussed. See 33 Am. Bar Ass'n R. 76 et seq.

[2] Thus it has been held that while an agreement to pay half of the amount recovered is void, an agreement to pay a sum equal to half the amount recovered is valid. Wilhite v. Roberts, 4 Dana (Ky.), 172.

[3] Boyle v. Great Northern Ry. Co., 63 Fed. 539.

[4] Storey : *Reform of Legal Procedure*, page 53 ; Doerfler: *Duty of the Lawyer as an Officer of the Court*, 24 Green Bag, 74, 76 ; 73 Ann. Am. Ac. Pol. & Soc. Science, 112, 167 ; Thompson: *Expert Testimony*, 23 Massachusetts Medical Society Communications, Article XXI ; Burr: *Extortionate Fees*, 3 Am. Bar Ass'n Journal, No. 1, p. 52.

[5] From an address on "The English Bar" before the New York State Bar Association in 1907. See Choate : *American Addresses* (1911), page 308.

our labors as aids to them in the administration of justice, if they have reason to suspect us of having bargained for a share of the result?"

The denial of justice, caused by this difficulty of the expense of counsel and by the abuses growing out of it, was so clear in this class of cases that when the compensation acts were adopted, it was hoped that the lawyer might be eliminated altogether.[1] This failed, as it was bound to fail, because the attorney's function, in all but limited types of cases, is indispensable to our method of administering justice. But the compensation acts and the industrial accident commissions have worked great changes. A double process of limiting the need for counsel on the one hand and of supplying counsel on the other may clearly be seen.[2]

Restriction of the attorney's function has been accomplished in several ways. In lieu of writs, summonses, and declarations, there are notices of injury and claims for compensation whose forms have been simplified and standardized. There are no details of service of process, for the mails are used. Questions of jurisdiction and venue have no importance, for one commission acts for the entire state. There are no pleadings and no interlocutory proceedings worth mention. Trial lists and calendars are not used; every case is assigned for hearing at a specific hour on a specific date, and notice is sent by the commission to all parties. Thus all preliminaries up to the point of trial, which in common law tort litigation required the services of counsel, are performed either by the party himself or by a clerk of the commission.

The law itself is infinitely more simple. The whole question of damages, on which many a lawyer has exercised his utmost ingenuity, is reduced to mathematical precision, and in a given case the precise award is determined by consulting a table which a grammar school child could understand. The issue of liability is shifted from the doubtful and contentious ground of negligence complicated by contributory negligence, assumption of risk, and the fellow-servant rule, to injuries "arising out of and in the course of the employment."

Although when a definition is widened it still has limits, so that marginal cases arise in plenty to cause disputes, under the compensation plan thousands of cases are so clearly within the law and the damages are so easily computed that settlements are made automatically and as a matter of routine. These settlements are in the form of agreements to pay a stated sum each week until disability ceases. They are all checked by investigators of the industrial accident commission and are not binding without its approval. Whereas under the former system an injured workman in settling a claim was obliged either to employ counsel to advise him as to his rights and damages, or else trust himself to the mercies of a usually pitiless and shrewd casualty company adjuster, and was bound by any release he signed, now thousands of claims are concluded promptly and accurately, with fairness guaranteed by the commission's

---

[1] Storey: *Reform of Legal Procedure*, page 79; Parry: *The Law and the Poor*, page 298. Cf. Field *v.* Longden, 1902; 1 K. B. Div. 47, 56.

[2] Cf. *Report of New York Industrial Commission* for 1916, pages 115, 118.

supervision, the entire process costing the employee not a cent.[1] Statistics in Massachusetts reveal how large a proportion of matters are thus settled.[2]

Period	Cases Automatically Settled and Approved	Cases wherein a Hearing was Claimed
July 1, 1912–November 30, 1913	7,000	584
December 1, 1913–November 30, 1914	13,856	799
December 1, 1914–November 30, 1915	15,496	1,201
December 1, 1915–November 30, 1916	15,864	1,600
December 1, 1916–June 13, 1917	15,135	1,007
Totals	67,351	5,191

This signifies that the compensation act plus proper administration has been able in the large majority of cases to secure absolute freedom and equality of justice to injured workmen. When it is remembered that seventy-five per cent of injured employees earn less than fifteen dollars a week[3] and would under the common law system have been obliged either to settle at the insurance company's terms, or employ counsel under an unfavorable contingent fee contract, or suffer a total denial of justice, it can be appreciated that the present order of things is little short of a revolution in the administration of the law.

Even if the case is not settled, the commissioners employ, as we have seen,[4] the method of conciliation where opportunity offers, so that a further number of cases are brought to a fair conclusion speedily, and without requiring the services of counsel.[5]

As to cases which go to trial, the traditional functions of an attorney are first to investigate and prepare the facts, second to prepare the law, and third to conduct the trial according to the rules of procedure and evidence. At hearings before industrial accident commissions the last function is rendered negligible. Rules of evidence have been cast to the four winds,[6] the commissions themselves are sovereign as to the procedure before them, and they are able to guarantee that no case is lost by technical error in presentation. In the mechanics of putting parties on the stand and questioning them, a timid and ignorant workman would be at a disadvantage, but the commissioner generally undertakes that responsibility for him. On the preparation of the facts, the commission has its investigating staff. These investigators talk with the witnesses, examine the locus, photograph the machinery, and file an impartial report which generally covers all the basic facts. This is supplemented by the employ-

---

[1] *Report of Massachusetts Industrial Accident Board* for 1913–14, *Public Document No.* 105 of 1915, page 20. See also *Report* for 1912–13, *No.* 105 of 1914, page 24. Cf. *Bulletin of the Industrial Commission of Ohio* for December, 1917, vol. iv, No. 13, p. 11, note ; *Report of New York Industrial Commission* for 1915, pages 24, 120 ; Indiana *Industrial Board R.* (1916–17), page 3. All but 2.1 per cent of the cases were adjusted by agreement.

[2] These figures were furnished by Mr. Broderick, Chief Statistician of the Massachusetts Industrial Accident Board. They are published in part in the 1913–14 *Report* cited above.

[3] The percentage of injured employees in Massachusetts earning less than $15 per week is known to be 78 per cent in 1913, 73.8 per cent in 1914, 72.9 per cent in 1915, and 72.8 per cent in 1916.

[4] See *ante*, Chapter IX, § 4, page 64.

[5] *Report of Massachusetts Industrial Accident Board* for 1913–14, page 18 ; the *Report* for 1912–13 (page 25) shows that 3000 claims were so adjusted, and that in 182 cases, even after hearing had been claimed, conciliation brought about a settlement. *Report of New York Industrial Commission* for 1915, page 124; *Ibid.* for 1916, page 114.

[6] 3 Am. Bar Ass'n Journal, No. 1, p. 57. The Ohio Law is typical. 1 Supplement to Page & Adams Ohio General Code, §§ 1465–91 (page 543).

er's detailed report of the accident, filed with the commission as required by law. The medical evidence is contained in the impartial physician's report. In New Jersey a compensation aid bureau has been established[1] to investigate and certify the facts. Thus the case is prepared without requiring the employee to engage counsel. In most cases this preparation is entirely adequate as to the facts.

Legal issues are not so satisfactorily cared for. The investigators are not lawyers, so that they may fail to appreciate legal difficulties and are incompetent to brief the law. Until recently this gap has not been serious, for the hearing is essentially one on facts, the substantive rules were simple, and there were few precedents. A real difficulty, however, did exist on appeals. An appeal is almost always on a question of law, and most commissions had no way of securing representation for employees in the appellate courts except by coöperation with the legal aid societies. In Ohio, in certain cases, the Commission itself takes the appeal for the employee[2] and the county prosecutor acts as counsel, and in New Jersey it is provided that counsel may be assigned,[3] but in most states when a case passes from the commission to the court, it becomes subject to the traditional method of administering justice, which pays but little heed to the inequality between the parties. Commissioners recognize this and have grappled with it by incorporating in their findings points of law with authorities in support.[4] As this becomes part of the record it serves as a brief, but at best it is a precarious way of ensuring the equal administration of law.

The statement that the industrial accident commissions wholly remove the need for the attorney is not warranted. They are fallible, and they have made errors which have been corrected through the investigation of counsel for the injured employee.[5] There is an inherent limitation which appears in cases which present a sharp conflict of testimony or raise a complicated question of law, and which call for a delicate weighing of facts and arguments and decision thereon. Obviously the commission cannot itself secure the evidence, brief the law, present the facts, and argue the case with whole-hearted zeal and at the same time decide the case with judicial impartiality. Where the functions are in conflict the judicial must be maintained, and as the employee is unable to present his own case, if fairness is to be preserved resort must necessarily be had to the attorney.

Rights of injured employees cannot be perfectly secured unless the commission is able, in necessary cases, to ensure for them adequate representation. The same need occurs in certain cases presented to small claims courts and domestic relations courts. Inasmuch as it is neither economical nor necessary for each court and each depart-

---

[1] New Jersey *Session Laws of* 1916, chap. 54.

[2] 1 Supplement to Page & Adams Ohio General Code, §§ 1465–74 (page 520). Cf. *Report of New York Industrial Commission* for 1915, page 140; *Ibid.* for 1916, page 40.

[3] New Jersey *Session Laws of* 1916, chap. 54.

[4] For an excellent example see Travelers' Insurance Co. *v.* Bowden, No. 26571 Equity, in the files of the Massachusetts Supreme Judicial Court for Suffolk County.

[5] See 7 Cincinnati L. A. R. 6; similar cases in the files of the Boston Legal Aid Society are *In re* Charles Cellin, No. 3; *In re* Benjamin Langer, No. 1017 and No. 4199.

ment to have its own staff of counsel, the ideal arrangement would be some central legal agency, like a legal aid society, existing as a department of the administration of justice, to which all courts and departments could refer such cases as needed the special care of counsel.

In discussing court costs it has been pointed out that a reduction, when coupled with proper court organization, did not mean an increased burden to tax-payers. So under the compensation acts, although the industrial accident commissions perform most of the services for which employees formerly have had to pay counsel, it does not appear that any increased cost to the state results. By a careful computation of the most accurate statistics obtainable it appears that the Commonwealth of Massachusetts, by having so many cases taken out of the courts, was saved in 1914 a sum of approximately $150,000.[1] During the same year the entire appropriation for the Industrial Accident Board was $87,400.[2] In considering the reorganization of the administration of justice with a view to making the position of the poor more equal before the law there need be no bugaboo about prohibitive cost to the state or intolerable burden to the tax-payer.

§ 3

There cannot be much expansion of this sort of administrative tribunal as regards injured workmen. Most states now have workmen's compensation acts. The recent

The Future of Administrative Tribunals

decision of the United States Supreme Court[3] depriving longshoremen and others engaged in maritime work of the benefit of state compensation acts was promptly remedied by Congressional legislation.[4] Employees in interstate commerce and sailors on American vessels[5] are still unprotected, and the compensation plan might well be extended to them.

It would not be surprising if justice by administrative tribunals were extended into an entirely new field through the provision of a compensation plan for injured passengers on railways, including street railways. If this were done, a second great group of cases would be taken out of the courts, out of the sphere of the traditional administration of justice, and placed under administrative commissions. This plan has been advocated by eminent jurists.[6] It has very recently received a thorough analysis and presentation by Arthur A. Ballantine, of the Boston Bar.[7] The idea was en-

---

[1] *Report of Massachusetts Industrial Accident Board* for 1914–15, *Public Document No.* 105 of 1916, page 70.

[2] Massachusetts *Acts of* 1914, c. 434.

[3] Southern Pacific Co. *v.* Jensen (May, 1917), 244 U. S. 205; 37 Supreme Court Reporter, 524.

[4] *Public Acts No.* 82 of the 65th Congress. Approved October 6, 1917.

[5] Cf. 13 N. Y. Legal Aid Review, No. 3, p. 7.

[6] Taft: *Administration of Justice*, 72 Central L. Journal, 191, 197. In discussing the compensation plan Mr. Taft included passengers. Storey: *Reform of Legal Procedure*, page 82. Mr. Storey develops the idea in some detail.

[7] 1 Mass. Law Quarterly (1917), 265; reprinted from the *Harvard Law Review* for May, 1916; see also, Ballantine: *Modernizing Railway Accident Law, The Outlook* for November 15, 1916.

dorsed by the Massachusetts Bar Association,[1] and pursuant to its suggestion a resolve was introduced into the legislature in 1917 calling for the appointment of a
commission to investigate the feasibility of the project. The resolve was defeated on
several grounds,[2] not the least of which was the opposition by a certain type of lawyer
which called it an "anti-lawyer" bill. The objection is in reality one of the strongest
arguments for extending the plan to railway accidents. Elimination of the contingent
fee lawyer is not derogatory to justice; and the administrative method under which
lawyers are often unnecessary is a great step toward a better realization of freedom
and equality of justice.

The future development of this type of administrative tribunal perplexes all jurists.
It is undoubtedly true that some of its present advantages are due to the fact that
it occupies an extra-legal position[3] and that temporarily it escapes from the limitations of justice according to law and judicial justice. It is closely analogous to the
rise of equity,[4] with the exception that instead of entrusting justice to priests in place
of judges, our recourse has been to laymen. New agencies enjoy a sort of hiatus when
rules and precedents are few, when the liberalizing spirit is strong, but this is transitory.[5] It is certain that the administrative tribunals must ascertain and administer their justice according to law, and it is likely that they will ultimately become
part of the regular judicial system.[6]

In any merger, and in developments in that direction, there is nothing to compel
a giving up of the use by administrative tribunals of investigators, impartial physicians, simple procedure, simple forms, mail service, and the automatic settlement of
claims. These are permanent improvements. They conflict with nothing basic. If they
interfere with parts of the traditional machinery, such parts ought to be scrapped.
Administrative tribunals have much to teach judicial tribunals about promptness,
inexpensiveness, and limiting the attorney to clearly defined functions.

Under the industrial accident commissions the lawyer's services are neither entirely
limited nor supplied. As time goes on, this gap will steadily increase. The burden of
work will force the commissioners more and more back on their judicial function to
the exclusion of their work in behalf of employees. As the law becomes defined in a
thousand cases, precedents and rules grow up which require that each side be represented if the trial is to be fair. Under the older compensation acts this is already felt.
Commissioners are reversing their attitude and are preferring to have employees represented by counsel. With regard to the difficulty of the expense of counsel, the net
result of the administrative plan will probably be to provide machinery for automati-

---

[1] 2 Mass. Law Quarterly (1917), 61.

[2] The great difficulty in this plan is the fixing of any schedule of damages which will fairly compensate injured persons whose vocations and incomes vary infinitely.

[3] Pound: *Organization of Courts,* American Judicature Society, *Bulletin VI,* page 4.

[4] *Ibid.,* page 5.

[5] Pound: *Justice According to Law,* page 11.

[6] *Ibid.,* page 42; *Report of Dean Pound to the President of Harvard University* for 1915–16, page 2.

cally adjusting many cases, and for conciliating a few more, but as to cases requiring hearing or trial, the attorney will be increasingly necessary.

§ 4

The public service commissions represent a group distinct from the industrial accident commissions. In function, purpose, and in the reasons leading to their creation

The Interstate Commerce Commission

they present points of difference. To meet the difficult questions of regulation of public utilities, individual action by injunction or mandamus was an unsatisfactory way to protect general public interests, so that some administrative machinery became imperative. Further, the issues involved in supervision of rates and service are essentially complicated questions of fact calling for investigation rather than points of law requiring decision. The function is much more administrative and much less judicial than is the case with the accident commissions. The public service commissions came into existence not as a revolt against justice according to law, but to fill a new administrative need.

The relation of such commissions to our problem is best illustrated by the United States Interstate Commerce Commission.[1] This Commission in its general work of securing fair rates and adequate service through its investigators, experts, and attorneys, is incidentally bringing justice to millions of persons who could never afford the expense of private litigation to secure redress in their own behalf. The Commission, however, does more than secure justice in general. It has power to investigate and redress individual cases of overcharge and similar matters. It has erected a machinery tending to secure more equal justice for the poor litigant against his powerful adversary by its promptness, by no requirement of costs, and by the double process of limiting the need for counsel to an extent and likewise, to an extent, supplying him.

The Commission gives much legal advice to shippers by correspondence.[2] A small shipper may thus be advised of his rights and, if he is unable to secure a settlement with the carrier, he may complain informally to the Commission. This is placed on the informal docket, and the Commission endeavors by correspondence, or otherwise, to secure a satisfactory settlement.[3] The Commission thus does exactly what the private attorney, in analogous cases, does in negotiating for a settlement.

If this proceeding, which is akin to conciliation, fails, the shipper is instructed to file a formal complaint. A standardized form is sent him, together with a copy of the Rules of Practice before the Commission, which contains an offer[4] to " advise any

[1] For an excellent presentation of the advantages of the administrative machinery of the state public service commissions, see an article by Max Thelen, President of the California Railroad Commission, in *The Utilities Magazine*, vol. iii, No. 1 (January, 1918), p. 3.
[2] *Thirtieth Report of the Interstate Commerce Commission* (for 1916), page 2. In this year about 50,000 enquiries were answered.
[3] *Twenty-ninth Report* (for 1915), Part I, p. 1. For the year ending October 31, 1915, 6500 such complaints were received.
[4] *Rules of Practice before the Commission* (1916), Rule XX.

party as to the form of complaint, answer, or other paper necessary to be filed in any proceeding." If the complaint is incorrectly filled out, notations are made and it is returned. When properly filed, the Commission itself obtains service on the defendant.[1] The Commission itself investigates the facts through its investigators, a hearing is had before one of its Examiners, and at the hearing rules of evidence are not enforced and the procedure is informal.[2] As the burden of proof is on the carrier,[3] in the simpler sort of dispute the shipper is entirely able to carry on his case without aid of counsel. The facts are then certified to the Commission, which enters its finding. If the shipper wins, and the railroad declines to pay, the shipper may take the case to the federal courts without payment of costs,[4] and if he is successful, he is reimbursed for his attorney's fee.[4]

Among the cases of the poor, matters of this sort are a very small item. The work of the Interstate Commerce Commission is valuable, however, as one more illustration of how much the courts could do toward securing a more equal justice by simplifying procedure, eliminating costs, and particularly if they were equipped with auxiliary administrative departments.

§ 5

In the five agencies and methods thus far discussed we have seen freedom and equality of justice furthered by simplification of procedure which conduces to despatch, and by elimination of court costs which, in actual operation, has not at all *Summary* served to foment fraudulent litigation. With regard to the root difficulty of the expense of counsel we have seen that small claims courts, conciliation, and arbitration solve the problem by making the attorney unnecessary in such proceedings, and that domestic relations courts and administrative tribunals afford a middle solution of rendering his services unnecessary in part and of supplying his services in part. We now pass to a third group of agencies, dealing with cases from which the attorney cannot be eliminated, which recognize this situation and frankly undertake to relieve it by supplying the attorney, or persons to perform his functions, without expense to the litigant.

[1] *Rules of Practice before the Commission* (1916), Rule III.
[2] All of the laws on this subject up to January 1, 1917, have been collected by the Interstate Commerce Commission and published in separate form as *The Act to Regulate Commerce*. See § 17, p. 36.
[3] *Ibid.*, § 15, p. 30.
[4] *Ibid.*, § 16, p. 33.

CHAPTER XIII

ADMINISTRATIVE OFFICIALS

> A New Jersey act creating a bureau in the labor department to
> assist injured employees . . . is an interesting provision for state
> aid to that class of litigants least likely to possess the initiative
> or the money necessary to begin and prosecute an action in the
> courts. PARKINSON: *Important Legislation during 1916.*[1]

§ 1

THE distinction between administrative tribunals and administrative bureaus
or officials is not always clear. Substantially, the difference is that the administrative tribunal as part of its work exercises an important judicial function, it passes
Definition judgment on contested and disputed states of fact, applies the law to the
facts as found, and enters an order accordingly, whereas the administrative official exercises an executive function, he enforces the law, but if he secures evidence of a violation, his only authority is to repair to a regularly constituted court
and ask for its judgment. Examples of the latter are insurance, tax, and labor commissioners. Both administrative tribunals and officials vary greatly in type and often
approach a point where it is impossible to distinguish them. Sometimes both are
united in one body as a state Board of Labor charged with enforcing the labor laws
and administering the compensation act. In their bearing on our problem it may be
said that the administrative tribunal is analogous to a court and the official to a
lawyer.

§ 2

The poor man may to-day obtain free legal advice and a certain amount of assistance
in divers branches of law by applying at the appropriate state departments. The in-
General surance commissioner will advise him whether his policy of life or
Assistance by fire insurance is in accordance with law and as to his rights there-
Administrative under. The tax commissioner will explain to him his obligations, if
Officials any, under the tax laws.[2] A deputy banking commissioner will instruct him as to the usury laws, the rates of interest permitted on
small loans, and the restrictions on assignments of wages given as security. In each
important port there is a United States Shipping Commissioner who advises seamen.[3]
He has authority, upon agreement of parties, to arbitrate disputes. In fact he has a
wider jurisdiction because almost invariably his informal recommendation as to payment of wages, deductions, discharge, and the like will be accepted by the captain

---

[1] Professor Thomas I. Parkinson of the Legislative Drafting Bureau of Columbia University in his *Review of Important Legislation in the United States during* 1916, 3 Am. Bar Ass'n Journal, No. 2, pp. 168, 172.
[2] See *Requirements of the Massachusetts Income Tax Law* (1916), *Bulletin No.* 1 of the Income Tax Commissioner,
§ 15, p. 26.
[3] See United States v. The Grace Lothrop, 95 U. S. 527.

of any American vessel. Immigration commissions are coming into existence which give much legal assistance to newly arrived immigrants. The best illustration is afforded by the California Commission on Immigration and Housing, which maintains a bureau of complaints, and does its best to adjust legal disputes in which immigrants are involved.[1]

The service afforded by these bureaus and officials includes advice and an attempt to adjust controversies, but stops there. They do not render assistance in litigation. Thus, if the insurance commissioner or the immigration commissioner finds that a complainant has been wronged, and is unable to secure redress by negotiation, there is nothing to be done except to refer him to some other official, or to a legal aid society, or to a private attorney.[2]

§ 3

There is a growing number of administrative officials empowered to render direct legal services in litigation. The New Jersey workmen's compensation bureau,[3] after

Legal Services in Litigation

its investigation, certifies the facts to the county court. This in fact operates as a petition and starts the litigation. It goes no further, but the statute permits the court to assign counsel to carry the case on. The Minnesota Department of Labor gathers facts in compensation claims and is authorized by law[4] to send its investigators into the district courts, where all decisions are made, to aid and counsel any party.

In Virginia a recent statute[5] gives the commissioner of agriculture supervisory authority over licensed commission merchants. A farmer who is not paid for his produce may complain to the commissioner and obtain a hearing. If the facts warrant, the commissioner is empowered to revoke the merchant's license and to bring suit to recover for the complainant the money due him.[6] Similarly, the supervisor of small loans in Massachusetts has authority to entertain complaints for violations of the law regulating interest charges and the small loans business in general, to conduct hearings, and to bring actions in the courts for violations of law.[7] In most cities there are legally constituted boards of health to which a person can complain as to the unsanitary condition of his neighbor's backyard, and the board will itself institute proceedings, thereby saving the party the expense of bringing a private suit to abate a nuisance.

[1] *Second Annual Report of the California Commission on Immigration and Housing* (1916), pages 95, 108, 117 a. In 1915 legal advice was given in 388 cases and 174 matters were adjusted. Massachusetts has very recently created a similar Commission, which has its own attorney to assist immigrants.

[2] See *Ibid.*, pages 98, 103, 117 a.

[3] New Jersey *Session Laws of* 1916, c. 54.

[4] *Fourteenth Biennial Report of the Minnesota Department of Labor* for 1913 and 1914, page 39. The precise number of cases in which court assistance is given is not known. It is estimated at fifty cases a month.

[5] Virginia *Acts of* 1916, c. 77.

[6] Parkinson: *Review of Important Legislation in the United States during* 1916, 3 Am. Bar Ass'n Journal, No. 2, 172.

[7] Massachusetts *Acts of* 1911, c. 727.

§ 4

The most striking example of state aid to parties in private litigation is afforded
by the Massachusetts Labor Commissioner in his authority to enforce
Collection of payment of wages. The plan, as it has been built up, is so unique and
Wages by has been so successful that it deserves thorough presentation.[1] The
Administra- Commissioner is the executive officer of the State Board of Labor and
tive Officials Industries,[2] which has general supervision over the labor laws regulating hours of work, sanitary provisions, safety appliances, employment of minors, and
the like.

Since 1886 there has existed in Massachusetts a law requiring corporations to pay
wages weekly and providing for criminal proceedings against employers for violations.[3] In 1895 the law was extended to include individual and partnership employers.[4]
Before making this important amendment the legislature asked the Supreme Judicial Court whether such a law would be constitutional. The Court filed an opinion that
the law would be valid.[5] Although there are contrary decisions in other states, the
point of constitutionality has never been raised in an actual case.[6] The original law
has been amended nearly every year, but always in the direction of widening its operation and including within its provisions additional classes of employees.[7] The scope
and plan of the law appears from its text:[8]

> "Every person, firm, or corporation engaged in carrying on a hotel in a city, or
> a factory, workshop, manufacturing, mechanical, or mercantile establishment,
> mine, quarry, railroad or street railway, or a telephone, telegraph, express or
> water company, or in the erection, alteration, or repair or removal of any build-
> ing or structure, or the construction or repair of any railroad, street railway,
> road, bridge, sewer, gas, water or electric light works, pipes or lines, shall pay
> weekly each employee engaged in his or its business the wages earned by him to
> within six days of the date of said payment, but any employee leaving his or her
> employment, shall be paid in full on the following regular pay day; and any
> employee discharged from such employment shall be paid in full on the day of
> his discharge. . . .
>
> "Whoever violates the provisions of this section shall be punished by a fine of
> not less than ten nor more than fifty dollars."

Enforcement of this law was first in the hands of the state police, and in 1912 was
transferred to the Labor Commissioner.[9] The rigor of the law is self-evident:

---

[1] For a commentary on the Massachusetts law, and similar laws of other states, see United States Bureau of Labor
Statistics, *Bulletin No.* 229 (1918), pages 70 *et seq.*

[2] Massachusetts *Acts of* 1912, c. 726, § 2. See United States Bureau of Labor Statistics *Bulletin No.* 229 (1918), pages
70, 73.

[3] *Statutes of* 1886, c. 87.   [4] *Ibid.,* 1895, c. 438.   [5] Opinion of the Justices, 163 Mass. (1895) 589.

[6] See Commonwealth *v.* Dunn, 170 Mass. (1898) 140.

[7] Revised Laws of 1902, c. 106, § 62; Acts of 1909, c. 514, § 112; Acts of 1910, c. 350; Acts of 1911, c. 208; Acts of 1914,
c. 247; Acts of 1915, c. 75; Acts of 1916, c. 229.

[8] General Acts of 1916, c. 229.

[9] Acts of 1912, c. 726, § 5; Acts of 1916, c. 14.

"The state board of labor and industries may make a complaint against any person for a violation of the provisions of the preceding section. Complaints for such violation shall be made within three months after the date thereof, and, on the trial, no defence for failure to pay as required, other than the attachment of such wages by the trustee process or a valid assignment thereof, or a valid set-off against the same, or the absence of the employee from his regular place of labor at the time of payment, or an actual tender to such employee at the time of payment of the wages so earned by him, shall be valid. The defendant shall not set up as a defence a payment of wages after the bringing of the complaint."

The Commissioner has two deputies, twenty-four inspectors, a chief clerk, and an attorney on his staff. Whereas most labor commissioners can only try conciliation, and if that fails refer the employee to a legal aid society[1] or leave him without any assistance, it is apparent that the Massachusetts Commissioner has the legal power and equipment to assist unpaid wage-earners as far as is necessary. The proceeding being under the criminal code, its process is summary, there are no costs, and the attorney is supplied by the Commission without expense to the employee. The machinery is so effective that it seldom has to be used. Wholesale non-payment of wages does not exist in Massachusetts as it does elsewhere. Unfortunately, the statistics of the work done are available only since 1915. They show:

Year	Number of Wage Complaints	Adjusted by Legal Department	Sums Collected	Prosecuted in Court
1915[2]	896	698	$3,192.22	198
1916[3]	1,746	1,586	12,374.61	160
1917[4]	—	1,432	8,885.32	—

The effectiveness and success of this plan are well attested by the fact that relatively few persons apply to the legal aid society in Boston for assistance in collecting their wages. Of those that do apply the larger number are domestic servants who are not included within the act, or persons whose claims are more than three months old and so barred by the statute. Comparative statistics for 1916 make this clear:

Legal Aid Organization in	Total Cases	Wage Claims	Per Cent
Boston	2,608	314	12
Chicago	10,697	3,134	29
Dallas	1,464	476	32
Kansas City	6,202	2,118	34
Los Angeles	2,571	1,938	75
Newark	2,152	804	37
New York	41,646	15,922	38

---

[1] Cf. *Fourteenth Biennial Report*, Minnesota Department of Labor (1913–14), pages 135, 201; 8 Pittsburgh L. A. R. 17.

[2] *Third Annual Report of the State Board of Labor and Industries, Public Document No.* 104, of 1916, page 20. These figures cover only the last five months of the year.

[3] *Fourth Report, Ibid., Public Document No.* 104 of 1917, page 25.

[4] From January 1 to September 30. These figures were furnished by Miss Andrews of the State Board of Labor and Industries.

In 1911 California attempted to provide the same machinery for wage collections, by passing the weekly payment law,[1] with criminal penalties for violation, and by placing its enforcement in the hands of the State Bureau of Labor Statistics. This law, on November 23, 1914, was held unconstitutional on the ground that it conflicted with the constitutional prohibition against imprisonment for debt.[2] The Board, like most commissions, has a general authority to summon in parties, and under that provision it has proceeded to aid unpaid wage-earners to the best of its ability. It has rendered great legal assistance, as appears from its statistical reports.[3]

Year	Claims Filed	Claims Collected	Amounts Collected
1912	1,899	1,292	$24,445.59
1913	3,573	2,213	36,450.69
1914	7,330	4,904	110,911.93
1915	9,320	5,249	153,804.20
1916	10,167	5,672	179,132.22

The higher percentage of claims enforced during the first two years as contrasted with the last two years is an immediate reflection of the court's decision in 1914, which necessarily deprived the Board of its final power. To-day, if an employer refuses to pay, the Board cannot institute litigation for the employee, it can only refer him to the Public Defender in Los Angeles and the Legal Aid Society in San Francisco, and elsewhere to no one.

That the Board is able to accomplish as much as it does is a tribute to the effectiveness of the method of conciliation under official conduct. The Board is like a poor man's court,[4] without power to render a judgment or to enforce its own finding. It can secure a result only through the mutual consent of the parties, which is conciliation.

§ 5

The complexity of government in the modern state will undoubtedly call for a steady development of the administrative arm. As officials, bureaus, and commissions are

Future Development
necessarily added, there will be an increase in the fields of law as to which poor persons can secure legal advice and certain preliminary legal assistance without consulting private attorneys.

Of more immediate importance is the possibility of extending the Massachusetts plan for the collection of wages. The poor man's case more often relates to wages than to anything else. A state board empowered to use the summary criminal process is, in many respects, of more assistance than the small claims court. The plan, if it could be extended, would probably stop non-payment of wages almost entirely, but

[1] See *Statutes of* 1911, page 1268.
[2] *Ex parte* Crane, 145 Pacific R. 733. This is a decision of the District Court of Appeals for the First District. No final appeal to the Supreme Court was ever taken. The constitutional provision is Article I, § 15.
[3] See *Seventeenth Biennial Report of the California Bureau of Labor Statistics* for 1915-16, pages 9-16; also *Sixteenth Biennial Report, Ibid.*, page 15.
[4] *Seventeenth Biennial Report, Ibid.*, page 9.

the constitutional prohibition against imprisonment for debt, which in most aspects is wholly desirable, stands as a barrier.[1] It is likely that the states would refuse to amend that provision; and it is certain that it could only be done after a long educational campaign. The only warrantable conclusion is that while here and there the idea may be adopted and while it serves to exemplify one strikingly successful solution for an important part of the problem, no general reliance can be placed on it as the best immediate solution of the nation-wide difficulty of the poor in collecting their wages through the processes of the law.

---

[1] For a recent case in Arizona holding that criminal process to enforce payment of wages is valid as against corporations, see Arizona Power Co. *v.* State (1917), 166 Pacific R. 275.

CHAPTER XIV

ASSIGNED COUNSEL

KENT: This is nothing, fool.
FOOL: Then 't is like the breath of an unfee'd lawyer, you gave me
nothing for 't.   *King Lear, Act I, Sc.* 4.

OF the nine agencies securing a more equal administration of the laws which are under consideration, the only one which is not of recent origin is the system of assignment of counsel to indigent persons in civil and criminal cases. This, together with the provisions for bringing suits in forma pauperis, constitutes the sum total of the machinery provided by our traditional administration of justice for safeguarding the rights of poor persons.

This matter of the assignment of counsel by courts to represent persons unable to employ their own attorneys raises several questions of the highest importance. A determination of the law on which the system is built answers the now disputed issue as to the relationship between the bar and legal aid organizations; on the workability and feasibility of the plan depends in large measure the argument about the public defender. These matters must be relegated to their appropriate chapters.[1] In this chapter our concern is to examine how far the difficulty of the expense of counsel has been solved by the assignment method and, on that basis, how far it ought to be incorporated into any thorough plan designed to remedy the existing inequalities. It is convenient to divide the discussion into assignments in civil cases, the divorce proctors, and assignments in criminal cases.

§ 1

The system of assignment of counsel looms large in the books, but has amounted to very little in practice. Analytically, it would appear that this power of the courts to

Assignment of Counsel in Civil Cases
assign attorneys to assist poor persons in cases where representation was necessary was a complete answer to the difficulty of the expense of attorneys. Practically, it has been no solution at all.

In addition to the inherent power of courts to assign attorneys, on the general theory that they are agents of the court and ministers of justice, there are statutes in many jurisdictions expressly conferring this authority on the judges, to be used in their discretion. Following the ancient precedents, the authority is generally contained in the laws permitting suits in forma pauperis.[2] For some reason this power seems never to have been used. Judges who are thoroughly familiar with the practice in the New York and Chicago municipal courts state that within their

---

[1] See *post*, Chapter XXIV, Legal Aid and the Bar, page 226; and Chapter XV, The Defender in Criminal Cases, page 111.
[2] Examples of these statutes are *New York Code of Civil Procedure*, §§ 460, 463; Hurd's *Revised Statutes of Illinois* (1905), page 555; Missouri *Annotated Statutes* (1906), § 1545; Carroll's *Kentucky Statutes*, § 884.

recollection counsel have never been assigned in civil cases. When counsel for the New York Legal Aid Society petitions in behalf of a client for leave to sue without payment of costs, the petition contains a prayer that he be assigned as counsel, and this is granted as a matter of course; but the rule that the courts of their own initiative do not designate members of the bar to assist needy suitors is not controverted by any other evidence. The system is so thoroughly in disuse that in many quarters its very existence is denied. The large majority of attorneys do not realize that there is any authority which can require them as a matter of duty to give their services without charge to poor persons.

It is not easy to state with precision why a system so deep-rooted in the history of our legal institutions should both in England and in the United States fall into such neglect. Doubtless it is in part due to the general failure to realize how the changed conditions of life had put the employment of counsel beyond the reach of so many persons. Probably even more important has been the fact that the system contains a certain unfairness. As the bar has developed, most of its members have been obliged to work hard to earn their living. To force such an attorney to undertake litigation without remuneration seemed a hardship which a court naturally would hesitate to impose. The highest courts in Indiana and Wisconsin have considered the unfairness so great as to constitute deprivation of property without due process of law, and have declared unconstitutional statutes requiring attorneys to serve under assignments without compensation.[1] In this situation is revealed the great weakness of the plan. If an attorney, obliged to earn his livelihood by practice, is compelled to serve a poor person without hope of reward, all the probabilities of human nature are that he will neglect that case in favor of cases brought by paying clients.

Because of this fact and of our experience, one would be tempted to cast the assignment plan aside and to hold that no good could come from it; but no such summary dismissal is justified, for elsewhere it has been made to operate with great success. The legal aid societies in Philadelphia, Duluth, and Los Angeles[2] have built up very careful systems under which they assign to outside attorneys such cases as they are unable or forbidden by rule to undertake. They have had no difficulty in obtaining a sufficient number of attorneys to serve, and by carefully selecting their list and by a slight amount of supervision they have been able to make the plan work satisfactorily to all parties concerned. What the legal aid societies, informally and without authority, can do ought not to be impossible for the courts.

The entire legal aid system in Scotland and France has for centuries been operated by a combination of the bench and the bar using the assignment plan as part of the in forma pauperis proceeding.[3] In Scotland about two thousand persons a year apply

---

[1] Webb v. Baird, 6 Ind. 13; Dane County v. Smith, 13 Wis. 585.

[2] The Los Angeles plan is described in detail in the San Francisco *Recorder* for September 8, 1914, and in 5 Journal of Criminal Law and Criminology, 601.

[3] This subject of judicial legal aid is considered in further detail *post* in Chapter XXV, A More Equal Administration of Justice, page 246.

for this assistance; the assignment of counsel goes on in daily practice, as a glance at the reports shows.[1] In England, where there has recently been a great awakening to the inability of the poor to utilize the machinery of justice, the assignment system is being made the chief reliance in the comprehensive reform undertaken by the courts.[2] In 1913 the English High Court of Judicature, after conferences with the bar, issued a series of rules making provision for poor persons' cases and calling for the formation of lists of solicitors and counsel who would accept assignments. Despite the complications resulting from the war, the most recent information is to the effect that the plan gives promise of being successful.[3] Before their numbers were depleted by enlistments, there were three hundred barristers and five hundred solicitors throughout England who stood ready to undertake assigned cases.[4]

While there are drawbacks to the assignment idea, it is too valuable to be given up altogether. In America it ought to be revived. There should be such a lively sense of obligation on both bench and bar that no civil suitor should be forced by poverty to do without counsel in cases requiring skilled preparation and presentation. Whenever such cases appear the judges should feel at perfect liberty to assign the cause either to the legal aid organization or to other counsel. Although in most respects an organized and specialized legal aid bureau is far more efficient than any assignment system, the latter can be made an effective auxiliary, and a last safeguard, in any complete plan for securing rights to the poor.

§ 2

In some states there are attorneys, known as divorce proctors, who intervene in divorce matters under assignment from the court. This work is done to safeguard the interest

Assignments in Divorce

of the state, not to assist needy parties, and the practice is mentioned here merely to establish the fact. It is valuable because it affords one more precedent for the state's concerning itself and lending its assistance in matters that are generally regarded as "private" litigation.

The idea originated in England, where the office of King's Proctor was created to prevent collusion in divorce cases.[5] The first attempt to establish a similar position in America was made in New York in 1901, but failed.[6] In a few states this function is performed either under statute as in New Jersey[7] and the District of Columbia,[8] or

---

[1] The Scotch system is presented in 105 Contemporary Review, 559, 562, and in 47 Law Journal, 49; for cases arising out of this practice see Ross v. Ross, 1 Scots Law Times (1914), 299; McGregor v. Kinloch, *Ibid.*, 474.

[2] Rules dated April 28, 1913, and published in the 1914 Rule Book. See Order 16, IV, §§ 22-31.

[3] *Law Times* for March 18, 1916.   [4] 49 Law Journal (1914), 362.

[5] For the acts see 23 & 24 Vict. c. 144, § 7; 36 & 37 Vict. c. 31; for a discussion see Halsbury: *Laws of England*, vol. xvi, tit. Husband and Wife, §§ 1125-1132.

[6] For the bill see State of New York Senate Bill No. 82, reprinted No. 837; see also printed report of the Committee on Amendment of the Law of the New York City Bar Association, dated March 14, 1901.

[7] Biddle: *New Jersey Divorce Practice* (2d ed.), page 134.

[8] District of Columbia Code, § 982; for a similar statute in Massachusetts see *Acts of* 1907, c. 390.

simply under the general authority of the court to assign counsel as in Denver and Kansas City.

Generally the duty of such an officer is to appear in default divorce cases to ascertain whether the proceedings are fraudulent and whether the defendant had proper notice. Indirectly this may occasionally serve to benefit some poor person, but the design is simply to protect the interest of the state that divorces should not be granted except for valid cause.

§ 3

Assignment of counsel in criminal cases is as common as it is uncommon in civil cases. In the federal courts and in the majority of the state courts of general criminal jurisdiction the law provides that the court must, on request, appoint counsel to represent the accused. It is the universal rule that no man is permitted to stand trial for murder unless he has counsel to represent him. In the inferior courts counsel are not assigned.

Assignment of Counsel in Criminal Cases

In most states the right to counsel is guaranteed by the constitution. Also the Sixth Amendment to the Constitution of the United States provides:

"In all criminal prosecutions the accused shall enjoy the right to a speedy and public trial; . . . to have compulsory process for obtaining witnesses in his favor; and to have the assistance of counsel for his defence."

In a number of states the constitutional provision has been supplemented by statutory enactments giving express power to the courts to assign counsel.[1] The systems in vogue vary infinitely. In some states counsel are paid, in others not. Some courts assign counsel in all matters, others only when requested.

The general statement is warranted that in criminal matters the courts and the bar have viewed their duty in an entirely different manner than in civil cases. The power of assignment and the duty to serve are clearly established. That the courts have acted on their own initiative and that the assignment practice is regularly established is due to the fact that the injustice of requiring a person to present his side of the story in a criminal matter without the advice of counsel is much more apparent than in civil controversies. When liberty is at stake, the desire that there should be fair play is more easily aroused.

It might appear, therefore, that we might confidently look to the assignment system to secure equality before the law at least in the more serious criminal cases. Unhappily this is not the case. The truth about the assignment system in criminal cases is that as a whole it has proved a dismal failure, and that at times it has been worse than a failure. Because of this breakdown, there has been sweeping over the country during the past five years a movement, commonly known as the public defender move-

---

[1] Thus see New York Code of Criminal Procedure, § 460.

ment, which is probably destined to supplant, or radically alter, the assignment practice. The details of the failure of the assignment system in criminal cases are so inextricably bound up with the discussion about the public defender that they can best be considered in that connection in the next chapter.

It must be recorded that the traditional administration of justice failed utterly to make the assignment system — the only machinery it provided — any kind of a satisfactory solution for the inequality caused by the inability of the poor to pay the fees of attorneys. In civil cases, the plan fell into disuse, so that legal aid organizations were found necessary to fill the gap in the machinery of justice. In criminal cases, use by the courts, through lack of supervision, degenerated into abuse by attorneys, so that the public defender, which is only another name for legal aid in criminal cases, was required to supplant a part of the machinery that failed to perform its function.

CHAPTER XV

THE DEFENDER IN CRIMINAL CASES

In criminal cases, the defence of the poor and destitute is a necessary obligation devolving upon the county, and to the extent of providing counsel for them the court is agent for the county. How-*ard County Commissioners* v. *Pollard.*[1]

HERE for the first time we are confronted with the question of the position of the poor before the criminal law. Thus far we have dealt almost exclusively with the law on its civil side, and with agencies designed to secure more equal rights in the bringing and defending of civil matters. It is the object of this chapter to examine the administration of justice on its criminal side, to see how far it guarantees freedom and equality to poor persons accused of crime, and to determine what betterments may be made.

In recent years our criminal law and procedure have been subjected to violent and persistent attacks. In no other field has the cry of one law for the rich and another for the poor been more exploited or more thoroughly believed. The proceedings in certain notorious trials of rich men for serious offences have aroused indignation and served to degrade all law in the opinion of hosts of persons. There is something dramatic about criminal trials which excites popular imagination and focuses public attention on the criminal rather than the civil law. The new office in criminal cases, generally called that of public defender, has had more written about it and is more generally known than all the other remedial agencies combined. There being a wealth of discussion,[2] our problem here is not so much one of simple exposition, as it has been in earlier chapters, but rather one of analysis. This is particularly necessary because much of the discussion thus far has been at loggerheads. It has not settled anything because frequently the essential issues have been overlooked or confused and the close relation between this particular problem and the whole problem of injustice to the poor, between the defender in criminal cases and the other remedial agencies, has not been observed.

§ 1

The term "public defender" is itself a source of confusion because its meaning has become ambiguous. The office of the first defender in Los Angeles was created by statute and supported by the county treasury, so that "public defender" at once acquired

---

[1] 153 Indiana, 371, 372.

[2] The best arguments for the agency are Wood: *The Place of the Public Defender in the Administration of Justice* (1914), and Mayer C. Goldman's book, *The Public Defender* (1917); contra, *Fifth Report of the Law Reform Committee of the New York City Bar Association on The Necessity and Advisability of Creating the Office of Public Defender* (1915), and *Majority Report of Sub-Committee on Public Defender of the Committee on Courts of Criminal Procedure of the New York County Lawyers' Association*, which was published in *Bench and Bar*, n. s., vol. ix, p. 309. These adverse reports are discussed in the *Minority Report* published in 5 Journal of Criminal Law and Criminology (1915), 660; and in 6 *Ibid.* 18. Citations to the most helpful of the other articles are made in following pages.

Preliminary Definitions

the connotation of a public official paid at public expense. However, when a private attorney in Houston offered his services to poor persons accused of crime, the press entitled him "public defender." The New York organization, being financed by subscription, consciously took the name of Voluntary Defenders Committee, but the man in the street knows it only as the "public defender" office. Articles that condemn the public defender as unnecessary and then praise the voluntary defender[1] have bewildered most readers and, what is worse, they have side-tracked the discussion.

In the hope of avoiding these pitfalls, the words "public" and "private" will be eliminated from this chapter. The official or agency under discussion will be called the defender in criminal cases, or, more simply, the defender.

The fundamental issue is whether our administration of justice is unfair to the poor accused of serious crimes, so that some agency for their better protection is required. In their bearing on that question all the defender organizations which have been established may be considered together, for in function they are all identical. The subordinate problem of whether they should be supported publicly or privately has interesting legal and political aspects, but as it is precisely the same issue which must be faced later in discussing public versus private legal aid organizations,[2] it, together with other collateral matters, will be relegated to the appropriate place in the subsequent chapters on legal aid work.

This substantial identity of the defender and the legal aid organizations is not realized. Well-informed writers have treated them as distinct agencies far removed from each other, so that a second confusion has resulted. Reports have been made that defenders are not necessary, but recommending that legal aid societies extend their assistance in criminal matters. This is tracing a circle around the question without answering it. To advise a man who is debating whether he requires a lawyer or not that he should not have lawyer A because he needs no attorney, but that it would be well for him to secure lawyer B, does not resolve his main doubt. The distinction arose from the historical fact that legal aid societies generally confined themselves to civil matters. Analytically the two agencies are as alike as two sessions of the same court; both were called into being by the same general causes, both exist for the same purpose, and both stand in the same relation to the administration of justice. While they have operated in different fields, evolution is fast breaking down this distinction, for many legal aid organizations are giving defence in criminal cases, and the defender agencies are giving their aid in civil cases.

Finally, it is necessary to distinguish between that part of criminal law which deals with serious crimes such as murder, burglary, larceny, assault and battery, and that part which is concerned with relatively trivial matters such as selling without a license, violations of the road law, of the building or sanitary codes, in short, public

---

[1] For example see an article in the New York *Evening Sun* for March 26, 1917.

[2] Chapter XIX, Types of Legal Aid Organizations, § 6. Public *versus* Private Organizations, page 180.

torts, and with such lesser crimes as drunkenness, street-walking, and vagrancy. In a rough way the line of cleavage is between the inferior courts and the superior courts of general criminal jurisdiction. The defender is concerned primarily with the more serious offences and with the defence of persons in the superior criminal courts. The following discussion deals with that field. There are defenders in some inferior courts, but they stand on quite a different footing and their consideration will be taken up in a separate section.

§ 2

Whether the defender in criminal cases is necessary to secure equal justice to poor persons accused of serious crimes depends on the answers given to these three questions:

The Argument

1. Do we believe that persons accused of the more serious crimes should have adequate representation?
2. If so, does the existing law and practice secure such adequate representation?
3. If the existing system is inadequate, is the defender a sound plan for securing proper representation?

The first question answers itself. When our general principle of the right of accused to have counsel is combined with the principle of freedom and equality of justice, the conclusion is inevitable. Nowhere has any one openly declared that poor persons in serious criminal cases should be left without adequate representation. Such a claim would be tantamount to arguing for a return to the harsh English criminal law, as it existed prior to the American Revolution, forbidding accused persons to have the assistance of counsel. In its effect on the individual poor person standing accused, in its effect on the administration of justice, and in its political effect there is no distinction between precluding an indigent by law from having counsel and erecting a system which in fact precludes him from obtaining counsel. There is unanimity of opinion that the administration of the criminal law should guarantee that no one shall be convicted of a serious crime without a fair trial, and without adequate representation.

§ 3

In weighing the fairness of the existing system there are two half-truths which have served too often to tip the balance, but which must strictly be ruled out of account because they beg the question and prejudge the issue. The first is the widespread impression that people are not arrested unless they are guilty;[1] that when the blue-coated officer of the law takes a man into custody, there "must be something in it." The second is that too much protection

The Existing System

[1] Cf. 73 Ann. Am. Ac. Pol. & Soc. Science (1917), 198.

is afforded already because the guilty sometimes escape conviction. A sound judgment cannot be predicated on such biased premises, but must be arrived at from an examination of what protections are actually accorded poor persons accused of crime.

Eight distinct protections may be discerned in our present administration of criminal law. Stated in the order of procedure they are: (1) at the preliminary arraignment a case against the accused must be made out; (2) if he is held, the district attorney reviews the case and may, if the evidence is insufficient, dismiss or nol pros the complaint; (3) thereafter the grand jury deliberates and will not indict except for cause shown; (4) an investigation is made by an impartial probation staff; (5) at the trial the judge guards the defendant's rights; (6) the law lends its assistance by presuming innocence and requiring proof beyond reasonable doubt; (7) the prosecuting attorney is a judicial official, so that in theory he is interested only in the whole truth and thus acts for the defendant; (8) if persons are too poor to employ counsel, provision is made for assigning counsel in their behalf.

This last is the crux of the situation. The other seven do not of themselves afford adequate safeguards. Standing alone and without counsel for the accused to call them into action, they would be of doubtful efficacy. This is because they are qualified, not absolute, protections. Singly or in combination they provide no sure test of guilt or innocence. They were never designed for that purpose. They are useful in winnowing out the clearer cases of innocence, but all other cases pass beyond them to a final determination by jury verdict. Through them many innocent persons have been released, but likewise through all these seven stages have gone many cases in which innocence did not appear until it was brought out by counsel for the defence at trial.

A brief review shows these statements to be true and why they are true. The preliminary hearing before a magistrate is intended to determine only whether the accused is so palpably innocent as to be entitled to immediate release, or whether there is sufficient evidence to hold him for further investigation and action by the grand jury, in technical language whether there is "probable cause." Not only does the law expect persons, if there is any sufficient evidence, to be held, but the magistrates, particularly where the charge is serious, hesitate to free a man if there is any evidence against him and incline to pass the responsibility on to the higher court.[1] At these hearings no counsel are assigned.

In New York in 1914, of 13,327 men and women arraigned for serious offences, 7088 were held for trial. That forty-seven per cent were discharged demonstrates the need for this protection. Further, it proves the falsity of the generalization, based on a lack of understanding as to how easily the organized power of society can be started in pursuit of an individual,[2] that most persons who are arrested are guilty. The fairness of our existing system cannot be supported by lightly assuming that it deals

---

[1] 5 Journal of Criminal Law and Criminology, 661; 6 Ibid. 21; Train: The Prisoner at the Bar (2d ed. 1915), page 56.

[2] Annual Report for 1914 of the New York City Magistrates' Courts, page 150. Statistics from 1905 to 1914 are given.

only with criminals who deserve no protection, but must depend on the provision it makes for an impartial determination of guilt or innocence after a full hearing at which both sides are adequately represented.

The second protection is the review by the district attorney. This is aimed primarily to ascertain whether the state can make out a case. It does not purport to be a thorough review of both sides.[1] The district attorney cannot know all the facts favoring the accused, for rare indeed is the prisoner who will confide in the man who is to prosecute him. Similarly, the grand jury hearing is ex parte. Neither the accused, nor his counsel, nor his witnesses are heard.[2] Their presence is prohibited. The proceeding is summary—seven minutes per case is the average deliberation of the grand jury in New York—and it is of so little value for any purpose that its abolition is seriously considered.[3]

In jurisdictions where a probation staff is attached to the criminal courts its investigation is unquestionably impartial. But it is an enquiry into the prisoner's personal history, past record, associations, and environment (of importance in assisting the court to fix a just sentence) rather than into the facts constituting the crime charged. The probation officer does not testify at the trial; his lips are sealed until after verdict.[4]

At the trial the judge presides over the proceedings and guarantees, so far as it is within his power, that they are conducted fairly and in accordance with the prisoner's legal rights. It was long maintained in England that this was a complete protection in itself, so that the accused needed no counsel.[5] In practice, however, it proved demonstrably inadequate and was abandoned in 1903.[6] This safeguard through judicial control is in reality very limited in scope. It is not because our judges are dishonest, unwilling, or incapable. They desire to follow Bacon's adjuration:[7]

"A judge ought to prepare his way to a just sentence, as God useth to prepare his way, by raising valleys and taking down hills; so that when there appeareth on either side an high hand, violent prosecution, cunning advantages taken, combination, great power, great counsel, then is the virtue of a judge seen, to make inequality equal, that he may plant his judgment as upon an even ground."

The trouble is that under our existing system the judge has so little opportunity to "make inequality equal." His hands are so much tied that he is more of an aloof umpire than an active protecting official.[8] He rules on objections made by counsel, but does not himself interpose objections to testimony. Except in the federal courts he is forbidden to express any opinion or to instruct the jury on the facts. In an ob-

[1] *The Office of the Public Defender* (Los Angeles, 1914), page 8.
[2] 5 Journal of Crim. L. 661; 6 *Ibid.* 22; Train: *The Prisoner at the Bar*, page 56.
[3] Olson: *Efficiency in the Administration of Criminal Justice* (1917), pages 14 *et seq.*
[4] 6 Journal of Crim. L. 22; *Probation Manual*, published by the Massachusetts Commission on Probation (1916), page 17.
[5] Fultz: *Public Defender*, 31 American Law Review (1897), 394.
[6] After much agitation the Prisoners' Defence Act was passed in 1903 to provide counsel to represent the accused.
[7] Francis Bacon: *Essays on Counsels Civil and Moral*, LVI, Of Judicature.
[8] 5 Journal of Crim. L. 495; 6 *Ibid.* 22.

vious miscarriage of justice he can order a new trial, but the practice is seldom to interfere with jury verdicts. The judge labors under the further difficulty of knowing only those facts that are introduced in evidence. A defendant, who was unrepresented and could not secure the attendance of witnesses, might have a valid defence of which the judge would be ignorant because the facts would not be before him. He could not learn the facts for himself, since he is neither empowered nor equipped to conduct any investigation.

The law attempts to throw its protecting mantle over the prisoner by means of three rules which in books are strongly in his favor, but which in action are uncertain quantities. It presumes the defendant innocent up to the moment when the foreman pronounces the jury's verdict. This rule in practice has little, if any, effect. The whole criminal system runs counter to it. If it were taken seriously, the state would long since have placed at the disposal of the accused resources, comparable to those arrayed against him, to enable him in fact to defend or assert the innocence which in law presumably attaches to him.[1] A second rule requires guilt to be proved "beyond a reasonable doubt." Although every defendant's counsel urges this in his argument and every judge states it in his charge, it is a matter of conjecture whether juries clearly understand it or its equivalent of "moral certainty," and, if they do, whether they follow the legal line closely enough[2] to make it a factor of any importance in their deliberations. The third rule, that the defendant's failure to testify is not to be construed against him, is commonly disregarded by juries[3] and is fast becoming a dead letter.

That the prosecuting attorney is a judicial officer is a sound statement of law, but the deduction that he therefore acts as much for the accused as for the state is not warranted. To an extent he may aid the defendant by his review of the case and by fairly presenting the evidence to the grand jury as has been indicated,[4] but at the trial he acts primarily as advocate for the government. He may aim to produce the whole truth, but he seldom knows, or can know, the defendant's story. In every populous district he is an extremely busy, generally overworked man, necessarily occupied in trying cases to the best of his ability, and with little time or opportunity to look out for the other side. In the heat of trial and in his zeal to convict, the prosecuting officer has often gone such lengths that new trials constantly have to be ordered by courts of last resort because of his unfairness.[5] An epitome of adjudicated cases reveals that he "has misstated the facts and obtruded improper matter into his opening statement to the jury, has impressed the jury by the suggestion of crimes other than the one charged, has attempted to get improper matter before the jury, has abused

---

[1] Cf. *Report of the Massachusetts Commission on Immigration* (1914), page 112; *Minority Report of Special Committee on the Public Defender of the New York County Lawyers' Association* (1914), page 11.

[2] Train: *The Prisoner at the Bar*, pages 159-161; Storey: *Reform of Criminal Procedure*, page 214.

[3] Train: *op. cit.*, pages 207 *et seq.*

[4] See *ante*, page 109.

[5] *Preliminary Report for the National Economic League on Efficiency in the Administration of Justice*, page 27.

witnesses, injected his personal and unsworn and damaging statements into the testimony, called the defendant all the vile names in his too plethoric Billingsgate dictionary, and has resorted to all sorts of reprehensible devices to awaken prejudice."[1] Much of such unfair conduct is due to the peculiar difficulty under which the district attorney labors. He is pitted against lawyers who are willing in their defence to use every trick, strategy, subterfuge, and device in their repertoire to delay or defeat him. He is forced to adopt an aggressive, distrustful, partisan attitude which is not consistent with the theory of his official impartiality.[2] In short, to expect him adequately to represent both sides is, as every lawyer knows, to expect the impossible.

These seven safeguards are essentially latent, not active, in their nature. The shrewd criminal supplied with money and able counsel may employ them and the technicalities which accompany this procedure to such an extent as to set the whole system at naught. Because some such striking instances are known to most people, when these several protections are stated one after the other, there is a temptation to jump to the conclusion that the law is already too considerate of defendants. It is overlooked that in the cases of the poor, standing alone without counsel and without funds, they may prove unavailing.

The great defect, which is common to them all, is that they are effective only in a negative way. Everybody who investigates the case for trial—from the complainant on through the police, bureau detectives, and the district attorney—is on one side. If the evidence shows the defendant to be not guilty, the protections operate; but nowhere in this system is any provision made for ascertaining the facts or the law in favor of the accused. Many defences are affirmative in their nature, as character evidence, self-defence, alibi, and the bias or malice of the complaining witness. The type of case in which innocence fails to manifest itself at one stage is precisely the type of case in which innocence will not be discovered by these protections at any stage of the proceedings.

These are the reasons why the foregoing checks and precautions fail to secure to the poor as adequate protection as we believe to be the right of every individual accused of serious crime. Adequate protection, in last analysis, depends on adequate representation, so that if our criminal procedure, as it stands, is to be found sufficient, it must be on the ground that it does provide proper representation to the poor through its system of assigning counsel.

§ 4

After a case has reached the superior court and passed through the preliminary stages, the prisoner is required to plead guilty or not guilty to the indictment, and

---

[1] With only a change of tense, this sentence, every phrase of which is supported by decisions, is to be found in Fultze: *The Public Defender*, 31 American Law Rev. 395. More recent cases are cited and quoted in Goldman: *The Public Defender*, pages 28–31; Wood: *The Place of the Public Defender in the Administration of Justice*, page 9.

[2] 5 Journal of Crim. L. 662; McCulloch: *Here is Justice*, 31 Everybody's Magazine (1914), 248, 249; Goldman: *The Public Defender*, chapter iii, Public Prosecution and Prosecutors; *The Office of the Public Defender*, page 9; *The Place of the Public Defender in the Administration of Justice*, page 8.

at this time, if he has no counsel and is too poor to employ his own counsel, it is the
The System of Assigned Counsel practice in the majority of American jurisdictions for the judge to assign him some lawyer to act in his behalf at the trial. In this one particular department the traditional administration of justice has recognized that the function of the attorney is essential, that there are persons who cannot afford attorneys, and that therefore in the furtherance of its justice the state must gratuitously furnish such persons with counsel.

The assignment system varies from state to state, but its important features are these. Counsel are always assigned in murder cases, and this is true even in those states, such as the New England States, where there is no general assignment system. In murder cases assigned counsel are paid and in many jurisdictions have an additional allowance for expenses.[1] In about half the states counsel are assigned in all felony or more serious cases, that is, to practically all defendants who appear in the superior criminal courts without their own counsel. In all but seven states counsel in such cases are not paid and have no allowance for expenses.

Although there are local exceptions due to the fairness of the law in reimbursing counsel or to the exceptional pains of the judge in making assignments, the following generalization as to the system is warranted: in murder cases the assignment of counsel has been reasonably successful, often brilliantly so, and in all other cases it has been a dismal failure. This is no paradox; the reasons for this partial success of themselves show why in the main the system has been, and was bound to be, a failure.

Counsel assigned in murder cases work with great zeal. They generally earn a greater fee than the state pays and expend more than they are reimbursed. But it is recognized that the newspaper publicity which attends a murder trial gives a lawyer the best advertising he can ever have and is just as valuable as a cash payment. The fact that the defendant's life is in his hands naturally spurs the lawyer on. In a word, the case appeals simultaneously to the lawyer's self-interest and to the best traditions of his profession.

The situation is reversed[2] in other cases. The prisoner arrested for burglary, rape, or assault may arouse no sympathy, in fact the matter may be revolting. More important, the average lawyer, however honest and desirous of performing his professional obligations, cannot afford to give a thorough defence. Even if he could devote several days' time to the trial, he cannot pay out of his own pocket for investigators, detectives, and medical, handwriting, or other experts. Witnesses may be in other states, and he can neither pay their travel expenses nor engage counsel to take depositions. The situation forces on the conscientious lawyer the ugly dilemma of either spending largely of his own funds or of giving an improper defence. Few lawyers are

---

[1] This is so in Massachusetts, where counsel are assigned only in capital cases. *Revised Laws of* 1902, c. 157, §§ 16, 17.

[2] District Attorney Smith, of Nassau County, New York, wrote to the Committee on the Public Defender of the New York County Lawyers' Association: "I find that attorneys assigned to defend persons charged with crime other than capital cases do not always take the same interest in behalf of their clients as attorneys do who are retained."

in a position to take the former course. The more well-to-do attorneys are entirely
out of criminal practice, and as they lack experience in this work are virtually exempt
from assignment.[1]

In the light of reason and in the face of the evidence which has been adduced it
is clear that the assignment system in all but capital cases is unfair to the attorney,
unfair to the accused, and that it does not work.[2] The adverse report on the public
defender by the New York City Bar Association admits, "There is considerable force
in this contention" that "a poor man's defence is seriously hampered and often prevented by the failure of our laws to make any provision for the expense of investigating and obtaining evidence, or for compensation to assigned counsel, except in murder cases."[3] The adverse majority report of the New York County Lawyers' Association makes the statement that "juries are prone to extend sympathy to defendants
when it appears that counsel has been assigned to defend them."[4] As an argument,
this is an admission which gives the case away. As a fact, the jurors cannot know
whether counsel is retained or assigned except in rare instances. Once they did know,
for a frank advocate closed his address to the jury with: "This man has no lawyer. I
am only assigned counsel. I get no pay. My only reward is in heaven, and how can I
ever get there!"

Courts have made spasmodic efforts to whip the assignment system into shape by
enlisting the leaders of the bar, but the attempts have not succeeded and have been
short-lived. Assignments as a rule, except in murder cases, fall either to very young
members of the profession who are willing to serve for the sake of the experience, or to
a peculiar class which has arisen in response to our curious condition of affairs. However amusing to the bar the custom of assigning criminal defences to its most recent
accessions may be, the proceeding on its face is unfair. With legal education as it is,
the fledgling is little more qualified to defend than the prisoner is to conduct his own
defence. Every lawyer remembers his first cases. However great his zeal or untiring his
efforts, the inexperienced attorney labors under an enormous handicap. It cannot be
said that where liberty and disgrace are the stakes a contest between an experienced,
capable district attorney armed with all the resources of organized society and a young,
untried, resourceless attorney, generally embarrassed and often frightened, is a fair
trial.[5]

A consideration of the second class of attorneys to whom assignments fall brings

[1] See *Prospectus* of New York Voluntary Defenders Committee, published in the New York *Law Journal* for March
19, 1917, and also separately in leaflet form.

[2] See 5 Journal of Crim. L. 496, 927; 84 Independent (1915), 86, 94; *Prospectus* of the New York Voluntary Defenders Committee; Wood: *The Place of the Public Defender in the Administration of Justice* (1914), pages 5–8; Goldman: *The Public Defender*, chapter ii, The Injustice of the Assigned Counsel System; J. P. Schmitt: *The Duty of Society to the Poor before the Law* (1914); *Minority Report of the Public Defender Committee of the New York County
Lawyers' Association*, containing letters from judges and district attorneys.

[3] *Fifth Report of the Law Reform Committee of the New York City Bar Association* (1915), page 15.

[4] This statement in the *Majority Report* may be found in *Bench and Bar*, n.s., vol. ix, p. 313. It is quoted and pointed
out on page 18 of the *Minority Report*.

[5] Wood: *The Place of the Public Defender in the Administration of Justice*, page 6; 5 Journal of Crim. L. 496; Goldman: *The Public Defender*, page 20.

us to one of the sorest spots in all our administration of justice. Just as the neglect to appreciate the position of injured workmen brought in the contingent fee with its train of abuses, so the impossibility—to the honest lawyer—of the assignment system has given rise to the "professional" assigned counsel. Less polite terms, such as "jail lawyers," "shysters," and "Tombs runners," are often used as descriptive of this class. Every lawyer who has the slightest acquaintance with the criminal side knows that this condition exists; it is frankly admitted even by those who disbelieve in the necessity for a defender in criminal cases.[1]

These men have learned how to make a living out of assigned cases. On days when the grand jury returns its indictments, and the prisoners are brought to the rail to plead, these lawyers may be seen sitting within the bar enclosure expectantly waiting.[2] Sometimes they are easily identified by their "lean and hungry look." They are willing to take assignments because they have succeeded by intimidation, threats, extortion, and even worse, in putting the assignment system on a commercial basis. They know how to strip a prisoner and his relatives of every last cent. For one whose conscience permits him to magnify the crime, the sureness of conviction (unless he is paid to defend), the severity of the judge, and the horrors of prison, the process is simple and produces results. They have procured fees in devious ways, ranging from compelling the mortgage to some shark of all the household goods to forcing the prisoner's wife to sell herself on the streets. That this degradation exists in connection with the administration of criminal justice is common knowledge. And back of the professional assigned counsel have grown up runners and straw bondsmen, who have worked their way into the jails, corrupted officials, and preyed on the prisoners.[3]

A system of justice which entrusts one of its essential functions to such men is a bad system. If well paid, the professional assigned counsel undertakes a defence that knows no bounds of honesty or propriety. It is largely this sort of conduct which has forced prosecuting attorneys out of their impartial position into an attitude of hostility and distrust. In these cases it would be ridiculous to consider the lawyer as a minister of justice. If not paid, he is perfectly willing to betray his client by neglecting the case, or forcing him to plead guilty, or deserting him altogether.

The assignment of counsel in criminal cases, except when the offence charged is murder, has been a general failure. In part it has become a means of extortion. As a system, both in plan and operation, it deserves unqualified condemnation.

---

[1] See *Fifth Report of the Law Reform Committee of the New York City Bar Association*, page 14.

[2] *Prospectus* of New York Voluntary Defenders Committee, page 2.

[3] For statements as to the existing situation see Wood: *The Place of the Public Defender in the Administration of Justice;* Goldman: *The Public Defender*, page 19; *Report of the Massachusetts Commission on Immigration*, page 111; *Report of the Boston Municipal Court* (1916), page 15; Train: *The Prisoner at the Bar*, pages 72–77; *Report of the Chicago Bar Association* (1916), pages 29, 75 *et seq.;* 7 Journal of Crim. L. 596; *Final Report of the New York Commission to Inquire into Courts of Inferior Criminal Jurisdiction*, Assembly No. 54 *of* 1910, p. 70; Chicago *L. A. S. Bulletin*, 1912–13, No. 1, p. 7; 1 Kansas City L. A. R. 10; 27 N. Y. L. A. R. 34; 33 *Ibid.* 13; 35 *Ibid.* 11, 22; 15 N. Y. Legal Aid Rev. No. 3, p.3; *Proceedings of Fourth Convention of Legal Aid Societies*, page 20.

§ 5

Because of this breakdown the idea of a defender in criminal cases came into being and in the last few years has grown apace. Some attempt has been made to discredit *The Genesis* the plan by stamping it as visionary, as a prelude to complete social- *of the De-* ization of the bar, and as subversive of fundamental rights. The pro- *fender Plan* posal to establish a definite defender is not revolutionary, nor is the thought new.[1] It is not an untried experiment, but one that can be subjected to the test of accomplishment. The essential underlying ideas in the proposition are two: first, that the official or attorney responsible for the defence of indigent prisoners should be paid for his services and his expenses defrayed; second, that instead of having counsel changing from case to case, all the work should be centralized in the hands of one official or organization.

The criminal procedure of other countries shows that elsewhere much progress has been made in these two directions. For centuries in Scotland there has been an arrangement whereby the bar associations (both of advocates and solicitors) each year designate certain members to act for the poor, and to this group all assignments are made, thereby securing responsibility and a certain amount of centralization.[2] In New Zealand, the magistrate, if satisfied after examination of the poverty of the defendant, assigns him counsel from the list furnished by the Law Society. Such counsel receives the same fees as the local Crown solicitor for the prosecution, and is allowed money to defray expenses.[3] In Rome, there is a Society for the Gratuitous Defence of Accused Persons, composed of counsellors and attorneys, which was licensed as a charitable corporation in 1904 and represents the plan of a legal aid society for criminal cases.[4] In the Argentine Republic, the defence is entrusted to counsel appointed by the Supreme Court for life at a monthly salary; in Norway, the expense of counsel for the defence is borne by the state; and in Denmark, the court appoints for each case a prosecutor and defender, both being selected from a list of public attorneys appointed by the King.[5]

In America, the idea was urged at the end of the eighteenth century. Concurrently with the work of the constitutional conventions, which did much to put accused persons in a more favorable position, Benjamin Austin wrote:[6]

"As we have an Attorney General who acts in behalf of the State, it is proposed that the Legislature appoint another person (with a fixed salary) as Advocate

---

[1] 6 Journal of Crim. L. 559; *Fifth Report of the Law Reform Committee of the New York City Bar Association* (1915), page 2.

[2] Keedy: *Criminal Procedure in Scotland*, American Institute of Criminal Law and Criminology, *Bulletin No. XI* (1913), page 11.

[3] 48 Law Journal (1913), 538; 19 Virginia Law Register (1914), 788.

[4] Chicago *Legal Aid Review*, vol. v, No. 3 (October, 1908), p. 7.

[5] Goldman: *The Public Defender*, pages 9–13.

[6] Honestus: *Observations on the Pernicious Practice of the Law*, page 26.

General for all persons arraigned on criminal prosecutions; whose business should be to appear in behalf of all persons indicted by the State's attorney."

After a period of quiescence the idea was revived, and by 1896 legislation pointing toward public defence had been introduced in a dozen states.[1] Since then the movement has gone forward with accelerating velocity. In 1906, Arthur Train in his famous *The Prisoner at the Bar* wrote of the imperative need for relief in criminal cases and advocated an organization analogous to the legal aid society.[2] Two years later Dean Wigmore wrote, "Ultimately we shall have a public defender, appointed and paid by the state, precisely like the public prosecutor."[3] In 1909, the New York Legal Aid Society was petitioned to undertake the defence in criminal cases.[4] During 1909 and 1910, the proposition was urged in Cleveland by the Legal Aid Society.[5] A year or two later, a pamphlet[6] was prepared by J. P. Schmitt of the New York Bar strongly advocating the idea, which is of especial interest because it names Judge Latshaw of Kansas City as "one of the ablest advocates of the establishment by the State of a public defender." The significance of this statement lies in the fact that Judge Latshaw, as presiding Justice of the Kansas City Criminal Court, has done everything within his power to make the assignment system successful, and unquestionably in his court it has operated more satisfactorily than in the large majority of other courts. His endorsement, therefore, is that of one who has seen the assignment system at its best. In 1914, the Massachusetts Immigration Commission reported squarely for the public defender and proposed a bill.[7] From 1914 on, there has been a flood of articles in both legal and popular magazines, bar associations have appointed special committees to consider the plan,[8] and a large number of bills have been introduced into the various state legislatures.[9]

An examination of this literature reveals the fact that the defender idea, in last analysis, is nothing more revolutionary than a plea for the extension of what is best in the assignment system and for reorganization along modern lines of efficiency. As payment of a reasonable sum for services and expenses in murder cases has worked well, let it be extended to the other cases, for assignments in all cases rest on the same principle and are used to secure the same result. As centralization of work makes for economy, efficiency, and responsibility, let there be, instead of a shifting group of attorneys, one definite official or organization charged with the duty of defending the poor, to whom all assignments may be made.

[1] Fultz: *The Public Defender*, 31 American L. Rev. (1897) 393.
[2] Train : *The Prisoner at the Bar*, page 77.
[3] Chicago *Legal Aid Review*, vol. v, No. 3 (October, 1908), p. 7.
[4] 7 N. Y. Legal Aid Review, No. 2 (April, 1909), p. 1.   [5] 3 Cleveland L. A. R. 12 ; 4 *Ibid.* 12.
[6] *The Duty of Society to the Poor before the Law*. This is undated. It was published in 1914.
[7] *Report of the Massachusetts Commission on Immigration*, pages 112, 228.
[8] In addition to the two New York Committees whose reports have already been cited, see 1915 *Report of the Chicago Bar Association*, page 63 ; 1916 *Ibid.*, page 75; 1917 *Ibid.*, page 69.
[9] For a chronology of the legislation from 1913 to 1916 see Goldman : *The Public Defender*, pages 87–96. Since 1916 legislation has been introduced in Connecticut, Colorado, and Virginia.

§ 6

Provision for the first[1] defender in criminal cases was made by the Los Angeles County Charter[2] which, after adoption by the people and ratification by the legislature, went

The Defend- into effect in June, 1913. After civil service examinations, Walton J.
ers and Wood was selected for the position, and his office was opened on Jan-
their Work uary 7, 1914. In February, 1915, a defender in the municipal court was
provided in Portland, Oregon,[3] in July a defender in the superior court was established in Omaha;[4] and in November the city of Los Angeles created a police court defender.[5] In February, 1916, the city of Columbus under its Home Rule Charter made provision for a defender in the municipal court.[6] In New York a splendid organization under the name of the Voluntary Defenders Committee began work on April 2, 1917.

Under the impetus of the movement several states have passed laws entitled acts to establish " public" defenders, but the provisions only go half-way, so that it is somewhat inaccurate and rather misleading to consider them as establishing definite officials or organizations, though they are unquestionably steps in that direction. Thus Virginia in 1916 provided for the appointment of a defender in Richmond by the presiding justice, to hold office for two years, but to be paid no salary unless the city council should see fit to appropriate a sum for that purpose.[7] Such a law secures centralization, but still leaves the old difficulty of putting an unfair, if not impossible, burden on the attorney. The Connecticut legislature in 1917 authorized the judges of the superior court to appoint an attorney as defender for the term of court, his services and expenses to be paid out of public funds.[8] This makes possible adequate representation, but loses the advantages of permanent responsibility.

As the work in Omaha is relatively small, and as no reports have been issued, the test of the defender in the superior court on the basis of accomplishment is best made by examining the work done in Los Angeles and New York. An idea of the extent of the work is gained from the following record of cases undertaken: [9]

City	Period	Cases
Los Angeles	January 7, 1914–June 30, 1914	200
Los Angeles	July 1, 1914–June 30, 1915	450

[1] In 1911 Oklahoma provided its Commissioner of Charities with an official who was called a "public defender." The title was a misnomer. His function was not to conduct the defence of poor persons in criminal cases but, as defined by the statute, to "institute, prosecute, or defend any suit or action in any court on behalf of any minors, orphans, defectives, dependents, and delinquents." This office was abolished in 1914. See *Fifth Report of the Law Reform Committee of the New York City Bar Association* (1915), pages 4-8, 26.

[2] Los Angeles County Charter, § 23.   [3] City of Portland, Ordinance No. 30,107 of 1915.

[4] The law was passed by the Nebraska legislature in 1915. Session Laws of 1915, c. 165. In July, 1915, the Governor made an ad interim appointment. Since November, 1915, the office has been elective.

[5] City of Los Angeles, Ordinance No. 33,348, new series.

[6] *Proceedings of Fourth Conference of Legal Aid Societies*, page 135.

[7] Virginia, *Acts of Assembly of* 1916, c. 204. See also c. 373.   [8] Connecticut *Public Acts of* 1917, c. 225.

[9] The Los Angeles figures are taken from the annual reports to the County Board of Supervisors, the New York figures from the published report for April-May-June, 1917.

City	Period	Cases
Los Angeles	July 1, 1915–June 30, 1916	431
Los Angeles	July 1, 1916–June 30, 1917	522
New York	April 2, 1917–June 30, 1917	195

The large majority of these cases involve felony charges; a few matters of parole and pardon are included. Owing to the newness of the work, accurate or standardized classifications are lacking. By translating the figures into percentages, some idea of the nature of the work may be obtained. In Los Angeles, the work is divided as follows:[1] felony cases 64 per cent, non-support matters 19 per cent, juvenile offences 9 per cent, the remainder representing inebriety and insanity cases, paroles, and consultations. In New York, the felony cases are subdivided and are:[2] burglary 38 per cent, larceny 30 per cent, robbery 12 per cent, assault 8 per cent, homicide 3 per cent, and the balance miscellaneous crimes.

Of greater significance is the record as to what happened in these various cases. By keeping the figures in percentages a more accurate idea is gained.

Disposition	Los Angeles	New York
Pleas of guilty entered	68.0%	76.0%
Tried and convicted	13.0	2.6
Tried and acquitted	5.7	5.3
Jury disagreed	1.9	—
Case dismissed	11.0	5.3
Discharged on recognizance	—	10.5

After a plea or finding of guilt the defender's work still continues. When sentence is to be imposed, an excessive or unmerited prison term may constitute as great an injustice as an erroneous verdict. At this stage it is the duty of the defender to inform the court of all the surrounding circumstances, the condition and past history of the prisoner's life, to ask mercy where it is deserved, and to assist the court in arriving at a just disposition of the case.[3] In Los Angeles, of 258 persons who pleaded or were found guilty, probation was granted to 107; in New York, of 121 persons who came up for sentence, 46 were released under suspended sentences. People *v.* Harris is a California case which illustrates the need for adequate representation after determination of guilt, if the court is to be enabled to mete out justice.[4] Harris was arraigned as a burglar, pleaded guilty, and claimed that he had entered the house to secure food. The defender's investigation revealed that he had been unable to secure work, had applied to the chief of police and secured a job for one day, had nearly starved for two days before committing the crime, and that his record was clear. As he had not actually stolen anything, the question of restitution was not involved. He

---

[1] From the 1916 *Report* to the Board of Supervisors.

[2] *Report of Voluntary Defenders Committee, April–May–June,* 1917.

[3] Cf. *Prospectus* of the Voluntary Defenders Committee, page 3; *The Place of the Public Defender in the Administration of Justice,* page 10.

[4] This case is reported in *The Place of the Public Defender in the Administration of Justice,* page 11; see also 50 Review of Reviews (1914), 742.

was released on probation, which disposition was unquestionably fairer to him and more in the interests of society than a term in the state prison.

How far the defender will prevent the conviction of innocent persons cannot, in the nature of things, be answered with precision or by statistics. The question is based on an imaginary premise, for we rarely know whether the accused is guilty or innocent. In the more serious cases there are seldom impartial eye-witnesses to the act. Only the accused, and sometimes his accuser, has absolute knowledge, and the word of neither can be accepted as final. There is no standard of comparison, for it is impossible to determine how many verdicts of guilty are erroneously found under our present system. From time to time cases come to light where error appears to have been committed,[1] but this again is conjectural, for we lack even a court adjudication as a guide. We have no proceeding, such as that in France,[2] whereby a man once found guilty and his case closed can some time later secure a new trial and be pronounced innocent. With us, he may be pardoned or paroled, but never acquitted.

It is unquestionable that the existence of the defender must prevent some unjust convictions. We believe that by a jury verdict after a fair trial we approximate the truth as closely as is possible. The defender reduces the danger of error to a minimum because he guarantees a fair trial to every one.[3] This is the fact in Los Angeles. Although the defender instructs more of his clients to plead guilty than did assigned counsel under the former régime, and although he tries only cases where he has faith in the defendant, he has secured a substantially larger number of acquittals.[4]

The case for the defender rests primarily on the fact that such an office performs an essential function in the administration of justice more efficiently, more economically, and with all-round better results than any other plan. The increased efficiency can readily be appreciated. It is apparent that, if other factors are anywhere near even, the attorney who devotes all his time to criminal work is more familiar with the law and the details of procedure than the attorney who is occasionally assigned a case. Centralization of work makes specialization possible. The office learns the easiest method of conducting the work, it develops its own staff of investigators, and knows the proper authorities to consult as points arise. The defender becomes an expert in criminal law just as we have experts in patent, or mining, or corporation law. The result is the same as the greatly increased efficiency in caring for the civil cases of the poor which has resulted from centralizing all such work in a well-organized legal aid society.

A defender's office, whether supported by the state or by contributions, obviously costs more than assigned counsel who are paid nothing. If, however, adequate representation is to be had, assigned counsel must be paid and their expenses reimbursed,

[1] Of these the most recent is the Stielow case in New York, New York *Times* for May 12, 1918, page X 5. See also 106 Outlook (1914), 660; Boston *Herald* for October 10, 1917; and the statement of Judge Crist in 52 Ann. Am. Ac. Pol. & Soc. Science (1914), 179.

[2] For an explanation of the French review proceeding see Richard W. Hale: *The Dreyfus Story* (3d ed. 1899).

[3] *The Place of the Public Defender in the Administration of Justice*, page 13.

[4] The statistics are given *post*, page 123.

so that the true comparison to determine the more economical method is between the defender and paid assigned counsel. During its first ten months the expense of the criminal department of the Los Angeles office was about $8400; during 1915, $9400; and during 1916, $11,161.40.[1] The average cost per case was respectively $23.86, $20.88, and $21.38, or a flat average for three years in 1324 cases of $21.87 per case. In the superior criminal court for Milwaukee, where assigned counsel are paid, the expense over a period of four years ending 1913 averaged $4934.25 per year for 121 assignments each year, or an average cost per case of $40.86.[2] It is probably not inaccurate to estimate that to secure adequate representation for indigent prisoners by paying assigned counsel is twice as expensive as by the defender plan.

Undoubtedly a further saving accrues to the state from the greater despatch with which the defender conducts his cases, thereby reducing the enormous overhead expense of maintaining the judicial machinery. The defender has no outside conflicting engagements; both he and the district attorney are available for trial when reached. He saves time in not raising formal or interlocutory questions for purposes of delay. His position and his relationship with the district attorney are such that cases are tried to the merits rather than on technicalities. The delays which at times have amounted to an open scandal are not utilized by him, because that is not his duty. Mathematical demonstration is based on such involved computations that it would be an unjustified digression in this study. In his 1916 report to the Board of Supervisors, Mr. Wood undertakes an extended analysis of these figures and reaches the conclusion, which is warranted by the facts, that his department saves Los Angeles County, over and above all expenses, a sum of about two thousand dollars each year.[3]

Before passing to a consideration of some of the further particular results of the defender plan, it is necessary to advert briefly to certain questions about the conduct of the work which always obtrude themselves in the discussions. They are mostly philosophical or ethical in their nature, such as " Will the defender defend men whom he knows to be guilty?" and " Should he require defendants to take the stand against their will?" Such questions are admittedly difficult, but they are not peculiar to the defender in criminal cases. They are precisely those questions which confront all lawyers, and which the codes of ethics can answer only in generalities. So far as the lines of conduct are clear they will be better observed by the defender than has been the case with retained criminal lawyers. He may not be able to prevent his clients from using perjured defences, but certainly he will not be a party to manufacturing them. It is his duty, as it is that of every attorney,[4] to refuse to permit evidence, known to

[1] These figures are taken from the reports to the Board of Supervisors. They are not absolute because, as the public defender also does civil work, some administration expenses had to be prorated; but if they err, it is not on the side of underestimation.

[2] These figures were furnished by the Milwaukee Bar Association, and are published in *The Place of the Public Defender in the Administration of Justice*, page 18.

[3] See also 8 Journal of Crim. L. 230, 597.

[4] For a discussion see *In re* Palmieri, 162 N. Y. Supp. 799. The case was reversed on the facts but not on the law in 221 N. Y. 131.

him to be false, to be introduced before the court. Though he may believe the defendant guilty, it is his duty, under all codes of ethics, to represent the defendant at the
trial and give him an honest defence. Mere belief gives to the lawyer, acting under a
court assignment, no right to constitute himself judge and jury. If he has independent knowledge of guilt, it must be from facts which would make it his duty to be
witness and not advocate.

The most troublesome question is as to his duty when his knowledge comes from
his client's confession, which is privileged. In practice this issue has not presented
itself. In New York, all defendants who have admitted guilt have been persuaded to
be honest with the court and plead guilty.[1] When the problem does arise its solution
will have to be left to the individual conscience deciding on the facts of the particular case. It is the strongly prevailing present opinion of the bar that in such cases
it is the lawyer's duty to defend, refraining from introducing any false evidence, permitting no perjury known to him, but requiring the state to prove fairly the truth
of its charges. More instructive than any abstraction is the story of what actually
takes place. William Dean Embree, in his first report as counsel for the Voluntary
Defenders Committee, makes this frank statement of his experience in New York:[2]

> " Of the twelve cases actually tried there were eight acquittals and four con-
> victions; of the twelve men who went to trial all asserted their innocence to
> counsel. Of the eight acquitted we believed in the innocence of six. Of the four
> convicted two were clearly guilty: the evidence against the third was over-
> whelming; and the evidence against the fourth was not strong but he had all the
> subjective evidences of guilt."

§ 7

In addition to the essential features of the defender's work, which are to advise prisoners as to their legal rights, give them honest representation at the trial, and submit
Further Re- to the court the facts by which a just sentence may be fixed, there are
sults of the certain further important results. The whole tone of criminal trials
Defender has been raised. The superficial but common remark that it is absurd
for society to employ one man to convict and another to acquit has
been shown to be wholly beside the point. The administration of justice gives to each
merely the function of presenting his side of the case in the belief that in the clash
truth is best discerned. Instead of working at odds, it has been possible for the two
attorneys to work in harmony to a common end.[3]

In both Los Angeles and New York the defender has the cordial support of the dis-

---

[1] *Report of Voluntary Defenders Committee, April–May–June,* 1917, page 3. For the same experience in Los Angeles,
see Clary: *The Public Defender,* 7 Pomona College Quarterly, 49, 56.

[2] *Report of Voluntary Defenders Committee, supra.*

[3] See *Report of Voluntary Defenders Committee, April–May–June,* 1917, page 4; *The Office of Public Defender,*
page 16; *The Place of the Public Defender in the Administration of Justice,* pages 16–20; 107 Outlook (1914), 828.

trict attorney. The defence is conducted without resort to trickery or deliberate false-hood, and the knowledge of this fact permits the prosecution to adopt an equally high plane of conduct. This is well demonstrated by the attitude of the two officials in insanity cases. In murder cases the defence of insanity has at times been so much abused as to become a by-word. It has been said that alienists could be secured to testify to anything. Certain it is that the spectacle of six experts testifying for the government that the accused is wholly normal and an equal number swearing for the defence that he is violently insane has not been edifying. It has tended to turn a trial into a farce and, as developed by the press, it has thrown discredit on the entire administration of law. When such a case arose in Los Angeles and the defender interposed the defence of insanity, the prosecutor knew the claim was bona fide. The two officials asked the court to appoint three disinterested physicians as experts, and it was stipulated that no other alienists would be called at the trial.[1] Such a method is fair, economical, and calculated to dignify the whole tone of our criminal procedure.

That the defender tries his cases on their merits without resort to technical objections taken chiefly for purposes of delay, and that this course saves time and expense to the state without prejudice to the defendants, is borne out by such figures as are available. In such a field as this, it is, of course, impossible to attain mathematical precision; all that can be done is to submit facts from which reasonable inferences may be drawn. An idea as to the use of technicalities is gained by reviewing the work of the Los Angeles defender in 1914 in contrast with that of paid attorneys in Los Angeles during the same year.[2] The figures as to demurrers are striking.

	Paid Attorneys in 1914	The Defender in 1914
Number of felony cases	514	260
Number going to trial	147	58
Demurrers filed	40	2
Demurrers sustained	2	2
Motions to quash	21	0
Motions granted	2	0
Motions for new trials	27	6
Motions granted	1	0
Appeals taken	27	3

As to the time consumed in trials the same comparison shows the following facts:

	Paid Attorneys in 1914	The Defender in 1914
Number of trials	147	58
Number of days in trial	239	59
Average time in days per trial	1.626	1.017

[1] G. Smith: *Making the Law work Both Ways*, 84 Independent (1915), 94; 7 Journal of Crim. L. 597.
[2] These figures were submitted by Mr. Wood to the Board of Supervisors as a part of his report for 1916. They were subsequently published in 7 Journal of Crim. L. 230.

The time saved by the defender being on an average slightly more than half a day per case tried, it is easy to see that in the course of fifty or one hundred trials quite a saving is effected when it is remembered that the daily cost to the state of a criminal jury trial is from one hundred and fifty to two hundred dollars.[1]

That the defender's conduct is not a deprivation of substantial rights, and that it does not militate against the accused's chances to demonstrate innocence, is reasonably well borne out by the following table. The inference is warranted that persons represented by the public defender have fared as well as those represented by their own attorneys, and better than those represented by assigned counsel before the advent of the defender.

	Work of Assigned Counsel in 1913	Work of the Defender in 1914	Work of Paid Attorneys in 1914
Number of cases	115	260	514
Pleas of guilty entered	71	183	250
Their percentage	62%	70%	48%
Defendants given probation	31	87	154
Their percentage	28%	33%	30%
Number of trials	30	58	147
Per cent going to trial	26%	22%	28%
Verdicts of not guilty or disagreements	6	20	54
Their percentage	20%	34%	36%

The above table contains a clue to the greatest immediate benefit which the establishment of the defender has brought about. In Los Angeles he has taken over all work formerly done by assigned counsel, and yet it appears that in 1914 more than twice as many cases came to him than reached the assignment stage in 1913. The chief reason for this is that under the former system, as counsel were assigned only at the time of arraignment in the Superior Court, prisoners had no one to advise them while in jail, they faced the preliminary hearing without any one to represent them, and so very easily fell prey to the jail lawyers and their "runners" who infest the jails. The defender has fought fire with fire. Each day a deputy visits the jails, cards stating that the defender is available for advice or help are in the cells, prisoners pass the word around, and the turnkeys are willing to forward notes. The jailers have coöperated because when the chance is given them they prefer to recommend the unfortunates in their custody to an honest attorney rather than to sharpers.

As the influence of the defender increases, that of the jail lawyer wanes. In Los Angeles that species of lawyer has been eliminated.[2] It has always been recognized that the establishment of an organization for public defence was certain to have this effect,[3] but the importance of the result has not been fully appreciated. It is no ex-

---

[1] Mr. Wood estimates the cost in Los Angeles at $200 per day. The Massachusetts Industrial Accident Board in its report for 1914–15 (Massachusetts, *Public Document No.* 105 of 1916, p. 71) estimates the cost of a civil jury trial in Massachusetts at $248.89 per day.

[2] *The Place of the Public Defender in the Administration of Justice*, page 14; 7 Journal of Crim. L. 595.

[3] Cf. *Fifth Report of the Law Reform Committee of the New York City Bar Association*, page 14.

aggeration to say that if no other reason existed, the defender plan would be more than justified by its success in stamping out these serious evils and thereby protecting from these "shysters" and "jail lawyers" not only the prisoners but the administration of justice itself.

One further result deserves mention here. The defender in criminal cases will be able to accumulate a fund of experience and data which will cover new fields and complement the facts gathered by probation staffs and the courts themselves, all of which will be invaluable in pointing the way to the betterment of our criminal procedure and our treatment of the criminal.[1] This opportunity is similar to that afforded by the legal aid organizations, so that its signifiance may conveniently be treated more fully in a later section devoted to this subject.[2]

§ 8

Whether or not the defender plan ought to be extended to the lower courts is a question that does not admit of easy answer. As to that part of the work of inferior crim-

The Defenders in the Lower Courts

inal tribunals which relates to preliminary arraignments and probable cause hearings there may be need of a defender, but he should be the same official who works in the superior court. This original jurisdiction of the police and municipal courts includes felonies, and the proceedings constitute the first stage in all serious criminal charges. If the defender is later to be called upon to represent the accused in the superior court, he clearly ought to have the right to appear at every step in the procedure, and therefore as to this limited field there may be need of his services. Certainly the Los Angeles charter provision which precludes the defender from acting in the lower courts in such instances is a mistake.[3]

As to misdemeanors and all other cases over which the lower courts have final jurisdiction (subject only to appeal), by having power themselves to impose a fine or prison sentence, the situation is entirely different. Many of the reasons for the defender in the superior courts do not obtain in the inferior courts. Very often there is no prosecutor, or if there is, his work is purely formal, so that there is little or no inequality in not furnishing counsel to the accused. Formal trials are the exception. The procedure is simple: in the absence of counsel the judge follows the rules of evidence only loosely, and generally the judge himself conducts the proceedings, bringing out the facts on both sides. It is possible for the defendant to tell his own story in his own words. As to many of the offences which bulk large in the work of the lower courts, such as drunkenness, street-walking, selling without a license, vagrancy, and overspeeding, the arresting officer is himself the witness and, except in those courts

---

[1] See Introduction by Dean Wigmore in Train: *The Prisoner at the Bar* (2d ed.), page xvii.

[2] Chapter XXII, *Legal Aid and the Community*, § 3, Preventive Law, page 214.

[3] *The Place of the Public Defender in the Administration of Justice*, page 20.

where the dangerous practice obtains of making the police act as prosecuting attorneys, which at once forces them into an aggressive and partisan attitude, such evidence is generally free from the taint of spite or malice or revenge which may characterize the evidence in complaints sworn out by private parties.

On the other hand, it can properly and with much force be urged that these are the courts of the people, that it is here that the great majority of persons have their only contact with the administration of justice, and that in accordance with the treatment they receive—particularly is this true of the immigrant population—will they judge our institutions.[1] Further, as to cases where representation is necessary, the only possibility is to have a defender because the inferior courts never have exercised the power of assigning counsel. Finally, it is truthfully said that the evil of jail lawyers, "runners," unreliable interpreters, and preying bondsmen, exists in its most malignant form in connection with the inferior courts.[2]

There is need for some one to assist the foreigner, the ignorant, and the terrified, if their side of the story is to be fairly heard. Undoubtedly a responsible intermediary who talked with the prisoners before their cases were reached could present the facts more intelligently and with a great saving of time to the court. It does not follow, however, that such a person must be an attorney. As in the small claims court, the attorney's function in the inferior criminal court is slight. There are few questions of law, the facts are generally simple, and the procedure is informal. It is likely that so far as representation is concerned, all that is needed or desirable could be secured through the probation officers. Much of the work done by the existing police court defenders finds its counterpart in other states in the work of the probation staff. After its study of the Columbus Municipal Court, the Bureau of Municipal Research recommended that the office of defender be abolished on the ground that the work was a duplication of that of the probation officer.[3] In Cleveland an intermediate plan was tried. The Legal Aid Society asked Newton D. Baker, then City Solicitor, to appoint a defender for the police court. It was arranged with the court that if parties needed or asked for advice, they might be assigned attorneys from the civil side of the City Attorney's office.[4]

The best examples of defenders in the lower courts are to be found in the police court of the city of Los Angeles, and in the municipal court of Portland, Oregon. For nearly a year the work was performed in Portland by a voluntary committee, until in 1915, by ordinance, the position was made official.[5] David Robinson was appointed as defender and began work in March, 1915. No reports, other than monthly state-

[1] Cf. *Final Report of the (New York) Commission to Inquire into Courts of Inferior Criminal Jurisdiction, Assembly No. 54 of 1910*, page 86; 9 Legal Aid Review, No. 2, p. 5.

[2] *Final Report of the (New York) Commission*, etc., page 70; *Report of the Massachusetts Commission on Immigration* (1914), *House Document No. 2300*, page 107; *Report of the Boston Municipal Court* for 1915, page 15; Train: *The Prisoner at the Bar*, page 74.

[3] *Report of the New York Bureau of Municipal Research to the City Council of Columbus*, dated January 31, 1917. See page 28.

[4] Baker: *Police Court Prosecutions and a Public Defender*, 2 American City (1910), 266.

[5] Ordinance No. 30,107 of 1915. To be appointed by the Council to hold office at its pleasure at an annual salary of $1800.

ments to the Mayor, have been made. From an examination of such reports and the files the following facts appear: From May 1, 1915, to December 31, 1915, 1998 cases were undertaken, and during the year 1916 the number was 1363. The great decrease was due to the prohibition law which took effect January 1, 1916. An analysis of 3077 of these cases (May, 1915, to November, 1916) shows the following results:

No. of Cases	Discharged	Held for Grand Jury	Punished by Fine or Imprisonment	Continued for Sentence[1]
3077	997	79	544	1457

In Los Angeles the great success of the defender for the county led to the passage of an ordinance on November 18, 1915, creating the position of city police court defender.[2] James H. Pope qualified under the civil service law and began his work February 14, 1916. Up to November 1, 1916, there had been 883 cases. No analysis of these figures is available.[3]

The methods employed by both officials are nearly identical and may be stated together. Neither attempts to represent all persons, but confines his activities to those who are too poor to engage their own counsel. Those who have obtained bail are considered able to pay fees. In Portland, there is the further precaution of requiring an affidavit of poverty; in Los Angeles, the prisoner's property slip, made out by the jailer, affords the basis for decision. Each night the jailer makes out a list of persons who have been arrested and transmits it to the clerk, who checks off those released on bail. Early each morning the defender receives this list from the clerk and then goes through the jail, hearing each man's story, advising him how to plead, and often further advising him as to his future conduct. As the cases are called in court the defender again suggests as to the plea, states the facts briefly to the judge,[4] and suggests a proper disposition. If the plea has been not guilty, the process is nearly the same. There is a marked absence of formal trials, of cross examination, argument, and the like. It is for these reasons that an adequate probation staff ought to be able to perform the necessary work as well as an attorney.

Many of the same advantageous results which have already been noted in connection with the defender's work in the superior courts can be observed in the inferior courts. There has been a saving of time with its consequent economy. Prisoners are properly advised, their cases are brought promptly before the courts so that they are not unnecessarily detained in confinement, trials are more honestly conducted, for the defender is never party to perjured or manufactured defences, and by reason of this the relationship with the prosecuting officer is one of cordial coöperation. Finally, the jail lawyers with their runners and bondsmen have been practically eliminated.

---

[1] Continued for sentence is analogous to release on probation under a suspended sentence.

[2] Ordinance No. 33,348, new series. The office was later put under civil service. The appropriation for the first year was $2710. The defender's salary is $1680.

[3] The only report is a typewritten statement made to the Mayor on September 20, 1916. This deals with the work generally.

[4] See 84 Independent (1915), 95, 99.

All of these results, except possibly the last, can be secured by an adequate probation staff.[1] As the probation branch is indispensable to every criminal court, the sounder line of development would seem to be to entrust this service to the probation officers rather than to duplicate the work and create new officials. There remains the great and growing evil of the jail lawyer. Thus far it has not been met by any agency as successfully as by the defender. There is not at present sufficient experience to warrant a final statement. If, however, after intelligent coöperation between court, jailer, and probation staff, the mischief caused by the shyster is not abated, there will exist an irrefutable argument for establishing defenders in the municipal and police courts.

§ 9

The defender in criminal cases, whether publicly or privately supported, is unquestionably the best immediate method for securing freedom and equality of justice to poor persons accused of serious crimes. It is a complete solution of the difficulties in the existing administration of the criminal law which have placed poor prisoners at a serious disadvantage, and it remedies some of the most glaring abuses which have brought the criminal law into disrepute.

Future Development of the Defender

The plan has gained great popular favor. An interesting reflection of this is to be found in recent political campaigns in which district attorneys have asserted that, if elected, they would themselves be public defenders.[2] Five years ago the phrase would have been meaningless. The idea gives promise of rapid development. Since 1914 it has spread very generally throughout the country, and has made more headway in legislatures and in the community at large than the proposed reforms in court reorganization and simplification of procedure. In three years it has made more impression on the public mind than its more ancient ally, the legal aid society, has been able to make in forty years.

It is not unlikely that the superior court defender will become recognized in the near future as an integral part in the administration of criminal justice. In the east the initiative is more likely to come from private than from public sources. If the legal aid societies possess the requisite vision and strength, they may be expected to extend their work into the criminal field and establish departments which will afford to the poor, who are accused of serious offences, the services of a skilful, well-equipped, and honest defender.

---

[1] After an examination of the Women's Night Court in New York, where there is an excellent probation service, made by Mr. Embree, counsel for the Voluntary Defenders Committee, and the writer, and after consultation with Judge Frothingham of that court, it seemed evident that there was no need for a public defender.

[2] During the 1916 November election the hoardings in Denver carried this advertisement: " Vote for Foley for District Attorney — A Public Defender not a Persecutor."

CHAPTER XVI

LEGAL AID ORGANIZATIONS

The purpose of this Society shall be to render legal aid, gratuitously if necessary, to all who may appear worthy thereof, and
who are unable to procure assistance elsewhere.[1]

THE last and the greatest remedial agency is the legal aid society. Though it stands as an extra-legal institution, unrecognized by the traditional administration of justice, it has done more to place the poor in a more equal position before the law than all the other agencies combined. For years it was alone in combating the denial of justice. Now it is supported and aided by the recent development of the other agencies which have already been described.

The legal aid organization is not a thing unto itself; its tremendous importance consists of the direct part which it takes in the administration of justice. For this reason the only true definition of legal aid work is in terms of relationship to the administration of justice and to the various remedial agencies. Only such a definition can ascertain the principles common to all legal aid organizations, prevent our being led astray by apparent differences in work in different cities, and establish a standard by which we can gauge the success and failure of legal aid work as far as it has developed.

A summarization of what has gone before brings us to a precise definition. We have seen that our present inequalities are the result, not of an unfair substantive law, but of the procedure which we have inherited and built up for administering that law. We have seen that the defects in the machinery of justice which cause the denial of justice to the poor are delays, court costs, and the expense of engaging counsel. We have seen that delays and procedural difficulties will be eliminated in due course as the reorganization of courts and simplification of procedure makes its inevitable headway, and that costs can be taken out of the way whenever we have the courage and will to do it. We know that the great difficulty, the difficulty which is inherent in our system of administering justice and cannot easily be done away with, is the expense of engaging counsel for advice or assistance in litigation.

We have examined eight groups of agencies and methods which are attempting the equalization of justice by solving, in one way or another, the problem of the expense of counsel. Discarding the system of assignment of counsel, which has amounted to little and which contains but small promise, we have found that the four types of cases which make up the chief burden of the poor are beginning to be taken care of through six agencies. Through the small claims court wage claims and miscellaneous small cases are beginning to receive suitable treatment. By conciliation and arbitration a start has been made in the employment of a new method of caring for

---

[1] Constitution of the New York Legal Aid Society, Article I, § 2.

small claims and domestic disputes. In the domestic relations courts a vast number of domestic difficulties are securing proper disposition. Under the administrative tribunals great progress has been made in the settlement and adjustment of suits growing out of industrial accidents. From administrative officials much legal advice is obtainable, and in a few instances direct assistance in litigation, notably in connection with wage claims, is available. Analysis has shown that, on the one hand, the agencies are capable of large expansion both through their adoption in more jurisdictions and through an increase in their functions; and that, on the other hand, they are not and probably never will be complete solutions for the difficulty of the expense of the attorney.

As to all cases in certain fields of the law and as to certain types of cases in all fields, the attorney is a necessity. To secure equality of justice in such cases, the only possible solution is to supply the attorney gratuitously to poor persons. Thus in the field of criminal law there is no possibility of eliminating the attorney, and the problem of how best to supply him is answered by the seventh agency considered,—the defender in criminal cases. What is true of the criminal law is equally true of great parts of the civil law. The only possible solution is to supply counsel, and here the legal aid society makes its appearance.

The function of the legal aid society is to furnish counsel to poor persons; to undertake their cases when no other assistance elsewhere is available. This definition fixes the relationship between legal aid organizations and the other remedial agencies and the entire administration of justice. Before these other agencies came into being the whole burden was thrust on legal aid organizations, to be met by them as best they could. Their load is lightened and their particular work changed as the other remedial agencies are established and developed. The Boston Legal Aid Society must supply attorneys for miscellaneous small suits in the Municipal Court; the Cleveland Legal Aid Society can refer such causes to the Small Claims branch of the Municipal Court. The Kansas City Legal Aid Bureau must be prepared to undertake proceedings to collect wages; in Boston they need merely to be referred to the State Board of Labor and Industries. While the work varies radically from city to city, the function everywhere is the same. A steady change in the cases requiring assistance from legal aid organizations is inevitable because of the part they play. As the domestic relations courts widen their functions and take over illegitimacy and separate maintenance, such cases will disappear from the legal aid offices; and as the industrial accident boards become less able to take care of disputed compensation cases, injured workmen will appear in increasing numbers among the legal aid applicants.

If, in the language of the day, we conceive of organized society at war with the inequalities in the administration of justice, then the first six agencies—small claims courts, conciliation, arbitration, domestic relations courts with their probation staffs, administrative tribunals, and administrative officials—constitute the first line of attack. It is for the legal aid organizations, including the defenders in criminal cases, to constitute the second line, to sweep up all that may evade or break through the first line, and to go forward on the points which the first line cannot reach.

Having, in this general way, defined the relationship of legal aid work to the other agencies and its relation to the entire administration of justice, we now turn to a more detailed examination of how legal aid organizations came into being, of what they have accomplished, of their present position, their future, and of their effect on the law, on the bar, and in the community.

PART III
LEGAL AID WORK IN THE UNITED STATES

Chapter XVII

ORIGIN AND DEVELOPMENT OF LEGAL
AID ORGANIZATIONS

> The founders of the Legal Aid Society, whose original intention it was to pro-
> tect a certain class of poor immigrants from the rapacity of runners, ticket
> speculators and the like, certainly had no idea of the majestic proportions
> which their enterprise would assume. Like an avalanche it has gathered strength
> and increased in proportions as it advanced. ARTHUR V. BRIESEN.[1]

§ 1

LEGAL aid work of an informal, unorganized, individual sort has always existed. The first legal aid work in the United States was undoubtedly done in the first law office established in the American colonies. The various charity organizations,

Preliminary

some of which were established early in our history, have always done a measure of legal aid work as the need arose by calling upon some individual attorney to give legal assistance in a particular case. In a real sense the service rendered, whether by law office or charity, may be called legal aid. Such work by the individual lawyer is still to be found in any smaller city or town, and many of the charities, even in the larger cities, still continue to give legal as well as material assistance.

All work of this nature, though it must be recognized, lies beyond the scope of our enquiry. Our concern is with the administration of justice as it affects the poor, with agencies which are playing a part in the betterment of that administration, and with any movement that seems to offer some solution for the existing denial of justice. Informal and individual legal aid work, from its nature, is transitory and fleeting. However much it may have aided the individual poor person here and there, it failed to affect the administration of justice, it offered nothing permanent on which to build, and when the enormous demand for legal assistance came with immigration and the growth of great cities in the last quarter of the nineteenth century, it collapsed. Then arose organized legal aid work which, being possessed of permanence and rapidly taking on the character of an institution, steadily grew in every direction and dimension. Our concern is with this organized legal aid movement because it offers one great solution for the inherent difficulty of the expense of counsel, and because it bids fair to exercise a profound effect upon the administration of justice itself. For our purposes, the distinction between individual and organized legal aid work may be likened to the difference between the personal charity work of a physician for individual patients and the establishment of hospitals and dispensaries. Or, to come more nearly to our own subject, judges have from time to time tried to adjust small disputes by conciliation or informal hearing, but such isolated instances

---

[1] From the *Twenty-fourth Annual Report of the President of the New York Legal Aid Society*, 24 N. Y. L. A. R. 5.

left no impression on the administration of justice and afforded no solution for the general problem of securing justice in a multitude of small matters. It was only the organized small claims court that had the power to alter the course of judicial administration and to offer a general solution for the general problem.

We have already seen that legal aid work consists of giving legal advice and legal assistance in negotiation and litigation to poor persons, without cost to them or at a minimum cost which they can afford, in matters where no other assistance is available. In the light of modern developments this may be spelled out to mean the furnishing of lawyers in cases where lawyers are necessary if justice is to be done, and where no other agency, as the state or the court, provides the attorneys or persons to perform the attorney's functions. A legal aid organization is simply an organization which has undertaken that responsibility. The organization may be a corporation, or a voluntary association, or a department of a larger organization such as a bar association, a municipality, or an organized charity; but there is implied something more than individual effort, there must be some elements of association, combination, and coöperation, through which are secured continuity and permanence.

As the primary object of this study is to set out the functional importance of the various agencies which are equalizing the administration of justice, the history of these movements is of importance only as it makes clearer the part which each plays or may be expected to play. With over forty legal aid organizations in the United States, a volume could be written on the one subject of their history. All that can be attempted here is to present the broad outlines of the rise and development of legal aid organizations in order that from such a background the work itself and its possibilities may be better appreciated and estimated.

§ 2

Organized legal aid work began its history in the city of New York in the year 1876. For nearly a century there had been in that city an association called The German Society, which had an especial interest in German immigrants. *The First Period 1876-99* Following the Civil War there was a great German emigration, and to meet the legal questions which were constantly arising, particularly with reference to the protection of newly arrived immigrants, The German Society appointed a special legal committee. By 1875 the burden of legal work had become so great that it was suggested by Sigismund Kaufman and Charles Hauselt that a separate society be formed.[1]

Accordingly, early in the year 1876 a group of American citizens of German birth and members of The German Society in New York met at the law office of Edward Salomon, an ex-governor of Wisconsin, for the purpose of forming an association, and on March 8, 1876, their organization was incorporated under the name

[1] Holls: *The Legal Aid Society*, 8 Charities Review (1898), 15.

of "Der Deutsche Rechtsschutz Verein." Their purpose, as the original constitution stated,[1] was "to render legal aid and assistance, gratuitously, to those of German birth, who may appear worthy thereof, but who from poverty are unable to procure it." Ex-Governor Salomon was elected president, offices were opened at 39 Nassau Street, and an attorney, who had his own law practice, was paid a salary to take charge of the cases of the new organization.[2]

This was not a legal aid society within the modern meaning of that phrase. It existed to protect German immigrants from the rapacity of runners, boarding-house keepers, and a miscellaneous coterie of sharpers who found that the trustful and bewildered newcomers offered an easy prey. The purpose was relatively a narrow one.[3] There was no conception of furnishing legal assistance in general, of preventing injustice except in this limited field, or of taking any part in the administration of justice. The organization was proprietary in its nature; it was supported entirely by The German Society, by German merchants, and by persons interested in assisting Germans. At the outset there was no vision of the future. There was not even an intention to try to develop into a general and far-reaching organization. But it was a beginning which was strong enough to weather the distrust and jealousy at first manifested by the legal profession,[4] and which did in fact, albeit unconsciously, lay a firm foundation for the great development that was to come.

The organization was made efficient and businesslike. Careful records of the cases and of sums collected for clients were made, and excellent reports, written in German, were published each year.[5] In 1879 the directors voted that on all collections of over twenty dollars the Society should charge a commission of ten per cent, and in 1881 the charge was extended to all collections above ten dollars. It is interesting to note that at the very outset two types of cases clearly predominated. Out of 212 cases received in 1876, there were 113 claims for wages and 51 matters concerning domestic relations; and in 1877, out of 750 cases, 281 related to wages and 61 to domestic difficulties. Until 1890 the work grew steadily, but it remained routine in nature.

At about this same time a similar but entirely independent and unrelated movement was taking place in Chicago. As in New York the frauds perpetrated on immigrants called attention to their legally defenceless condition and led to the formation of a society to help them, so in Chicago the great number of seductions and debaucheries of young girls under the guise of proffered employment aroused the women of the city[6] and led, through the instrumentality of the Chicago Woman's Club, to the formation in 1886 of an organization which was the next year incorpo-

---

[1] Constitution of 1877, Article I, § 2.

[2] *History of the New York Legal Aid Society* (1912), page 4.

[3] 11 N. Y. Legal Aid Rev. No. 2, p. 2.

[4] Holls: *The Legal Aid Society*, 8 Charities Review (1898), 15, 17.

[5] The first report was published February 28, 1877.

[6] Conover: *The Chicago Protective Agency*, 8 Charities Review (1898), 287.

rated under the title of The Protective Agency for Women and Children.[1] Like the New York society, there was no vision of a general rendering of legal assistance to poor persons. By force of circumstances, however, the work did outgrow its original limits, and although still confined to assistance for women and children, it was extended to include all legal difficulties presented by such persons. From an extremely small beginning of about six cases a month, the work rapidly grew to formidable proportions. In 1890 there were 1455 cases, of which 349 were claims for wages. It was from the outset the policy of this Protective Agency to charge no fees of any description. Careful annual reports were published.

In 1888, on the initiation of the Ethical Culture Society of Chicago, there was established in that city a second organization, which was named the Bureau of Justice.[2] This was in fact the first true legal aid organization. It undertook to supply legal services in all cases to all persons, regardless of nationality, race, or sex. It was in no sense proprietary; its leadership, control, and support were not derived from any particularly defined group, and its income came from charitably disposed persons in the general public. It adopted the policy of charging some fees to its clients. By reason of its wider scope, its work increased by leaps and bounds, so that by 1890 it was thrice the size of its sister agency. According to the third annual report for the period March 1, 1890, to March 1, 1891, the cases numbered 3783, and the sum of $10,658.45 was collected for clients. Had the society in New York continued along its original lines, the leadership in the legal aid movement would have devolved on the Bureau of Justice, but even while these twin Chicago organizations were making their first brave experiments, changes destined to affect profoundly the whole future development of legal aid work everywhere were quietly taking place in New York.

Emerson has said, "Every institution is but the lengthened shadow of some one man," and nowhere is the truth of the statement more clearly illustrated than in the relationship of legal aid work to Arthur v. Briesen. No history of legal aid work could be complete if it failed to pay tribute to his courageous vision, his faithful leadership, and his untiring labors in bringing justice within the reach of the poor, whom he knew and loved. Mr. Briesen was not one of the original incorporators of the New York Legal Aid Society. His connection with the work began in 1884, when his name appeared on the slender membership roll. During 1889 he was a member of the law committee, and at the annual meeting he was elected president for the year 1890, a position to which he was annually reëlected during the space of twenty-six years, and which was terminated only by his resignation so that, in his own words, "younger and stronger hands might take the helm."

To understand the situation which confronted the new president, it is necessary to review what the Society had accomplished up to 1890. The work had gone forward steadily, increasing from 212 cases in 1876 to 3413 in 1882, and remaining nearly

---

[1] *Report of the Proceedings of the Fourth Conference of Legal Aid Societies* (1916), page 137.

[2] Wigmore: *Additional History of Legal Aid Work*, 1 Mass. L. Quarterly (1916), 288.

constant at about that figure through the next seven years. Monies collected for clients had steadily increased from $1000 in 1876 to $12,460.71 in 1882 and $20,104.20 in 1889. The Society had had great difficulty in collecting money for itself. Its total expenses had been nearly $38,000, of which The German Society had contributed one-fourth. The balance, except for a small income from fees, was contributed by a few members, whose number averaged sixty-four. During these thirteen years the Society had six times closed the year with a deficit. Until 1890 all the annual reports were published in German, and from a statistical table showing the nationalities of applicants, published for the first time in 1889, it appears that of the 3500 clients in that year 2438 were natives of Germany, 346 were Russian Poles, 148 were Russians, 147 were Hungarians, and 31 were Americans.

Mr. Briesen not only breathed new life into this wavering institution, but he brought to it a new vision of its wider usefulness. From his own struggles he knew, and as he looked about him he saw, that injustice was not confined to Germans. He saw that all nationalities, even native-born Americans, were daily obliged to lose clear legal rights which they had no means to enforce. It was his creed that as all these persons, whatever the country of their birth, had come to America to be Americans, so the legal aid society should extend to all of them, irrespective of nationality, its protection and guidance up to the furthest limit of its ability. By such stars was the true course of legal aid work finally charted.

He at once set about to put these changes into effect. The annual report for 1890, which was printed in German, following the usual custom, he translated and republished in English. By the act of translation the somewhat forbidding and formidable title which the Society had borne was presented to the public in the more understandable form of "The German Legal Aid Society." Under the charter provisions persons other than Germans had no right to assistance, and legally the Society had no authority to expend its funds in their behalf, but by 1889, such persons finding no relief in the courts or from law offices were seeking the Society's help in large numbers, and, as Mr. Briesen wrote in his report,[1] "without special instructions, the attorney, following the dictates of humanity, found himself obliged to extend his field of operations to all sufferers." To regularize this situation and in accordance with his belief, he persuaded the directors to change the constitution by omitting the words "of German birth." Inasmuch as the policy of charging small fees had for some time been determined upon, a further minor change of qualification was made. The amended purpose clause, as adopted in 1890, read:[2] "Its object and purpose shall be to render legal aid and assistance, gratuitously if necessary, to all who may appear worthy thereof and who, from poverty, are unable to procure it." This was the language of a real legal aid organization; but the change was not made without a struggle. Many of the directors did not understand Mr. Briesen's belief; The German Society withdrew its support; but his faith was rewarded, for by the end of the year

[1] 15 N. Y. L. A. R. 3.   [2] Constitution of 1890, Art. I, § 2.

1890 the Society's support had widened and its membership increased from 81 to 170 subscribers. Mr. Briesen saw that the Society not only had a direct contribution to make to the administration of justice, but that it stood in a peculiar relationship to the bar. He spread the knowledge of this new organization among lawyers, and from them he asked assistance. For the first time the bar began to get an inkling of what its purposes were, and slowly, by dint of much persuasion, the larger firms were enrolled as members. In the report for 1890 a table was submitted, showing the size of the claims collected for clients, which serves as an interesting reflection of the character of the work. Of 507 claims collected, 350 were under ten dollars, 127 were between ten and fifty dollars, 13 were between fifty and one hundred dollars, and 17 ranged upwards to about five hundred dollars.

Although from its inception the Society was obliged to face much criticism and indifference, its first enemy appeared in 1893 in the guise of a fraudulent legal aid society. Such an attack was inevitable, and it was the precursor of similar attacks, which were repeated in following years until stopped by legislation.[1] As the Society built up its reputation for honesty and square dealing, the phrase "legal aid" came to carry a very clear connotation of safety and relief to the minds of the poor. The shyster element at the bar was not slow to see that there was a magic in the words which could be capitalized into a cash value. A number of associations, carrying the phrase "legal aid" as a part of their title, sprang up, and like wolves in sheep's clothing went about seeking whom they might devour. It was a difficult moment for this relatively new and generally unrecognized Society. Had it failed to stand its ground, its fair name, its greatest asset, and its only way of reaching the poor, would have been lost and "legal aid society" would have become a term of obloquy even as it has in England. The directors fought this dangerous situation by seeking relief in the courts, and it is to the credit of the judges that they perceived the true condition and protected the Society in its title by enjoining the use of the words "legal aid" for any purpose calculated to deceive or mislead the poor.[2]

In 1894 the legal aid idea took root in Jersey City.[3] No definite organization emerged for many years and the work remained small in scope, but the circumstances of its establishment reveal how local the legal aid plan was even after eighteen years and how slowly it made headway. Although Jersey City is directly across the Hudson River from New York, and although the society in New York had existed since 1876, the Jersey City organization was created in entire ignorance of its near neighbor. It was modeled after the "Poor Man's Lawyer" at the Mansfield Settlement House in London, which was known to the founder of the Whittier House Settlement in Jersey City because she had lived in London. For years the two kindred efforts existed side by side, each without knowledge of the other.

---

[1] See 18 N. Y. L. A. R. 7; 23 *Ibid.* 9; 28 *Ibid.* 8; 31 *Ibid.* 16; 32 *Ibid.* 11; 6 N. Y. Legal Aid Rev. No. 3, p. 19.

[2] For the injunction in the case of The Legal Aid Society *v.* The Coöperative Legal Aid Society, see 28 N.Y.L.A.R. 8.

[3] Cf. *Twenty-second Annual Report of the Whittier House Association* (Jersey City, 1916), page 14.

Several noteworthy developments took place in New York during 1896. For the first time a retaining fee of ten cents was asked of applicants who were able to pay that amount. The directors expressed their purpose to be that "of removing the sting of charity from the applicants, and of making the client feel that the assistance rendered was in the nature of a regular business transaction."[1] This fee has been continued ever since. The Society's internal organization was placed on a better basis. Originally, the attorney had received a salary and was allowed to engage in private practice. Later, the attorney was given a lump sum, out of which he engaged all his assistants and paid all expenses, retaining the balance plus a proportion of the fees as his salary. In 1896 the Society placed the attorney on a definite salary, required all his time, and itself paid all expenses under a budget. This plan was adhered to, and served as a precedent for other organizations in later years as to the proper relationship between a society and its attorney. Most important, the idea of Americanizing the Society, which Mr. Briesen had steadily advocated,[2] was finally consummated by a charter amendment under which the Society dropped its German title and became simply "The Legal Aid Society."[3] By this act renewed emphasis was placed on the fact that the organization offered its assistance to all persons irrespective of nationality and, reciprocally, it asked for wider support from all persons. This was not promptly forthcoming, but it managed by diligent work to increase its income sufficiently to meet its fast rising tide of applications.

The records show a decrease in cases in 1897, but this is due only to a change in the recording system whereby advice cases were not listed or recorded.[4] In fact, the increase was so great that in 1899 it was found necessary to open three branch offices:[5] a Seamen's Branch, which instantly took a commanding position and proved to be a very haven of refuge for "poor Jack;" a branch in the University Settlement, which later became the East Side Branch; and a Women's Branch, which later moved and became the Up-Town Branch.

When the nineteenth century drew to its close, the idea of organized legal aid work had been in existence for twenty-four years, and yet it had taken root in only three American cities. Of its span of life from birth up to the present moment, more than half had passed with a record of achievement of only three legal aid organizations established, whose combined work in 1889 aggregated only 10,425 cases. Each was struggling with financial difficulties, and the general outlook was by no means hopeful. Perhaps the most encouraging fact that appeared at the close of this first era was the statistical record, which proved that Mr. Briesen's belief that Americans needed assistance as well as Germans, that citizens as well as immigrants were the victims of injustice, was absolutely correct and that his desire to make the legal aid society

---

[1] *History of the New York Legal Aid Society*, page 15.
[2] See his statement in 1891 in 16 N. Y. L. A. R. 14.
[3] Constitution of 1896, Art. I, § 1: "The name by which this Society shall be known in law is The Legal Aid Society."
[4] 22 N. Y. L. A. R. 3.   [5] 24 *Ibid.* 7.

an American institution was realized. In 1889 the application lists showed 2569 natives of Germany and 2317 natives of the United States. From that time on, in steadily increasing measure, the largest number of applicants were Americans, who sought a relief which their own institutions failed to provide.

§ 3

The first decade of the new century gave indications that organized legal aid work was to develop into a national project. The expansion was not rapid, but it went on *The Sec-* steadily, and by 1910 organized legal aid work was reasonably well estab-
ond Period lished in all of the larger cities of the east. This development was not
1900–09 due to any propaganda or missionary work. There was no central organization which consciously planned, or led, or built up the movement. The growth came about because in the larger cities persons in different walks of life and in their various associations, such as the charities, churches, bar associations, women's clubs, and the like, found themselves confronted with the pressing problem of how to obtain justice for poor persons who came to their attention. The older solution of taking the individual case to some kind lawyer was not only becoming unsatisfactory to all concerned, but was rendered out of the question by the greatness of the demand, which no private office could undertake to meet. There was a certain vague knowledge abroad that something was being done in New York, no one understood precisely what it was or exactly what Mr. Briesen was driving at, but to New York they all turned for instruction.

It is this fact which makes the development of ideas about the work in New York of such great importance, for those conceptions were largely copied, often for no other reason than that New York did its work in that particular way. The mistakes of New York became the faults of the entire movement, but as most of its plans and rules and tendencies, under Mr. Briesen's inspiration, were of the highest order and in the main correct, the New York pattern of organization, which was widely copied, proved an excellent model. It is due to this fact, and not merely because of its size, that New York has deservedly been supreme in the legal aid world. As one reviews the history and sees the accomplishments of this society and that society it becomes increasingly clear that the New York organization has justly earned its title of *The Legal Aid Society*.

In 1900 a group of attorneys in Boston, all closely identified with the Bar Association, felt a clear demand by the poor of the city for the assistance of counsel, and decided to form an organization like that in New York. In April a charter of incorporation was granted, which stated the title to be "The Boston Legal Aid Society." Up to this time there was no standard nomenclature; there was one Legal Aid Society, one Protective Agency, one Bureau of Justice, and one Poor Man's Lawyer. With its adoption in Boston, and later elsewhere, the term "legal aid" grew into the standard and uniform name for this sort of organization. It has become something akin to a trademark. The new society in Boston took over what appeared to be the New York policy and decided to reject criminal cases.[1] The most important thing about this society is the fact that its initial impulse came entirely from the bar.[2] For the first time an object lesson was afforded of the definite relationship between legal aid work and members of the bar. It is true that the relationship was put on the narrow ground of providing an agency to relieve private offices of their charity cases, but it did plant a seed which is now beginning to bear fruit throughout the country.

The New Jersey Legal Aid Association came into existence in 1901. The facts about this organization are not entirely clear. Plans were begun in 1897 to bring about a state instead of a city organization, and this was carried through in name, but the object was not realized. The Association became in fact the legal aid society for Newark, and although when the society was incorporated in 1907, the state name of "The New Jersey Legal Aid Society" was retained, the organization was, and is, a local organization doing its work in Newark. It does not control the work in Jersey City or Hoboken, and it never established societies in Trenton, Paterson, or elsewhere. It conforms more to fact, and is less confusing, to consider this organization as the Newark Legal Aid Society.

In March, 1901, the New York Labor Secretariat, a specialized form of legal aid work which has failed to make headway in this country, was formed. Germany had learned of organized legal aid work from New York, and the idea had promptly been put into general effect, with the modification that the agencies which established legal aid bureaus were religious groups, political parties, and labor unions. From Germany the conception of a labor union legal aid society came back to New York and the Labor Secretariat was created. Its work is in every respect like that of a legal aid society, but its membership is restricted to persons in unions which have joined the plan. It is a coöperative idea closely resembling the similar arrangement more generally in vogue for providing physician's services. The Secretariat plan was never formally extended beyond New York, and it is perhaps fortunate, for if legal aid work had developed along class or group lines, its real position in the administration of justice, the essentially public nature of its service, would have been obscured.

Philadelphia was next in line, following closely the New York pattern, and getting under way in September, 1902. A description has been written[3] which merits quotation, for it conveys a picture of the meagre way in which most legal aid organizations were obliged to begin, and of the precarious hold which they had in the community at their start.

"All of the multitude of charitable organizations for which the city of Philadelphia is famous, agreed that there was no opening or necessity for such a society. One of them, the Society for Organizing Charity, showing that its bark

[1] 1 Boston L. A. R. 9.   [2] See *A Lawyers' Legal Aid Society*, 23 Case and Comment, 1008.
[3] *Report of the Proceedings of the First Conference of Legal Aid Societies* (1911), page 7.

was worse than its bite, loaned the Legal Aid Society a room down in the slums for use without charge two evenings during the week. There the first attorney met clients at a temperature which hovered somewhere near zero, as the Society for Organizing Charity was not able to supply heat. The attorney was accustomed to advise clients in an ulster and gloves. The Provost of the University of Pennsylvania subscribed the sum of $25 for incidental expenses, such as postage, stationery, and costs. On this equipment, namely, a fireless room, $25, and a couple of enthusiastic young attorneys, the Legal Aid Society of Philadelphia began its work."

In the same year a committee was formed in New Rochelle to furnish legal assistance in that city and in Westchester County. In October the Educational Alliance of New York, located on the East Side, where it was in a position to reach the vast Jewish and Russian immigrant population, undertook legal aid work, for which it had felt the need for several years but had lacked the necessary funds, by establishing within its organization a Legal Aid Bureau.[1] It was planned to confine the services to advice, conciliation, and arbitration. It soon appeared, however, that such a limitation was untenable,[2] for in the worst cases of injustice court action is generally the only solution. Curiously enough, while this effort to reach the Jewish population in New York's East Side by means of an independent organization instead of by extension of the existing organization was being undertaken, a parallel development was taking place in Chicago with a view to bringing legal assistance to the large Jewish population in Chicago's West Side. The Bureau of Personal Service, which had started in 1897, had not found its proper sphere of usefulness until in 1902 it saw the great existing need and entered the field of legal aid work. From the point of view of ideal arrangement it is regrettable that this duplication of organizations arose, but in fact there was no duplication of work, for the new organizations entered new fields. As the older organizations in both New York and Chicago lacked the financial strength to answer completely the great demand for legal assistance, these new agencies became valuable allies, and justified their creation by accomplishing a vast amount of work.

Two important contributions on the side of more accurate records were made by the attorneys for the Boston society during 1902. Up to this time the records of the work included only the number of clients, their nationalities, the nature of the cases presented, and the amounts collected for clients. To this the Boston attorneys added a table showing the sources from which the clients came.[3] The value of this information to the proper development of the work was quickly appreciated. It was adopted in New York in 1905,[4] and thereafter was generally utilized. Even more valuable, there was added a table showing the disposition of all cases.[5] Other organizations had recorded the dispositions of court cases, but none had classified and published the results of the work in all cases. Logically, it would seem that a complete record of dispositions is a necessary complement to a record of cases received, as necessary as the disbursement

---

[1] 7 Educational Alliance R. 20 ; 10 *Ibid.* 31.   [2] 13 *Ibid.* 48.
[3] 3 Boston L. A. R. 24.   [4] 30 N. Y. L. A. R. 35.   [5] 3 Boston L. A. R. 12.

side of a cash-book, if any balance or estimate of results is to be had; but this importance has never been grasped. Boston itself discarded the method, and not until 1907 was it definitely established. The older organizations and the majority of the newer have never adopted any classification of dispositions, chiefly because New York was the recognized leader and its system was generally followed.

During 1903 no new organizations were formed. An innovation was made in New York by the publication of a quarterly review of legal aid work. The directors believed the subject was of such intrinsic worth that if information about it could be brought home to the public, the needed financial support would be forthcoming. A printed monthly statistical report was sent to all members as a first experiment, but this proved dry reading. The idea of a quarterly review which should contain, in addition to a statistical statement, the stories of interesting cases and leading articles was hit upon, and in April, 1903, *The Legal Aid Review*, of eight pages, made its initial appearance. The *Review*, which has ever since been continued, proved to be of more than local value. It carried notes on the development of the work in other cities and provided a medium for many excellent articles dealing with legal aid work and its significance. It was analogous to any trade or professional journal and it served the same purposes. To the existing organizations there was made available information concerning methods for conducting the work, of which they needed all they could get, a community of interest was fostered, and the message in this compact and readable form was carried far and wide into new fields.[1]

Three organizations were added to the growing list in 1904. Atlanta produced a society which did good work and gave every promise of a sturdy development.[2] Interest subsided, however, and the enterprise languished and disappeared. This was the first death in the otherwise healthy legal aid family, and it was the more unfortunate because this was the first foothold in the South. In Cleveland a group of lawyers and the Jewish Federated Charities, both finding an imperative need for some definite plan for providing legal services, happily discovered each other and in combination set up the splendid Cleveland Legal Aid Society.[3] Up to this time nearly all of the organizations were of the same mould and conformed to type, but in Denver a departure was made of much interest in the field of legal education,[4] when the local law school started "The Legal Aid Dispensary of Denver." The instructor in practice was made the attorney and the senior students were used as his assistants. The plan was too successful and had to be abandoned. The character of the service given was so high that hundreds of persons applied. The rising cost entailed thereby

---

[1] Chicago at one time published a *Legal Aid Review*, which was discontinued, and since 1912 has published a *Bulletin*. This is issued only at irregular intervals. It has never attained the position or exercised the influence of the New York *Review*.

[2] Atlanta *Constitution* for September 5, 1904, quoted in 2 N. Y. Legal Aid Review, No. 4, p. 2.

[3] Work was begun in January, 1904. The Society was incorporated in May, 1905.

[4] This is the first "legal clinic." This matter is beyond the scope of this report, but is discussed in a separate pamphlet entitled "Legal Aid Organizations and Legal Education."

exceeded the funds at the disposal of the law school, and as neither the lawyers nor the charities would help, the project was discontinued in 1910.

During the next five years, from 1905 to 1909, both inclusive, the progress continued steadily. On June 15, 1905, the Bureau of Justice and the Protective Agency were wisely consolidated into the Chicago Legal Aid Society. As each had widened its scope to meet the increasing demands, the jurisdictions of the two became nearly identical, so that the merger was the only sound business course. Later developments demonstrated the fact that the strength of one combined organization would exceed the total strength of its component parts. As these two original Chicago organizations do not again enter into our discussions, it is convenient at this point to summarize their accomplishment. The Bureau of Justice in its seventeen years[1] entertained 66,676 cases, collected $87,067.05 for its clients, and expended $75,449.11 in the prosecution of its work. The Protective Agency for Women and Children during nineteen years, with one year's figures missing,[2] cared for 39,341 matters, collected for clients a total of $38,844.98, and expended $52,469.39.

New York opened its Harlem Branch in 1905, and in 1906 tried to start a Criminal Branch, or at least to provide some assistance in the inferior criminal courts, but as the needed funds could not be secured, the criminal work was reluctantly abandoned. The failure of the Society to extend its legal aid into the criminal field and thereby to meet the need which in recent years has called the public defender into being was not due to lack of perception but to lack of funds. Nevertheless the fact gave the legal aid movement a twist away from criminal work. Other societies, lacking in experience and not clearly understanding the position of legal aid work in its relation to the administration of justice, saw that criminal cases did not appear in the New York reports and blindly adopted what they supposed was some rule or policy against such work.

In 1907 New York opened an office—its fifth branch—in Brooklyn. Financial stringency caused this to be closed the next year, but in 1910 it was permanently reopened. Cincinnati set up an organization in 1907, Pittsburgh followed in 1908,[3] and Detroit in 1909. This last is of interest because it was established and supported by the Association of the Bar of the City of Detroit. Thus for the first time, after thirty-three years, the bar in its collective capacity took a part in this movement for making justice more accessible to the poor.

---

[1] These figures are complete except for the half year January 1, 1905–June 15, 1905, for which period no report was ever made.

[2] The report for the period April 1, 1893–April 1, 1894, being the *Eighth Annual Report*, is missing.

[3] In 1908 an association bearing the legal aid name was formed in Los Angeles. No reports were ever published. No attorney was ever put in charge of the work. It did render a certain amount of service until 1914, when the Public Defender's office took over all such work. From such evidence as is available it is proper to exclude it from the field which is of concern to us as not being a definite organization.

§ 4

The third era consists of a four-year period in which the territorial expansion of the work went ahead very rapidly. Whereas in 1909 there were fourteen definite organizations in existence, by the end of 1913 the number had doubled to twenty-eight. As the preceding period marked the establishment of legal aid organizations in the East, so this is primarily the period of extension into the Middle West—Kansas City in 1910, St. Louis, Akron, and St. Paul in 1912, Duluth, Minneapolis, and Louisville in 1913. A further penetration of the eastern field went on at the same time. Baltimore and Rochester were added in 1911. New York, now possessed of two organizations with five branch offices, added further to its legal aid equipment by the establishment of the National Desertion Bureau. This organization, created by the National Conference of Jewish Charities to combat the growing evil of family desertion, represents a specialized legal aid organization and affords a striking illustration of the efficiency that attends specialization of work. In 1912 a strong society was started in Buffalo, and in the same year two young men who had learned of the idea in the East started a small but valuable society in Colorado Springs.

The Third Period 1910–13

The year 1913 marked the second attempt to plant legal aid work in southern fields. In New Orleans an organization was fostered by the Louisiana Bar Association, which has managed to hold on although its development has been disappointing. In the industrial city of Birmingham a legal aid bureau was opened as a branch of the Lawyers' League, an association of lawyers formed for social and civic betterment. The bureau was never very active and when the Lawyers' League died it also succumbed.

Students in the Harvard Law School organized in 1913 a legal aid bureau in Cambridge, which not only served as the first representative of a new type of organization, but also brought into life again the question of a possible coöperation between legal aid and law schools. In Minneapolis, which has already been mentioned, under the guidance of Dean William R. Vance of the University of Minnesota School of Law, an alliance was made between society and school which operated to mutual advantage and served again to bring into prominence the question of a legal clinic, which by this time had been reluctantly given up in Denver.

An outstanding fact of the development during this third era was the change which took place in the predominant type of legal aid organization. Up to 1910, of the fourteen societies that attained permanence, ten were organized as private charitable corporations. From 1910 through 1913, of the fourteen societies that lasted, eight came into being as departments of organized charities. Leaving aside Colorado Springs, which represents a venture of eastern men rather than any western impulse, a glance at the map shows that, with one exception, the legal aid movement had not pushed farther west than the Mississippi River by the end of 1913.

Kansas City, Missouri, was the exception, and it was also an exception in a more important than a territorial way. Hon. Frank P. Walsh, then a practising attorney in Kansas City, and later Chairman of the United States Commission on Industrial Relations, was interested in the work of the Board of Public Welfare which had been created by the city to take care of prisoners and to supervise parole. Mr. Walsh had visited the legal aid societies in New York and Chicago, and he knew from his own practice that there was a similar need in Kansas City. He conceived of the idea of placing such work under the supervision of the city's Board of Public Welfare. Six attorneys were found who were willing to devote two hours each on one day a week. Under this plan the office was opened on August 10, 1910. On the first day there were twenty applications, and the volume of the work clearly showed that a more permanent arrangement was necessary. Accordingly on September 15 the Board of Public Welfare appointed one attorney to devote all his time to the work, gave him a salary, and supplied him with assistants.[1] No special ordinance was passed; the Welfare Board acted under its general authority and drew the necessary money from its general funds.[2]

This was a step of profound importance, destined to influence the entire history of legal aid work and probably destined to affect the whole course of the administration of justice. This public Legal Aid Bureau challenged the long accepted conception, on which our civil administration of justice was built, that the state's duty ends when it has provided judge and court house, and that it has no interest and no right to take a part in private litigation. Here in Kansas City for the first time an American community put the ideal of the fundamental law into practice and saw that no one was denied justice because of inability to employ counsel. As it has rather aptly been put, "By the organization of the Legal Aid Bureau, justice in this city has been placed on the free list with religion, education, and health."[3] The significance of a public society was not at once grasped, nor was it followed for a while. But the vigor of the idea proved itself when at the end of its first full year the Kansas City Bureau took third rank among the then existing nineteen legal aid organizations, easily outdistancing societies in larger cities which had had more time for growth, as in Boston, Cleveland, and Philadelphia. This undertaking of legal aid work by a municipal government and the payment of expenses out of the public treasury made a deep impression in the legal aid world. It is not to be wondered that its full significance was not at once appreciated, for it is a long step from thinking of a legal aid society in terms of a charity and as a place where lawyers may send their charity cases, to conceiving of it as a department of government and a part of the public administration of justice. Kansas City stood as an object lesson, and because of it the thought of the leaders in the movement in various cities began to crystallize as to the true function and position of a legal aid organization.

[1] 1 Kansas City L. A. R. 3.
[2] *Report of the Proceedings of the Third Conference of Legal Aid Societies* (1914), pages 38, 39.
[3] 2 Kansas City L. A. R. 1.

One other important development took place during this period. Very slowly there had been growing up among the various organizations a feeling of comradeship and a realization that all were engaged in a common enterprise. In 1911 this took the practical shape of an invitation from Pittsburgh to meet to discuss common problems and the advisability of a central organization. Thirteen societies responded by sending delegates. The discussion[1] disclosed that there were many practical reasons for the formation of an alliance. A central office could lead in propaganda work in new fields and could provide a clearing house through which cases could be transferred for action from one city to another. Legal aid work was developing in Europe and the movement had assumed an international character, so that there was need of some official to whom foreign legal aid societies could send cases for reference to the proper local society. It was further pointed out that, by combining, the legal aid societies might take a part in national problems and in remedial legislation. Such beneficial results were so obvious—indeed they had earlier been presented by New York[2]—that it is remarkable that the union was not effected sooner than it was. As a result of this first conference in Pittsburgh a committee was appointed to draw up a plan for a permanent central organization.

A second conference was held in New York in 1912, at which time the National Alliance of Legal Aid Societies was formed, and a constitution and by-laws were adopted.[3] As has generally been the case in the history of American institutions, this initial attempt at federation resulted in producing a very weak central body, lacking both the funds and the power to provide any real leadership. Legal aid work having developed entirely as a local growth, it was inevitable that local feeling should run high in the sense that each organization was afraid to surrender any authority to a central governing body. The Alliance has called two conventions, one at Chicago in 1914 and one in Cincinnati in 1916, and its president has done some work in foreign cases, but beyond that it has amounted to nothing.

§ 5

The fourth period, consisting of the last four years up to 1918, constitutes the most remarkable chapter in the entire history. The idea spread very rapidly, reaching out to the Pacific Coast and into the Southwest, until nearly all of the larger cities in the United States had established legal aid organizations. Whereas in 1914 there were twenty-eight societies, in 1917 there were forty-one societies, among which number are included two public defender organizations doing civil as well as criminal work, and in addition there

*The Fourth
Period
1914–18*

---

[1] The complete discussion is contained in *Report of the Proceedings of the First Conference of Legal Aid Societies* (1911).

[2] 31 N. Y. L. A. R. 19.

[3] These are contained in *Report of the Proceedings of the Second Conference of Legal Aid Societies* (1912), page 17.

were four public defender's offices confining themselves to criminal work. In nineteen other cities the idea was welcomed and, although definite results are not yet apparent, from some of these places new organizations will soon emerge. In all cities where legal aid had been established the work continued to increase steadily.

The most important fact in this last period is that the prevailing type of organization shifted to that of the publicly controlled, publicly supported bureau. In 1914 the Los Angeles Public Defender's office, charged also with the responsibility of civil work, was opened, and the work in Duluth was taken over by the city. In 1915 the municipalities took over the work in St. Louis and Dayton, and in Dallas the Board of Public Welfare created a Free Legal Aid Bureau. During the same year public defenders were established in Los Angeles (for the police court), in Omaha, and in Portland, Oregon, in which last city the official was so besieged by applicants for civil assistance that perforce his office became a regular legal aid society. In 1916 the city of Omaha established a public society, the people of Hartford voted on referendum to have a municipal legal aid bureau, and in Columbus a public defender was provided.

In Washington and New Haven the Harvard plan of a law school legal aid society was put into effect by students in the George Washington and Yale Law Schools. Strong organizations came into being in San Francisco and Milwaukee, and lesser but still important societies were started in Columbus, Nashville, Plainfield, Richmond, and San Diego. In Jersey City the work, which can be traced back to the "Poor Man's Lawyer" at the Whittier House Settlement in 1894, blossomed out and produced a full-fledged society. The last event in the period covered by this report was the establishment in New York in 1917 of a splendid organization to provide legal aid in criminal cases, called "The Voluntary Defenders Committee," which serves to round out the legal aid equipment of that city by carrying the work into the criminal field, which none of the other societies had been able to reach.

§ 6

The history of the movement for organized legal assistance to the poor is that of a conception possessing great intrinsic value which could earn appreciation only with *Review* the passage of time. After a painfully slow beginning during a period of twenty-four barren and almost stagnant years, the idea pushed forward gradually, but nevertheless steadily, for the space of ten years, and then for seven years raced ahead with constantly accelerating velocity. From period to period the advance has been in geometric progression.[1] The high tide of territorial expansion has been passed, but the momentum has by no means subsided.

Side by side with this territorial expansion, and keeping pace with it, there has

---

[1] See the table showing the increase in number of organizations and in cases, *post*, page 152.

gone on a steady evolution of thought about the work. The beginnings of a technique as to how the work may most effectively and efficiently be done have been made. More important, there has gradually been dawning a clearer conception of the meaning of organized legal assistance to the poor. The movement has passed through three stages and is entering a fourth. From its original position as a sort of proprietary organization with the narrow mission of aiding only a limited group, it broadened out and took on the stature of a charity, anxious to help all who needed its assistance, but still viewing its object as that of dispensing legal assistance as other charities dispense material assistance. Thence it emerged onto a higher plane, where it understood that in its daily work it was not so much giving anything to the poor as it was obtaining for them their just dues; that it was not dispensing charity, but was securing justice.

The mind of the bar and of the community in general has not advanced beyond the second stage. To most persons a legal aid organization is still a charity. The directors of legal aid societies and the attorneys in charge have nearly all, through their closer contact with the work, come to an appreciation of the fact that they are engaged in essentially a public undertaking, and that they have a part in the administration of justice.

The last development, which is the fourth stage in the evolution, regards the organized legal aid movement not as a thing apart or as a thing unto itself, but rather as an important and contributing factor in a greater movement—a movement embracing the reorganization of courts, the simplification of procedure, and all the remedial agencies and methods examined in Part II of this study—for the betterment of our administration of justice. It recognizes that legal aid work, even at its best, is not the whole solution or the only solution, and that it can reach its own maximum strength only in alliance with the other forces and agencies about it, preferring them where they are the more efficient, supplementing them where they fail. In this light legal aid work ceases to be an end in itself; it becomes merged in a great design according to which the whole administration of justice is to be rebuilt and reshaped to the end that denial of justice, so far as we now understand it, may cease. The majority of those identified with the work have not yet recognized or consciously accepted this last conception; but in the reports which are now being published and in the character of the work being undertaken there is ample evidence that shortly it will be accepted as the guiding principle for the future.

NOTE: In this chapter all the definitely established legal aid organizations have been mentioned. For a complete list, both of organizations in existence and those in process of formation, alphabetically arranged and giving the names of officers and addresses, see 15 N. Y. Legal Aid Rev. No. 3 (July, 1917), pp. 13–15; 24 Case and Comment (August, 1917), 216–218. The earlier lists published in 8 Pittsburgh L. A. R. 27; 11 Chicago L. A. R. 37; and *Report of Proceedings of the Fourth Conference of Legal Aid Societies* (1916), page 156, are now inaccurate.

Chapter XVIII

WORK OF THE LEGAL AID ORGANIZATIONS

I have known about the Legal Aid Society for some years, but
it conducts its affairs so quietly and so unostentatiously that
I did not know, until the other day, how extensive is the work
it is doing. It stirs one's blood and compels one's deep homage
to read the great figures! MARK TWAIN.[1]

§ 1

THE final test of any organization lies in its accomplishment. This challenge the
legal aid organizations are not afraid to meet. To make a compact presentation
of the work that has been done, one is necessarily driven to the use of statistics, but it
should be remembered that figures, however great, are incapable of por-
Introductory traying results in terms of human happiness and welfare. An idea of
this larger benefit can be obtained to a limited extent by examining the individual
cases that are presented in the reports of the legal aid organizations. These, if collected, would fill several volumes, and still they would represent only an infinitesimal
part of the good which has been achieved. This human side of the work, the splendid
efforts that have been made, the encouragement, comfort, and help which have been
brought to those in trouble, the far-reaching effects of this practical ministration in
accordance with the American ideal of justice and fair play,—such things will never
be presented in their full force until there appears a Dickens to write a twentieth
century version of *Bleak House* or a Hugo to depict the struggles of a modern Jean
Valjean.

The essence of the work of legal aid organizations is the rendering of legal advice
and legal assistance to the individual in the individual case. It is for this purpose that
they exist, and it is with such work that we are here concerned. Out of the individual case work there grows other work, more general in its nature, such as the support
of remedial legislation, coöperation with the charities, and service to the community
in driving out the loan sharks. These matters are secondary and may be postponed
for later consideration.[2]

If ever there was an occasion for the use of statistics without an apology or justification, it exists in connection with legal aid work. It is high time that the figures
were presented and that attention be called to them. Feeling themselves bound by
professional ethics, the societies have never exploited their work in individual cases,[3]
and as a matter of policy they have preferred to do their job "without noise or osten-

---

[1] From a letter written December 12, 1905, to Mr. Louis Windmüller, Treasurer of the New York Legal Aid Society.
[2] Chapters XXI to XXV deal with work in this broader field and with the relationships between legal aid organizations and the law, the community, the charities, and the bar.
[3] See *A Lawyer's Legal Aid Society*, 23 Case and Comment, 1008; *Report of Proceedings of the Fourth Conference
of Legal Aid Societies*, page 36.

tation."[1] As a result, in the community at large and even among the members of the bar, the work is very little known and has received but scant acknowledgment. It has been done so silently and it has gone ahead so quietly that a statement of the dimensions to which it has attained is in the nature of a revelation.

§ 2

The forty-one legal aid organizations of the United States, as their contribution toward making more equal the position of the poor before the law, have provided at-

The Total Work torneys to 1,133,700 persons, have collected for their clients sums aggregating $3,590,681, and to accomplish this work they have expended $1,573,733. These are minimum figures. All estimates and conjectures have been excluded. If all the figures could be known, the number of clients would be considerably increased. If it were possible to estimate the amount which clients have received from weekly orders secured for them by legal aid societies, the figure representing collections would probably be doubled. Orders and decrees for the support of wives and children and findings under the compensation acts all call for weekly payments. The former run indefinitely, they may remain in force as long as the person lives, but it is impossible to know or estimate with any accuracy how much is paid in accordance with their terms, for these payments by husbands are both irregular and uncertain. The latter continue throughout the period of disability up to ten years, payments are certain, but as the date when an injured man returns to work and compensation stops is almost never known to the society, no computations are possible. All that can be offered is opinion, and the best opinion is that if such actual payments were known, they would swell the total collections to seven million dollars. Taking the figures as they stand, they offer ample evidence of the inadequacy of the traditional administration of justice in itself to protect the rights of the poor through law. Without organized legal aid, what would have been done for these hundreds of thousands of persons who were justly entitled to several millions of dollars?

While the height of territorial expansion has been passed, the volume of work has by no means reached its zenith. In the last six years the work has doubled, and the increase is due not only to the creation of new organizations, but also in a very appreciable measure to the growing work of the older societies. How vast the work will be at the end of the next decade no one can foretell, but it is certain that the development is still going on apace. Complete figures showing the increase in case work, in collections for clients, and in expenses, year by year for each organization and in total for all organizations, are contained in the three statistical tables appended to this report. A condensation of these tables shows that the work has grown as follows:

---

[1] This description was applied in an editorial in the *Outlook* for July 18, 1903. Quoted in 1 N. Y. Legal Aid Rev. No. 3, p. 3.

Year	Number of Organizations	Cases	Collections for Clients	Expenses
1876	1	212	$1,000	$1,060
1885	1	3,802	17,711	2,870
1890	3	9,316	47,580	11,953
1895	4	16,128	66,341	14,312
1900	5	20,896	101,970	21,669
1905	12	33,352	80,020	42,734
1910	15	52,644	166,851	76,602
1912	21	77,778	217,532	119,705
1914	32	109,048	268,849	160,189
1916	41	117,201	340,199	181,408

§ 3

The nature of legal aid work has already been pointed out in general terms in earlier connections. Writing in the light of experience gained in a hundred thousand cases, the attorney for the New York Society thus expresses it:[1]

Nature of the Work
"What is Legal Aid Work? What kind of work do you do? How often these questions are asked each year, and surprising as it may be to some, there are thousands in this City of ours, who are not only unfamiliar with our purposes, but to whom our existence is unknown.

"From birth to death, the poor man is the prey of a host of petty swindlers. He is educated to believe that justice is free and he finds that to get it, he must pay a lawyer a price he cannot afford. It has often been said that only the poor know the sorrows of the poor. This may be so, but I believe that only the Legal Aid Society knows their wrongs. Unless injuries and unfairness to the poor man are punished, he feels that justice is not for him, and that he has not the same opportunity and protection as the rich man; he becomes anarchistic. The fundamental object of our Society, therefore, is to see that all, no matter how poor, or how oppressed, shall get justice. We care nothing for race, sex, color, creed, or previous condition of servitude; we do believe that the laws mean something and our work is to see that they mean the same for the poor that they do for the rich. Let me emphasize that the Society does not give charitable support to needy persons, but only justice and the enforcement of just and honorable claims."

The scope of the work is confined to the field of legal action. The societies are engaged in the practice of law and not in social service work as that phrase is generally used. More closely than anything else, the work resembles the work of an attorney engaged in general practice, the chief points of difference being in the matter of fees and in the number of cases. To many of the innumerable questions which are asked the attorneys give answers based as much on common sense as on law, but the bar will admit that this is not a peculiarity confined to legal aid practice.

Proceeding to a more specific examination of just what cases are brought to the legal aid societies, it is at once apparent that claims for wages and domestic difficul-

[1] 38 N. Y. L. A. R. 23.

ties far outnumber any other classes of cases. Almost universally the collection of wages comprises the greatest work, then come the husband and wife difficulties with suits for separation (not divorce) and proceedings to enforce support, and beyond these two great groups the cases presented range widely over the whole field of civil law, except that poor corporations have not yet sought legal aid, so that there is little practice in corporation law.

The societies have kept accurate records of the nature of their cases, and although the classifications have never been standardized, it is possible to compile an intelligent table showing the kind of work presented by clients to organizations in seven different typical cities during the year 1914, which was a normal year.[1] As the volume of work varies from city to city, the relative importance of the groups of cases is best seen from percentages. This table is on the following page.

Legal aid work varies from city to city, but the average percentage figures in this table give an accurate idea of the general run of the cases and in what sorts of work the organizations are engaged.

There are five particular classes of cases about which some doubts have been raised as to whether they could properly be entertained by legal aid organizations. These are criminal cases (other than family desertion and non-support and bastardy), personal injury cases, divorce libels, complaints against attorneys, and bankruptcy proceedings. The last two admit of summary disposition. There are only three societies which refuse bankruptcy cases as a matter of rule. The organization in Nashville, which is allied to the Commercial Club, is its chief exponent.[2] There is every reason for discouraging voluntary bankruptcy, but there is no reason for flatly refusing to file schedules as a matter of rule. Until the small claims courts evolve a successful court trustee plan,[3] bankruptcy is often the only relief allowed by law. In cases where a vindictive creditor is harassing his debtor, causing him to lose his job as fast as he finds employment, making it difficult to support his family and impossible to pay other creditors, neither ethics nor morals enjoin resort to the bankruptcy court.

Only three societies refuse to give any consideration to complaints against attorneys. It is a common policy to refer all such matters directly to the proper Bar Association. The soundness of such a policy depends entirely upon the condition of the local Grievance Committee. In New York there is excellent reason for promptly referring complaints to the Grievance Committees of the City and County Bar Associations, both of which maintain investigators and attorneys for just such cases and do excellent work. Of few other Grievance Committees can this be said; reference to many of them results in pigeonholing the complaint. In general, it would be well for legal aid organizations to accept and prosecute cases against attorneys. The societies deal

---

[1] This is not true of workmen's compensation cases. Many of the compensation acts were not passed until 1914 or later. The societies are just beginning to find their function in this new field of litigation.

[2] *Report of Proceedings of the Fourth Conference of Legal Aid Societies*, page 111.

[3] See *ante*, Chapter VIII, Small Claims Courts, § 7-3, page 57.

TABLE SHOWING CLASSIFICATION OF LEGAL AID CASES

Classification	Boston	Chicago	Cleveland	Kansas City	New York	Philadelphia	St. Louis	Total
Cases analyzed	2,229	16,121	2,399	6,503	40,430	3,874	1,859	73,415
	per cent	per cent	per cent	per cent	per cent	per cent	per cent	Average per cent
Bankruptcy	—	.1	.3	—	.8	—	—	.17
Bastardy	2.5	.6	—	—	.02	—	—	.44
Children's cases[1]	2.8	2.3	2.9	.2	.1	2.3	—	1.5
Criminal cases	1.8	.9	5.2	.5	.4	4.5	.8	2.0
Domestic relations	16.6	16.3	16.0	13.0	8.5	19.0	7.9	13.9
Estates of deceased	2.3	1.3	1.4	.7	2.2	3.5	1.1	1.78
Employment agencies	—	.7	1.0	.2	.02	—	—	.27
Insanity	.5	.1	—	—	—	—	—	.08
Insurance	—	1.1	1.4	1.3	.8	3.6	2.1	1.47
Landlord and tenant	2.4	2.7	14.0	1.9	1.8	6.5	.3	4.2
Lawyer's misconduct	2.4	2.0	1.1	—	.3	1.6	1.6	1.28
Loan sharks	1.4	8.0	25.5	7.5	.05	—	7.6	7.15
Personal property	8.9	3.9	2.3	10.6	7.5	4.8	6.2	6.3
Seamen's cases	.7	—	—	—	3.8	—	—	.6
Torts in general	5.2	.5	1.2	.6	2.0	—	—	1.3
Personal injuries	[2]	2.1	4.0	.8	4.0	3.7	2.2	2.4
Wages	11.2	25.4	15.5	44.1	31.4	17.0	41.8	26.6
Workmen's compensation	.9	2.1	—	—	—	—	—	.4
Advice[3]	15.2	3.4	—	2.5	22.3	20.3	7.5	10.17
Contract, debt, and money claims[4]	24.3	16.2	7.7	15.7	13.3	7.7	20.4	15.0
Miscellaneous	—	9.5	—	—	.08	4.8	—	2.05

[1] Matters concerning children as custody, guardianship, adoption, support, protection, and as distinguished from general family problems, which are grouped under "Domestic Relations."

[2] Boston in 1914 classified its personal injury cases simply as "Torts," so that they are included under that heading.

[3] "Advice" is used differently by different organizations. Those showing higher percentage figures classify as advice all general enquiries which are received and matters which are closed at the first interview; the others classify the case under the subject-matter to which the advice relates.

[4] "Contract, debt, and money claims" is a catch-all classification which includes a variety of kinds of cases in which the clients may be either plaintiffs or defendants.

with the poor, who are most easily imposed on and taken advantage of; they are more likely to encounter certain types of abuse than any other agency; and they may work in excellent coöperation with the local Grievance Committee. When the misconduct is so gross that disbarment is warranted, the complaint and the evidence should go to the Bar Association, for it is desirable that any court proceedings should be instituted in that name, but as to all other matters the legal aid organizations can render invaluable service to the community and to the bar itself by investigating complaints and fearlessly prosecuting the cases where action is warranted.

In divorce matters there is a clear and well-justified rule to refuse to institute divorce proceedings. Of thirty-one organizations doing general legal aid work and having existed long enough to have settled rules of policy, twenty-two decline to represent divorce libellants, and in addition two, though accepting the cases, use every means to discourage such proceedings. There is a strong public policy against making divorces easy and cheap. The argument for costs as a deterrent can be well made in this field. The issue is not between divorce and no relief; non-support proceedings will secure support and separation proceedings will protect against brutality or physical abuse. The issue is between legal action which breaks up a home forever and legal action which preserves the home or leaves the path open for reconciliation. Organizations, as in Jersey City and Boston,[1] have attempted to accept divorce cases and have found that their assistance was abused, and so have changed their tactics. While exceptions are sometimes warranted in unusual circumstances, the rule is a wise one, for its very existence puts the legal aid attorney in a firm position in dealing with such applicants. The reason which justifies declining the institution of divorce proceedings requires that such libels, when brought by other attorneys, be defended by legal aid attorneys in all cases where there is a proper defence. The extension of the original rule to include refusing to represent libellees in divorce matters is entirely without justification. The desire to preserve the integrity of the home, which is the reason for not bringing divorces, requires the representation of the wife, whose husband seeks a divorce, in order that the home may be broken up only for cause shown and not for lack of representation or for default. Most organizations perceive and follow this distinction.

In reviewing the history of legal aid organizations we have already seen that in New York the legal aid society was unable to undertake general criminal work. New York's leaders saw that the need for legal assistance was as great in criminal as in civil matters,[2] but as the necessary funds for the proposed Criminal Branch were not forthcoming, and as the District Attorney sent deputies into the magistrates' courts who, it was hoped, would act impartially, the society gave up its venture into the criminal field.[3] The Chicago organization in its earlier years did a good deal of work in

[1] 4 Boston L. A. R. 17.
[2] 35 N. Y. L. A. R. 11; 36 *Ibid.* 38.
[3] This is further discussed in 7 N. Y. Legal Aid Review, No. 1, p. 2; No. 2, p. 1; No. 3, p. 19.

the criminal courts, but gradually abandoned it.[1] In Boston it was early determined to refuse criminal cases.[2] Buffalo started out to undertake criminal work,[3] but has felt obliged to change its policy. In fact, the situation to-day is that of the thirty-one organizations having any clear policies or rules, twenty-one refuse criminal cases, and those which have no rule do very little, if any, such work. Three considerations have brought about this unfortunate result. First, as has been pointed out, many societies adopted the rule because in doing so they thought they were following a precedent based on experience in New York. Second, all societies are overworked and undermanned, so that they have feared to be swamped if they opened the flood-gates of criminal applications. Third, as criminal practice has grown into a specialized field, requiring expert investigators, and specially trained and experienced counsel, the societies have recognized that they lacked the proper equipment to conduct criminal cases, especially the more serious matters, properly.

The legal aid organizations have failed to develop in this direction as they should have developed. The public defender movement is the result of their shortcoming. Legal aid societies in general should bestir themselves and strain every effort to provide assistance in this important field. They will do well to take advantage of the momentum of the public defender idea, and merge it with themselves, by establishing public defender departments. To have two sets of organizations existing side by side will entail unfortunate results in duplication of work and increased expense to be borne by the public or the community. As it is always difficult to merge established organizations, it is highly desirable that the legal aid societies secure the requisite funds, equip themselves properly, and then let it be known that they are prepared to accept assignments from the court or direct applications from persons charged with the more serious offences. How far the legal aid societies should attempt to practise in the lower courts is the same question which has been considered in connection with the police court public defender.[4] This is a local question for each society to answer in accordance with local conditions.

The chief point of contention among the organizations is with regard to accepting personal injury cases. Of the thirty-one organizations, twenty-four refuse such cases unless they be claims for trifling amounts. The rule is a result of the contingent fee system. The majority position is that to do such work is to enter into competition with the bar. The injured person who is able to retain his own counsel is, of course, not entitled to free assistance from a legal aid organization. It is argued that by virtue of the contingent fee any injured person, no matter how poor, can secure the services of counsel. The minority hold to the proposition that a poor man does not cease to be entitled to the services of a legal aid organization because he has suffered a serious injury. They regard the contingent fee, as it is used in practice, as an ex-

---

[1] This may be seen by reviewing the attorney's reports in the Chicago Legal Aid Society *Reports* from 1905 to 1910.
[2] 1 Boston L. A. R. 9. [3] 1 Buffalo L. A. R. 5.
[4] See *ante*, Chapter XV, The Defender in Criminal Cases, § 8, page 124.

ploitation of the unfortunate position of the injured person and not as a method of giving him proper relief.[1] The organizations which decline personal injury cases are forced into a most uncomfortable position. An injured poor person applies for assistance, which is refused; he then asks to whom he should go, and this information cannot be given him. This second refusal is a necessary result of the first, for the reference of personal injury cases to selected members of the bar forces the society into discrimination and gives rise to a practice more objectionable to the bar than is the practice of accepting the cases. The result of the double refusal either to accept the case or to recommend an attorney is disastrous. The injured party may not know anywhere to go and so fail of relief altogether, or, what is more likely, will fall into the hands of a "runner" or lawyer's agent, and will then pay the larger proportion of any settlement or recovery in fees. To combat this evil, many of the organizations have qualified their rule by accepting such cases for arbitration or settlement, but not for litigation. The New York Legal Aid Society, which first laid down the rule against personal injury cases, illustrates all these propositions. The Society has always refused to accept these cases and logically has refused to recommend applicants to any named attorney, but in recent years it has been willing to entertain the cases for purposes of settlement only.[2] This modification of the rule, although a step forward, is in violation of the principle on which the rule itself is based. Lawyers charge contingent fees in settled as well as litigated cases, the bar derives more income from the settlements than from the verdicts in negligence cases. The poor man can as easily get an attorney to undertake his case for settlement as for litigation, and the legal aid society in accepting the case for settlement is just as directly competing with the bar as if it accepted the case with a view to litigation. The situation brings about a clash between the two principles that legal aid organizations should assist the poor and that they should not compete with the bar. In any such conflict the proper interests of the poor should be given priority. It is their need which is the very reason for the existence of legal aid organizations. If the legal aid societies had been strong enough at the outset to accept these cases generally, and thereby to ward off the contingent fee system, they would have rendered an invaluable service to American justice and to the bar itself. Having failed of that, they should not now acquiesce in the situation, but should have the courage to minimize the bad condition by accepting the personal injury cases of poor persons and by giving complete legal assistance in this as in any other kind of case. This position finds support in the remarks of one of the best attorneys of the New York Legal Aid Society:[3]

"However much we may vary in our opinion that attorneys may be unfair or unjust, we must admit that there is about the negligence case, an atmosphere

---

[1] The arguments are set out in *Report of Proceedings of the Second Conference of Legal Aid Societies*, pages 43-52.

[2] *Report of Proceedings of the Second Conference of Legal Aid Societies*, page 51.

[3] See *Report of Proceedings of the Second Conference of Legal Aid Societies*, page 51.

that is totally different from any other kind of case, and as a matter of fact negligence cases, personal injuries, have taken on an atmosphere of gambling; and I do think that our Legal Aid Society or any other, might well take up that class of case, simply for the purpose of getting the profession generally back to a more wholesome view of that kind of case, and make all attorneys realize that those are cases which can be treated like other cases."

As most of the personal injury cases offered to legal aid societies are those of injured workmen, the passage of the workmen's compensation acts, which have so largely done away with contingent fees, would have rendered this argument academic were it not for the fact that several societies have carried over their rule and applied it to cases under the new law. Thus the rule tends to reinforce the too common opinion that attorneys are unnecessary under the compensation acts, so that the legal aid societies are keeping out of a field where their services are sorely needed. Not all, but many of them are making their original mistake over again. An injured workman, receiving one-half or two-thirds of his former pay, is not in a position to pay largely for lawyer's services. As his compensation comes in weekly instalments, instead of in one sum, the contingent fee is less applicable. With the passage of time there will inevitably be an increasing necessity on the part of injured workmen for representation at hearings in all contested cases. It will be tragic if the legal aid organizations, through blind adherence to an originally doubtful and now clearly outworn rule, persist in refusing their assistance to a large class of poor persons who stand in dire need of that assistance.

§ 4

Inasmuch as the legal aid societies do no advertising, feeling themselves bound by the traditions of the profession in that regard, it is interesting to ascertain how the *Sources of the Cases* vast army of clients finds its way to their offices. Nearly all the organizations keep records of the channels through which their cases come, but the records are in a form which leaves much to be desired. From the point of view of the individual society, properly classified source records are indispensable to an intelligent direction of the work. By a classification of source names which represent the various elements and groups in the community,—as the organized charities, the courts, the newspapers, the churches, etc.,—it is possible to determine where the society is known and where it is not, and then take steps calculated to bring its existence to the knowledge of the latter group. Our concern here is merely to ascertain how clients learn of the legal aid societies and what groups in the community are using the societies. There is an utter lack of standardization, which precludes any comparison between cities, or the taking of any general average, as was possible in considering the nature of the cases in the preceding section. On the basis of existing information no satisfactory table can be compiled. It is probably better than nothing, however, to take the records of four of the older and better established organizations for the year 1914 which has already been used, and with some slight rearrangement to submit the figures as they stand. It will readily be seen that such general headings as "Friends" made percentage figures valueless. It should also be noted that, except in New York, the heading "Former Clients" includes not only persons themselves former clients, but persons referred by former clients. The number of clients who themselves return to the legal aid society in the course of a year is relatively small.

Classification of Sources	Boston	Chicago	Cleveland	New York
Judges, clerk of courts, public officials	423	2,557	494	4,233
Lawyers, including legal aid societies	177	299	37	776
Organized charities	343	1,093	128	449
Newspapers	73	925	518	882
(By) Former clients	560	2,088	552	2,019
Doctors and hospitals	18	—	13	—
Ministers and churches	32	—	12	—
Direct applications	—	2,555	608	5,470
By friends	551	5,824	—	17,754
Consuls for other nations	—	30	—	401
From foreign sources	—	—	—	1,646
Miscellaneous	52	750	178	6,800
Total cases analyzed	2,229	16,121	2,540	40,430

The most interesting figures are those relating to the courts. Although generalizations based on this table alone must be made with caution, there is extrinsic evidence which corroborates the above figures showing that from judges, clerks, and other officials the Boston Legal Aid Society receives 19 per cent of its clients, Chicago 16 per cent, Cleveland 19 per cent, and New York 10 per cent. It is a fact that the legal aid organizations have everywhere earned good reputations before the courts, and that the judges and clerks are glad to refer needy persons to them. It is not unusual for a judge to stop a case in which it becomes apparent that an unrepresented party needs counsel and instruct the clerk to give him a card to the legal aid society. Up to the present time, a splendid foundation has been laid for a coöperation between the judiciary and legal aid organizations which ought to grow steadily closer as time goes on.

§ 5

If complete figures were available, the most valuable would be those telling what results the organizations have obtained in the matters entrusted to them. Such figures *Disposition of Cases* do not exist. A few organizations, mostly smaller societies, compile and publish their dispositions of cases. A number of organizations state the results in litigated cases, but as these are only a fraction of the total intake, the facts have only a limited application. Too many societies present as their annual balance sheet a statement of cases received and money expended. Proper accounting should show to the community the funds received (by subscriptions or public grant) for carrying on the work and what has been done with that money in terms of results accomplished in their cases. From such a comparison the societies have nothing to fear. Their work can stand the test. The omission to make proper records of results is due to a failure to think the situation through and to appreciate the necessity for such a tabulation, but it is none the less a bad failure.

No clearer proof of the extremely local nature of the development of legal aid work could be desired than the chaotic condition of the most basic records. As to the nature of the cases, the classifications are not standardized; as to their sources, there is not even proper classification; and as to their disposition, in the great number of instances there is no classification whatever. So far as concerns the records on which reports to the public are based, all cases except those taken to court might have been thrown in the waste basket. There never having been any central organization which had power to unify, relate, and standardize the work of the various local societies, each has built up its own system or lack of system with the inevitably resulting confusion. This deplorable condition will probably continue until the National Alliance of Legal Aid Societies is made over into a living instrument with some power to influence and mould the general course of legal aid work.

The disposition figures of the few societies which keep such records admit of simple classification and, in percentage form, give a very fair picture of what becomes of the cases. In the following table the results of the work done by six organizations during 1916 is analyzed.

TABLE SHOWING DISPOSITION OF LEGAL AID CASES

	Boston	Detroit	Milwaukee	Minneapolis	Newark	San Francisco
Cases analyzed	2602	452	847	2633	1673	229
Classification of disposition	*per cent*	*per cent*	*per cent*	*per cent*	*per cent*	*per cent*
1. Advice given or papers drawn	25.4	27.8	9.3	28.6	12.2	37.5
2. Prohibited by rule[1]	3.1	4.6	—	2.7	5.1	7.8
3. Client not entitled to aid	4.3	—	10.5	—	—	—
4. Referred to appropriate agency	6.5	—	2.6	6.6	5.5	15.2
5. No legal relief possible[2]	16.6	5.7	19.8	3.4	3.5	11.3
6. Investigated, no merit in case[3]	2.0	—	15.0	10.4	10.7	—
7. Lapsed by client	15.3	4.6	18.5	18.1	6.4	10.0
8. Relief by settlement or adjustment	17.4	47.5	24.2	22.1	52.9	10.0
9. Relief by court proceedings	6.4	9.5	—	} 7.6	3.4	7.0
10. Defeat in court proceedings	.9	—	—		—	.8

[1] "Prohibited by rule" refers to such matters as criminal, personal injury, and divorce cases, and to persons able to retain their own counsel.

[2] "No legal relief possible" means either that the facts disclosed no cause of action or that relief was impossible, as where a defendant had left the jurisdiction or was without assets.

[3] "Investigated, no merit" means that the organization investigated the claim and found it to be without merit. This is primarily used where the evidence is conflicting and the investigation leads the attorney to believe that his client is in the wrong or cannot prove his case.

The percentages in the foregoing table give a wholly accurate idea of what happens when the cases are passed through the legal aid office. If statistics from the larger organizations could be presented, they would show very much the same results. Out of one hundred cases brought to a legal aid organization, one-quarter are requests for advice or for the drawing of instruments, as wills, notes, or mortgages, and these are quickly disposed of. Five applicants cannot be accepted because their cases relate to criminal, divorce, or personal injury matters, or because they are able to engage their own attorneys. Three persons the society declines to represent because they do not deserve assistance, regardless of the strict merits of the case, as where they desire to institute litigation and garnishee a debtor's wages for reasons of spite or vindictiveness. Six persons, either at the outset or later as the case develops, prove to need medical or charitable more than legal assistance, and so are put in touch with the appropriate agency. In ten of the complaints it quickly becomes apparent that legal action will afford no relief, as where the facts fail to constitute a cause of action, or the defendant is beyond the jurisdiction, or the defendant is judgment-proof, or the plaintiff lacks the necessary money to pay the court costs and other expenses called for by the necessary litigation.

This leaves fifty-one cases requiring further investigation or action of one sort or another. Such investigation discovers that in eight cases the additional facts brought to light fail to confirm the client's story or so weaken it as to give rise to a reasonable inference that he himself is in the wrong. In ten cases the society's efforts go for nothing, because the client fails to return when he is later needed to take further steps in the prosecution of the case. Sometimes this is because the society's work has brought the defendant to terms and he makes his settlement directly with the client, often it is because the clients move, or lose interest, or find the law too slow, or for any one of a thousand reasons. These are the most discouraging cases in legal aid work, but because of the class of people among whom the society's work lies, it is inevitable that a certain number of clients will allow their cases to lapse. There remain thirty-three cases requiring action and in which the society is satisfied on investigation that the claims are well founded. Of these it is possible to settle or adjust twenty-five. Eight opposing parties are obstinate or refuse to attempt to reach a fair compromise so that suits are brought against them. Of these eight litigated cases, one is lost and seven are won. Multiplied out to the proper proportions, these figures show the grist of the legal aid mill.

§ 6

The office of a legal aid organization is like any ordinary private law office. The only objective signs of difference that impress the observer are the modesty of the appointments and the steady procession of persons coming and going. In general the organizations, through their attorneys, conduct their cases just as any attorney conducts his practice. In a few offices the work, up to the point of litigation, is taken

Principles in the Conduct of the Work

charge of by persons who are not lawyers, but these instances are exceptions to the prevailing rule.

As the legal aid organizations stand in a quasi-public position, as they are charged with the responsibility of expending the sums entrusted to them only for proper purposes, they are confronted with certain peculiar problems which have led to the adoption of several interesting principles concerning the conduct of the work. Realizing that their work was in the field of the law and that they were taking a part in the administration of justice, the organizations have wisely refrained from erecting any moral standard which applicants must satisfy before being entitled to assistance. The only test is the intrinsic merit of the claim plus a due regard for those restrictions which good ethics impose on all members of the bar. Suits for reasons of spite, vexatious proceedings taken for delay, technical defences to just claims, will not be undertaken. The main principle may be illustrated in an extreme way by stating that if the worst man in the world was actually owed ten dollars by the best man, the society would undertake the collection for the former, provided he was too poor to engage his own attorney. It is a tribute to the clear-sightedness of the leaders in the movement that the societies early took this stand. Had they undertaken to lay down rules concerning the morality of applicants, they would have arrogated to themselves the right to define justice differently than the law defines it, and they would have lost sight of their main objective of securing the legal rights of persons unable to obtain assistance elsewhere.

There are very few exceptions to this rule. New York refuses to accept claims from domestic servants who have left without reasonable notice. This is only a half exception, for the custom of notice is now so clearly established in that occupation that it would surprise no one to have the law hold that the week's notice is an implied condition of the contract. Servants who are discharged without a week's notice constantly seek recovery of pay for that week, so that the New York rule is simply making the principle work both ways. In domestic tangles, particularly where children are involved, the organizations make careful investigation of the client's life and history, and decline to act if he or she proves unworthy. In these cases the moral test is itself the legal test. In a proceeding for guardianship or custody of children the fitness of the petitioner is put in issue by the law. Morality as a test of exclusion is sometimes applied in illegitimacy cases. The society will assist a woman in such a case, no matter how much she herself may have been to blame, in the first such instance, and probably in the second, but after that the society will decline to act.

In all their work the organizations earnestly endeavor to refrain from competition with the bar. They have been so anxious on this score that at times they have gone too far, they have refrained from what seemed competition even at the expense of their clients, as in personal injury cases. In this relationship to the bar the societies have kept their record remarkably clean. The number of clients who are able to impose on them is so trivial as to be negligible. No serious charge has been made by responsible members of the bar that the societies were representing persons able to pay for their legal services. When it is considered that the societies do the work more economically than a private office could and yet lose from five to thirty-five thousand dollars a year, it is self-evident that they are engaged in a class of work which would represent a dead loss to the profession if its members were called upon to perform the necessary services.

The only criticism which requires consideration is that the societies "feed" cases to certain attorneys. By this it is meant that the society refers such cases as it declines — criminal, divorce, personal injury, and paying cases— to a limited number of attorneys. It is because of this criticism that many of the societies which decline negligence cases also decline to refer the applicants to any attorney. What to do with cases which are rejected has always been a difficult question. If a society is to refer cases at all, it must refer them to attorneys whom it knows and trusts, for it unavoidably pledges its reputation that the case will be rightly conducted and that no excessive fee will be charged. This results in discrimination. Here again there is a conflict between two principles, and in such a conflict the interests of the clients should be held superior, they should not be sent empty away; if the society cannot itself act for them, it ought at least to see that they come into proper hands. It therefore becomes largely a question of how the reference system can be made least objectionable.

There are three plans in existence. In Los Angeles, the bar association certifies a list of attorneys who are willing to take cases, and civil matters are referred to them in rotation, following the alphabetical order, by the public defender's office. The list is extensive, so that the element of discrimination is reduced to a low point, but correspondingly there is a real danger that some attorney will prove incompetent, or neglect his case, or charge an improper fee. Whenever this happens it injures the society's reputation, deters persons from seeking its assistance, and lessens its power in the community. In Philadelphia, cases are referred to a limited list consisting of eleven attorneys. Their work is reviewed by the legal aid attorney, he meets with this informal staff regularly and checks up the progress made in their cases, and all fees charged are communicated to him and recorded. This method is highly efficient, it protects the society entirely, but the element of discrimination becomes large. The plan has been so well conducted in Philadelphia that criticism has not been heard, but if attempted elsewhere, it might easily meet with disfavor and arouse hostility. In Chicago, Boston, and several other cities, the cases are referred to attorneys formerly on the legal aid staff. This is perhaps the least objectionable method, for it very completely guards the society's position and good name, and, on the other hand, as the group of ex-attorneys in those cities is constantly enlarging and changing each year, the discrimination does not appear great. There is no complete solution of this difficulty, which is precisely like that confronting judges in their selection of masters, auditors, receivers, and referees.

Litigation is always the last resort in a legal aid society. Conciliation and arbitration are the favorite means employed, as has earlier been pointed out.[1] Many of the cases of the poor are against other poor persons who are equally unable to pay attorney's fees. The societies have, in their respective communities, earned such reputations for fair dealing that the opposing party is very often willing to come to the office and fully relate his side of the story. The legal aid attorney changes his attitude from that of advocate to that of arbitrator. Force of circumstances gives his decision the validity of a legal judgment because neither party can afford to pay counsel to fight his decree. The attorney in this function closely resembles the judge of a small claims court, and the results obtained have been as gratifying. It is the rare case where the parties are not willing voluntarily to abide by the decision. Although the societies bring justice to thousands of persons whose claims otherwise could never be heard, there is much warrant for the statement that the net result of the work, because of the manner in which it is conducted, is to decrease rather than increase litigation.

Figures based on records for 1915 show that in Boston out of the total number of cases received only 9 per cent were taken to the courts, in Cleveland 8 per cent, in Kansas City and New York 6 per cent, and in Chicago 4 per cent. Examining further into the New York work, which is the largest and of longest duration, it appears that year after year the proportion of cases in which proper relief could not be obtained without resort to litigation has been less than one-tenth of the total number.[2] These figures are not accidental; they are the result of a policy consciously adopted and followed. The attorney for the society in his report for 1907 gives it clear expression:[3]

" Since the first day of January, 1907, there has hung in each of the six offices of The Legal Aid Society a neatly framed placard containing an extract from the writings of Abraham Lincoln — who was not only a great lawyer, but a great friend of the poor — words which seem particularly appropriate to guide and inspire the work of the attorneys of the Society.[4] . . .

" The poor applicant who makes his plea for legal aid, and the person against whom he lodges his complaint, each knows that behind the advice and counsel which is given by the Society's attorneys lies the sanction of the law and the resort to the tribunals established by the law. Nevertheless, these tribunals are sought only as a last resort. The truth so forcibly expressed by Lincoln has more and more come to be recognized as a principle which should be followed in business relations, and it is the working rule of The Legal Aid Society."

The societies institute or defend cases in court only when they are reasonably convinced that the truth is on their side. Their appearance in court depends on the

[1] See ante, pages 63 and 70.

[2] History of the New York Legal Aid Society, page 29. For detailed figures and statements see 32 N. Y. L. A. R. 30; 34 Ibid. 7; 36 Ibid. 10; 37 Ibid. 24; 38 Ibid. 24; 41 Ibid. 8.

[3] 32 N. Y. L. A. R. 29.

[4] Here follows the quotation of the famous saying as to the discouragement of litigation which has earlier been quoted on page 60.

merits of the case as they understand it and not on the payment of fees. They have established a standard of conduct which is likely to exert a powerful influence in the future. The standard accords with the best ethics, but it unquestionably is far in advance of the average attitude of the bar. They deal with the old and vexing question of duty by frankly placing their duty to the court before their duty to the client. There is to-day a steady trend of thought which is shifting the emphasis of the lawyer's duty from one owed primarily to his client to one owed to the court whose minister in the search for truth and the administration of justice he is.[1] The legal aid societies are putting this hopeful theory into practice, and if they should become the training schools in practice for law students, their influence on the next generation of lawyers would play an important part in bringing about a more general realization and acceptance of this higher definition of professional obligation.

§ 7

Whether or not legal aid organizations are justified in charging fees has been a fruitful topic of discussion at all their conferences.[2] The fees called into question are of two

The Charging of Fees

sorts. First, there is a fee which is charged when clients apply for assistance, commonly called a retainer fee, and ranging in its amount as used by different organizations from ten to fifty cents. Second, there is a charge by way of commission on sums collected for clients, which also varies, but never exceeds ten per cent. New York adopted the policy of charging small fees early in its history. In 1879 it put into effect the commission charge, and in 1896 it instituted the retainer fee. Nearly all of the older organizations followed the plan. The newer organizations, particularly the public bureaus, have adopted a contrary policy. At the present time the societies stand very nearly evenly divided in opinion and practice. A careful investigation made in 1916 by the Chicago Legal Aid Society ascertained that of thirty-nine organizations, eighteen charged fees and twenty-one did not. Analyzing the figures more closely, it appears that of fifteen organizations of the private corporation type (representing in the main the older and larger organizations), nine made charges and six did not; of fifteen organizations existing as departments of charities, five did and ten did not; and of five public bureaus, one did and four did not.

If the charging of fees prohibited deserving clients from securing the assistance of legal aid societies, or if it worked serious hardship on them, or if it was contrary to any fundamental principle of legal aid work, then fees ought to be wholly abolished. The evidence indicates that none of these three bad results follows from a proper system of charges. If the retainer fee were an absolute condition precedent, it would

---

[1] Cf. *Public Service by the Bar*, an address delivered by Elihu Root as President of the American Bar Association at its meeting on August 30, 1916.

[2] *Report of Proceedings of the First Conference of Legal Aid Societies*, page 57; *Ibid.*, *Third Conference*, page 39; *Ibid.*, *Fourth Conference*, page 89.

work great hardship. The universal rule is that it may be abated or entirely waived in the discretion of counsel. No charge is made in cases of deserted wives. In fact, the charge is only collected from about one out of every three clients. The figures of cases received give no indication that the fees make any difference. When the New York Society rearranged its fees in 1902, it had this possibility in mind and appointed a special committee of the Board of Directors to make an investigation. They reported that the fees as charged did not keep clients away.[1]

It does not seem that the fees charged work any hardship on the clients. Chicago found cases where, after it had charged fees, the client was obliged to seek charitable assistance.[2] If that were generally the case elsewhere, it would be a final argument, but there is rather interesting evidence in existence which points in a contrary direction. In Detroit the policy has been followed of making no charges, but of permitting clients to give as a donation any sum they desire. This affords a test of what clients feel willing and able to give in payment for services rendered. It may be contrasted with Boston, which has always charged fees by way of commissions on amounts collected. The criterion is the percentage relationship which the fees or donations from clients bear to the amounts collected for them. The following table shows for a period of six years the percentage of sums recovered which clients donated in Detroit and the percentage which was charged in Boston:

Year	Percentage of Collections	
	Donated in Detroit	Charged in Boston
1910	14.7	7.6
1911	12.5	6.0
1912	12.0	10.0
1913	4.5	7.5
1914	18.3	6.3
1915	18.3	5.3
1916	6.6	5.9

It is a fair inference that if clients in Detroit felt able to give $1.24 out of each $10 collected for them, no hardship was done in Boston in charging its clients .69 on each $10 collected. Where discretion is vested in counsel to make the charge according to the nature of the case and the needs of the client, it is unlikely that injustice will be done. The fee is fixed at the end of the case, by which time the attorney knows the client and his situation well. As attorneys are paid fixed salaries and receive no part of any fees collected, no personal interest is involved. The fact that two-thirds of the organizations operating as departments of charities do not charge fees might give rise to an inference that the charities regarded any fee as working a hardship. In the absence of more direct evidence no such general inference is warranted, for it appears that in 1916 the Cleveland Federation for Charity and Philanthropy instructed the Legal Aid Society that it would do well to give more attention to requiring the payment of fees in proper cases.

[1] 27 N. Y. L. A. R. 6.   [2] *Report of Proceedings of the Fourth Conference of Legal Aid Societies*, page 90.

The charging of fees is not contrary to any fundamental principle. The proposition for which legal aid organizations stand is equality before the law. The world of clients is not to be divided between persons able to employ their own counsel and persons able to pay nothing. The larger number of legal aid clients are not applicants for charity—many of them would refuse to apply for assistance if they considered that they were being given charity;[1] they are mainly self-supporting, self-respecting persons, whose income does not give them a sufficient margin to pay the fee which a private attorney must charge. The ideal of the legal aid organization is to give to the poor man at a price he can afford to pay, whether it be two dollars or fifty cents or nothing, as competent legal services as the rich can buy.[2] If it were able to do that, it would secure complete equality. Its aim would be fully realized.

The dispute is not one of principle, but resolves itself into practical considerations. It was on practical grounds and not on any matter of principle that the Women's Committee of the Chicago Legal Aid Society advocated the abolition of fees.[3] It was felt that it was impossible to devise a system which worked with justice and uniformity. It is possible that clients may deliberately impose on an attorney and thus avoid the small fee, and so a discrepancy or lack of uniformity may result. Such instances ought to be very rare because most clients have no desire to reward good deeds with bad, or honest dealing with trickery, and also because the attorney, by virtue of his position, knows so much about the client that he cannot readily be imposed upon.

Most practical considerations weigh in the balance in behalf of charging fees. The request to a client that he pay a retainer fee of ten, twenty-five, or fifty cents is only asking him to defray the incidental cash expenses to which the society is at once put. To conduct the case, the society incurs expense for postage, telephone, and carfares, and there is no reason why a client, when able, should not defray such items. This is directly in accord with the universal rule of all organizations to require clients, when able, to pay court costs and witness fees. This type of fee is negligible as a source of income, but many of the older organizations, as those in New York, Philadelphia, Boston, and Cleveland,[4] believe that a small initial charge is worth while because it puts the relationship between client and society on a more businesslike basis, it tends to maintain self-respect, it prevents a tendency to pauperization, and it gives the client a greater sense of responsibility toward the society. Cases which the society is forced to close as "lapsed" are generally those where it alone has expended money, time, and effort; rarely does the client who has invested his cash, however little, fail to see the case through.

The income from the second kind of fees, commissions on collections, though not

[1] See post, Chapter XIX, Types of Legal Aid Organizations, § 5, page 178.
[2] Cf. Report of Proceedings of the First Conference of Legal Aid Societies, page 7; Ibid., Fourth Conference, page 100.
[3] "The committee makes this recommendation on practical grounds." The report is quoted in Report of Proceedings of the Fourth Conference of Legal Aid Societies, page 90.
[4] 12 Cleveland L. A. R. 9.

large of itself,[1] is sufficient, because of the low cost per case, to enable an organization to undertake many more cases than it otherwise could afford to accept. It has been pointed out that New York is thus enabled each year to undertake seven or eight thousand more cases.[2] As every organization works up to its financial limit, this is a practical consideration of importance. In actual result it means that clients, who are able to do so, return to the society a small portion of the benefits which the society has secured for them, not in order that the society may prosper or its attorneys be enriched, but so that the society may be able to do more work for less fortunate clients who are unable to pay anything whatsoever for the services that they receive.

[1] The fees charged by legal aid organizations by way of commissions on collections are set out in their annual reports. The following table gives an idea of their amount. The figures are for 1916 except as to Chicago, whose figure is that for 1915.

Organization	Commissions Charged	Amount Collected for Clients
Boston	$1,354.73	$22,808.31
Buffalo	275.30	2,881.67
Chicago	716.25	18,528.99
Cincinnati	49.45	2,271.38
Cleveland	145.85	unknown
Hartford	12.35	323.70
Minneapolis	467.05	7,401.54
Newark	612.25	6,704.10
New York:		
Legal Aid Society	7,631.89	128,005.10
Educational Alliance	844.14	16,537.62
Philadelphia	383.93	11,286.34
Rochester	3.40	689.38
St. Louis	591.94	5,109.00

As the organizations conduct their work at a cost of from $1.50 down to .50 per case, it is apparent that these commissions enable them to do a substantially larger work than their income otherwise would permit.

[2] *Report of Proceedings of the Third Conference of Legal Aid Societies*, page 43.

Chapter XIX

TYPES OF LEGAL AID ORGANIZATIONS

Private agencies lack the essential quality of this new (public) office: the recognition of the whole community's obligation to the man in court and to its own self-respect as a democracy. The Independent for October 18, 1915.[1]

§ 1

IN the development of the work thus far there have emerged five distinct types of legal aid organizations. They are:

The Five Types

1. Private corporation societies.
2. Public bureaus.
3. Departments of organized charities.
4. Bar association societies.
5. Law school societies.

There are one or two organizations which do not fit into these classes, and within the groupings there are many varieties, but these clearly are the *types* of organization now in existence. Before taking up and weighing the respective merits of these various types, it is worth while to mention briefly the few special organizations that are engaged in legal aid work.

§ 2

The standard legal aid organization would be one which rendered to all persons who were unable to procure assistance elsewhere that legal advice and assistance which

Specialized Organizations

they needed in any case in any branch of the law, excepting only the instituting of divorce proceedings. The test should be the inability of the client to employ counsel, and only very rarely the nature of the case.[2] We have seen that the large majority of organizations give general civil relief except in personal injury and divorce cases, but that they give no criminal relief.

There are a few organizations which specialize in limited kinds of work and accept nothing else. Most of the public defender organizations confine themselves to criminal matters. This is not true in Los Angeles or Portland, but it applies to the defenders in Omaha and Columbus and to the Voluntary Defenders Committee in New York. There is no reason for this divided jurisdiction. Ultimately this specialized work ought to be merged with the general legal aid work so far as organization is concerned. That we have this specialized form of legal aid service is due to the historical fact that the legal aid organizations themselves never met the demand in the crimi-

---

[1] From an article by Geddes Smith entitled "Making the Law Work Both Ways," 84 The Independent, 94, 95.

[2] There might occasionally have to be some qualification. If such cases were presented, the societies might well be justified in refusing breach of promise and alienation of affection cases, which too often are only cloaks for blackmail.

nal field. Hence arose the necessity for some one to do that particular work to complement and carry to completion the legal aid idea. To fill that particular need came the public defender rendering that particular service. The same thing would happen if all legal aid societies were to-morrow to refuse all domestic relations cases. The need for legal assistance in that field would soon manifest itself, and we would see either the domestic relations courts extending their functions by adding attorneys to their probation staffs, or the erection of organizations providing legal assistance in that special field.

An illustration of this same process is afforded by the National Desertion Bureau. The legal aid societies have done reasonably well in meeting the problem of non-support, but, with the exception of Kansas City, they have failed to cope with desertion. When a husband deserts or abandons his family he very often goes into another state, so that the case against him presents the practical difficulty of ascertaining his whereabouts and the legal difficulty of extradition. The National Desertion Bureau was established in New York in 1912 by the National Conference of Jewish Charities. It is a legal aid organization confining its work entirely to desertion and abandonment cases. This specialization has resulted in maximum efficiency. The Bureau has been amazingly successful in locating deserters, it has coöperated with the prosecuting attorneys in securing their return to the jurisdiction, and by thus compelling husbands to perform their obligations of support it has saved to the United Hebrew Charities thousands of dollars which formerly it had to pay out for the support of abandoned families.[1]

This Bureau, with the admirable technique of work which it has devised, stands as an example to all legal aid organizations. Desertion and abandonment ought to be sternly combated in every community, and it can best be done through efficient legal aid work. It would, however, be a mistake for every city to have its own special bureau for this special work. It can far better be done as a part of the work of the existing legal aid organizations. Much of the success in desertion work depends upon having reliable, efficient, coöperating agencies throughout the country. This is ready at hand if a strong enough central body is created to bring the local organizations into closer alliance and to provide the necessary clearing house for the transmission of cases and information.

The few greatest cities may need special organizations for special purposes, but the general development should be in the direction of merging all branches of legal

[1] The records show quite clearly, particularly when the growth of population is remembered, the effect produced by the National Desertion Bureau since its creation in 1912.

Year	Number of Persons given Charity Relief	Amount granted by United Hebrew Charities
1910	521	$31,251.00
1911	431	24,950.00
1912	313	18,319.00
1913	298	18,160.27
1914	234	17,384.49
1915	267	17,094.87
1916	195	14,803.77

aid service in any community into one definite society or bureau. This involves no loss of efficiency. Specialization should continue, but it should not be specialization of organization, but specialization of work within the one organization. Specialization is imperatively needed for desertion cases and criminal cases. It is just as much needed for seamen's cases, workmen's compensation cases, loan shark cases, in fact, for any extensive branch of the law giving rise to many cases among the poor. The one organization, if properly equipped, can secure the same efficiency through departmental specialization, and in addition it secures unity of purpose, control, and policy, better coöperation, less duplication, and it effects many economies in the overhead and administrative expenses.

§ 3

The legal aid system of Germany is very largely built on group lines. There are political, religious, and class bodies or associations which provide legal assistance for

Legal Aid by Employees and Employers
their members. Fortunately, the development in the United States, due chiefly to the influence of Mr. Briesen, which has already been noted, has been in an entirely different direction. The type of organization that extends its assistance to all poor persons in a city, regardless of politics, religion, or class is more democratic and it is sounder. As its function is to play a direct part in the administration of justice, it should no more be founded or carried out on partisan, or sectarian, or any other lines of cleavage than should the administration of justice itself.

There are two organizations in America which act for definitely limited groups rather than for the community in general.[1] The Labor Secretariat in New York is a coöperative legal aid society giving its assistance to the members of its constituent labor unions. The plan of itself is an entirely worthy one. It has never grown to any size nor has it extended itself into other cities. Though it has existed since 1902, it has been so far outstripped by other types of organizations that it has been lost sight of. In such an organization inevitably the fundamental conception of legal aid work is lost. It does not represent an extension of the administration of justice. It represents only a plan for securing, through combined purchasing power, the services of a private attorney. Had most of the organizations been of this type, the true position of the legal aid society in the administration of justice would have been clouded, and its influence in bettering and equalizing that administration, which has clearly been at work since the establishment of public legal aid in 1910, would not have been strong if it had been felt at all.

As a sort of complement to the Labor Secretariat, which typifies legal aid by employees, there is in Detroit the Ford Legal Aid Bureau, which represents legal aid

---

[1] It is interesting to note that in Havana, Cuba, legal aid is furnished by Wage Earners' Clubs. See 9 N. Y. Legal Aid Review, No. 3, p. 2.

by employers. This Bureau was started in March, 1914, as a part of the general welfare work which is carried on in the Ford factories. The Bureau is a division of the company's legal department. It has its office in the main factory building, and has a staff of four attorneys. The Bureau is chiefly interested in searching titles for men buying their homes under the profit-sharing plan, in protecting them from fraudulent insurance agents and others, in taking care of garnishment suits, and in facilitating naturalization proceedings.[1] The Bureau gives general advice, but does not usually undertake litigation.[2] It is a fair criticism that the Bureau is more interested in matters which affect or concern the company than in matters which affect the employee alone. Thus, if a man is sued and his wages are garnisheed for a debt of ten dollars, he will be given representation, but if he is owed ten dollars, he will not be given an attorney to bring suit in his behalf. The following table, covering an eight months' period from June, 1916, through January, 1917, shows the nature of the work done:[3]

Nature of Cases	Number of Cases
Titles examined	723
Appraisals of real estate	568
Advice on real estate matters	7,917
General legal advice	8,109
Citizenship cases	403
Protection in fraudulent transactions	316
Garnishments	1,982
Orders to show cause	223
Representations in court	528
Summons served	376
Total	21,145

In general the idea deserves the highest commendation. If it is developed along the lines of other legal aid organizations, it is capable of doing great good with its vast clientele of nearly one hundred thousand workmen. If it develops as a proprietary organization, its efficacy will be seriously impaired. It is a striking illustration of a principle that is steadily gaining better recognition in the business world.[4] It is known that a sick employee is an inefficient employee. Methods for safeguarding health and providing medical assistance are common. It is equally true that the mentally worried or harassed employee cannot do his best work. Worry impairs efficiency, but it is not realized how many men and women are troubled by domestic difficulties, by fear of the loan shark, or by other problems which, because they involve the law, terrify persons who do not know where to turn for advice and counsel. It is both humanitarian and good business for employers to afford legal as well as medical assistance. It is almost certain, however, that this can best be arranged not through

[1] This is set out in *Helpful Hints to Ford Employees* (1915), pages 32–34.
[2] This statement is made in a prospectus of the work prepared by the legal department for publication.
[3] Compiled from the daily reports of the Factory Legal Department to the Department of Education.
[4] The Manufacturers' Association of the City of Bridgeport: *Report on Welfare Work in Bridgeport* (1918), pages 70, 124.

a bureau controlled by the company but through the independent legal aid organization existing in the city. Because of a reticence which can easily be understood, men are slow to reveal their troubles to their "boss" or to attorneys responsible to him. They would be unlikely to admit having troubles at home, or having borrowed money, or being in debt. In dealing with an independent legal aid attorney there is no such reluctance, at least no more than there is with any attorney. The legal aid organizations are not now in a financial position to add largely to their work, but the company could properly pay the increased cost of its increased work by a subscription, which would be less than it would cost to run its own legal aid department.

It is not unlikely that in the future the large employers of labor will enter into some relationship with legal aid organizations. The Legal Aid Bureau of Nashville is a department of the Commercial Club, and its existence is due in large measure to the interest and activity of business men. Its secretary has emphasized the services that legal aid organizations may render to business organizations.[1] A step in this direction has been taken in Boston. The Edison Electric Illuminating Company has always permitted its employees to consult its own counsel, but recognizing that "it is a question whether all of our employees who might take advantage of this do so," it has made an extended statement concerning the Boston Legal Aid Society, and offers to give any employee a letter of recommendation from its Welfare Bureau to the society.[2]

§ 4

Returning to a consideration of the five types of legal aid organizations proper, it is desirable first to fix the extent to which each type has been used. We have earlier

In General of the Five Types
seen in studying the history of legal aid work that during the first two periods of its development the private corporation society was the favorite type, that during the third period the departmental type prevailed, and that during the last period the public bureau predominated. There have been fifty-eight distinct times when the question of organization has presented itself. This includes organizations which have been founded and then lapsed, mergers, and reorganizations. The various types have been employed to the following extent:

Type	Number
1. Private corporation societies	15
2. Public bureaus	9
3. Departments of organized charities	17
4. Bar association societies	5
5. Law school societies	5
6. Miscellaneous	7

[1] M. G. Denton: *The Services of Legal Aid Societies to Business, Particularly to Employers of Labor, Report of Proceedings of the Fourth Conference of Legal Aid Societies*, page 108.
[2] 8 Edison Life, No. 8 (August, 1917), pp. 257–259.

With the miscellaneous group we are not concerned. They are in the main organizations whose work has never become extensive or which have not yet had time to decide on their final form of organization. Of the fourth and fifth types — the bar association and law school societies — there are fewer organizations, and as they raise no difficult questions and may be easily described, it is advisable to deal with them first.

The law school type, though of great interest in connection with legal education, is not of importance in the general field of legal aid work. With the exception of the Harvard Legal Aid Bureau, they have proved weak and have done only a small amount of work.[1] The limitations of this type are inherent and obvious.[2] A staff of untrained men, not members of the bar, limited as to the time at their disposal, and all dispersed during the summer vacation, is not a model to be followed. These organizations have done no harm, much good to the comparatively few cases which have come to them, and a great deal of good to the men who have done the work. This last is the great asset of this type. It will leave its mark on the rising generation of lawyers. In discovering and developing this asset—an asset both to legal aid and legal education — the law school society has made an important contribution. The idea is one to be treasured and not lost. Fortunately it can be preserved and carried out more effectively in connection with other types of legal aid organizations which have permanence, trained supervision, and better equipment.

The bar association type has been employed only to a limited extent. In St. Louis the Bar Association established an excellent society. As it was soon afterward taken over by the city and operated as a department of government, it does not offer any final test for this type. The Birmingham attempt failed, so that New Orleans, Columbus, and Detroit are the only remaining societies of this sort. From the experience afforded in these three fields the bar association type is found wanting. Apparently the bar associations thus far have not had a proper vision of the opportunity and they have proved a weak instrument to which to entrust this important service. In New Orleans and Columbus the work has gone forward but slowly and the organization has hardly crystallized at all. In Detroit, where the society was started in 1909, despite an enormous growth of the city, the Bar Association has methodically gone on year after year appropriating five hundred dollars for the legal aid work, never grasping the opportunity or perceiving the need growing around it, and never giving more than perfunctory attention to the work. The result has been that despite the efforts of an able attorney in charge, the work has sunk to a low level. Detroit, conceded in 1917 to be the fifth city in the country, in legal aid work ranked twenty-fourth. There are several reasons for the failure of this type. The greatest is undoubtedly the general

[1] The Legal Aid Society of the George Washington University Law School ranks second and has done reasonably well under adverse conditions; the Yale Legal Aid Bureau has never attained strength; and no information is available as to the Legal Aid Bureau of the University of Tennessee. The Denver society is no longer in existence.

[2] For an extended presentation and discussion of this subject see *Report of Proceedings of the Fourth Conference of Legal Aid Societies*, pages 11-20; and *Third Annual Report of the Harvard Legal Aid Bureau*.

indifference with which the bar has thus far regarded legal aid work. There is further the natural conservatism of the bar, which makes the development of the bar associations themselves a tedious process, with the result that any activity of the association also grows slowly. There are two other limitations which also appear in other types and are more fully considered in their connection. They are: first, that an organization does better when it is independent and has to stand on its own responsibility; and second, that although legal aid work is primarily a legal affair, its best control and direction are secured when to the lawyer's point of view there are added other opinions representing other elements in the community.

The private corporation societies, the public bureaus, and the departments of organized charities constitute the three great types of organization. Not only do they greatly outnumber the other types, but by them is borne the burden of the work. In 1916, out of a total of 117,201 cases, they cared for 116,099 cases.

These three types raise two great questions. The first is as to the respective merits of the independent society, on the one hand, and, on the other, of the society or bureau which is not independent, but is a department of some larger charity organization. This is a question relating solely to organization, and it is the chief question from the point of view of how legal aid work may best be organized. The private corporation represents the independent form and the charity bureau the departmental form. On this issue the public bureaus afford examples of both kinds. There are independent public bureaus, and bureaus that are departments of welfare boards.

The second question is as to the respective merits of private and public organizations. This is the precise point which has been so much debated in the public defender discussions. It is more than a question of organization, it reaches down and calls into consideration the fundamental principles and meanings of legal aid work. On this question the private corporation societies and charity bureaus unite to present one side and the public bureaus to present the other.

Before analyzing these questions and weighing the arguments it is helpful to ascertain the present situation. The following table, arranged according to the size of cities, sets out where each type is to be found and the number of cases received by each organization in 1916. It is readily apparent that the private corporation societies predominate in the larger cities and the charity bureaus in the cities of the second class. This is made clearer if we add the cities where the work is still in indefinite shape, but where the charity bureau type has been adopted, as in Bridgeport, Des Moines, Grand Rapids, Indianapolis, and Seattle. It is further apparent that the private organizations are to be found mainly in the east, and the public organizations mainly in the west.

City	Population[1]	Type	Cases in 1916
		Private Corporation	41,646
New York	5,670,167	Private Corporation	957
		Department of Charity	5,788
Chicago	2,521,822	Private Corporation	10,697
		Department of Charity	4,685
Philadelphia	1,750,000	Private Corporation	4,845
St. Louis	850,000	Public Bureau	1,235
Boston	767,000	Private Corporation	2,608
Cleveland	750,000	Private Corporation	4,946
Los Angeles	600,000	Public Bureau	8,848
Baltimore	595,000	Department of Charity	376
Pittsburgh	590,000	Private Corporation	684
San Francisco	530,000	Private Corporation	242
Buffalo	480,000	Private Corporation	1,516
Cincinnati	450,000	Private Corporation	1,698
Milwaukee	448,000	Private Corporation	1,174
Newark	401,000	Private Corporation	2,155
Minneapolis	370,000	Department of Charity	3,029
Kansas City	300,000	Public Bureau	5,270
St. Paul	290,000	Department of Charity	1,749
Portland	275,000	Public Bureau	1,363
Jersey City	270,903	Private Corporation	447
Louisville	265,420	Department of Charity	78
Rochester	265,000	Department of Charity	382
Omaha	210,000	Public Bureau	1,318
Hartford	150,000	Department of Charity	134
Dallas	135,000	Public Bureau	1,480
Dayton	135,000	Public Bureau	922
Akron	130,000	Department of Charity	20
Duluth	104,000	Public Bureau	5,629
San Diego	90,000	Department of Charity	28
Plainfield	20,550[2]	Department of Charity	150

§ 5

Reason and experience unite to indicate that the independent organization, which generally is synonymous with the private corporation society, has many points of superiority over the departmental and dependent organization. It is *Independent* v. essential in this connection to stick to facts and not to be misled by *Departmental* terminology. There are departmental bureaus which are independent *Organizations* in all but name. There are private corporation societies which are not independent as to certain aspects of their work. The truth of the propositions

[1] The population figures are taken from the *World Almanac* for 1917, page 762.
[2] Figure given in 1910 Census.

hereinafter advanced receives excellent corroboration from this very situation, for invariably in so far as an organization is independent the advantages of the independent type are found, and in so far as it has surrendered its freedom of action the corresponding disadvantages appear.

The independent type of organization, as exemplified by the private corporation society, makes for greater responsibility and at the same time permits greater freedom of action. It must stand on its own feet. It cannot hide in the shadow or stay under the protecting wing of any other organization. Before the community, the courts, and the bar it must stand or fall according to its own reputation. The issue cannot be beclouded by any intermediary. That this fact inculcates a feeling of responsibility is undeniable. The executive committee of a general charity has no such interest in, and feels no such responsibility for, a legal aid bureau which is merely a department of the greater organization, as has the board of directors of the incorporated society. It is not without significance that as a rule the best societies are to-day of the independent type and that the work of an independent legal aid organization has never been given up. A very great failure in legal aid work is chargeable to charity organization management in Bridgeport; in Baltimore and Rochester the work has not developed as it should have during a space of six years ; and in Des Moines, Grand Rapids, and Indianapolis the charity control has failed to produce any definite or enterprising legal aid undertaking. It was the realization of these advantages which led Philadelphia in 1916 and Richmond in 1917 to become independent incorporated societies.

Legal aid work, when conducted as a department of charity, has less freedom of action. In funds, which are its sinews for work, it is often throttled by a charity budget in which it is but a small item. Its appeal for support, being through the charity, lacks direct force with the bar which should be its main source of reliance, and the response depends less on what it has accomplished and more on what the charity in general has accomplished. If the charity fails to earn public approval, the legal aid work is also doomed, as it has so resulted in Portland, Oregon. The reports of the legal aid departments are swallowed up in the general charity reports, and are confined to very brief compass. The legal aid attorneys in Minneapolis and Dayton have submitted excellent reports about the nature and significance of legal aid work which have never been published or given to the community in any form. A few paragraphs are selected by the general secretary or director of public welfare for incorporation in their annual report. The greater portion of the attorney's report never reaches any other person. For three years the Bureau in Kansas City published its own reports and in them is contained much invaluable information; during the last three years, however, its reports have been published as a part of the general report of the welfare board, with the result that they have shrunk both in size and value and contain little more than a bare statistical record. For nine years the Cleveland incorporated society published annual reports which still rank among the best contributions to legal aid literature, but since it has turned its financial control over to the Cleveland Federation for Charity and Philanthropy, its annual reports have dwindled to a leaflet, and in the Federation's Year Book it occupies a scant two pages. In a young movement such as legal aid is, and in one which is not at all understood, it is essential that the work have adequate presentation. Even the persons engaged in the work need all the information and assistance that can be gained from experience in other cities. The burden of leadership in thought and in making the movement known has fallen entirely on the independent corporation societies. They have been, and still are, the producers and disseminators of the only legal aid literature that there is. Had it not been for them, the legal aid movement would never have been known and its spread from city to city could hardly have been accomplished.

With the departmental type of organization there is less freedom of thought and less initiative. This results from the nature of the arrangement under which the departmental bureau is customarily conducted. There is a general secretary or director who stands between the legal aid attorney and the controlling board which alone can do things. Thus in Minneapolis the attorney reports to the general secretary, and he in turn reports to the controlling board. This is an unwise arrangement, for no general secretary is competent to pass on the issues presented. Legal aid work is a distinct thing from general charity work, it requires the legally trained mind acting in the light of a knowledge of legal affairs to understand much of its significance and to chart wisely its course of activity. The general secretary of a charity organization is disqualified from passing expert opinion on such matters, he lacks the legal training to apply to them, and he approaches them from an entirely different background. The same difficulty applies, in most instances, to the controlling board, which has the final word and determines the budget. A board quite competent to supervise the traditional charity departments is incompetent to determine the peculiar questions presented by legal aid work. This checks growth and tends to retard the development which normally takes place with an intelligent counsel dealing directly with a board picked because of their peculiar fitness for and interest in directing legal aid work. The independent organizations always have been and still are blazing the trail.

The greatest flaw in the departmental type is that its power for good is lessened by the fact that it tends to reach a smaller group of persons than does the independent type. The legal aid bureau of an associated charities or federated charities generally has its offices with that organization. Often the offices are in the local charity building. It is the customary and the natural arrangement for all applicants to go to a central application desk, and there to be referred to the proper office or person. These facts give rise to an impression in the community which confuses legal aid with charity, which in turn has a marked effect in limiting the legal aid clients to persons who are applicants for charitable assistance. The self-supporting class, able to pay its own way in the ordinary affairs of life, but unable to meet the unusual expenses called for by any litigation, is strongly inclined to stay away. This tendency has often been suspected,[1] but until 1916 there was no corroborative evidence.

In April, 1916, the Legal Aid Department of the United Charities of St. Paul moved its offices from the Wilder Charity Building, where it had had offices with the other charity organizations of the city, to an office building given over largely to lawyers' offices. Immediately the number of clients doubled. The test is a fair one. Both buildings are accessible, the Wilder Charity Building is a beautiful modern structure and the Society's present quarters are in an old, third-class office building. There are no other or unusual circumstances to account for this almost automatic doubling of the work. The same attorney remained in charge, and the work was carried on as before. The increase was no temporary flurry, as an analysis of the cases shows. The change was made April 22, 1916. A comparison of the cases accepted during the five months ending April 30, 1916, and during the five months following April, 1916, makes this clear.

| In Charity Building | | In Office Building | |
Month	Cases	Month	Cases
December	61	May	113
January	42	June	85
February	50	July	102
March	50	August	85
April	50	September	109
Total	253	Total	494

This cannot be accounted for by any seasonal variation. The peak of the load for most organizations comes during the winter months. The sums of money collected for clients also increased from $2533.47 to $3280.71.

It is possible to ascertain where this increase came from. The number of cases sent by the charities and the courts remained constant and other sources very nearly constant with the exception of the State Labor Department. From this channel there came 319 cases as against 128 during the five months' period before the change. This is reflected in the records of the nature of the cases, which show that the increased work is mainly accounted for by wage claims, which jumped from 165 to 376 cases. For a matter of this sort the evidence is remarkably clear and convincing that formerly persons who applied at the State Labor Board for assistance in securing their wages and were referred to the legal aid society, when they went to the address given and found it to be a charity building, declined to enter and went away, and that now the same sort of persons with the same sort of cases, having the same feelings and ideas about themselves, are quite willing to go to the legal aid bureau in its new location.

All these arguments are minimized in so far as the departmental societies are given autonomy. If a legal aid bureau of an organized charity has in fact its own offices, its own executive committee empowered to decide and act, its own budget, and the con-

[1] Cf. 15 Boston L. A. R. 18; 1 Hartford L. A. R. 3; St. Louis (Bar Ass'n) L. A. R. 3; 1 Baltimore L. A. R. 5.

trol of raising its finances, no harm is done by adhering to the name. These statements are necessarily generalizations. In a given locality they may be outweighed by
peculiar local conditions. Nor are they to be taken as a disparagement of the work
performed by the departmental bureaus. Some of them, particularly those in Minneapolis and St. Paul, have done extremely well. It is the sole purpose of this examination to state such conclusions as are demonstrable by facts, so that legal aid work may,
in the light of experience, develop as soundly as possible.

§ 6

In the all-important issue between publicly supported, publicly controlled legal assistance to poor persons and privately supported, privately controlled legal assistance

*Public v. Pri-
vate Legal
Aid Organi-
zations*

no distinction need be made between the "public defender" organizations and the "legal aid" organizations. The conflicting principles
presented by the Los Angeles Public Defender and the New York
Voluntary Defenders Committee are in no wise different from those
presented by the Kansas City Legal Aid Bureau of the Board of Public Welfare and the New York Legal Aid Society. In the ensuing discussion no distinction will be made, and the phrase "legal aid organizations" will be used to include
both groups. The only issue is which type is superior, which type should be selected
for the future development of legal aid work,—the publicly controlled or the privately controlled legal aid organization?[1]

Theoretically, the argument for public legal aid is irrefutable. The basis of the
argument takes us back to the beginning of this report, where our ideal of the freedom and equality of justice was set forth. Equality before the law is the crux of the
situation; the ideal of freedom is a reinforcing principle which plays a part in so far
as it is necessary to secure the essential principle of equality. Justice must be equally
accessible to all persons, and the administration of justice must deal equally with all
persons. Where equality can be secured only by reducing the price of justice, the cost
must be reduced; where equality can be secured only by making justice free, then
there must be freedom of justice. In the issue which confronts us these ideals take
on concrete form and demand practical application.

Legal aid work is part and parcel of the administration of justice. It is not dispensing charity. It is simply giving or securing to each applicant what is his right.
Historically we can see that the administration of justice by the state as we now have
it has come about by a gradual process of the state's taking over to itself the performance of the various functions which make up the administration of justice.[2] At

---

[1] Control and support almost always go together. All publicly controlled bureaus are supported out of public funds.
All privately controlled societies, except three, are exclusively supported by private subscriptions. The Buffalo
Legal Aid Society receives financial assistance from the City of Buffalo and the County of Erie. The Richmond Legal
Aid Society receives free rent in the Juvenile Court Building. The Voluntary Defenders Committee in New York re-
ceives free rent in a municipal building.

[2] Zane: *Bench and Bar in the Golden Age of the Common Law,* 2 Illinois Law Review (1907), 1.

one time the function of the judge was in private hands. The lord of the manor was the judge for his tenants. The church exercised its ecclesiastical jurisdiction over marriage and the administration of estates. In the time of Henry II a step forward was taken when the greater part of the judicial function was entrusted to judges, responsible only to the king, who as sovereign occupied the position of the modern state. Many of the ministerial functions were originally in private hands. After a judgment for damages the plaintiff himself satisfied his judgment by taking away the defendant's property. Now the levy of execution is exclusively in the hands of the sheriff, a public officer. Arrests and service of process in criminal cases were for years made by private persons until the police systems were established. In the not far distant past prosecutions for crime were in private control. A private individual made his complaint and paid his own attorney to prosecute the case in court.[1] This function was taken over by the state acting through its district attorneys and prosecuting officers. To-day all the basic component parts of the administration of justice are in the control of the state, except the part taken by attorneys in bringing and defending civil suits and in defending criminal matters.

The state enacts the laws, controls the judges, the clerks, the bailiffs, the sheriffs, the probation staff, the police, the district attorneys, the jurors, and provides the court houses. If this were enough to secure equality before the law, there would not be the slightest case for public legal aid bureaus. But we have already seen that in many cases in many fields of law, the inequality resulting from the inability to employ counsel vitiates the equality of the whole machinery. We know that this is so because it is the attorney who supplies the motive power to make the machinery of justice move. If one were to use a homely analogy, the administration of justice might be likened to an automobile, in which the law represents the engine, the judge the control, and the attorney the gasoline. To give to two men exactly the same type of car and supply one with gasoline and the other with none and then to expect a fair race is obviously preposterous. So long as the attorney is made necessary by the form of the machinery, equality can be had only if the attorney's services are available to every one.

The last step in the extension to its natural completion of the state's control over judicial proceedings is the taking over, so far as may be necessary to secure equality, of the control of the attorney, thereby guaranteeing that poverty shall bar no one from securing the attorney's services. It is the accomplishment of this step which the public legal aid organizations represent. The conception of a judicial proceeding in which equality is guaranteed by having every participant an officer of the state is no longer a dream, it may be seen any day in Los Angeles. A deserted wife tells her story to a district attorney. He makes out a complaint and transfers it to the Public Trustee, who makes a preliminary investigation. The clerk draws a warrant, which is given to an officer for service. The defendant is brought into court for arraignment and

---

[1] Hyde: *Reorganization of the Bar*, 8 Illinois Law Review (1913), 239, 240; 5 Journal of Criminal Law and Criminology, 926.

trial before the judge. The state and the prosecuting witness are represented by an assistant district attorney and the defendant by the Public Defender. If there is a verdict or finding of guilt, the defendant is put under the supervision of a probation officer and pays the weekly amount ordered by the court to the Public Trustee.

This is not an argument for the socialization of the bar. It is an argument for equality. For persons who are able to employ their counsel, no change is necessary, but for the vast multitude who cannot, some readjustment is imperative. It is not a claim that the state should pay all lawyers. It is a claim that the state should pay for lawyers to represent poor persons in proper cases where the attorney's services are necessary to secure equality before the law. It must be made clear that the case for such state paid attorneys is not based on sentimentality, or charity, or kindness, or anything of the sort. Nor is it a progressive proposition in the sense that it is opposed to a conservatism that cherishes the good in our existing institutions. It is based on fundamentals as to which citizens of all opinions — conservatives and radicals — are in accord.

The point is that in all litigation the state is the great silent party in interest. This is clear in criminal cases, in divorce matters, and in disbarment proceedings. It is equally true in all so-called private litigation.[1] If this were not so, why should the state require that parties to private litigation use its laws, its courts, and its judges to determine their private quarrel? Originally the state was compelled to take a hand to preserve the peace, to prevent private vengeance, self-help, self-redress, all of which disturbed the King's peace. With the rise of the ideals of democracy a far better reason was supplied. Our government was designed to secure through its laws the individual rights to life, liberty, and property, and the more newly conceived social interests. The laws are able to effect these purposes only through the administration of justice. When a man by his labor has accumulated property there are persons who would like to take it away from him by force or trickery. To permit it would be to sanction anarchy. The law forbids, and it attains its end through the administration of justice, which enjoins the wrong, or gives redress, or punishes the offender. If, for any reason, the man were prohibited from obtaining the assistance of the law through the processes of the administration of justice, his rights would be worthless, the law would be an impotent sham, and his property could be taken with impunity. Yet this is precisely the position of the poor.

To the conservative the proposal that the state should provide counsel for the poor seems class legislation. By this he means that it is unjust to tax those who have accumulated property by their energy, frugality, and enterprise in order to help those who have not. In other words, he feels that equality of opportunity becomes meaningless if those who take their opportunities are to be penalized in favor of those who do nothing. When properly applied these points have great force, but they have

[1] Cf. Blackstone's statement: "Besides, the public is in nothing so essentially interested as in securing to every individual his private rights." 1 Blackstone's Commentaries, 139.

no application within the realm of justice. Exact justice is the basis of equality of opportunity. It is as repugnant to the conservative as to any one that a man should prosper by employing persons to work for him, taking the profits of their labor, discharging them without pay, and being enabled to pursue such a course with impunity because of the inability of the workmen to invoke the machinery of justice in their behalf. Yet this non-payment of wages has happened in hundreds of thousands of cases.

There is no justification for saying that justice should be denied if a person cannot pay the price fixed. No one would claim that the only persons entitled to protection are those who are able to defray the cost of that protection by paying the judge and clerk their salaries, the jurors their fees, and by renting the court room. The cost of justice is variously estimated. In Massachusetts the expense to the state of a civil jury trial has been fixed at $248.89 per day.[1] The Public Defender in Los Angeles has reported that the salaries, fees, and overhead expenses in a criminal jury trial amount to $200 per day.[2] The daily cost of the Philadelphia Court of Common Pleas is about $150.[3] The expense of a jury trial in the Chicago Municipal Court is not less than $75 per day.[4] Any serious proposal to restrict the use of the courts to only such persons as could defray these expenses is inconceivable. Justice is not merchandise; it cannot be granted or withheld according to the purchasing power of the applicant. It is the affirmative duty of the state, at public expense, to do all that is needful to secure justice to every one. In the main this is perfectly recognized. The state does afford all that is necessary with the exception of the attorney. As this omission is fatal in certain cases, the argument concludes that the state must administer its justice better by supplying the attorney in such cases.

Emergencies and times of stress often serve to make clear the injustice of a course of conduct which is tolerated in every day life. After the great explosion of ammunition at the Jersey City wharves, known as the " Black Tom " explosion, the City Attorney's office publicly offered to accept the claims of the families whose men had been killed and to bring suits for negligence without any charge to the clients whatsoever. The injustice of leaving these destitute families without redress or of compelling them to seek relief through the usual channel of the contingent fee became so clear that the public appreciated and undertook its responsibility. The federal government, in coöperation with the states, has undertaken to furnish free legal aid to the ten million men of draft age in connection with the legal problems raised by the new classifications of men under the selective draft law.[5] The attorneys who are giving the advice are not to be paid out of public funds, but they are under govern-

[1] *Report of the Massachusetts Industrial Accident Board of* 1914–1915 (Public Document 105 of 1916), page 71.
[2] In a supplemental report to the *Report of the Public Defender to the Board of Supervisors* for the year 1915–16.
[3] *Address* of Judge Charles L. Brown to the Men's Club of the Market Square Presbyterian Church (1914), page 12.
[4] *Eighth and Ninth Chicago Municipal Court Reports*, page 130. For a general article see Rood: *The Cost of Public Justice*, 12 Illinois L. Rev. (1918) 540.
[5] A concise presentation of the regulations is contained in 2 Mass. Law Quarterly, 563 *et seq.*

mental control and the clients are not to pay fees. This is public legal aid work in one limited field. It is the assumption by the government of the responsibility which during the first draft the legal aid societies all over the country met to the fullest extent of their resources.

If this position is well taken, and the logic behind it is undeniably strong, it follows that it should be the state, and not any private group, which should provide and control the attorneys for the poor. The administration of justice is a public affair, every part of which must be subject to public control. These attorneys for the poor stand on the same footing as the judges. Both are supplied by the state because only through them can the administration of justice operate. Such attorneys should no more be left to private selection or made subject to private control than should the judges. Further, it is a fact that the privately supported agencies are unable to meet the entire need because they lack the necessary funds. The state can recognize no such limitation. In its supreme duty of administering justice, the state cannot permit a condition under which its administration is equal or unequal, a success or a failure, according to the ability or inability of a handful of private persons to raise a certain amount of money.

In passing from the theoretical to the actual we leave an argument that is all in favor of publicly controlled and publicly supported legal aid organizations and are immediately confronted with a practical situation which gives rise to grave doubts. All of the public bureaus are controlled by municipal governments except that of Los Angeles, which is a county office. It is a commonplace that many American municipalities possess improper and inefficient governments in which politics play an undue part. It is always a question whether it is safe to entrust an essential service, such as legal aid, to such a government. The privately incorporated societies in the larger eastern cities have frankly been afraid to surrender any part of their autonomy to political control.[1]

Certain direct advantages have resulted from the fact that a legal aid bureau was a public undertaking. St. Louis affords an excellent illustration because, during its history, it has been both a private and a public organization. The investigator reports that since the society came under public control her position has carried with it much greater dignity and power, enabling her to use channels formerly closed and to do more efficient work. The Bureau has the whole-hearted coöperation of the other public departments. As a private society there was great difficulty in getting justices of the peace to accept in forma pauperis affidavits, thereby waiving their costs, but now they offer no objection.[2] There was a further difficulty in that the jurors' fees in the justice's court amounted to nine dollars, and these had to be paid. Now, if a jury is claimed, the Bureau is not obliged to pay the fees because the jurors are

---

[1] The New York Legislature has authorized the Board of Estimate of the City of New York to appropriate $25,000 for the Legal Aid Society. The New York Society has not used this fund. It has always been afraid of political control. See 23 N. Y. L. A. R. 13; 32 *Ibid.* 10; 11 *Ibid.* No. 4, p. 2; *History of the Legal Aid Society*, page 48.

[2] *Report of Proceedings of the Fourth Conference of Legal Aid Societies*, pages 86, 88.

required to serve as a public duty. Even more important, the public bureaus are unquestionably better known, they reach a wider field, and they are answering the demand for legal assistance with a nearer approach to completeness than the private societies. This fact appears very clearly in the later discussion as to how far the legal aid organizations are meeting the full need.[1] It may here be noted that since the Hartford society became a public bureau on January 1, 1917, its work has more than tripled.[2] In St. Louis the work has likewise made a substantial increase.[3] Detailed records are available and from them it appears that the nature of the cases, the sources of the cases, the nationalities of the applicants, and the fees charged, are almost exactly the same under public control as they were when the work was controlled by the Bar Association.

The public legal aid bureaus started out with a splendid record. Most of the positions in the legal aid staffs were put under civil service regulations, high standards were set, and there was no sign of political interference. It has been felt by persons who were closely watching this development that any original success was not conclusive, that the real test would come only after the bureaus had been in existence a few years, long enough for the novelty to wear off and for public interest to wane.[4] Until 1917 the outlook was most hopeful. Los Angeles, Portland, Kansas City, St. Louis, Dallas, Duluth, Dayton, Hartford, and Omaha were doing splendid work, they had placed excellent attorneys in charge, and in several respects they were proving more successful than the private societies. Thus, in Kansas City, the Legal Aid Bureau established a much higher standard in the treatment of desertion cases than any private society had attained. In one year thirteen deserting husbands were traced and brought back from Missouri, Oklahoma, Colorado, Nebraska, and Washington at an expense of six hundred dollars. The Bureau officially stated that if a deserting husband could be found, no expense would be spared in bringing him to justice. The private societies have been prohibited by financial considerations from even attempting this work. Most of the attorneys in the public legal aid bureaus were placed under the civil service, and were selected after examinations into their fitness. Politics did not venture to meddle in their offices. There was a change of administration in Kansas City, the Republicans replacing the Democrats, but the legal aid attorney was not interfered with, the budget appropriation was kept up, and the Bureau's work went along uninterruptedly.

In 1917, however, the danger of this public type of legal aid organization was made clear. In May a new administration took over the city government of Dallas.

[1] Chapter XX, Present Position of Legal Aid Work, § 1, page 192.

[2] The work in Hartford is naturally small. For three years the organization was private. During the first year it averaged 6 cases a month, during the second 7 cases, and during the third 8 cases. The public bureau has averaged 27 cases a month.

[3] This does not appear from the records in the Appendix because since the Bureau became a public undertaking no record of cases is made in which advice only is given.

[4] Cf. statement of Rudolph Matz, late President of the Chicago Legal Aid Society, in *Report of Proceedings of the Fourth Conference of Legal Aid Societies*, pages 51, 52.

The Mayor dismissed the director of the Department of Public Welfare under which the Legal Aid Bureau operated. He then sought to appoint a personal friend as attorney for the Bureau, and when that gave rise to a storm of public protest he abolished the Bureau entirely. Legal aid work no longer exists in Dallas. In July a new administration was elected in Portland, Oregon. The attorney holding the office of Public Defender had attained the highest rank in a competitive civil service examination for the position and had received a permanent appointment. He had not supported the newly elected Mayor in his campaign, however, and on July 13 the City Council, at the Mayor's request, without any public hearing and without notification to the Public Defender, abolished the office. In both instances the evidence is clear that the bureaus were doing good work, that the attorneys were superior men, and that the discontinuance of the work was due solely to petty political considerations. As if to furnish a striking contrast, the year 1917 also witnessed the establishment by private enterprise in New York of a privately controlled, privately supported, Voluntary Defenders Committee, which by virtue of its personnel, equipment, and work ranks among the very best legal aid organizations in the country.

Because of this unhappy discrepancy between theory and fact, the only conclusions that can be drawn as to the respective merits of public and private legal aid organizations are local rather than general in application. Where local political conditions permit, there is every reason for organizing legal aid work as a public affair under public control. On the other hand, in cities where private legal aid organizations are well established, there is every reason for them to remain as they are. They possess a freedom of action, a liberty in taking risks in making experiments, which will leave in their hands for several years to come the duty of leadership in the development of legal aid work.

Nevertheless, there should be a clear consciousness on the part of all legal aid organizations that they are engaged in the performance of a public function, and that their ultimate goal is to become a part of the state's administration of justice. Thus far the only attempt at public control has been through the municipality, which is undoubtedly the weakest part of our entire structure of government. It is easily conceivable that some plan may be devised whereby the value of public control may be secured without paying the price of diminished efficiency through political interference. As legal aid work relates itself to the administration of justice rather than to municipal government, it is preferable that the work should be organized and controlled as a part of the judicial machinery which is increasingly being taken out of the field of partisan politics. In the last chapter of this report, dealing with the future of legal aid work, a suggestion of this sort is considered.[1]

---

[1] See post, Chapter XXV, A More Equal Administration of Justice, § 3, page 246.

CHAPTER XX

PRESENT POSITION OF LEGAL AID WORK

The largest law office in the United States is the Legal Aid Society of New
York, with nearly 40,000 new cases annually. The next largest office is the Legal
Aid Society of Chicago, with 12,000 new cases annually. JOHN H. WIGMORE.[1]

§ 1

Present Extent of the Work

THE present extent of organized legal aid work involves two considerations.
first, measured by geography and by the size of cities, how far have the legal aid
organizations been able to extend themselves? second, measured by
the need, how far have the organizations been able to extend their
assistance in the cities where they exist?

If the cities in which legal aid organizations are to be found were marked on a
map of the United States, the eye would at once see that there are two great areas
wherein legal aid work is non-existent. One is the far west. Bounded by lines running Duluth–Minneapolis–Omaha–Dallas on the east and Portland–San Francisco–Los Angeles on the west, there is an enormous extent of territory without
legal aid organizations. This is all newer country, there is as yet no great need for
the work, for there are almost no large cities.[2] The extension of legal aid work into
this field is only a question of time. If a need manifests itself, societies or bureaus will
be formed and the work undertaken in due course.[3]

The second area is that of the southeast. South and east of a line running Richmond–Louisville–Nashville–New Orleans no legal aid work is done. The organizations in these boundary cities have not flourished as well as elsewhere. The situation
here differs radically from that of the far west. There is great need of the work, for
there are large cities with much poverty. It is not a question of orderly extension in
due course, for the attempt to plant legal aid institutions has already been made, but
without success. In Atlanta and Birmingham societies were started under the inspiration of small local groups, did well for a while, and then were allowed to lapse. In
Chattanooga, Knoxville, and Memphis some steps for the formation of organizations
were taken, but the plans have accomplished practically nothing. Here is to be found
the only general failure of the legal aid idea. No satisfactory explanation of this condition has ever been offered. Apparently there is need for the assistance of some
strong central organization to coöperate with local groups and to assist the work
until it shall have won local interest and support.

This geographical examination reveals the extent of the work only in a most general way. A far better test is afforded by cities, for organized legal aid work is es-

---

[1] From an editorial in 12 Illinois Law Review (1917), 38.

[2] A movement to start an organization is underway in Salt Lake City. Denver once had a flourishing society which
does not now exist.

[3] Letters from attorneys in Washington, Montana, and Utah have already come to some of the larger eastern organizations asking for information about the work.

sentially a city problem. We have earlier seen that the growth of urban population was a prime factor in bringing about the breakdown of the administration of justice, and that it is in the large cities that the great denial of justice exists. The chief defect in our traditional administration of justice which causes hardship to the poor is the expense of counsel. In the country towns and smaller cities this difficulty is overcome by the charity work of the lawyers. It is the general opinion that it is rare indeed for an inhabitant of a small town to be denied legal assistance even if he is unable to pay for it. Just where the line of demarcation is to be drawn is not certain, but there is good authority for fixing it at cities with a population of one hundred thousand. In connection with this study letters were sent to the charity organization societies (also called "associated," "federated," and "united charities") in all cities and towns in the United States where there were no legal aid organizations, asking if they experienced a need for organized legal aid work. The replies indicate that the one hundred thousand population mark is as accurate a dividing line as can be fixed. There seems to be a tacit agreement that this is the point at which a city becomes a large city and at which those problems that are essentially "city" problems make their appearance.[1]

In considering how far the legal aid movement has been able to cover the large cities we face three situations: cities with no legal aid work, cities with very little legal aid work, and cities having definitely established organizations doing substantial work that gives every indication of steady, consistent development. The following table presents the facts in summary form. We know that legal aid work started in New York and Chicago, our two largest cities, so that the question is how far the legal aid movement has been able to work downward into the cities with smaller populations. In order to indicate this, the cities are divided into five groups, each lower group including the higher group, so that the total number of cities having a population over the specified figure may appear.[2]

Class	Total Cities of this Class in the United States	Legal Aid Work		
		None	Very Little	Definitely Established
1. Cities over 350,000	18	0	0	18
2. Cities over 300,000	21	0	2	19
3. Cities over 200,000	33	3	4	26
4. Cities over 150,000	41	6	6	29
5. Cities over 100,000	71	27	10	34

For the purpose of this test, which aims to ascertain to what extent legal aid organizations have been established in our large cities, we may consider that the situ-

[1] Dr. King in his book *Wealth and Income of the People of the United States*, in discussing the growth of large cities (page 20), fixes the line at cities with a population of over one hundred thousand.

[2] The table is based on the legal aid situation on January 1, 1917. The cities are grouped according to the population credited to them on that date by the *World Almanac* for 1917. For this purpose the 1910 Census figures are too old to be accurate.

ation in cities having no work or very little work is unsatisfactory, and that in cities having definitely established work it is reasonably satisfactory. A recapitulation in percentage terms, based on the preceding table, shows very clearly the present extent of legal aid organizations.

Class	Total Cities of this Class in the United States	Percentage of Cities in which Legal Aid Work is	
		Satisfactory	Unsatisfactory
1. Cities over 350,000	18	100.0	.0
2. Cities over 300,000	21	90.0	10.0
3. Cities over 200,000	33	78.8	21.2
4. Cities over 150,000	41	70.7	29.3
5. Cities over 100,000	71	47.9	52.1

There is still much room for the extension of legal aid work into new fields. The large cities are by no means completely covered. When it is remembered that the idea did not begin to spread until 1900, it is remarkable that it has been able in seventeen years to take definite shape in all the largest cities and in three-quarters of those having over two hundred thousand inhabitants. The problem of expansion for the immediate future—and one which will call for intelligent direction from some central body—is to establish organizations in the twenty-five cities having none and to strengthen those in the nine cities where the movement is still weak. This is essentially an extension into a new class of city, one whose population is above one hundred thousand but below two hundred thousand.

In taking up the question of the extent to which the legal aid organizations in the cities where they exist have been able to meet the full demand of the poor for legal assistance, we at once encounter a difficulty because we have no objective standard by which to measure their work. We can estimate the number of the poor in the larger cities, but there is no way of knowing how many of them each year are involved in litigation or need legal aid. It is possible, however, to work out a reasonably accurate standard suitable for our immediate purpose. The public legal aid bureaus, in localities where they exist, are well known to, and very generally used by, the poor of the city. The Kansas City Legal Aid Bureau is the oldest of this type, and unquestionably is the best locally known legal aid organization in the United States. In 1915, which was a normal and average year, one out of every 64 persons in the total population[1] applied to it for assistance. The Los Angeles office is the second best known, and in 1915 it received one application from each 78 in the population.[2] On the basis of this Kansas City–Los Angeles record, we may say that the standard annual legal aid clientele would consist of one person for each 75 inhabitants. There are no data anywhere which would show this estimate to be materially in error and, on the other hand, there is evidence to indicate that it closely approximates a true

[1] The Bureau serves a population wider than that within the city limits, which in 1915 was fixed at 400,000.
[2] Los Angeles is a county office serving the entire county population, which in 1915 was fixed at 800,000.

standard. Thus, according to our criterion, Kansas City and Los Angeles were receiving as many applications as they should, so that during 1916, which was a year of more steady employment giving rise to fewer wage claims, they should have received somewhat fewer applications. Their records show this to have been the case.[1] Considering the cities where private societies have longest been established: the New York organization in 1915 extended assistance to one in each 116 of the population, and it is known that there is a large demand for legal aid which is not being met because of inadequate finances. The Chicago organizations in 1915 received cases from one in each 162 of the population: the Chicago Legal Aid Society has stated that if funds permitted, it could double its work; and the Chicago Bureau of Personal Service, with increased resources, did in fact during the next year extend its work 85 per cent.

In many ways it would be preferable to measure the extent of legal aid work by the 1915 figures, but as this would exclude organizations formed in 1915 or early in 1916, it is necessary to take the fiscal year of 1916. In the following table are set out, first, what the standard clientele of each legal aid organization should be on the basis of one client for each seventy-five inhabitants;[2] second, the actual number of cases received during the fiscal year of 1916; third, the percentage that the actual number bears to the standard; and fourth, in an outside column, the per capita amount expended in each city for legal aid work, for there is a close relation between the financial condition of the societies and the extent of their work. Such local factors as enter in to make the table inaccurate for comparative purposes are set out in the notes.

TABLE SHOWING PRESENT EXTENT OF LEGAL AID WORK

Legal Aid Organizations in	Standard Clientele	Cases in 1916	Per Cent of Standard	Per Capita Amount Spent in Cents
Kansas City	5,333	5,270	99.0	1.05
Los Angeles	10,666	8,848	83.0	2.35
Dallas	1,800	1,480	82.0	1.78
Duluth	1,386	3	80.0	3
New York	75,602	48,391	64.0	1.11
Minneapolis	4,933	3,029	61.0	.93
Plainfield	274	150	54.0	4
Dayton	1,800	922	51.0	.97

[1] The work in Kansas City decreased from 6202 cases in 1915 to 5270 in 1916; in Los Angeles from 10,277 in 1915 to 8848 in 1916; the decreases being 15 per cent and 14 per cent respectively.

[2] Since 1910 there have been such great changes in urban population, as notably in Cleveland and Detroit, that the Census figures are wholly antiquated. The figures for population on January 1, 1917, as given in the *World Almanac*, are used.

[3] The Duluth Free Legal Aid Bureau case figures include the Municipal Court probation cases, so that they cannot be used in this connection. For the same reason the expense apportionable to the legal aid work is not known. A careful estimate, however, shows that Duluth ranks no lower than 80 per cent.

[4] Legal aid expense not known, as the figures are not separated from the general budget of the Charity Organization Society.

Legal Aid Organizations in	Standard Clientele	Cases in 1916	Per Cent of Standard	Per Capita Amount Spent in Cents
Cleveland	10,000	4,946	49.0	.43
Omaha	2,800	1,318	47.0	.31
Chicago	33,624	15,382	46.0	1.73
St. Paul	3,866	1,749	45.0	.63
Newark	5,346	2,155	43.0	.78
Portland [1]	3,666	1,363	37.0	.71
Boston [2]	10,234	2,608	25.0	.84
Buffalo	6,400	1,516	24.0	.49
Cincinnati	7,517	1,698	22.0	.30
Philadelphia	23,333	4,845	21.0	.25
Milwaukee	5,983	1,174	20.0	.45
Nashville	1,853	260	14.0	[3]
Jersey City	3,612	447	12.0	[4]
Rochester	3,533	282	11.0	.49
Columbus	2,800	300	11.0	[5]
St. Louis	11,333	1,235	11.0	.68 [6]
Cambridge	1,466	104	7.0	[7]
Hartford	2,000	134	6.7	.08
Richmond	2,133	121	5.6	.02
Pittsburgh	13,904	684	4.9	.32
Baltimore	8,782	376	4.2	.17
Detroit	11,000	410	3.5	.06
San Francisco	7,133	242	3.4	.18
San Diego	1,200	28	2.3	.01
Louisville	3,539	78	2.2	[8]
Washington, D. C.	4,904	75	1.5	.00
New Orleans	5,333	74	1.4	.02
Akron	1,733	20	1.2	.00
New Haven	2,133	18	.8	.00

Eliminating those organizations whose case figures for one reason or another are not closely accurate, it appears that the general average attained by thirty cities is 28.1 per cent. In other words, it is undoubtedly true that thus far the legal aid organizations as a whole have not developed sufficient strength to satisfy the entire need. They have been able to accomplish only one-third of their whole aim. As many

[1] The case figure represents only the public defender's criminal work. No statistics of civil cases were kept.

[2] The standard is not strictly applicable to Boston because in that city wage claims are collected by the State Commissioner of Labor. *Semble* Chicago and Cleveland, owing to the existence of the small claims courts.

[3] The Nashville expense figures could not be secured.

[4] Complete expenses for the year are not known.

[5] In Columbus the attorneys volunteer their services and pay the incidental expenses, so that no total expense figure can be computed.

[6] In St. Louis cases calling only for advice are not recorded. If these were known, it is probable that St. Louis would rank at about 50 per cent.

[7] Law school students constitute the staff in Cambridge. Expenses are nominal and are not stated.

[8] The expenses of the Legal Aid Committee are not kept distinct from those of the Associated Charities.

of the organizations are new, the result of this test is not surprising; but the fact remains that if organized legal aid work is to solve the problem of the denial of justice, it must in the near future find the means and the resources to extend its assistance to this great group of persons who thus far have not been reached.

A division of the organizations according to their various types gives interesting results that bear out some of the observations made in the preceding chapter. It is obvious that the public bureaus are far better known and that, because they have larger funds at their disposal, they are more nearly able to satisfy the demand. It is also clear that the independent private corporation societies are able to reach and to care for a much wider field than the bureaus which are organized as departments of charities. A résumé, based on the preceding table, shows in percentage terms how far the organizations, grouped according to type, have been able to attain the standard.

Type	Per cent of Standard
1. Public Bureaus	72.4
2. Private Corporation Societies	30.6
3. Departments of Charities	18.7
4. Law School Societies	3.1
5. Bar Association Societies	5.3
6. Miscellaneous	10.0

§ 2

While it is true that the legal aid movement still has a long road to travel, it is equally true that already the existing organizations hold strong positions in their *Legal Aid Staffs* respective communities, and that more than any other agency they are striking at the root difficulty in our administration of justice by placing at the disposal of poor persons their staffs of skilled attorneys.

The legal aid organizations of the United States are to-day providing a corps of one hundred and seventy-five attorneys, all members of the bar and admitted to practice in all courts. Of these, sixty-two devote their entire time to the work and one hundred and thirteen are employed for part of their time, which ranges from one-third to one-half of the working day. These attorneys are assisted by sixty-three clerks and stenographers on full time, six on part time, and by thirty-three investigators and social workers who spend their entire time in legal aid service. This force of two hundred and sixty-seven persons, especially trained in legal aid work, constitutes a mighty force for making the position of the poor more equal before the law. In addition to these paid staffs, there is a much larger number of volunteer attorneys and workers who give a measure of their time which in the aggregate forms no inconsiderable item.

Legal aid work is essentially a young lawyer's work. It has been said with much truth, "In such excellent work every member of the bar might well bear a part. But it appears that the older members have left it all for the young ones."[1] There are twenty-eight organizations that have attorneys in charge of their work, and these executive attorneys, on an average, have been members of the bar for only seven years. As a number of these attorneys have been in charge for several years, if figures had been compiled three or four years ago, they would have shown a still younger group of leading attorneys. The assistant attorneys on the staffs are almost entirely even younger men.

All praise is due to the loyalty of these young attorneys to the cause of legal aid work. As Mr. Briesen has written, "Its success depends entirely on the purest devotion of its attorneys, upon an almost religious denial of every particle of self-interest on their part." They have been faithful to their trust. The present position of legal aid work is due almost entirely to them. They have been the leaders, the organizers, the workers, the thinkers, and the developers. If any older member of the bar is entitled to take credit unto himself, it is Mr. Briesen, and yet he has repeatedly taken occasion to pay his tribute to the efforts of the younger attorneys.[2] No one fact impresses the observer who sees one office after another more than the courage, zeal, and devotion which they everywhere manifest. To these men, invariably overworked, generally underpaid, struggling with insufficient equipment, sacrificing their opportunity to build up any private practice of their own, the entire profession owes a great debt. Legal aid work is what it is to-day, it has advanced as far as it has, its reputation is clear and free from suspicion because of them.

§ 3

The greatest weakness of organized legal aid work, the one great factor which constantly bars its path, and which may ultimately prove its undoing, is its lack of funds.

Poor Finances

The reason that the existing organizations have not more completely answered the demand of the poor for legal assistance is that they are grossly under-financed. This ever present condition of an impoverished treasury has forced the two greatest mistakes in the development of the work. It deterred the organizations from accepting the cases of injured workmen,[3] and it has precluded them from entering the criminal field.[4] Inadequacy of support compelled the New York Legal Aid Society to give up its work in Brooklyn for a while and still makes it impossible to open sorely needed branch offices in the Brownsville and Williamsburgh districts and in Queens County.[5] Mr. Briesen in a speech on "The Future"[6] pointed out the great obstacle when he said, "Our hands are tied." The Chicago Legal Aid Society, adopting the high courage of its leader, the late Rudolph Matz, determined to accept its full responsibility, and to meet the entire demand, with

---

[1] From an article in 18 Case and Comment (1912), 463, quoting the St. Louis *Republic*.
[2] 23 N. Y. L. A. R. 3; 25 *Ibid.* 17.   [3] See *ante*, page 85.   [4] See *ante*, page 155.
[5] 41 N. Y. L.A.'R. 28.   [6] 11 N. Y. Legal Aid Rev., No. 4, p. 3.

faith that its work would be appreciated and the necessary support would be forth-coming. In 1914 it had climbed well toward its goal,[1] but the financial support did not materialize, and it was forced to make drastic retrenchments. It is now able to keep its office open for clients only two hours a day, thereby mechanically reducing the number of applications, and it is forced to entrust much of its work to volunteers. Everywhere among the privately supported organizations the story is the same. Some of the public bureaus are in a stronger position, but even their finances are not yet adequate. The organizations all live a hand-to-mouth existence, which is not only de-pressing to the workers, but is a repressive force that keeps the legal aid work down and prevents it from accepting the great opportunity which awaits it.

Thousands of persons have been denied justice because the organizations were un-able to extend assistance to them. Within the organizations unfortunate results have been produced. Boards of directors have been forced to underpay their staffs. This has meant that young men, attracted to the work by their ideals of service, have at the end of a few years been automatically forced to abandon the work in order that they might earn their living. There has been a constant change of personnel which has greatly impaired the efficiency of the work,[2] and it has made more difficult the evolution of any science in its conduct. It has tended to narrow the conception of the work by keeping it intensely local. Few of the executive attorneys have ever had time to learn much more than how to conduct their own offices. About the time when they have mastered that and are beginning to observe what is going on in other cities, they are forced to leave the service and their experience and ideas are lost.

Taking the figures from the societies which pay their executive attorneys anything, it appears that seventeen organizations retain men for their full time at an average yearly salary of $2217. Excluding the salary of the chief attorney for the Voluntary Defenders Committee, which is the only organization thus far to be put on a straight-forward business basis, the average salary drops to $1887. The seven organizations that retain men on part time (one-half to one-third of their time) pay an average yearly salary of $628. It is perfectly apparent that at such figures the legal aid soci-eties cannot command or retain the services of the type and calibre of men they ought to have and must have if their work is to be properly conducted and successful.

When the nature of the work is considered, the extreme poverty of the organiza-tions is the more remarkable. They are engaged in an essential public service; they are performing for the community an obligation which comes before any duty to give charitable support. As careful an observer as Lyman Abbott has stated, "The first duty of society to the poor is not to give them charity but to secure them justice."[3] If the work were done at an enormous cost, an explanation would be afforded; but in point of fact legal aid work is the least expensive of all so-called charitable under-

---

[1] Measured according to our standard previously laid down, the work in Chicago in 1914 was answering 64 per cent of the entire need, as against 46 per cent in 1916.
[2] 14 Boston L. A. R. 5.   [3] 4 N. Y. Legal Aid Review, No. 2, p. 2.

takings. In the year 1916 the total cost of thirty organizations, which took care of over one hundred thousand cases, was only $181,408. As a part of this gross expense was met by fees paid by clients, the net average cost to the community for each case undertaken was about one dollar and fifty cents.[1] The annual expense of two or three first-class children's agencies or general charities would exceed the entire expense of these thirty legal aid organizations.

Legal aid work is carried on entirely by current subscriptions. The societies start each year with no balances, with no assured income, so that they are forced to measure the extent of their work from month to month according to the donations which they may receive. Of thirty-five societies from which accurate statistics are available, thirty have no endowment whatever. The endowments and invested funds of the societies in New York, Chicago, Philadelphia, Boston, and Pittsburgh amount to a total of only $37,356.86. How pitiably small this figure is may be seen by contrasting it with the endowment of a single well-financed agency such as the Massachusetts Society for the Prevention of Cruelty to Children, which has invested funds to the value of $352,198.[2]

Legal aid work in general does not receive any financial assistance from state or municipal governments. The few public bureaus are, of course, supported by public funds. Of the twenty-seven non-public organizations as to which accurate statistics are known, only three are publicly aided. The Buffalo Legal Aid Bureau receives an annual grant of $750 from the county of Erie and a like grant from the city of Buffalo. This exceptional situation is due to the earnest efforts of the Bureau's president, John Alan Hamilton, who requested the appropriations on the straightforward basis of services rendered, which it was easy enough to prove. The Voluntary Defenders Committee is given free rent, and the Richmond Legal Aid Society is permitted to use a room and the telephone in the Juvenile Court Building. The other private organizations—and it is this group which is still doing by far the greater portion of the work—receive nothing.

The work has had to be financed by periodic appeals to the bar and to the public. The results have been wholly unsuccessful. Various reasons are ascribed for this failure, of which two are most prominent. Financing is a matter for the boards of directors or executive committees. These boards, consisting in the main of lawyers, seem on the whole to have been sadly lacking in imagination and enterprise, so that they have failed to arouse any general interest in the work. It is certain that the legal aid idea has not been made clear, and that even to-day the work is very generally unknown. Although legal aid societies have existed since 1876 and the public defender offices only since 1914, the latter, due to two or three excellent publicists, are to-day far better known in the United States. Seemingly there has not been great difficulty in

[1] The figure varies from city to city. In New York it has been below one dollar per case for years; in Kansas City and Cleveland it has been as low as fifty cents per case.
[2] *Report of the Massachusetts State Board of Charity* for 1917, page 102.

securing legislative appropriations for the public defender's work, and in New York, where the undertaking is privately financed, the committee in charge was able to secure in a short space of time nearly as large an income as the Legal Aid Society has been able to acquire after forty-one years of service.

The second reason alleged is that legal aid work, from its very nature, lacks the appeal which other sorts of charities possess, so that its voice is lost in the multitude of appeals with which the public is deluged.[1] This reason must be accepted with some reserve. While the civil work of the legal aid organizations may not be as dramatic as the criminal work of the public defenders, it is full of vital interest if the proper persons could be found to give it adequate expression. Within the four walls of the legal aid offices human life is laid bare. More tragedies and comedies are enacted than can be seen on any stage. The people of the cities march in endless procession through the offices, leaving behind them a composite picture of life in our great cities. They are not the wrecks and failures of our civilization; they are self-respecting, self-supporting persons. As nearly as one group can, they represent the common people. What they think, how they fare, wherein they are handicapped, are matters of concern to every one, for it is to make the lives of just such persons somewhat brighter and fairer that we are trying to build a civilization founded on democracy.

That legal aid work fails to carry any appeal is true to this extent. For a definite appreciation of why the poor are denied justice and of how essential organized legal aid work is to a more equal administration of the laws, some background of knowledge concerning our legal institutions is necessary. Every one can understand that an abandoned family is likely to starve if it is not relieved; but it is not so self-evident that the calamity might have been prevented if the processes of the law could have been invoked, and that to seek redress through the law required somebody to provide free legal assistance. This very situation ought to constitute a strong and direct appeal to the members of the bar. Boards of directors have not thoroughly cultivated this field and so have met with but moderate success.[2]

This financial obstacle, ever present with every organization, is to-day the great limitation of legal aid work. It lacks the sinews of war. It is in leash, held in at every turn. Bad financing as to income is the rock on which all private organizations may go to pieces. All other factors in the present situation are decidedly hopeful. But this problem remains to be solved, and it must be solved quickly or else the organized legal aid movement must fail to go forward and gradually cease to be an important factor in the equalization of the administration of justice.

[1] Cf. 22 N. Y. L. A. R. 5, 17; 34 *Ibid.* 6.
[2] This is considered further in Chapter XXIV, Legal Aid and the Bar. See *post,* page 226.

§ 4

Legal aid work has not yet passed out of the stage of localized organization. We have already seen that the societies were started in the various cities by local groups act-
Lack of Cen- ing independently. If there was no such group, no society was started,
tral Control and if the group failed or dispersed, the society went with it. There never has been, as there is not now, any strong central agency in a position of leadership. There is no centralized responsibility or authority. The legal aid movement has not yet become a coördinated national undertaking.

There is a steadily growing realization among the local organizations of a community of purpose and of the need for closer coöperation. The feeling of comradeship became strong enough in 1911 to bring about a successful conference of delegates from the various societies then in existence. The discussion turned mainly on the advisability of some union, and while there was a feeling that such steps ought to be taken and excellent arguments for such a plan were advanced, there was also a certain holding back and a reluctance to be committed to anything definite. This was perhaps entirely natural at such a first gathering. The upshot of the meeting was to secure a committee to draft a form of alliance.

A second conference was held in 1912, at which the National Alliance of Legal Aid Societies was formed and a constitution and by-laws were adopted. From the point of view of organization this is as far as the development has proceeded. The Central Committee of the National Alliance has called two conventions, which have been productive of fruitful discussions and of a valuable interchange of opinions, but it has done nothing else. The weakness of the Alliance and the strength of the local tradition are well attested by the fact that even the conventions are in the main planned for and controlled by a local committee of the society which is the host, and the expenses of the convention are defrayed by that local organization. Thus if the local society delays the printing of the record of the proceedings (and these records unquestionably constitute the most valuable information about legal aid work in existence), the National Alliance can do nothing but wait, and if the funds of the local society permit the printing of only a limited number of copies, the National Alliance can do nothing but submit.

As it exists to-day, the National Alliance is like a federal government without power of taxation. It is impotent. There is a power to assess the local organizations, but it is not in use, partly because the local societies desire that the central body should not be strong and partly because they are poor. For all practical purposes the National Alliance does not exist except for a few days once in two years when a convention is in session.

The situation is unfortunate. It has retarded development and it may cause serious trouble. There is an imperative demand for such elementary things as standardized records of work, conventionalized classifications of the nature, source, and disposition of cases, and uniformity of financial accounting. It ought to be possible for one society to compare its work with that of any other in order to benefit from the lessons which accurate comparisons teach, but as there are as many systems as there are organizations, even the simplest comparison is a puzzle. There is great need for a central clearing house to provide for the proper reference of cases.[1] As commerce and business have overflowed all artificial state boundary lines, so legal aid work often runs beyond the confines of the city or state. With forty-one organizations in existence a substantial beginning could be made. A Boston creditor could collect from his debtor in San Francisco, and a wife deserted in Chicago could trace and locate her husband in New Orleans. Such a central agency could establish relationships with attorneys in smaller towns who were willing to do their share of legal aid work and thus provide a complete network, stretching over the entire country, so that no claims would have to be abandoned because of the absence of parties from the jurisdiction. The essential of any such plan is close supervision, which ensures that prompt attention be given to all matters so referred. One local organization cannot exercise such a control over another organization; it can be done only by a central body. As it is to-day, legal aid societies often refer cases to private attorneys rather than the legal aid societies in other cities because they have no guarantee that the latter will render prompt and accurate service.

There is no definite head, no leadership in the legal aid movement. Because of this no intelligent propaganda or missionary work is carried on. There is no attempt to bring legal aid work to the attention of bar associations or other groups in cities where there is an obvious need for such work. What happens at the present time is that persons desirous of having a legal aid society hear of the work in some one city, and so, when they establish their organization, copy the only plan which they know of with all its virtues and vices, or they may write to a number of larger societies and receive in reply such inconsistent information and such diverse models to follow that in despair they erect their own structure as best they know how. This is a slipshod way of conducting an important undertaking. A central bureau, with a field secretary, could place accurate information at the disposal of any organizers, could assist in installing a proper system calculated to take care of the work efficiently and economically, and could help new organizations through their first hard years. Intelligent leadership will be increasingly necessary as other remedial agencies develop and expand. It will be a distinct loss if the public defenders are allowed to grow apart from the legal aid organizations. Thus far no attempt has been made to bring the two together or to show that the two belong together and have much to learn from each other.

There are some enemies of the legal aid movement which can be attacked only through a powerful central organization. Abuse of the term "legal aid" may become a serious menace to a natural future development. Because of the universally high

[1] *Report of Proceedings of the First Conference of Legal Aid Societies,* page 34.

standard of the societies thus far the term "legal aid" has earned a connotation of fair play and square dealing. It has a good will that can easily be capitalized by unscrupulous attorneys. This is not a chimerical fear, for there are instances where it has already happened. In England the organization most nearly like our legal aid society is called "Poor Man's Lawyers' Association." There are a number of such organizations, but until 1913 they formed no alliance and had no concerted strength. As a result, there grew up all over England "Legal Aid Societies," which were simply catch names to draw business, serving the same purpose as the "runner," so that the term "legal aid society" became as much a term of reproach in England as it is above reproach in the United States. Such societies have been publicly denounced as wolves in sheep's clothing.[1]

Attempts to trade on the name have been made in New York, but were repressed by the vigorous action of the local society. In cities without societies the process can be and has been accomplished with impunity. There are to-day three legal aid societies in widely different parts of the country which are struggling under a heavy handicap because, before their existence, the name was used for fraudulent purposes. A wide-awake central body could have stopped such practices by promptly detecting them and enlisting the coöperation of the local bar association for their repression. Legal aid organizations may have no funds in their treasuries, but in their name they have an invaluable asset. They must guard it, for the chief strength of legal aid organizations in reaching the people who need help is the guarantee which the name carries.

There are further great possibilities for concerted action. There are national problems on which the experience of the legal aid organizations ought to be formulated. In many aspects of the divorce problem they could shed much light from the cases which come to them. If a study of non-payment of wages were to be made, their files together with the records of labor bureaus would furnish the best evidence. More important, they should play a direct part in the nation-wide movement for a betterment of the administration of justice by reorganization of courts and simplification of procedure. They should coöperate with such definite work as that of the American Judicature Society. In these subjects they are vitally concerned. They have the background from which to point out how the existing denial of justice to the poor may be lessened. They have a responsibility, second to none, in the planning and carrying through of our Americanization program. They possess the latent possibilities of becoming a mighty factor in the betterment of American justice.

None of these things are being done; none of these possibilities are being realized.[2] There is nowhere any responsibility or authority to undertake these larger projects. An adequate central organization is imperatively needed to make legal aid work a more concerted, aggressive, vital, and intelligent force.

[1] See an article in *Truth* for January 1, 1913 (No. 1880), page 12; also 47 Law Journal (1912), 48.
[2] See also *post*, page 217.

Chapter XXI

LEGAL AID AND THE LAW

It is precisely because the force of things tends always to destroy
equality, that the force of legislation ought always to tend to maintain it. Rousseau.[1]

§ 1

THE legal aid organizations throughout the country have steadily taken a deep
interest in legislation, they have made valuable contributions in many struggles to write wise laws on the statute books, and they have themselves secured the
enactment of several excellent pieces of legislation. The legal aid socie-
Legal Aid   ties are not legislative bureaus, they have no political affiliations, and
and Legis-   they are not vehicles for the promotion of any pet cause or panacea.
lation   Their primary work is confined to giving through their staffs of attorneys the legal advice and assistance in individual cases which poor persons need. It
early became apparent, however, that if they were to be effective in their fight against
injustice, they must from time to time take a part in the formulation of remedial legislation. They saw cases of injustice which the law was powerless to redress because
of the inadequacy of certain provisions or the lack of proper laws framed to meet the
changed conditions. In 1903 the New York Legal Aid Society amended the purpose
clause of its constitution so that it read:

> "The purpose of this Society shall be to render legal aid and assistance, gratu-
> itously if necessary, to all who may appear worthy thereof and who are unable
> to procure assistance elsewhere, *and to promote measures for their protection.*"

Language of similar import will now be found in the constitutions of the majority
of societies. The Chicago Legal Aid Society states as one of its objects:

> "Second. To take cognizance of the workings of existing laws and methods of
> procedure, and to suggest improvements."

Whether expressed in words or not, all the organizations, public and private, have
concerned themselves with legislation when their experience indicated a need for
improvement.[2]

It is worth while to enumerate in summary form the various legislative campaigns
which the societies have undertaken or in which they have played important parts.
Such a statement gives an idea of the sort of measures with which the organizations
have concerned themselves, and serves to indicate the general and intelligent interest
which they have taken in the matter of law-making. Maryland had had since the
eighteenth century a law regulating the support of illegitimate children which limited the amount of payments that could be enforced against the father to thirty

---

[1] Quoted in Roberts *v.* Boston, 5 Cush. (1849) 198, 204.
[2] 14 World's Work (1907), 9091, 9093.

dollars a year for seven years. The attorney for the Baltimore Legal Aid Bureau, together with a member of the local bar, drew a bill, which was passed in 1912, leaving the payments to be fixed in the discretion of the court up to the sum of thirty dollars a month.[1] In Boston, the attorney for the Legal Aid Society coöperated with a committee of judges which drafted the present Massachusetts law on illegitimacy, enacted in 1913. In 1916 the Society secured the passage of a law limiting the rate of interest on small loans to three per cent per month, and a second law safeguarding the assignment of wages.[2] The Legal Aid Bureau of Buffalo pointed out the harshness of the law governing the conditional sales of furniture on instalment payments and the inefficacy of civil proceedings to secure support for abandoned children, and recommended legislation.

The Chicago Legal Aid Society has entered largely into legislative activity. It has carried on the sterling work of the Protective Agency in the matter of providing adequate legal safeguards for the protection of children from abuse. A law secured by the Protective Agency in 1905 was declared unconstitutional, but was redrafted and reënacted through the efforts of the Society in 1907.[3] In the same year work was begun on legislation to regulate interest charges on loans secured by pledges,[4] which was continued on through the next year,[5] and a bill was presented and urged before the state legislature in 1909 which failed to pass.[6] A decision holding unconstitutional the act regulating wage assignments caused the Society to take up that fight and to frame a law which would stand attack.[7] Work on these and other matters was carried on during 1910, although the legislature was not in session.[8] When the legislature met in 1911 the bills received favorable committee reports, were passed by one house, and killed by the other.[9] In 1916, following sensational disclosures by the press as to the rates of interest charged poor persons on small loans, a group of organizations, including the Legal Aid Society, took up a campaign which led to the enactment in 1917 of a proper act regulating the business of small loans. The backbone of the fight was provided by a document, proving beyond question the extortions which the laxity of the law permitted, published by the City Department of Public Welfare.[10] This remarkable document was irrefutable because it was based entirely on the records of actual cases, of which the Legal Aid Society furnished nearly one-half.

As a part of the organization of the Cleveland Legal Aid Society there has always existed a most energetic legislative committee. Its greatest triumph is the Cleveland Small Claims Court. It not only sponsored this court, but conducted an investigation of the evils of the justice of the peace system that was published and led to the successful campaign, in which all the better interests in the city took part, for a mod-

---

[1] *Report of Proceedings of the Second Conference of Legal Aid Societies*, page 38.
[2] 16 Boston L. A. R. 10.   [3] 2 Chicago L. A. R. 12; 3 *Ibid.* 12, 16.   [4] 3 *Ibid.* 17.   [5] 4 *Ibid.* 8.
[6] 5 *Ibid.* 8.   [7] 5 *Ibid.* 9.   [8] 6 *Ibid.* 7.   [9] 7 *Ibid.* 8.
[10] *Bulletin* of the Department of Public Welfare, City of Chicago, vol. i, No. 4 (November, 1916), "Loan Shark Number."

ern municipal court.[1] The activities of the Legislative Committee have covered wage assignments, attachments of wages, desertion, and small loans,[2] delays in small causes, a summer criminal session to secure prompt hearings for prisoners held on serious charges, public defenders,[3] legislation to provide the court trustee plan,[4] service of process by mail,[5] and fairer provisions for an equity of redemption in chattel mortgages.[6] Not all of these matters were brought to the desired conclusion, but the Society has to its credit, in addition to its municipal court bill, five important accomplishments in the loan shark law, a provision for three days' notice before the attachment of a married man's wages, registered mail service, the reduction of court costs, and an amendment making the desertion of a pregnant woman an extraditable crime.[7]

The Cincinnati Legal Aid Society, being in the same state with Cleveland, has coöperated with that organization in successfully urging the loan shark legislation,[8] and in advocating the court trustee plan which thus far has met great opposition.[9] The public bureau in Dallas, before politics cut its life short, had pointed out serious flaws in the Texas laws and had advocated legislation of a modern type dealing with desertion and non-support (analogous to the Uniform Desertion Act), the requirement of some intervening period between the issuance of a marriage license and the performance of the ceremony, provision against fraudulent divorce, stricter usury laws, an exemption of a fixed proportion of wages from assignments, and safeguards against conditional sale abuses in instalment furniture contracts.[10] The first attorney for the Hartford Legal Aid Bureau was elected to the legislature, from which vantage-point he was able to urge many interesting measures. His work in connection with the Hartford Home Rule bill made possible the referendum vote by which the Hartford municipal Legal Aid Bureau was established. He drafted the so-called public defender law.[11] Other measures, which were not understood and so failed of passage, related to the establishment of a small claims court, the establishment of county legal aid societies with attorneys to be appointed by the governor, and in forma pauperis proceedings with assignment of counsel.[12]

The public bureau in Kansas City signalized its appearance as a new factor in the administration of justice by making an elaborate investigation of the abuses of the justice of the peace system. This led to an amendment of the Missouri law on garnishment of wages which had become a national scandal.[13] Forty railroads enter Kansas City, and under the law it was permissible to attach the wages of any employee of

---

[1] American Judicature Society, *Bulletin VIII*, page 5; *Justice for the Poor (First Report of the Cleveland Legal Aid Society)*, page 2; 4 Cleveland L. A. R. 19; 6 *Ibid.* 7, 16; 9 *Ibid.* 13.
[2] 2 *Ibid.* 11.   [3] 3 *Ibid.* 10, 15.   [4] 7 *Ibid.* 12, 16.   [5] 7 *Ibid.* 16.   [6] 8 *Ibid.* 12.
[7] See pamphlet published by the Cleveland Legal Aid Society entitled "All Men are Equal before the Law."
[8] 7 Cincinnati L. A. R. 5, and fly-leaf on cover.   [9] 6 *Ibid.* 9.
[10] *Second Annual Report of the Dallas Board of Public Welfare*, pages 9, 10.
[11] This has already been commented on *ante*, page 117.
[12] These matters are not set out in the Hartford reports. They were introduced in the 1915 session of the legislature and are House Bills Numbers 443, 442, and 480 respectively.
[13] 1 Kansas City L. A. R. 12 *et seq.*

these roads, wherever he might work, by service of process on the Kansas City office of the road. One employee was obliged to travel nine hundred miles to defend such a suit and prove that he owed no debt. As it was possible to bring suits in Missouri against employees in any part of the country, which they were obliged to default because they could not travel so far to put in an appearance, a wholesale collection business, permeated with fraud, sprang up. This traffic became a specialty of certain justices' courts, which became known as "Jack Rabbit" courts. As a result of the investigation, the abuse was stopped.

Only a few of the measures advocated by the New York Legal Aid Society during its long period of activity[1] can be mentioned. It has taken part in urging the kinds of legislation that have already been noted in connection with other organizations, such as the loan shark laws[2] and more stringent provisions to enforce payment of wages,[3] and in addition it has fought to better the condition of seamen. It sent one of its members to Washington to appear before the Congressional Committee on the Merchant Marine, and secured laws to prevent shanghaiing and peonage among sailors.[4] It has further argued for the extension of the United States Shipping Commissioner's jurisdiction, against allotments of pay to persons other than dependents, and against shipping fees which induced a form of slavery.[5]

In Pittsburgh the Society has studied unsatisfactory laws which work injustice, has noted how like defects have been cured elsewhere, and has publicly advocated legislation to reduce costs, to prevent fraud through the conducting of a business under an assumed name, to secure more stringent supervision of industrial weekly-payment insurance policies, and to empower the Labor Board to collect wage claims.[6] Of the work done in Philadelphia, the most important was the Society's inauguration of a campaign for a municipal court, which was persisted in for years and which finally, in coöperation with other agencies, gave Philadelphia its present admirable court.[7] It made an investigation of the situation on the waterfront which disclosed horrible conditions in the treatment of sailors.[8] It arranged for a hearing before the Congressional Committee on the Merchant Marine and, in coöperation with the New York Society, submitted evidence which brought about protective legislation. It also succeeded in having the powers of the insurance commissioner somewhat increased in supervising industrial insurance policies.[9] At the conferences of legal aid societies, matters of legislation and suggestions for improvements are the most common topics of discussion.[10] As yet, no combined attempt to work out national legislation in which all organizations might coöperate has been made.

It is apparent that the legal aid organizations have taken up the burden of try-

[1] 29 N. Y. L. A. R. 10; 40 *Ibid.* 20; 41 *Ibid.* 10.
[2] 30 *Ibid.* 37.   [3] 32 *Ibid.* 35.   [4] 31 *Ibid.* 10.   [5] 29 *Ibid.* 36.   [6] 8 Pittsburgh L. A. R. 14–21; also 7 *Ibid.* 27.
[7] *Report of Proceedings of the Second Conference of Legal Aid Societies*, page 24.
[8] 3 Philadelphia L. A. R. 9.   [9] 8 *Ibid.* 7.
[10] See *Report of Proceedings of the First Conference of Legal Aid Societies*, pages 15, 21, 23–26; *Ibid., Second Conference*, pages 24, 28, 38; *Ibid., Third Conference*, page 26; *Ibid., Fourth Conference*, pages 132, 140.

ing, through remedial legislation, to keep the law equal in the face of changes and new plans and devices which tend to destroy equality. It is clear that the societies come into contact with legal abuses which would not appear in the ordinary private law office, and which the community in general would not be in a position to detect or understand. Because of the position of the legal aid society and because it has accepted the responsibility of remedying defects as rapidly as it is able, it has unquestionably served to secure the enactment of wise measures which, without it, never would have become law. Two entirely different illustrations will show concretely why this is and how it works out.

For years there has been in California a curious rule about costs on appeal. A plaintiff might bring his action in the lower courts and obtain judgment. The defendant, thereupon, could claim an appeal by paying one dollar and twenty-five cents. This not only forced the plaintiff to try his case all over again and subjected the proceedings to delay, but it permitted the defendant to take no further action at all and to have the case pend indefinitely. The only recourse open to the plaintiff was to enter the defendant's appeal in the Superior Court himself, pay six dollars for such docketing, and also pay two dollars for having the case marked on the calendar. Unquestionably thousands of attorneys for plaintiffs in as many cases, when confronted with this situation, have felt the absurdity as well as the injustice of putting a premium on appeals and of compelling the plaintiff to pay the costs of an appeal which he did not take and did not want. Undoubtedly many of them felt that it ought to be set right, and perhaps a few jotted down notes to draft a bill in a leisure moment. Yet they must all have gone on to their other business and forgotten it, for no attempt to change the law was ever made.

The Los Angeles Public Defender had not been at his civil work for six months before he saw the defect in the law. He reported on it officially,[1] drew a bill, submitted it to the legislature, and in 1915 the procedural rule was amended.[2] The Public Defender not only was in a position to discover this little kink in the law, but also he felt that the responsibility rested on him, that it was his business to straighten it out, and he promptly proceeded to do so.

There are innumerable places in the law where just such betterments will make the course of justice run more smoothly. They are not glaring defects about which a public hue and cry can be aroused; reformers will never change them, for reformers will never know of them. The inevitable result of changing conditions and of a body of law which is gradually built up case by case is to leave some loose ends which cause needless friction and injustice. Many groups in the country are watchful for just such things, and they possess the coherence and resources to take care of themselves. The poor are not in a position to understand or to act. For that vast number the legal aid society must act as champion, for in the course of its daily work it finds

---

[1] *Place of the Public Defender in the Administration of Justice*, page 24.
[2] *Acts of* 1915, California Code, § 981.

these omissions and from the wealth of its experience it can easily determine just what remedial legislation is necessary.

The second illustration relates to a defect in substantive rather than procedural law, and shows an entirely different function which the legal aid society performs. The world has always had its usurers, but the modern loan shark, specializing in small loans and doing business among the very poor, is a by-product of our great industrial cities with their wage-earning population. In Massachusetts until 1916 the law permitted a lender to loan ten dollars and to charge interest on that loan at the rate of one hundred and eighty per cent per year. It also permitted an instalment house to sell a diamond ring and to take as security an assignment of wages which bound all future wages earned for a period of two years and exempted not a penny. When the assignment was filed, the employer was legally bound to turn all the employee's pay over to the creditor. The abuses were so gross that public attention was directed to them and the question became of immediate public concern. A wave of reform secured a law in 1913 concerning small loans which promptly proved not to have changed interest rates at all. Nothing was accomplished as to wage assignments in general. Year after year earnest attempts were made, but they all failed because the Committee on Legal Affairs was unwilling to recommend legislation until the proponents could prove their case.

The poor do not appear at legislative hearings to present evidence in their own behalf as to how they are exploited. Those who had appeared in their behalf were certain of their case, but they were unable to prove it. In 1916 the Legal Aid Society, cooperating with the Law Department of the City of Boston, the Russell Sage Foundation, and one member of the House of Representatives, entered the fight. The Society, because of its position, was able to make two invaluable contributions. First, from its files it was possible to produce records of actual cases whose authenticity could not be challenged, and which proved beyond question that the alleged abuses were being perpetrated daily. Second, the Society was able to serve as a centre around which all forces could unite and to undertake the leadership in a public campaign, for its attitude was known to be impartial, it had no selfish interests to serve, and the sincerity of its motives and the truth of its statements could not be impugned. After a five months' fight against a naturally bitter opposition both bills—one fixing the maximum rate of interest on small loans at three per cent per month and one safeguarding wage assignments by provisions for exemptions and the wife's consent—were made law.[1]

This achievement finds its counterpart in the work of other societies in other cities. It reveals a militant group of organizations. The significance of such work is that it denotes the presence of an organization that can speak for an estate in the community which by reason of its own limitations is inarticulate. This is an important contribution toward preserving the fairness of the substantive law which is the requisite foundation for an equal administration of justice.

[1] Massachusetts *Acts of* 1916, chaps. 208 and 224.

§ 2

Under our common law system the decision of a court of last resort not only adjudicates the rights of the particular parties to the action, but also fixes the law for
Legal Aid and Common Law
all future similar cases. In the generality of its application a case decision is as important as an act of legislature. It follows, therefore, that a proper and equitable decision may have as much effect in safeguarding the rights of the poor as a remedial statute. Precisely the same reasons which lead legal aid organizations into legislative work lead them to seek final adjudications in proper cases.

Thus far the societies have by no means taken as large a part in appellate work as they have in remedial legislation. They have been debarred by the expenses entailed in appeals for transcripts, records, briefs, and court fees. It is financially impossible for most organizations to undertake such disbursements. They have reasoned, and with much wisdom, that so long as the funds at their disposal are small, it is inadvisable to spend on one unusual case a sum which would enable them to extend their assistance to one hundred applicants with ordinary cases. As the limit of an organization's resources is an absolute limit, the societies have been, and still are, unable to secure to their clients as complete legal protection as wealthier litigants may avail themselves of. This is a clear limitation to the service which they can afford.

Because of our case system, however, it is imperative that somehow certain types of cases should be finally determined. It is one thing not to appeal from the ruling of a trial judge on a point of evidence which, though erroneous and prejudicial, cannot affect the settled rule of law and operates only to defeat the individual in the particular case. This is an injustice, and it is regrettable that such instances occur, but so long as the legal aid societies are poorly supported, instances of this sort are inevitable. It is a far different thing that a ruling which makes new law and affects many persons should be allowed to stand unquestioned if it is unfair or is deemed erroneous, such for example as a decision by an inferior court or tribunal that injured longshoremen are not within the provisions of the workmen's compensation act. In cases wherein new important points of law and matters of general legal or social interests are involved, it is essential that legal aid organizations should be able to carry the issue through to the highest court for its decision. Every society should have a "fighting fund" for this purpose.

There is an opportunity for the legal aid organizations to supply a much needed element, which has for some time been entirely lacking, in the steady development of our common law. The common law is the people's law; it has had its being in their life; it has been able to develop in a comprehensive way through the controversies of all classes of citizens, high and low, in all sorts of cases, big and little. This sturdy, all-round development is not so clear to-day. The poor cannot afford appeals, the small case does not warrant the incurring of large expense, and the large private offices, engaging in general practice and doing legal aid work as a part of that practice, no longer exist. A glance at the reports will show that the only cases of the poor which receive appellate attention are personal injury suits where the stakes are large enough to induce attorneys to assume the expense themselves. The highest courts are being largely confined to expositions of the law of negligence, of property matters such as wills and trusts, of corporation, banking, and business law, of taxation, and of procedure. In the main these are the only cases brought to them. Two generations ago Chief Justice Shaw of Massachusetts was called upon to decide whether a calf was subject to attachment,[1] and when the care with which he examined the issue evoked some merriment at the bar, he said with much emotion: "Gentlemen, this may seem to you a trifling case, but it is a very important question to a great many poor families."[2] One may search far in the reports of to-day without finding any comparable instance. It has in large measure been this inability of the mass of the people to secure a development of the common law suited to their needs that has driven them to act through their representatives and resulted in our endless legislation concerning both substantive and procedural law.

It has been said with much truth that the offices of legal aid organizations are the only common law offices that remain in existence in the large cities.[3] There the common law may be seen working itself out in its application to the people in their daily lives. Innumerable questions arise which have never been decided and which ought to be decided.[4] As an illustration, it is not clear under Massachusetts law whether the fictitious lease is a lawful method of ejecting a tenant at will without the two weeks' notice required by statute.[5] It is used every year in thousands of cases. It is not to the interest of landlords to dispute it, the poor who are ejected by it are unable to question it, and as a result it continues in existence. Slightly different in operation but tending to the same result is the too common practice in compensation cases where insurance companies take appeals and the employee is unable to file a brief and present his side of the case. One-sided argument cannot secure as fair a construction of the statute as a decision rendered after full hearing of both sides.

Just as the legal aid organizations are necessary to secure to the individual poor person his day in court, so they are necessary to secure his hearing on appeal. But the latter is more than a question of individual justice; on it may depend the right to protection and redress of countless other persons similarly situated. It is not of chief importance whether the legal aid organizations win or lose their appeals; the prime consideration is that our common law system should have a fair chance to work itself out by having points needing determination brought to the supreme courts, and by having those issues fairly argued, not from one, but from both points of view.

[1] Carruth v. Grassie, 11 Gray, 211.   [2] Chase: *Lemuel Shaw* (1918), page 280.
[3] Rowe: *Joseph H. Choate and Right Training for the Bar*, 24 Case and Comment (1917), 264, 273, 275.
[4] 30 N. Y. L. A. R. 48; cf. Parry: *The Law and the Poor*, page 175.   [5] Cf. page 14, *ante*.

What little work of this sort the legal aid societies have been able to do serves to indicate very clearly what a valuable work they might, if permitted, perform for the law. At the time of the loan shark campaign in New York a question arose as to the legality of the lenders' charging a ten dollar fee as "attorney's services" in drawing the papers taken as security for the loan. By such a device all the laws limiting interest rates could be set at naught. The plan is a very common one, and it must have been successfully employed in New York in thousands of cases. No borrower had ever been in a position to undertake the long fight necessary to test this subterfuge and to secure a final adjudication. In the case of London Realty Company v. Riorden the New York Legal Aid Society undertook to defend a suit based on such a transaction on the ground that the loan was in violation of law. The Municipal Court gave judgment for the plaintiff. The Society appealed and the Appellate term of the Supreme Court affirmed the judgment. The Society took a further appeal to the Appellate Division, where the court reversed the affirmed judgment, saying that the attorney's fee was "a device or pretext to evade the law." This time the lender appealed and the Society followed the case to the Court of Appeals, where it was finally ruled that the law had been violated and the judgment was set aside.[1] It is interesting to note that in the companion field of wage assignments the law concerning the requirement of notice to the employer, although that question must have been a decisive factor in innumerable cases, was never determined until the Russell Sage Foundation engaged counsel to take the necessary appeals.

The maritime law permits sailors to be fined for disobedience because strict discipline on shipboard is essential. In order that fines might not degenerate into abuse, the law required the master to make an entry in the log book concurrently with the imposition of the fine. This provision was not complied with, and it became an easy matter for unscrupulous captains to discharge their crews with little or no pay on the allegation that there were deductions for fines. No sailor was in a position to dispute the illegality of this conduct. When the situation came to the attention of the Seaman's Branch of the New York Legal Aid Society, a case was brought before the federal court where it was held that if entries were not properly made, there could be no deductions for fines.[2] Such a decision automatically carries the intended protection of the law to all seamen on American vessels.

A less important instance, which has a good deal of humor in it, is found in the practice of the Philadelphia Legal Aid Society. In its struggle against the loan shark the Society, failing at first to find any point of attack, set up as a desperate defence to a suit in the Court of Common Pleas the contention that an office where usurious rates of interest were charged was a disorderly house. By some weird reasoning this was sustained. It sufficed to keep the lenders at bay until the Society worked out the more tenable theory of enjoining all suits brought on usurious notes.[3]

[1] 36 N. Y. L. A. R. 26; 37 Ibid. 30; 38 Ibid. 27.   [2] The St. Paul, 133 Federal, 1002; 30 N. Y. L. A. R. 39.
[3] 8 Philadelphia L. A. R. 6.

In Hartford certain employers who had less than five employees contended that the compensation act did not apply to them. The Legal Aid Committee took a test case to the Supreme Court, where the general applicability of the act was upheld.[1] In Boston the Legal Aid Society has taken up for final determination cases involving the power of the Industrial Accident Board to control the fees charged by physicians to injured employees,[2] the construction of a statute requiring insurance companies to pay compensation to employees who had received an award from the Board, notwithstanding an appeal taken to the Supreme Court by the insurance company,[3] and the right of a seaman to libel a ship for his wages when the agreement under which the master had shipped his crew was in accordance with the custom of shares with a stipulated daily wage in addition.[4]

The most important ruling obtained by a legal aid society is the California decision, already referred to in connection with the question of costs as a denial of justice, in which the court held that in order to prevent a frustration of justice, courts of record have an inherent power to permit a suit without prepayment of costs when it appears that the enforcement of costs will preclude the party from all possible relief.[5] In this matter the attorney for the San Francisco Legal Aid Society appeared as amicus curiae. This decision at once opens the doors of the courts in proper cases to persons throughout the state who have hitherto been barred from seeking redress because of their inability to defray the required court costs and fees. Should a recognition of the simple truths on which the decision rests lead to its adoption in other jurisdictions, this case would mark an advance, second only to the original in forma pauperis statute of Henry VII, in the progress toward a more free and equal justice.

[1] 2 Hartford L. A. R. 4.   [2] Holland v. Zeuner, 228 Mass. 142.
[3] Insurance Co. v. Peloquin, 225 Mass. 30; 16 Boston L. A. R. 15.
[4] Holmes v. Schooner Mettacomet, 230 Fed. 308; 233 Ibid. 261.
[5] Martin v. Superior Court for Alameda County, 54 California Decisions (October, 1917), 422.

CHAPTER XXII

LEGAL AID AND THE COMMUNITY

Perhaps you may discover many things yet wanting in the Law; Mischiefs
in the Execution and Application of the Laws, which ought to be better
provided against; Mischiefs annoying of Mankind, against which no Laws
are yet provided. The Reformation of the Law, and more Law for the Reformation of the World is what is mightily called for. *From the First American Address to Lawyers.*[1]

§ 1

REMEDIAL legislation and the final determination of legal issues of general
application affect the entire community, and work in these two directions is
work for the community. The service which legal aid organizations render to the
community is, however, not confined to these two forms of activity,
but extends into many fields and its effects reach far and wide. As all
their work is legal in nature and pertains to law, the contributions
which the societies make to the common welfare are along legal lines. Because of their
peculiarly close contact with life no general legal wrong or fraud can long be perpetrated on the poor before some case, revealing the situation, comes to their office
and provides a point of attack. The organizations detect fraudulent schemes, suppress abuses, study conditions, educate persons in matters of law which they ought to
know, and are the first to act when some new need for legal assistance appears. So far
as these various activities can be reduced to one formula, it is that of law enforcement rather than of law making.

Community Service

The loan shark has been able to exist in spite of laws either by evading or ignor-
ing them. Important as remedial legislation is in curbing his power or in ousting him,
it is equally important to fight him by enforcing the laws against him, and making it impossible for him to practise usury by recovering back from him all excess
payments and preventing borrowers from overpaying on their loans. During the last
three years the Chicago Legal Aid Society has acted in 1266 cases, permitting the
payment of the legal rates, but cutting off all excess sums demanded by the lenders, which aggregated $16,884.88.[2] Everywhere the legal aid organizations have been
the most determined enemy of the loan sharks, driving them to cover by exposure
and thwarting their carefully concealed plans for evading the law.[3] Thus, in Massachusetts, after the new law regulating interest rates was passed, the lenders immediately
became incorporated and required all borrowers to agree to buy shares of their stock

---

[1] By Cotton Mather in 1710, quoted in Warren: *History of the American Bar*, page ix.

[2] Eubank: *Loan Sharks and Loan Shark Legislation in Illinois*, 7 Journal of Criminal Law, No. 1 (May, 1917),
reprinted by the Russell Sage Foundation. See page 11 of the reprint.

[3] The reports of the legal aid societies are full of statements as to this work. See particularly 8 N. Y. Legal Aid Rev.
No. 1, p. 1; 10 *Ibid.* No. 1, p. 1; 6 Pittsburgh L. A. R. 11; also *Bulletin of the National Federation of Remedial Loan
Associations* for November, 1916, page 7; Chicago *Legal News* for March 28, 1918 (whole No. 3293), pages 277, 280.

on the pretext that it was to afford security for the loan. This in effect served to break down the law and to restore the former high rates. Four test cases were brought by the Legal Aid Society, with the result that the lenders' licenses were suspended or revoked, and the subterfuge was abandoned.[1] In thus protecting and enforcing the law in all its vigor the Society was not merely aiding four individual borrowers: it was preventing the exploitation of the one hundred and fifty thousand borrowers of small loans in Massachusetts, and promoting the community welfare.

Attempts are steadily being made to perpetrate hoaxes or fraudulent schemes on the less intelligent members of the community. Where some element of gambling or of a lottery is included, the lure is strong and the trick works. In 1914 a most ingenious "club plan" for the sale of furniture, with the usual speculative accompaniments, was promoted in New York. Thousands of poor persons joined and paid in, in sums of twenty-five cents a week, the vast amount of one hundred and sixty thousand dollars. The Legal Aid Society secured warrants to which the defendants pleaded guilty, and then undertook in behalf of thirteen thousand victims to liquidate the business so that the purchasers might be saved as much as possible.[2] Following this experience the Society published a statement of schemes to be avoided by the poor.[3] The love of chance-taking is not the only human frailty that is capitalized. Vanity does just as well, and the concern which offers to make a "movie" star of any applicant finds willing listeners who cheerfully pay for a course of instruction.[4] The legal aid societies in the various cities are constantly on the watch for these fraudulent undertakings and combat them to the best of their ability.[5]

Other illustrations abound. The mere mention of some of them suffices to show the value of the service which the societies render. The Legal Aid Bureau of the Educational Alliance and the Legal Aid Society in New York coöperated to stop the illegal traffic in divorces which certain rabbis were carrying on among the Jewish immigrant population.[6] In Philadelphia it was discovered that a large manufacturing plant was in the habit of paying its employees, many of whom were minors, by check. These checks were cashed at the nearest place, which was a saloon. On the Legal Aid Society's representation the company discontinued its practice and paid in cash.[7] Special protective work in behalf of immigrants has been undertaken; the New York Legal Aid Society opened and maintained a special immigration branch until lack of funds forced it to be given up.[8] Conditions from which seamen have suffered, such as shanghaiing, crimping, and the exaction of fees for getting men jobs, have been steadily

[1] 16 Boston L. A. R. 10-14; *Report of the Massachusetts Supervisor of Loan Agencies* for January 1, 1917 (*Public Document No. 95* of 1917), pages 15-21.
[2] 39 N. Y. L. A. R. 19; *Report of Proceedings of the Fourth Conference of Legal Aid Societies*, page 133.
[3] 39 N. Y. L. A. R. 24.   [4] 40 *Ibid.* 36.
[5] 3 Buffalo L. A. R. 6; 5 Pittsburgh L. A. R. 13; 7 *Ibid.* 17-26; 16 N. Y. L. A. R. 6; 21 *Ibid.* 8; 22 *Ibid.* 8; 4 Philadelphia L. A. R. 4, 5.
[6] 11 Educational Alliance Report, 55; 22 N. Y. L. A. R. 10.   [7] 8 Philadelphia L. A. R. 10.
[8] 36 N. Y. L. A. R. 18; 37 *Ibid.* 10, 21; 38 *Ibid.* 12.

combated.[1] In 1907 the New York Society, through the attorney for its Seamen's Branch, secured evidence on which a boarding-house keeper was convicted of exacting a shipping fee. A notice of this conviction was issued by the United States Commissioner of Navigation and publicly posted in all American ports.[2] When this one conviction proved an insufficient deterrent, the Society promptly followed it up with further convictions.[3]

The societies have undertaken an amount of educational work in instructing the poorer classes as to their legal rights and liabilities by the publication of handbooks setting out the law in simple and easily understandable language. In 1912 the Kansas City Legal Aid Bureau published a forty-four page booklet covering the legal questions that most commonly arise in the lives of the poor. A first edition of two thousand copies was immediately exhausted, and a second edition, with translations into different languages, was printed.[4] The organization in Akron, finding that borrowers were paying interest rates greatly in excess of the legal maximum because of their ignorance of the law, prepared and distributed twelve thousand copies of a leaflet dealing with the provisions of law concerning loans, chattel mortgages, assignments, and the like.[5] The Bureau in Nashville has in preparation a pamphlet dealing with the law in general for distribution among the employees of the industrial plants of the city. The New York Legal Aid Society has published an edition of five thousand copies of a *Handbook for Domestic Servants*.[6] Its other publication of this sort, being a compendium of the maritime law and known as *The Sailors' Log*, has carried its name around the world. A first issue of five thousand copies in 1904 proved inadequate to meet the demand, a second edition was issued in 1906,[7] and a third edition is now ready for printing. Following the declaration of war by the United States, several of the societies met an obvious need and produced concise little volumes of *Law for Soldiers, Sailors, and their Dependents*.

§ 2

Nothing could indicate more vividly the value to the community of having in its midst organizations like the legal aid societies than the events which took place after America's entry into the World War. The complete story cannot be written yet, for much work which has been done by the legal aid organizations has not yet been reported on and so is unknown, but enough has come to light to prove the present point of legal aid service to the community, state, and nation.

War Work

In Boston a Lawyers' Preparedness Committee was formed to be in readiness for such legal problems as the vast changes were certain to produce. It was apparent to

---

[1] 8 Philadelphia L. A. R. 10; 27 N. Y. L. A. R. 29; 32 *Ibid.* 42.

[2] 32 N. Y. L. A. R. 3.   [3] 33 *Ibid.* 31; 35 *Ibid.* 28; 39 *Ibid.* 32.   [4] 3 Kansas City L. A. R. 5.

[5] *First Report of the Charity Organization Society of Akron*, report of the Legal Aid Committee, page 14.

[6] 31 N. Y. L. A. R. 48; 33 *Ibid.* 13.   [7] 29 *Ibid.* 10; 31 *Ibid.* 9.

this Committee that the best machinery for handling a large volume of cases was to be found in the Legal Aid Society, and therefore the Committee asked the Society to undertake all legal work for men entering service and their dependents. Through the press it was publicly announced that all such persons could secure free legal advice and assistance of any sort from the Society's attorneys.[1] As the situation developed, and as the Home Service Section of the local chapter of the American Red Cross found itself steadily confronted with legal questions concerning the government allotments, allowances, compensation, insurance, and cases under the Soldiers' and Sailors' Relief Act, it became clear that this mass of work could best be entrusted to the Legal Aid Society, which was effected through its becoming counsel for the Home Service Section. In New York there was evidence that a number of disreputable attorneys and others were preying on ignorant persons of draft age by holding out that they could secure exemption on payment of a large fee. For their own ends these shysters encouraged attempts to evade the selective draft law. To combat this evil it was decided to open a bureau where reliable advice about the law could be secured at nominal cost. Recognizing the reputation of the Legal Aid Society and its ability to provide quickly the facilities and machinery for taking many cases, the Mayor's Committee on National Defence and the War Committee of the Bar Association of the City of New York asked the Society to establish a bureau for draft information. This was immediately done, and the bureau continued its work throughout the period of the first draft.[2] In Milwaukee, following a statement of the governor of Wisconsin that men were being charged exorbitant fees in connection with exemption claims, the Legal Aid Society made arrangements with the Chairman of the District Board whereby any matters might be referred to the Society in the discretion of the Board.[3]

In carrying out their assignments, the societies soon saw that the chief difficulty which they had to combat was ignorance of law. Persons failed to safeguard themselves in the manner prescribed by law because they did not know that any legal steps were necessary. The provisions of the War Risk Insurance Act of October 6, 1917, and of the Civil Relief Act of March 8, 1918, were very generally unknown. To point out the difficulties likely to present themselves to the average man and his family and to urge proper legal action, the Society in Boston published a thirty-eight page pocket size booklet of *Legal Suggestions for Soldiers and Sailors and their Dependents.*"[4] Over one hundred and fifty thousand copies were distributed, the requests coming from every state in the Union; twenty-five thousand copies going to the Army and Navy; thirty thousand to Exemption Boards, thirty-five thousand to the Red Cross, fifteen thousand to Public Safety Committees; twenty thousand to War Camp Community Service Committees; and the balance on individual applications. The

---

[1] 24 Case and Comment (October, 1917), 400.   [2] 15 N. Y. Legal Aid Rev. No. 4 (October, 1917), 1.
[3] 1 Milwaukee L. A. R. 4.
[4] See Boston *Evening Transcript* for August 4, 1917 (editorial); *Ibid.* for October 10, 1917 (editorial); Boston *Advertiser* for August 2, 1917.

Council of National Defence recommended to the various State Councils that they publish similar pamphlets. Legal aid organizations in New York, Philadelphia, Louisville, Milwaukee, and Rochester[1] printed like pamphlets for their respective jurisdictions. In other states the idea, which was first conceived and acted on by the legal aid organizations, has been taken up by other groups and organizations.

The usefulness of the individual societies would have been greatly increased if they had been united under the control of some one central agency. When the federal government in 1918, through the Council of National Defence, made its comprehensive plans[2] to extend legal aid to every soldier and sailor and his family, the legal aid organizations should have been the first to offer themselves. By reason of their favorable location, their reputation for integrity, and their great experience in caring for a multitude of cases, they might easily have become in every large city the centre of legal work for men in service and their dependents. If they had possessed a properly empowered and alert central office, it would have been heard in the councils at Washington, and could have placed at the government's disposal a trained and equipped staff of attorneys with a going organization capable of indefinite expansion. Because they had failed to erect any central authority, the societies were unable to grasp the greatest opportunity ever presented them.

§ 3

There is a new movement in the realm of law which will prove of incalculable benefit to the community at large and in which the legal aid organizations are likely to play an important part. It may be called the science of preventive law. As physicians have made great strides in preventive medicine, as workers in the *Preventive Law* field of social service are placing their emphasis on the prevention of the factors which cause poverty and degeneracy,[3] so it is becoming recognized that the legal profession may perform a like service in the law. The science of prevention in all three branches means the same process of searching for the cause of the wrong condition and then of ascertaining the cure. As Henry Stockbridge, chairman of the Section of Legal Education of the American Bar Association, has put it:[4] "When an evil is once recognized, the first remedial step is to ascertain the cause and then to seek out and apply the antidote or remedy."

Our law has never had forehanded scientific development. This is the weakness of the common law method of building law case by case. Much legislation has been

---

[1] *Rochester L. A. R.* for 1917, page 8.

[2] *Official Bulletin* for July 15, 1918, vol. ii, No. 360; *Supplementary Bulletin No.* 84 of the Council of National Defence, August, 1918.

[3] Pear: *Social Values in Public and Private Relief*, published in *The Field of Social Service* (1915), pages 208-210.

[4] 41 Am. Bar Ass'n R. (1916) 659. Cf. Chief Justice Olsen of the Chicago Municipal Court: *Efficiency in the Administration of Criminal Justice*, page 29—"We shall try the modern methods of the medical profession—diagnosis and prevention, when cure is impossible."

necessary, but the statutes too often represent only opinion or snap judgment and not conclusions drawn from definitely ascertained facts. One reason for the failure of the law to deal with difficulties before they come to pass instead of always after they have happened is that the necessary basic material has not been ready at hand. The experience and data which the hospitals and clinics afforded in medicine, and which the charity organizations' files and records furnished in social service, were not to be found in the average law office. Court dockets possess a fund of information which the modern municipal courts are beginning to analyze and study for the purpose of suggesting betterments. Outside of the courts there has been no organization which afforded the cases by which the workings of the law could be observed and tested.

It may be said that American law at the present time stands in need of four great things. First, the reorganization of courts; second, the simplification of procedure; third, the equalization of the administration of justice so that denial of justice to the poor may cease; and fourth, a Bureau of Justice of the sort suggested by Dean Pound,[1] which shall provide the means for the scientific study of the law, for detecting its shortcomings, and for providing the necessary information by which alone constructive remedial work is made possible. If all the changes advocated by the leaders of the first three movements could be effected to-day, a new series of problems would begin to appear to-morrow. This is inevitable because no institution which is static can be satisfactory when all the life which it attempts to regulate is in constant flux. Only by a Bureau of Justice which can keep abreast of changing conditions and ascertain how and where new laws are needed or old ones call for different application can the recurrence of the old errors be avoided. It is unquestionably a tremendous task, but it is necessary if the law is to be a living science instead of a set of archaic dogmas and doctrines. Had there been such a Bureau during the last quarter of the nineteenth century, it would have known that the structure of our judicial organization was faulty, that the procedure was over-technical, wasteful, and slow, and that there was a necessity for supplying attorneys to the poor. With such knowledge it might have induced courts and legislatures to act so that the difficulties would have been met as soon as they arose.

The legal aid organizations cannot be such a Bureau of Justice, but they can be a part of it, and by their own preventive work in the field of law which affects the poor they can give an object lesson which will hasten its coming. No more appropriate point of departure could be made, for the need in this particular field is great and no organizations come closer to the life of the common people of the nation.[2] The legal aid organizations are beginning to realize that out of their vast volume of

[1] This was suggested by Dean Pound in his address before the Conference of Delegates of State and Local Bar Associations on September 3, 1917. The address has not been printed, but this point is mentioned in 24 Case and Comment, 422, 423.

[2] Cf. statement of Graham Taylor in his address to legal aid society delegates, *Report of Proceedings of the Fourth Conference of Legal Aid Societies*, page 130.

work they can develop this scientific by-product.[1] The proposition has been given excellent presentation by the Board of Directors of the Boston Legal Aid Society in these words:[2]

> "To be militant in placing needed laws on the books, and vigilant in securing their enforcement, are undoubtedly great services to the community, easily comprehended because of their dramatic appeal. What is even more sorely needed, however, is a sensitive instrument with which to detect the failures of our legal system, and a fund of social experience out of which to build anew.
>
> "The present system of the administration of justice is in the process of undergoing great and far-reaching changes by reason of the attempt to re-shape its antique framework to meet the needs of modern society. The great task is bringing about experimentation with new methods of administering justice, elimination of unnecessary cost and complicated procedure, and the recasting of the powers of the various courts. The rapid spread of administrative boards, the instituting of small claims courts in which court costs are eliminated, together with the lawyer, the project of a Domestic Relations Court combining the present jurisdiction in that field of the Divorce, Probate, Criminal, and Juvenile Courts, are all parts of the process of reconstruction. It is the readiness and ability to serve the community in this great task that has so suddenly thrust the Society into its present unique position.
>
> "The Legal Aid Society is often the only agent for collecting the needed data. How many people are denied justice because they cannot afford to advance the costs of court? Even the most systematically kept court records can disclose, at best, the number of small suits actually begun, but not those which were never brought because of poverty. The answer lies written in the files of the Society. What are the most common abuses in the legal profession, and can they be lessened or eliminated? How is the Workman's Compensation Act working out in practice from the employee's point of view? How far is the neglected wife, child, or parent, prevented, by defects in the laws, from securing the support which those very laws attempted to guarantee? These and many other vital questions can be answered in whole, or in part, only by an analysis of the material which is continually pouring into the offices of the Legal Aid Society."

Although the movement is only at its inception, tangible proofs of what it can accomplish are available and have been mentioned in earlier pages. The campaign in Illinois for better laws regulating small loans was built up on facts many of which were ascertained from data furnished by the Chicago Legal Aid Society. Similarly, the evidence which proved the flaws in the Massachusetts law concerning wage assignments, and which also showed just what was necessary to provide adequate safeguards, came from the cases of the Boston Legal Aid Society. It was the study of the evils of the justice of the peace system by the Legal Aid Society in Cleveland that pointed the way to the small claims court. In New York, when the question of abolishing arrest on execution for wage claims under fifty dollars was discussed, there

---

[1] *Report of Proceedings of the Second Conference of Legal Aid Societies*, page 20; *Ibid.*, *Fourth Conference*, page 63; 1 Philadelphia L. A. R. 8; 31 Chicago L. A. R. 13; 16 Boston L. A. R. 8; 15 N. Y. Legal Aid Rev. No. 2, p. 1.
[2] *Director's Report* for 1916, 16 Boston L. A. R. 3, 4.

was much generalizing, but the actual facts of the use of the body execution and of its effect were found in cases of the Legal Aid Society. On this one small point the Society was able to produce one hundred and eighty-four cases covering a period of two years.[1] Along precisely the same lines, in the field of criminal law the defender organizations can collect information which will give further assistance to the community in its ancient problem of crime and the treatment of criminals.

To do work of this sort, certain mechanical arrangements are indispensable. All records must be accurately arranged so that they are easily available, and they must be intelligently tabulated. Societies which have in the past prided themselves on "doing their work instead of keeping records" must make an abrupt face-about and fall into line with scientific progress. In the evolution of a technique of legal aid work the guiding principle must be the planning of case and other records so that they shall have definite meaning and can be utilized. This is one further reason why a central and governing legal aid agency is imperative.

Some of this preventive law work the societies can do alone. Much more they can do in coöperation with other agencies such as the courts, bar associations, labor commissions, charities, and the like. It is easy to see how much coöperation could do, and how necessary each would be to the other, in such matters respectively as denial of justice through court costs, professional misconduct, non-payment of wages, and the practical working of the laws governing support of families. Many of our community problems are not yet solved. Some we are only beginning to perceive. Before definite steps can be taken there must be the stage of straight thinking and interchange of opinion. This is an age of democracy, not only in government but in thought. Our problems are so complex that no one man knows enough to see the whole solution. Only by coöperation, by putting together the best thoughts from all sources, is the remedy to be found.

The community needs light from every angle. It sorely needs to learn that putting laws on the books is nothing. Enforcement is the test. If in actual application a law fails to accomplish its intended purpose, then it is not the remedy. Here the legal aid experience is invaluable, for in many instances the desired information can best come from the legal aid organizations.

§ 4

The greatest service which the societies render to the community is their promotion of good citizenship. By their protection of the immigrant and their securing to the
Good Citizenship
native born their legal rights, the legal aid organizations are each year proving to their hundred thousand clients the integrity and fairness of our institutions. This engenders respect for law, loyalty, and patriotism. A competent observer has remarked[2] that the legal aid society "has a

[1] 34 N. Y. L. A. R. 21.   [2] Editorial in 8 Charities Review (1898), 4.

field which presents direct possibilities of promoting good citizenship and faith in our institutions, especially among our immigrant population, such as are scarcely afforded in any other way."

It was the vision of this service which the legal aid society could render that inspired Mr. Briesen to transform it from a restricted to an American organization. A statement of this work for the making of good citizenship cannot better be presented than in his own words,[1] written after having seen the process steadily going on for twelve years: "It is not merely that we protect the weak from being wronged and defrauded of that which is their just due; that is a great deal to be sure, but there are other and collateral results which are of value to the community and the country.

"The Society's work makes good citizens and arouses a sentiment of respect for the laws, and also, I may say, a sentiment of patriotism. Many of our clients are persons of foreign birth—people, often, who are ignorant of the laws and of how to set the machinery of the law in motion. They have some vague idea that there is law for the redress of wrongs, but they have heard that it is too costly a luxury for the poor; that it is law for the rich and not for the poor. They know they have been defrauded and wronged, but redress may seem to them hopeless. They have no money to secure it, and therefore they think it is not for them. The consequence is that they become bitter, not only against the particular person who has wronged them but against society in general, against the country which permits society to be organized on so unjust a basis. Such persons—and they need not be confined to persons of foreign birth by any means—are ripe to listen to those social agitators and disturbers who are only too prevalent. They are ripe for enlistment in the ranks of those who are regarded as dangerous to the security of law and order."

[1] 17 Ann. Am. Ac. Pol. & Soc. Science (1901), 165.

Chapter XXIII

LEGAL AID AND THE ORGANIZED CHARITIES

> Workers in organized charity frequently find cases needing legal aid and
> no other relief—cases where legal aid is the only thing necessary to relieve
> suffering. Or it may be that material relief is needed; but in addition a legal
> redress of some wrong will effect the only permanent cure and reëstablish
> a family on a self-respecting, self-reliant footing. MARION HOUSTON.[1]

IN considering the services rendered by legal aid societies to the various charity
organizations we are concerned not alone with those societies which are departments of charities, but with the work of all organizations of all types. Even the departmental bureaus are not confined in their service to the charities of which they
are a part, although the form of their organization tends somewhat to restrict the
freedom with which other charities utilize them, but join with the independent organizations in giving their assistance and coöperation to all the charities in their
respective cities. This legal work consists not in advising the charity itself in its
corporate capacity on matters involving its entity or its policy, but in providing
legal advice and assistance in those cases which the charity has undertaken and
which present legal questions. For the sake of clearness we may also exclude the
relatively small number of cases in which the charity has no interest except to refer
them directly to the legal aid society. Thus we are not concerned with the case where
a man who has a wage claim goes to a charity because he does not know where else
to go and is forthwith sent to the legal aid office. Such a case does not differ from a
matter referred by a newspaper, or a private person, or from a direct application.
It requires no coöperation and implies no relationship. The situation, which it is
the purpose of this chapter to discuss, is that where a charity in trying to work out
some case problem presented to it finds itself confronted with a legal question which
may be the major or minor issue in the case, but which must be answered if the case
is to be properly diagnosed and treated, and which the charity worker himself is not
qualified to decide.

§ 1

The charities in their daily work with individuals and families constantly find situations that call for legal advice and assistance. Persons apply for charitable assist-

The Volunteer Counsel Plan
ance when they are in trouble, and that trouble invariably traces
its origin back to one or more of three causes—individual frailty
or weakness, which is the rarest cause; social or economic maladjustment, which is the commonest cause; and what may be called legal maladjustment or

---

[1] From an article on Coöperation in 2 N. Y. Legal Aid Review, No. 1, p. 2 (January, 1904), by Marion Houston, who
was at that time the representative of the Executive Board of the Council of Civic Coöperation in New York.

inability to secure redress by law, which is a very frequent source of trouble. Illness is an example of the first, unemployment of the second, and of the third an injured workman unable to secure compensation, a family whose breadwinner pays the greater portion of his wages to some loan shark, a deserted wife, or the mother of an illegitimate child.

It is the task of the trained social worker not merely to tide over any emergency which may exist, but, what is more important, to diagnose the case with a view to preventing a recurrence of the cause and of lifting the person or family out of a subnormal condition to one of independence and self-supporting self-respect. When the difficulty or a part of the difficulty appears to involve law, the social worker needs to be able to secure prompt, accurate, and expert advice. The charities have from their origin faced this difficulty if their cases were to be intelligently conducted, but it is only within comparatively recent years that the difficulty has become one of great concern. This is largely the result of two factors. First, the changed conditions which resulted in wholesale denial of justice to the poor at once increased the number of cases where the distress could be traced to legal maladjustment. Second, with the modern training of the social worker the emphasis has been laid on preventing the recurrence of the trouble, which in turn has called for skilled diagnosis, and this has uncovered the existence of situations calling for legal action which formerly would have been passed over. Whereas the charity worker was formerly content to supply material assistance to a destitute family, now the educated social worker makes an objective of finding the deserting husband, and of compelling him to perform his moral and legal duty to support his family. This changed point of view marks the development of charity into social service which is not the less sympathetic because it is the more intelligent.

In their endeavor to secure adequate legal advice and assistance, the charities have customarily adopted an expedient which is called the volunteer counsel or honorary counsel plan. They have placed on their directorates or committees one or more attorneys, prominent in the profession, who were supposed to hold themselves in readiness to give instruction on points of law. However satisfactory this arrangement may have been in earlier times, it has proved entirely inadequate under present conditions in the large cities. Just as the private law offices formerly cared for poor clients and did legal aid work in their own offices, and when the great demand for free legal assistance came were unable to cope with the need, and because of the altered conditions of law practice gradually gave up the legal aid work altogether, so much the same change has gone on with regard to the work of honorary counsel for charity organizations, except that the facts were not as quickly realized and the necessary readjustments were more slowly made.

Three flaws are clearly apparent in the volunteer or honorary counsel plan. It fails to provide as prompt or as much legal advice as social workers need. The lawyers who are chosen for the positions are men of reputation and extensive practice. They are extremely busy. Workers are very much disinclined to bother such men with what may seem petty questions. They do not feel free to go to such offices as often as may be necessary to have legal doubts in their cases resolved for them. When they do go they are quite likely to find the lawyer engaged in conferences or meetings which cannot be interrupted. This is not the fault of the individual lawyer; it is not that he attempts to evade his responsibility — nearly every one has rendered conscientious service; it is the fault of the conditions which attend the plan.

In the second place the charity work suffers because it is not the lawyer's first business to care for such cases. Modern offices work under pressure, and when a choice has to be made between the firm's business and the charity case, it is inevitable that the former should obtain precedence. The charity case is put by until a more favorable opportunity, or else it is turned over to one of the office "cubs," who has just graduated from law school, to experiment with. It is a general rule that the cases presented by the charities cannot afford to wait. The worker presents the problem in order to be able to plan the best possible relief in the light of the legal situation that is involved. If the legal answer or the legal action cannot be had promptly, the arrangements go awry and constructive progress is greatly hindered. For example, if the charity case is one of family destitution because the father has been injured and is not receiving compensation, the charity worker needs to know at once whether compensation will automatically be paid after two weeks, or whether a contest will be necessary, and if so, how long it will probably take, or whether there is no chance for any compensation. Only with these questions answered can the worker form any intelligent estimate of the best course to pursue. If compensation is to be available shortly, the problem is only one of tiding over an emergency; if there is no legal relief in sight, then the injured man must be trained in some lighter sort of work and a position be found for him; if a contest is necessary, then a very delicate balancing of probabilities concerning the chance of success and the time required has to be undertaken with the lawyer's close coöperation.

Finally, the volunteer counsel plan is not calculated to procure accurate or expert advice. If it does secure accurate advice, it is only in a most uneconomical way. The body of the law is now so vast that no one man knows it all or can keep pace with its growth. Specialization has necessarily resulted, and the larger offices, from which the honorary counsel are drawn, have generally specialized along lines of corporation, banking, business, and property law. The legal problems of the poor do not fall in these fields. It is not surprising that the patent expert knows nothing about a boarding-house keeper's lien or that the corporation expert knows nothing about the criminal procedure to enforce family support. Many of the cases that come to the charities from the poor are in the by-ways of the law in which most lawyers are not expert and about which they know very little.

To make this concrete, we may consider two typical situations. One great group of charities in our larger cities are known as the associated, or united, or federated charities, or charity organization societies. In their cases a common problem relates to the loan shark. A destitute family needs help because the wage-earner pays ten per cent per month interest on a loan. The precise question is whether there is any legal relief, and with this question the social worker goes to the charity's counsel. It is quite likely that he has only a vague knowledge of the law and therefore must needs look it up. As this subject has been a battle-ground of contention in the last five years, the statutes represent a series of acts, repeals, amendments, and revisions, with the usual embroidery of case interpretations, further supplemented in several jurisdictions by administrative rulings by loan supervisors or bank commissioners. In his search the lawyer finds his digests valueless, the statutes a maze, and perhaps he overlooks the administrative rulings which are unknown to many lawyers. If he decides that the rate of interest is in excess of law, he is confronted with procedural doubts. He may find that the most summary procedure is before an administrative official, but the nature of such proceedings is not familiar to him. When he finally gets his result, much valuable time of a valuable man has been wasted. The attorney for the legal aid society could be called on the telephone, and in many instances would have the accurate answer on the tip of his tongue. The contrast is not one of personalities, but of system. The legal aid attorney is probably the inferior lawyer of the two, but he has had several hundred cases of the sort, he has been through the procedure often, so that the entire law on this subject is an open book to him.

Our second great group of charity organizations are the children's agencies. A common problem with them is that of the illegitimate child. In planning the child's future, the primary considerations are whether the alleged father can be compelled to provide support and, if so, what order can be secured. The chances are that the honorary counsel cannot accurately estimate the situation because in his entire practice he may never have had a bastardy case. These matters are commonplaces in the legal aid office. Their attorneys have scores of such cases, they have been through bitterly contested trials and know the pitfalls, they have submitted briefs and know the law, and through frequent appearances they know the sort and kind of evidence which judges require to fix paternity and make orders for support.

These statements rest not alone on their intrinsic reasonableness. They are supported by direct evidence from the charities themselves.[1] In connection with this study letters were sent to the charity organization societies in all cities where there are no legal aid organizations, asking how they cared for the legal problems in their cases and if their arrangements were satisfactory. A few replied that they were able to use nearby legal aid societies; the vast majority stated that they used the volunteer or honorary counsel plan. As to the effectiveness of that arrangement, the opinion varies according to the size of the cities. Places having a population[2] of less than

---

[1] *The First Report of the Legal Aid Bureau of the Federated Charities of Baltimore* contains an excellent statement, pages 1–7.

[2] Population figures are based on the 1910 Census figures.

ten thousand report that they have few, if any, legal problems. The charity societies in cities with populations ranging up to forty thousand find that for such legal matters as are presented the voluntary counsel plan is generally satisfactory. In the replies from charities in cities with from forty thousand to seventy thousand inhabitants, there is a note of doubt. The remark is repeatedly made that the plan can be only temporary in its success and will be outgrown if work increases. The charities in cities above seventy thousand, with one exception, report a need for a more definite method of caring for their legal problems. The one exception is Denver, where the Social Service Bureau is able to avail itself of the services of an attorney who was for several years chief attorney for the Chicago Legal Aid Society. Such an exception tends rather to prove the rule.

§ 2

The volunteer counsel plan in the larger cities fails to give the service which the charities ought to have. There are two alternative remedies, one for each charity to

Service by Legal Aid Organizations

retain and pay its own attorney, and the other for the charities to utilize the staffs of the legal aid organizations. A few of the largest charities, particularly the Humane Societies, have adopted the former course. Most of the charities, however, are now obtaining their legal advice from the legal aid societies.

The various legal aid organizations do a great amount of work for the charities in their respective cities. We have noted earlier in examining the sources of legal aid work that a very substantial number of cases came from the charities. These numbers refer only to clients, and do not include calls from social workers for advice. In St. Paul the record of such calls which has been kept shows that in 1913 workers sought the legal aid society's assistance in forty-seven instances, in 1914 two hundred and eighty-seven times, in 1915 seven hundred and seventy-six times, and in 1916 nine hundred and fifty-four times.[1] This last figure represents over three calls each working day. The legal aid reports contain frequent references to this particular phase of their work.[2] Perhaps the most advanced step has been taken by the Children's Aid Society in Boston, which has retained the Legal Aid Society as its special counsel and thereby is able to command a definite amount of time for its workers. It has given the proposition this clear expression:[3]

"It is desirable that our workers have easy access to lawyers having a wide knowledge of all laws affecting our work, and it is also desirable that this knowledge and experience be concentrated in the office of an organization such as the Legal Aid Society. Our legal problems are uncommon in the average law office.

[1] *Report of Proceedings of the Fourth Conference of Legal Aid Societies*, page 107.
[2] *Report of Proceedings of the Fourth Conference of Legal Aid Societies*, page 104; *Ibid., Second Conference*, page 29; *Ibid., First Conference*, page 7; 19 N. Y. L. A. R. 26; 8 Philadelphia L. A. R. 3, 10; 6 Chicago L. A. R. 6; 3 N. Y. Legal Aid Rev. No. 2, p. 4; 11 *Ibid.* No. 1, p. 4; 11 *Ibid.* No. 3, p. 4.
[3] Boston Children's Aid Society, *Report* for 1916, page 26.

"The Legal Aid Society is also used as counsel by many of the other social agencies in the city. It is therefore acquiring an experience in the handling of such work as to make it of unusual help; first in the treatment of immediate legal needs and second in the analysis of defective procedure and the devising of remedies."

The legal aid organizations are qualified to give to the charities accessible, prompt, and expert legal service. Their attorneys are always available for consultation, because that is a part of their duty. For a like reason the necessary work can be promptly performed. Cases brought by the charities are a part of the work which it is the business of the legal aid society to undertake. Charity cases are carried through by a legal aid office just as a paying client's case is conducted by a private law office. The service is expert because the legal aid attorneys, through long and repeated experience, become specialists[1] in the law which is most commonly involved in the cases of the poor.

§ 3

Each large city now has its several charities dealing with the various kinds of problems which are presented. The addition of the legal aid society completes the circle.[2]

Coöperation   The system of coöperation whereby the charities bring their cases to the legal aid society is not only better than that of the volunteer counsel plan but, for several reasons, it is preferable to having each organization retain its own attorney.

Centralization fixes responsibility, avoids duplication[3] and waste of effort, and reduces cost. The situation here is like that discussed earlier, when it appeared that various courts, tribunals, and administrative departments needed from time to time to refer cases to attorneys. Here as there, it seems sounder to have one central bureau to which all similar matters may be referred rather than a decentralized system of one attorney for each organization or department.[4] This is so because the problem is a unit and the cases, from wherever they are referred, are of the same nature.

Coöperation by the charities operates to increase the advantages which the legal aid societies of themselves can give. As the charities send in all their legal cases to the one central agency, its experience is automatically increased, its staff becomes more expert, and consequently its service to the charities reaches a higher plane of proficiency. Both the legal aid societies and the charities are serving the same community. Each needs the other, and their close coöperation brings about mutual benefits.[5]

The pooling of all experience in one office furthers the preventive work which the legal aid society can do by affording it more material from which to diagnose legal ills and ascertain their remedies. If each charity were to have its own attorney,

---

[1] *Report of Proceedings of the Fourth Conference of Legal Aid Societies,* pages 107, 118, 119.
[2] 24 N. Y. L. A. R. 17.   [3] 3 Chicago L. A. R. 12.
[4] See *ante,* page 89.   [5] 15 N. Y. Legal Aid Rev. No. 2, p. 5.

devoting only a part of his time to such work, there would be a wealth of material so divided up in a number of offices that it would be unintelligible. Two hundred wage assignment cases in one office afford a sound basis for constructive reasoning; if split up into twenty offices, the salient facts appear less clearly and there is hardly enough experience in any one place to afford a satisfactory test for any conclusions.

While the legal aid organizations undertake preventive law work primarily for the benefit of the community at large, the charities profit from all such work. As the poor are better protected from extortion, and as the application of the law is made more prompt and certain in bringing redress, the area within which legal maladjustment is a provocative cause of distress is narrowed, the burden of the charities is lightened, and for the future they are able to bring about more permanent results in such of their cases as come within the added protections secured by the legal aid organizations.

CHAPTER XXIV

LEGAL AID AND THE BAR

It is the sense of this Conference that bar associations, state and
local, should be urged to foster the formation and efficient administration of legal aid societies for legal relief work for the worthy poor,
with the active and sympathetic coöperation of such associations.[1]

THERE is a direct relationship between legal aid organizations and the members of the bar, both as individual attorneys and as a collective body. Out of
this relationship there spring reciprocal obligations to be observed by each and services to be rendered to each. While the responsibilities are bilateral, the performance
is still very much one-sided. The legal aid societies have recognized their position and
have served the bar to the limit of their ability; the lawyers are only dimly aware
that they owe a debt to legal aid work, and as yet they have not taken the part which
may fairly be expected of them. Where there ought to be the closest possible alliance,
there is not a semblance of ordered and sustained coöperation. It is profitless to attempt to fix or apportion the blame for the past; but it is of high importance both
to the cause of legal aid work and to the reputation of the profession, that the wholly
unsatisfactory nature of the present situation be stated and that steps, calculated to
improve it, be suggested.

§ 1

The services which legal aid organizations have rendered, and are rendering, to the
bar may be first considered, as they are undisputed and can be simply explained. Summarily stated, the societies are performing for the bar its legal and moral
Legal Aid responsibility to poor persons needing legal assistance, by virtue of their
Services to work and their position they are strengthening the reputation and pop-
the Bar ularity of the profession in the community, they are disclosing and bringing to the proper authorities cases of abuse and misconduct by individual attorneys,
they are from time to time advising and assisting individual lawyers on matters in
which they have become specialists, and they are more and more coöperating with the
bar in its efforts to better the administration of justice, to keep the profession clean,
and to secure proper educational training.

Most of these points have already been considered in their appropriate connections.
The profession is admittedly interested in legal education and in standards for admission to the bar. Many state bar associations have special committees on legal education. The Section of Legal Education of the American Bar Association is working
with the bar examiners to erect and maintain suitable standard educational require-

---

[1] From a resolution unanimously adopted by the Conference of Delegates of State and Local Bar Associations at
their meeting, held in conjunction with the American Bar Association, on September 3, 1917. 3 Am. Bar Ass'n Journal, No. 4, p. 592; 42 Am. Bar Ass'n R. (1917) 437.

ments for admission to the bar. Their encouragement of the Carnegie Foundation's study of legal education, of which the present volume is a part, has been more than generous. One mooted and perplexing question has been the requirement of training in practice. Here the legal aid society steps forward, partakes in the discussion, and offers a tangible solution. It was through the legal aid society that the articles on the legal clinic by Dean Wigmore and William V. Rowe were brought to the attention of all the bar associations in the country. So far as its position warrants, the legal aid society is contributing its thought on those aspects of the question which are peculiarly within its knowledge, and it stands ready to assume its fair share of the burden in bringing about the clinical training of law students in its offices.

The bar is closely concerned with the administration of justice and with its betterment. We have seen that the legal aid societies have played an important part in the shaping of the law,[1] and that they have developed as far as anybody within the profession the science of preventive law.[2] In all such work they are in fact coöperating with the bar and furthering the bar's interests. Of less importance but deserving mention is the assistance to individual lawyers in particular cases. Legal aid attorneys have become experts in the law governing certain types of cases, such as workmen's compensation, separation between husband and wife, assignments of wages, small loans, illegitimacy, criminal proceedings to enforce support, and most recently in the laws concerning men in military service. It is a common thing for attorneys in private practice to ask for advice and suggestions when such a case is brought to their office. All assistance of this sort the societies gladly furnish.

Discipline is a primary concern of all bar associations. In this unpleasant and difficult work the legal aid societies have proved themselves valuable allies. They serve to supplement the jurisdiction of the bar associations by bringing to light abuses which would not otherwise be known. In the great cities, where the bar is so large that the members do not know one another, where personal acquaintance is limited to one's own circle of practice, the legal aid societies deal with a class of attorneys who are unknown to the leaders of the bar, they negotiate with them, try cases against them, and come into contact with them in daily practice, so that they are in a position to detect improper and unlawful conduct. They can also observe those collection agencies, dealing in the smaller claims against the poorer people, which carry on their business in a manner perilously close to the line prohibiting the practice of law by corporations, and which secure their collections in devious ways including the use of demand notes, forms of complaint, and summonses that approach abuse of legal process. It must never be forgotten that the legal aid organizations act and speak for those who are particularly defenceless and who, when they are imposed upon, or cheated, or charged extortionate fees are completely at a loss as to what they should do, and have no money to engage counsel to institute proceedings for redress in their

[1] See *ante*, Chapter XXI, Legal Aid and the Law, page 200.
[2] See *ante*, Chapter XXII, Legal Aid and the Community, § 3, page 214.

behalf. At this most needed point the legal aid societies can best stand as guardian. They have won the confidence of these poorer classes and are generally known to them. The societies, very fortunately for work of this sort, are in an impartial position which is respected. They have no private interests at stake, they do not act to earn a fee, and the lawyer whom they call to render an accounting knows that they are acting only in accordance with their duty. Just as they have served to extend the administration of justice into this great field at the bottom of society, so they have extended the watchfulness and discipline of the bar association.[1] They have brought hundreds of cases to grievance committees in all parts of the country. They are in a position to do even more, and if accorded a measure of encouragement, they will do more.

What have thus far been presented may be called minor contributions. There remain for consideration two great services which are performed by all legal aid organizations everywhere for the benefit and in behalf of the bar. They are a most powerful influence in preserving the faith of the common people in the integrity of the bar. The profession as a whole, particularly its better members, has no conception of the appalling number of persons who to-day view the lawyer with suspicion and distrust. The deadly parallel between the commentary of De Tocqueville on the American bar and that of Bryce, fifty years later, is well known.[2] The change from "the highest political class" and "the only enlightened class whom the people do not distrust" to "a part of the great organized system of industrial and financial enterprise" ceasing "to be so much of a distinct professional class" is a matter of history. The change is summed up in the saying that formerly lawyers had clients, now clients have lawyers.[3] Since Bryce, a period of forty years has elapsed, during which the pendulum might have swung back in a more favorable direction, but it has not. The distrust of lawyers to-day is marked,[4] but it differs from the dissatisfaction of earlier times in that it is not the product of jealousy or fear of a new ruling class, but proceeds from intelligent criticism founded on facts. In these forty years a generation has been born, grown up, and is now carrying on the affairs of the world and causing most of the cases which require legal treatment. This generation, at least that part born in the lower social stratas, has apparently been taught from infancy that lawyers are a class who prey on the weak, who profit out of their misery, and who are so strongly entrenched that the state cannot curb them. To this attitude the contingent fee, the commercialization of the profession, and the lowering of standards have, in their results, all contributed. Quite typical is the remark of the applicant for legal aid who, on being told that the society could not accept his case and that he should go to some honest lawyer, replied that he had never associated together the words "honest" and "lawyer." This man was not a tramp, or a dead-beat, or even a

---

[1] *Report of Proceedings of the First Conference of Legal Aid Societies*, page 48; 33 N. Y. L. A. R. 25.

[2] Brandeis: *Business—A Profession* (1914), pages 314-318.

[3] That the lawyer has tended to become an employee is noted by Dean Pound in his address, *Causes of Popular Dissatisfaction with the Administration of Justice*, in 29 Am. Bar Ass'n R. 395, 415.

[4] *History of the Harvard Law School* (1917), page 155.

charity applicant. He had been a painter for twenty years and had always supported himself and his family, until an accident disabled him and forced him to seek redress by law. That the large majority of their clients entertain a low opinion of the bar is the unanimous testimony of the legal aid attorneys. They do not speak in haste or with bitterness. They merely voice a conclusion forced upon them by the thousands of persons who annually pass in and out of their offices.

The legal aid societies strive to teach their clients not only that the law is fair, but that lawyers are not without honor and conscience. The work is done by men who are themselves lawyers, who hold high ideals of professional obligation, and who feel keenly the reproaches flung at their profession. Their work serves as a pledge of the bar's good faith, and they gladly give to the bar as much credit as can truthfully be ascribed to it. Were they in a position to state that in all their work they were acting for the whole bar, and performing for it its recognized collective responsibility to see that no one was denied justice because of inability to pay fees, they could implant in the minds of the multitudes who seek their assistance a renewed faith in the integrity of the bar in this country, and a renewal of the law-abiding spirit. The legal aid societies are undeniably popular. If the bar were more closely identified in the public mind with their work, the same good will would be reflected and attach to it. An eminent lawyer has written to his profession concerning the legal aid society:[1]

"But we can do nothing which will so surely increase public confidence in us collectively as to make this society flourish as a distinctively legal charity."

The last and greatest service which the legal aid organizations render is that in all their work they are relieving the bar of a heavy burden by performing for the bar its legal and ethical obligation to see that no one shall suffer injustice through inability, because of poverty, to obtain needed legal advice and assistance. Each case which a legal aid organization undertakes puts the bar in debt to it, for in the conduct of that case it is doing the work of the bar for the bar.[2] This fact discloses the essence of the relationship between legal aid organizations and the bar. It is commonly expressed in the narrow language of providing a place to which lawyers may send their charity cases, leaving themselves free to engage in remunerative work. This is but a small aspect of the situation; it fails to include the thousands of persons who never apply to private offices, knowing that they cannot pay the expected fees, and yet who need counsel and representation if they are to secure justice. With all these persons the members of the bar are concerned. As individuals and collectively as a profession, they are under obligation to give or provide them the necessary legal assistance. To-day the bar performs its obligation vicariously through the legal

---

[1] Holls: *The Legal Aid Society*, 8 Charities Review (1898), 21. Cf. 2 N. Y. Legal Aid Review, No. 4, p. 2. It is interesting to note that the same thing has been said to the English bar, 48 Law Journal (1913), 180.

[2] Cf. 8 Chicago L. A. R. 9; 7 Pittsburgh L. A. R. 11. By far the best presentation of this fact is contained in a letter under date of December 5, 1916, from George S. Hornblower of the New York Legal Aid Society to Bronson Winthrop, chairman of a special committee of the New York City Bar Association appointed to investigate the Legal Aid Society.

aid organizations. It is proper that it should be done in this organized way which secures economy and efficiency,[1] but it does not make an end of the responsibility resting on the bar. The very fact that the legal aid organizations are thus doing the bar's work places the bar under obligation to supervise and provide leadership for the legal aid work and to supply the necessary financial and moral support. These are the services which lawyers should render to legal aid work. The legal aid organizations are entitled to look to the bar for this leadership and support. Such assistance is accorded in scanty measure because the bar in general does not see the situation in this light, and apparently does not admit the premise that there rests on every lawyer a definite duty toward the poor litigant.

§ 2

With this present prevailing opinion it is impossible to bring home the obligation of the bar to legal aid organizations without first making clear the lawyer's duty to the poor litigant. It is the general rule that each attorney, on his admission as a minister of justice and agent of the court, becomes subject to assignments from the court to represent needy persons without charge or for any fee they may be able to pay. The theory of this obligation is not peculiar to our law; it is a characteristic of the lawyer's position in all civilized communities, and there is evidence that it has been recognized from the earliest times.[2] In criminal cases the legal nature of the obligation is clear because it is enforced. No statute is necessary to give the court this right to call upon the bar, its power is inherent, and statutes only declare it.[3] In civil cases, as we have already seen,[4] the power has fallen into such disuse that its existence is forgotten or denied. Because it is not employed there is an absence of authorities squarely on the point, but in a number of decisions the language shows unmistakably the court's opinion of the rule of law.[5] The reason for the rule is precisely the same in civil as in criminal cases,[6] and the court has the same inherent power to command the services of counsel in aid of persons unable to pay.[7] There are statutes expressly conferring this power in civil matters on certain courts in certain cases in Illinois, Indiana, Missouri, New Jersey, New York, and Tennessee; and Congress by

The Lawyer's Obligation to the Poor

---

[1] Cf. 3 Am. Bar Ass'n Journal (October, 1917), 589.

[2] Brunner: *Early History of the Attorney*, 3 Illinois L. Rev. 257.

[3] Presby *v.* Klickitat County, 5 Wash. 329, 332; 6 Corpus Juris, 727.

[4] See *ante*, Chapter XIV, § 1, page 100.

[5] House *v.* Whitis, 5 Baxt. (Tenn.) 690, 692; Matter of Kelly, 12 Daly (N. Y.), 110; Harris *v.* Mutual Life Ins. Co. 13 N. Y. Supp. 718; Todd *v.* Todd, 9 N. J. L. J. 342; Kern *v.* State, 35 Ind. 288; see the text statements in 16 Encyc. of Pleading and Practice, 690, and 3 Am. & Eng. Encyc. of Law, 417, 419.

[6] Cf. Goldman: *Public Defender* (1917), page 18.

[7] This opinion is confirmed by George P. Costigan, Jr., Professor at the Northwestern University Law School, who has just completed an exhaustive study of cases bearing on the lawyer's duty in all its aspects in connection with his source-book entitled "Cases and Other Authorities on Legal Ethics" (1917). Professor Costigan, in response to an enquiry, states: "It seems to me clear that there is a duty on every lawyer as an officer of the court to accept an appointment by the court to represent poor clients in civil as well as in criminal cases."

Act of July 20, 1892, in dealing with the in forma pauperis proceedings, authorized the assignment of counsel in the federal courts.[1] The assignment of attorneys to act as divorce proctors is a further illustration of the same power.[2] Under the provision of the Soldiers' and Sailors' Civil Relief Act every court in the land is empowered in all cases and required in certain cases to assign counsel to act in behalf of men absent in military service.[3]

That the attorney, because of the nature of his office, is under legal obligation to assist needy suitors finds confirmation in the laws and customs of other countries. In France, the obligation of service was early enunciated by a royal edict which said of the attorney, "He was not, under pain of being disbarred, to refuse his services to the indigent and oppressed." [4] The obligation is still recognized,[5] and on it is based the French system of securing legal assistance to the poor known as "l'assistance judiciaire." [6] In Spain, the attorneys on admission swear "to take charge of cases committed to them by the courts at the instance of litigants who could not find a lawyer; to defend gratuitously poor clients where there were no lawyers paid for that purpose."[7] Likewise in Italy, lawyers must give gratuitous service to the poor.[8] The German system known as "the privilege of the poor," which is analogous to the French judicial assistance and to our in forma pauperis, permits citizens in cases of exigency to demand from the government the services of a lawyer.[9] The two Scottish bar associations undertake each year to furnish solicitors and advocates, who are then assigned by the court in cases of indigent suitors.

In England the assignment system has for years been as little used in civil cases as in the United States. Concerning the common law, Chief Justice Hale is credited with the statement that if the court assigned a serjeant to be counsel and he refused to act, the court would make bold to commit him to prison.[10] During the last half century the English administration of justice failed as completely as that in the United States to secure equality and to provide for the cases of the poor. The failure was in many ways more serious because no organized legal aid movement developed to ameliorate this condition as it did in America. In 1913, however, the Supreme Court of Judicature issued rules providing a comprehensive plan for securing to the poor their day in that court with adequate representation. The power of assignment

---

[1] Whelan v. Manhattan Ry. Co. 86 Fed. 219.   [2] This has been stated ante in Chapter XIV, § 2, page 102.

[3] Public Act No. 103 of the 65th Congress, §§ 200 et seq.

[4] Carter: Ethics of the Legal Profession (1915), page 26.

[5] Fuller: The French Bar, an address delivered before the New York City Bar Association, and later published in 23 Yale Law Journal (December, 1913), 113, 120.

[6] See post, Chapter XXV, § 3, page 246. Cf. Parry: The Law and the Poor, page 147; 105 Contemporary Review, 562; Speech of M. Bruwaert, French Consul-General in New York, at the Legal Aid Society Banquet, Report of Speeches at Twenty-fifth Anniversary Dinner of the New York Legal Aid Society, page 28; Théry: French Legal Assistance for the Poor, 1 International Law Notes (January, 1916), No. 1, p. 12.

[7] Manuel Rodriguez-Serra: Admission of Attorneys from the Spanish Standpoint, 35 Am. Bar Ass'n R. 842; Cohen: The Law — Business or Profession? (1916), page 61.

[8] Cohen: Ibid., page 64.   [9] 7 N. Y. Legal Aid Rev. No. 3, p. 17.

[10] 3 Campbell's Lives of the Chief Justices, 20.

was revived. Because of the similarity in legal institutions, English precedents carry more weight with us than those of any other country, and for that reason the court's declaration of the attorney's duty is significant. No act of Parliament gave to the courts the control which they purpose to exercise. The High Court rightly considered that it had ample inherent power. The rules provide for the formation of lists of solicitors and barristers who volunteer their services and then continue:[1]

"Rule 26. . . . And the Court or Judge or proper officer shall assign to the applicant a solicitor and a counsel (whether named in the list kept pursuant to Rule 23 (2) or not), to assist him in the conduct of the proceedings. . . .

"27. A solicitor or counsel assigned under Rule 26, shall not be at liberty to refuse his assistance unless he satisfies the proper officer or the Court or a Judge that he has some good ground for refusing."

This obligation owed by every lawyer to the poor, which is stated with reasonable clearness in the American cases, and which is undisputed in other systems of law, finds unmistakable support in the accepted standards of ethics. In other words, this duty is in part a legal obligation because the lawyer is a minister of justice, and in part an ethical responsibility because of his membership in a profession. In matters of this sort accepted canons of ethics are entitled to as much weight as decisions in adjudicated cases and most attorneys so regard them.[2]

When the adoption of the present canons of ethics of the American Bar Association was under discussion, Mr. Justice Brewer pointed out that the most important part was the Oath of Admission, which included within itself the final statement of the lawyer's duty.[3] Of this Oath it is said in Part III of the Canons as adopted,[4] "The general principles which should ever control the lawyer in the practice of his profession are clearly set forth in the following Oath of Admission to the Bar, formulated upon that in use in the State of Washington, and which conforms in its main outlines to the duties of lawyers as defined by statutory enactments in that and many other states of the Union—duties which they are sworn on admission to obey and for the wilful violation of which disbarment is provided." The final clause of this Oath is:[5]

"I will never reject from any consideration personal to myself the cause of the defenceless or the oppressed, or delay any man's cause for lucre or malice. So help me God."

In these time-honored words the obligation of service is imposed.[6] Here there is no distinction between the duty in civil and criminal cases. This broad declaration is supported by similar statements in all treatises on ethics. The first code of ethics in America was probably that drawn up by David Hoffman early in the nineteenth

---

[1] These rules are contained in the 1914 *Rule Book*. They are Order 16, IV, Proceedings by and against Poor Persons.
[2] Cf. statement of the Missouri Bar Association concerning the canons of ethics adopted by the American Bar Association, 39 Am. Bar Ass'n R. (1914) 562.
[3] See 31 Am. Bar Ass'n R. 62; 33 *Ibid.* 570.   [4] 33 *Ibid.* 584.   [5] 33 *Ibid.* 585.
[6] The lawyer's oath in the Canton of Geneva, which has been in force for years, reads: "I swear before God not to reject, for any consideration personal to myself, the cause of the weak, the stranger, or the oppressed."

century. As he expressed it in his eighteenth canon:[1] "I shall never close my ear or heart because my clients' means are low. Those who have none, and who have just causes, are, of all others, the best entitled to sue or be defended; and they shall receive a due portion of my services, cheerfully given." Sharswood in the course of his celebrated lectures on ethics referred to this duty in several connections. Of the bar in general he said:[2] "It is indeed the noblest faculty of the profession to counsel the ignorant, defend the weak and oppressed, and to stand forth on all occasions as the bulwark of private rights against the assaults of power." And of the lawyer he said:[3] "There are many cases, in which it will be his duty, perhaps more properly his privilege, to work for nothing. It is to be hoped that the time will never come, at this or any other Bar in this country, when a poor man with an honest cause, though without a fee, cannot obtain the services of honest counsel, in the prosecution or defence of his rights." The Hon. Charles E. Hughes, formerly a justice of the Supreme Court of the United States, has said: "To take from the poor man a part of the burden which necessarily falls on him because of his poverty and see to it that he obtains in every proper case his legal rights has always seemed to me to be a part of the duty of the lawyer."[4]

By well-settled principles of professional ethics and by the voice of authority, so far as the courts have been called upon to express their judgment, the attorney is called upon to render services to the needy. This he has not done. The legal aid society has done it for him. The attorney for the Pittsburgh Legal Aid Society appeared as counsel for a woman, the prosecuting witness in a criminal case, only a few years ago. The attorney for the defendant in his address to the jury remarked that the legal aid appearance was unwarranted and that the entire county bar stood ready to assist such a needy woman. The facts were that the woman had consulted several members of that bar, who had relieved her of what little money she had without doing anything for her, and only then did she seek the help of the legal aid organization.[5] As a fact of general application it is not true that the members of the bar despoil the poor — some of them do, but they are a small minority; yet it is the fact that the bar as a whole has done almost nothing to assist the poor in securing that justice which our institutions profess to guarantee them. With the existence of organized legal aid work, blame does not attach to the bar for allowing such organizations to undertake the cases of the poor. This method of meeting the need is in every way desirable. But having permitted the legal aid societies to perform for them for their own professional obligation, censure justly attaches to the members of the bar for having failed to give something of their earnings for the support and something of their time for the leadership of this legal aid work.

[1] 2 Am. Law School Rev. 230, 232.
[2] Sharswood: *Professional Ethics* (fifth edition, 1884), page 53.   [3] *Ibid.*, page 151.
[4] 15 N. Y. Legal Aid Review, No. 1, p. 1.
[5] 2 Pittsburgh L. A. R. 18.

§ 3

By virtue of the position and work of the legal aid organizations in the community
the obligation of the bar to the poor may be said to have been hypothecated to the
Services of   legal aid organizations. They having performed and being equipped to
the Bar to   better perform the bar's responsibility to the weak and oppressed, the
Legal Aid   bar should feel that it is incumbent on it to render to the legal aid soci-
Work   eties the services of which they stand in need.

The legal aid societies need leadership, moral support, and financial
support. These three things go together and are of one piece. They are essential to
the well-being of every legal aid organization. One fact which very forcibly strikes
the observer of the work in different cities is that legal aid success or failure goes
hand in hand with good or bad support from the bar. Given the amount of interest
and coöperation accorded by the local bar, the strength of the legal aid work can be
accurately estimated and foretold. No society can flourish in the face of hostility, or
suspicion, or indifference from the attorneys of the city. In this situation there is no
middle ground; those who are not with the work are necessarily against it. To know
nothing about legal aid work, to care nothing about it, and to do nothing for it is
to doom it as effectively as by open opposition.

The vast portion of the bar has been in this middle position. They have paid little
attention to the work and its needs. One could read the proceedings of ninety-five
per cent of the various bar associations without finding a mention of legal aid work
in their discussions. The assumption would be warranted that the bar had no interest
in or concern for this great attempt to equalize the administration of justice. In September, 1917, something about legal aid work was made known at the Conference of
Delegates of State and Local Bar Associations, held in conjunction with the American
Bar Association. For the first time in forty years legal aid work, which is national
in scope, was given consideration by a national gathering of lawyers. The resolution,
proposed by Charles A. Boston of the New York Bar and unanimously passed by the
delegates, which has been quoted as the keynote of this chapter, expresses the duty
which the bar owes. Judged by the standard there set, the bar as a whole must be held
to have defaulted on its obligation.

The blame in part attaches to the legal aid societies themselves. Knowing the conservatism of the bar and its occupation in other worthy lines of endeavor, the societies have failed to present their case and to force the issue. Having failed to establish a central agency of their own, they have had no spokesman for their cause in
the general meetings of the bar. What should be made clear is that the legal aid
organizations represent one of the great legal reform movements of the times. It
ranks with the movements for reorganization of courts and for simplification of procedure. It needs the same study and requires the same support. There might well be
a section of the American Bar Association on legal aid or, better still, on the equal-

ization of the administration of justice, so that all the remedial agencies making for that end might be included. Were legal aid given the dignity and support which would attach from such consideration, their work would receive an enormous impetus. Aided by such prestige, they could more successfully consider with the local associations how the bonds between the two could be strengthened and the work of bringing justice to the poor be advanced.

The legal aid organizations need the best leadership which can be obtained. For the greater part of this guidance they rightly and necessarily turn to the bar. If their undertaking were a thing apart, they might be left to work out their own salvation or fail, as the case might be, but it is not. They are dealing with one of the most vexing problems in the law, and one which is immediately related to the entire administration of justice. The other reforms which are receiving the bar's attention aim to better our justice; this is concerned with bringing about justice where there has been none. If the legal aid organizations are to grow and develop along sound lines, if they are to attain their end completely and expeditiously, they require the highest wisdom in their supervision and control. As most of the issues which arise are legal in nature, they need for leaders men of legal training, with a thorough knowledge of existing defects in the administration of justice and of large vision as to how those difficulties may best be overcome. The actual case work can be left to the staffs of attorneys, but the matters of policy involved call for riper experience and more mature judgment.

Legal aid work in its present state of development gives rise to a host of questions, some of which have been answered wrongly, many of which are still disputed and unsolved. What is the line of legal aid jurisdiction, so that it may perform the service for which it exists and yet refrain from competition with the bar? Should divorce, criminal, bankruptcy, or personal injury cases be refused? Should fees be charged and, if so, to what extent and under what method? How far should the societies themselves pay court costs where clients are destitute and their cases pressing? What legislation should be advocated? Should the societies advertise in order that the thousands who may need their assistance may know of their existence? Are they warranted in exerting their influence in the election or appointment of officials to positions which are of great importance in their work, such as marshals, members of industrial accident commissions, and judges of the lower courts?

In the future development of the work more intricate questions, involving relationships with other bodies and fundamental matters of policy, are bound to arise. They are now on the horizon, if indeed they are not already here. Should the societies ally themselves with the law schools to establish the legal clinic and how may that be done? Ought they to try to incorporate within themselves the existing public defender offices and to establish criminal departments where no one is doing that work? How far should the organizations urge conciliation and arbitration as methods of settling disputes superior to those now employed? Is it desirable that they follow the ideas presented by the Labor Secretariat and the Ford Legal Aid Bureau, and undertake to do certain types of legal work for labor unions and employers? To what extent must the local societies surrender their control and become merged in one federal or central organization? How far is the small claims court a better method of securing justice in thousands of the cases which the legal aid organizations now care for themselves, and may they not best promote their own interests by urging the creation of such courts? Perhaps the supreme question of all is, Should the societies plan ultimately to become governmental agencies, as state controlled bureaus or as a department of the administration of justice?

It requires no intimate knowledge of legal aid work to appreciate that the wise settlement of such issues can be had only if the best intelligence is directed to them. Increasingly the bar must supply some of its best members for the positions of leadership or the whole movement will fail of its high purpose and possibilities. Only by steady, persistent, and intelligent guidance of the highest order will the work be reduced to a science, its proper place in our legal institutions be secured, and its development into a comprehensive national agency for the equalization of the administration of justice be obtained. If the bar is unable or unwilling to grant this leadership, the legal aid movement will retrogress, decay, and fall into disrepute. What is to-day our fairest hope as the solution for the existing denial of justice will be lost.

There are ample indications that lack or laxity of proper control by the bar will bring on these results. In Bridgeport inattention and indifference permitted an attorney to take over the legal aid work, to use it as a means of self-advertisement, and so to conduct its affairs that he was later questioned about the expenditure of trust funds and left the city. Shortly thereafter Bridgeport became a centre of munitions manufacturing and grew into a vast industrial city. It needs legal aid work badly and it has none. The task of establishing it is now rendered doubly difficult, and it will be obliged to encounter an atmosphere of distrust not only from lawyers but from those whom it will seek to help. The Newark organization, though to-day doing a fine work, has labored under a heavy handicap owing to a prejudice against it resulting from a course of conduct by an earlier attorney which would have been impossible under decent supervision. For a number of years before the present Society was established in San Francisco, the local bar permitted an attorney to hold himself out as a legal aid society for purposes of private gain. In New Orleans, and even more strikingly in Detroit, as we have already seen, bar associations have paid so little attention to the work that it has been unable to advance and remains wholly inadequate to cope with the need of the poor for legal assistance in those cities.

About a third of the societies have boards of directors, consisting mainly of lawyers, who have rendered admirable and faithful service. These are the organizations which have gone steadily ahead, which have been brought up to a high state of efficiency, and which lead in the development of legal aid work throughout the country. Satisfactory as this present leadership is, there is no guarantee of its continuance. When these men die or resign there is no reasonable certainty that worthy successors can be found. Collectively the bar is perpetual, and in its associations it has continued an uninterrupted existence. Were the bar associations to have active supervisory committees on legal aid work, an element of permanence could be secured.[1] It would be a task of such a committee to instill into the minds of all lawyers a more lively interest in the work, and it could be called upon to find in the profession and to draft for positions of leadership as the need arose the best qualified men in its membership. Such a supervision was contemplated by the resolution of the Conference of the Delegates of State and Local Bar Associations. In all probability it will first be acted upon in New York, where the Legal Aid Society has requested and the Association of the Bar of the City of New York has appointed a special committtee to enquire into the needs of legal aid work.

§ 4

The legal aid organizations should find their chief financial resource in the membership of the bar.[2] They ought not to be compelled to solicit contributions from the general public until they can truthfully state to that public that the bar *Financial* has done its appropriate share. It is common knowledge that the bar as *Support* a profession is not considered charitable. The contrast with the med- *by the Bar* ical profession is frequently drawn. It is asserted with much truth that the great surgeon, giving a part of every day to visitations in the hospitals, and performing the most serious operations for the poor without charge, has no counterpart among lawyers. Until the legal aid society became established there was an unfairness in the criticism because there was no way in which the average lawyer could render this public service. The poor clients never came to his office and there was no place where he could find them. As law is practised, it would be well-nigh impossible for a lawyer to set aside an hour or two a day for charity cases. Even if he could, its desirability would be doubtful, for it involves an unnecessary loss of time and waste of efficiency. The bar can most effectively render its charitable service in coöperation with the legal aid societies by enabling them to become powerful, well-equipped, and well-manned organizations.

The appeal of the legal aid societies to the bar rests not only on this charity basis, but may also properly be put on a basis of services rendered. It is the fact that the organizations are performing for the bar its duty to the poor. To do this they are spending money, and by their work they are leaving the lawyers free to devote themselves to the cases of paying clients. If the members of the bar are to have the legal aid organizations perform a duty which by law and ethics is primarily their own obligation, then they may fairly be called upon to meet the expenses necessarily incurred by the societies in doing that work.

[1] Cf. Holls: *The Legal Aid Society*, 8 Charities Rev. (1898) 15, 21.   [2] 11 N. Y. Legal Aid Rev. No. 3, p. 2.

Such financial support the bar has not given. The growth of legal aid work has been made possible by laymen and not lawyers. That the societies have found it less difficult to interest and to get subscriptions from the public than from the bar indicates a condition which is not healthy, and which is discreditable to lawyers in general. Precisely what the bar has done may be seen by examining the income figures of some of the larger legal aid societies for the year 1916. In the following table the subscribers and subscriptions are divided as between laymen and lawyers, and it appears that six societies in the largest cities of the country, with an aggregate income of sixty thousand dollars, received only twenty thousand dollars from lawyers.

City	Total Subscriptions		From Laymen		From Lawyers	
	No.	Amount	No.	Amount	No.	Amount
Boston	249	$5,789.00	122	$2,434.00	127	$3,355.00
Buffalo	157	1,524.00	106	974.00	51	550.00
Chicago	520·	14,870.25	446	10,683.25	74	4,187.00
Newark	167	1,513.00	86	1,133.50	81	379.50
New York	913	32,803.05	489	21,537.05	424	11,266.00
Philadelphia	432	3,156.00	387	2,835.00	45	321.00

The proportionate part of the expense borne by the bar appears from the following table, which gives the percentage of the society's total membership who are lawyers, and the percentage of the total income given by lawyers.

City	Percentage Borne by Lawyers	
	in Number	in Amount
Boston	51.0%	58.0%
Buffalo	32.4	36.0
Chicago	14.2	28.1
Newark	48.0	25.0
New York	46.4	34.3
Philadelphia	10.4	10.1

These figures show what a limited number of attorneys have done. What the bar as a whole has not done is disclosed by an examination of what proportion of the bar in these respective cities gives anything at all to the legal aid work. The following table states the total membership of the bar in these six cities according to the 1910 Census and the number which support legal aid work.

City	Number of Lawyers	Number of Lawyers Supporting Legal Aid	Per cent of Bar Supporting Legal Aid
Boston	1,360	127	9.3%
Buffalo	714	51	7.1
Chicago	3,896	74	1.9
Newark	390	81	23.0
New York	10,661	424	3.9
Philadelphia	1,843	45	2.4

These figures, which will probably come as a shock to the public-spirited portion of the bar, are not altered or bettered by any donations from the bar in its collective capacity. An examination of all financial reports for 1916 shows only two such instances of support—one in Detroit, where the entire budget of the Society consists of a five hundred dollar appropriation from the Bar Association, and one in Richmond, where after a sharp debate and with much opposition, the Bar Association voted two hundred dollars for the society just starting in that city. In 1917 the Rochester Bar Association gave one hundred dollars to the local Legal Aid Bureau.[1] It is fair to add that the new organizations in Jersey City and San Francisco have had the greater part of their expenses, which are still small, defrayed by individual lawyers.

When these facts were shown to the Conference of Bar Association delegates, and after a pointed statement by Moorfield Storey, the Conference voted to add to its original resolution on legal aid work a clause "that attorneys generally be urged to give such societies their moral and financial support."[2]

What the bar could do by its concerted action may be suggested by a simple computation. We have earlier estimated that if the legal aid organizations in the cities where they now exist are to meet completely the need for legal assistance, they must extend their work three and a half times. This would mean an annual expense of not more than $584,500. We know that organizations should be established in thirty-seven additional cities. These are nearly all places with populations of between one hundred thousand and two hundred thousand persons, and in a city of this size an adequate legal aid organization can be maintained for $2000. For extension into new cities, therefore, we should add $74,000. This would amount to a total annual national legal aid budget of $658,500. This income could be raised if every member of the bar in the United States would give, either directly or through his bar association, to legal aid work in satisfaction of his obligation to the poor about five dollars. There is nothing unreasonable in such a proposition. Even assuming that about half of the bar cannot afford that amount or never can be made to feel their responsibility, the annual expense to each lawyer in the remaining half would be only about ten dollars.

In other words, the American bar has it easily within its power to permit legal aid work to develop to its natural completion, to perform the full measure of the responsibility which rests on it as a profession, and thereby to put to an end the existing denial of justice to the poor in the United States.

On whether in the years to come, now that the Conference of Delegates of State and Local Bar Associations has given clear expression to the bar's duty, the legal aid societies receive the unstinted support of the whole bar will depend in large measure—on this more than on anything else—the future of legal aid work.

[1] Rochester L. A. R. for 1917, page 15.   [2] 3 Am. Bar Ass'n Journal, 597.

CHAPTER XXV

A MORE EQUAL ADMINISTRATION OF JUSTICE

> Equal and exact justice has been the passionate demand of the human soul since man has wronged his fellow man; it has been the dream of the philosopher, the aim of the lawgiver, the endeavor of the judge, the ultimate test of every government and every civilization. CHIEF JUSTICE WINSLOW *of the Supreme Court of Wisconsin.*[1]

§ 1

WE can end the existing denial of justice to the poor if we can secure an administration of justice which shall be accessible to every person no matter how humble, and which shall be adjusted so carefully to the needs of the present day world that it cannot be dislocated, or the evenness of its operation be disturbed, by the fact of poverty.

Immediate Constructive Action

The constructive methods which will enable our judicial institutions to realize their ideal are clear, first, because we know the precise difficulties to be remedied, and second, because there are already in existence many agencies definitely designed to obviate or overcome these difficulties and which, with proper development and expansion, can be made wholly successful. Of these the greatest is the already formidable group of legal aid organizations. They are, indeed, the key to the solution of the whole problem, for if we can speedily give them the resources which they need and deserve, they will move forward and become the instrument through which we can attain the desired end. Properly equipped, they will provide the necessary stimulus, they will furnish the requisite leadership, and they will devise the concrete detailed working plans and carry them through to completion.

In the existing machinery of justice there are three defects, which in their practical results destroy the impartiality of the administration of justice and thereby make impossible that absolute equality before the law which the ideal of democracy demands, which our form of government was designed to secure, and which it is trying to guarantee through a fair and sound substantive law. The first difficulty is that the machinery often moves so slowly, or can be made to move so slowly, that wholly unwarranted delays occur to rob the protection and redress vouchsafed by law of much of its efficacy and value. The second difficulty is that the wheels of justice cannot be set in motion simply by a complaint based on the commission of a wrong, but require, in addition, a certain amount of financial lubrication in the form of payments to the courts for costs and fees. If persons, because they are poor, are unable to satisfy this requirement, they are debarred from seeking redress, the whole law is powerless to afford its intended protection, and this is so even where poverty is the result of the very wrong which renders necessary the appeal to the processes of the law.

---

[1] From an *Address* delivered April 25, 1912, before the Northwestern University Law School; quoted in 4 Journal of Criminal Law and Criminology (1914), 650.

Though delays and costs have caused, and until eliminated will continue to cause, much injustice to the poor, they are only superficial defects in the technical structure of our legal institutions. Where intelligent rearrangements, suiting the administration of justice to the conditions of life which it is intended to control, have been made, as in the small claims courts, both difficulties have been successfully overcome. Complete solutions of general application are contained in the definite plans, now making headway, for the reorganization of courts and the simplification of procedure. By allying themselves with these great movements, the legal aid organizations can most speedily and effectively make justice prompt in all matters, summary in certain types of cases where quick relief is the only relief, inexpensive, and free in those instances where equality of justice can be had only by freedom of justice. Organized legal aid, in the capacity of a coördinated national undertaking, should work in close coöperation with such national agencies as the American Judicature Society and the American Bar Association Special Committee to Suggest Remedies and Formulate Laws to Prevent Delay and Unnecessary Cost in Litigation; and the local societies should join with the proper committees of local bar associations in all their activities along these lines. In this way they can best present the particular difficulties which they know, and can see to it that in the general plans for the betterment of the administration of justice ample provision is made to secure a form of structure and type of machinery which will be able to guarantee equality before the law to the poor.

The third difficulty results from the trilemma that the machinery of justice can be operated only through attorneys, that attorneys must be paid for their services, and that the poor are unable to pay for such services. This is the great, the inherent and fundamental difficulty — inherent because our legal institutions were framed with the intention that trained advocates should be employed, and fundamental in the sense that no amount of reorganization or simplification, short of a complete overturn of the whole structure, can entirely remove the necessity for the attorney. This is a difficulty rather than a defect, for in the main it is as undesirable as it is impossible that the proper functions of the lawyer in the administration of justice should be altogether eliminated. This problem differs radically from that relating to delays or costs, and calls for an entirely different solution. It is not well recognized or generally appreciated, and there are no definite movements or organizations which offer opportunities for alliances.

The task of the legal aid organizations is to present with all possible clearness this difficulty in its full force, to draw to themselves the interest and coöperation of judges, bar associations, and others concerned with the perfecting of justice, and to devote themselves patiently and unremittingly to a study of those agencies and methods which may be made to serve toward this end. There are now in existence three great agencies, operating in as many fields of law, illustrating two distinct plans for overcoming this obstacle, which have passed through the experimental stage so that immediate reliance may be placed on them. These are the small claims courts, the domestic relations courts, and the industrial accident commissions, which are so constituted and so operate that in the average small claim, the average complaint for non-support, and the average case of an employee injured at work the employment of counsel is unnecessary.

This is accomplished in the small claims court by the segregation of simple cases involving small amounts in one court, where the proceedings are without technicalities or formal rules so that there is no need for the performance of the attorney's function. These courts by virtue of their greater powers can deal with most small matters sounding in debt or contract far more effectively than can the legal aid societies. Organized legal aid, therefore, should everywhere advocate the establishment of courts of this type. If it can secure small claims branches of the municipal courts in all large cities, it will automatically obviate the difficulty of attorneys' fees, and incidentally the defects of delays and costs, and gain for the poor an entirely equal administration of a branch of the law which controls a very great number of the controversies to which they are party. The legal aid organizations are the natural bodies to undertake the development of the small claims court because they are in a position to understand its efficiency; to appreciate why it needs as complementary functions power to order instalment payments of judgments, control ejectment proceedings, act as trustee for debtors, and employ conciliation; and also to detect the point at which the method becomes unworkable and where the attorney again becomes necessary.

The domestic relations courts, as to most of the cases of desertion and non-support of wives and children which are now within their jurisdiction, have successfully met the difficulty of the expense of counsel by limiting the need for his services through standardization of forms and simplification of procedure, and by maintaining an administrative department of probation officers who perform the remaining necessary parts of the attorney's function. Such courts exist in the largest cities and in most of the large cities. They are unquestionably empowered and equipped to secure better redress than are the legal aid societies. The question for organized legal aid is how far they should attempt to have included within the jurisdiction of the domestic relations courts the kindred matters of divorce, separation, illegitimacy, guardianship, and adoption. This is debatable ground; it may well prove that in libels for divorce attorneys are indispensable. The experiment of this widened jurisdiction, in which the criminal processes and conciliation will be at the court's disposal, ought to be made. On the inside the judges can watch its operation; on the outside there is no organization better situated to detect any breakdown, or to ascertain the desirable limits of any such jurisdiction, than the legal aid society. These courts are as successful in domestic disputes as the small claims courts are in their field. In so far as the legal aid societies can secure their wise extension, to that extent will another great category of the cases of the poor be placed under an administration of justice which will be accessible and able to operate impartially in fact because free of the difficulties which have hitherto destroyed equality.

The industrial accident commissions, aided by a simplification of the substantive law on points of liability and damages, have erected an administrative machinery which accurately and quickly adjusts and disposes of the larger proportion of the cases of injured workmen which come within their jurisdiction. Such commissions now exist in nearly all states. The question for the legal aid organizations in this connection is not one of territorial expansion, but one of how far this new administrative method of securing justice can be extended into other departments of law. The automatic settlement of disputes by supervised agreements instead of through the traditional channels of judicial litigation unquestionably achieves an entire freedom and equality of justice. The method is easily capable of application to cases of interstate employees, seamen, and with some modifications to passengers on railroads and street railways. There are great difficulties in the way of its extension to cases where there is no contractual or other preëxisting legal relationship between the parties, as to the pedestrian run over by an automobile, or to the driver of a team who has a collision with a street car. But to the extent that it can be carried, it will serve to eliminate the inequalities of the traditional system, and its proper extension is therefore a matter of immediate concern to legal aid organizations.

At the same time the legal aid societies must bear in mind that there is a fixed point at which this administrative method breaks down. As to the cases which give rise to bona fide contests on law or facts, the administrative method, though it has developed some points of superiority, differs only in a superficial way from the traditional methods of litigation in the courts and is subject to the same limitations. There is the same need for the attorney and the same difficulty presented by the inability of the poor to pay for attorney's services. In all appeals this difficulty is accentuated. Here organized legal aid should play its part by supplying attorneys to all injured persons who are not able to retain their own attorneys. The ability of applicants to engage their own counsel should be determined in these as in any other cases, — by the fact of poverty and not by the speculative value of the claim. If the societies can thus supplement the administrative machinery, they will protect the community, the bar, and the courts from a recurrence of the dangers and iniquities of the contingent fee system.

There are other agencies and methods which cannot be immediately relied on, but which may, under intelligent study and guidance, develop into formidable instruments for the equalizing of the administration of justice. Conciliation and arbitration as judicial functions are still new and untried. How far administrative officials, particularly those empowered to lend their assistance in litigation, can be utilized to secure equal rights for the poor is a consideration involving many elements of doubt. Of these matters conciliation probably contains the greatest possibilities, but they all warrant close and sympathetic observation and the results of their experiments should be made known to the legal world. In such work the legal aid organizations may well play an important, if not a leading part. They have a direct interest, and they are in a position to see whether these agencies and methods perform in fact the promise which in theory they contain. New suggestions and proposals will steadily arise which in their turn will require this same observation and report.

In these ways the legal aid organizations can promote the necessary reconstruction of the administration of justice and thereby scientifically eliminate so much of the denial of justice to the poor as is caused by gaps, or flaws, or outworn parts, or imperfect adjustments in the organization of our administration of justice.

They must go further. In vast tracts of the civil law and in all of the criminal law relating to the more serious crimes, equality in the administration of justice can be had only by supplying attorneys to the poor. In civil matters this has always been the function of the legal aid societies; in criminal affairs it is now the function of the public defenders. This part of their task is well known to the organizations. The work of the public defenders must be carried on in all cities, and it is preferable that it should be done in conjunction with, and as a part of, the legal aid work. The legal aid organizations must extend themselves into all of the large cities, and must triple their staffs and undertake a threefold increase of their work. If these things can be done, that part of the denial of justice which is traceable solely to the inability of the poor to employ counsel will be eliminated, and it is only in this way that the great difficulty of the expense of counsel will be completely overcome.

§ 2

At the present time the legal aid organizations in the United States are equipped to do none of these things. They will be able to continue to care for a certain number of individual cases, but that is not enough. They will either go forward or backward. Either they will become the best instrumentality for the equalization of American justice, or they will fail, and be discarded, and some other plan will be utilized. Because of the work they have accomplished, the wealth of their experience, and the excellence of their record, it is in every way desirable that it should be made possible for them to succeed.

A More Efficient Legal Aid Work

For the success of organized legal aid work there are three imperative requisites — better leadership, a sound financial foundation, and the merger of all the individual societies and bureaus and public defender offices into a definite union with centralized responsibility and authority.

Of these three cardinal needs the greatest is leadership, for it may fairly be assumed that under intelligent guidance proper financing would be secured and a central legal aid bureau would be established. To ensure the wise direction and development of organized legal aid work there are needed for the boards of directors and executive committees men of high calibre, endowed with both vision and courage, who fairly represent the various elements in the community who are concerned in this work. Such groups are the judges, the charities, the churches, the employers, the labor unions, the law schools, and above all the bar, for in this undertaking the members of the bar have the greatest·responsibility. The societies cannot be expected to evolve the necessary leaders from within themselves. It is not only natural but inevitable that they should look to the bar. It is the duty and the privilege of the bar associations, which most nearly represent the bar in its collective capacity, to provide from among their own leaders a number of properly qualified lawyers who can constitute the nucleus of legal aid leadership and add to themselves persons representing other groups in interest. This alliance between legal aid work and the bar should reach from top to bottom. As a local undertaking it should have the supervision and support of the local bar associations, and as a national movement it should have the supervision and support of the American Bar Association.

The acute financial crisis which the legal aid societies face need not always remain a stumbling-block in the path of their development. If the pressing demands of the present were squarely met, arrangements could unquestionably be made which would care for the future. Legal aid work is not expensive, its needs are modest, but at the present time it is denied even this small support. If the organizations were given a clear track for a few years and provided with the necessary resources during this intervening period, they could rid themselves of the handicaps under which they now struggle and attain such a position of responsibility and strength that they would earn and attract their necessary income from available sources. The shoulders of the bar are broad enough to carry the whole load so easily that the individual member would scarcely feel its weight. If the work becomes, as it ought to become, a part of the bar's work, if the situation is made clear to the bar associations so that they feel their responsibility, there will be no great difficulty in securing small subscriptions from lawyers generally, made as a matter of professional duty, which in the aggregate will furnish the legal aid organizations with the greater part of the funds that they require. In addition there are many members of the community who are able and willing to give generously for this object, which they regard as a worthy charity. If the salient features of the work were presented to the public in an intelligible and sympathetic form, the number of donors could be materially increased. Once the legal aid societies obtain proper leadership and are given an opportunity for development, there is every reason to believe that finances will cease to constitute a menace always threatening their existence.

The need for some union of legal aid organizations that will nationalize the work and provide a central responsibility and authority is obvious. In their National Alliance the societies have erected a shell without substance. For the future, the work is too great to be conducted in a slipshod way, and its extension into new fields is too important to be left to a hit-or-miss policy. The combined experience of the societies must be assembled and a technique for the conduct of the work developed. A standard system of records and accounts must be devised and then installed. Matters of policy should become uniform as rapidly as possible. A clearing house, with power of supervision, is necessary for a free transference of cases throughout the country. Some initiative must be manifested in establishing societies where they are needed. There must be some central body authorized to represent and speak for the organized legal aid movement in the councils of the bar, at the meetings of the charities, and at the law school conferences, and to coöperate with such undertakings as the American Judicature Society. If there is to be any intelligent development in coöperation with the other remedial agencies, there must be a central bureau to disseminate information to all the legal aid organizations as to how such agencies operate, what their advantages are, and wherein they are limited. The present state of affairs, in which no society except the local society understands how small claims are cared for in Cleveland or wages collected in Massachusetts, cannot be allowed to continue. The administration of justice is a serious business, and its reconstruction requires infinite pains, well-considered suggestions, and judgment of the highest order. Because they have undertaken the responsibility of championing the cause of the poor, the legal aid organizations are vitally concerned in any reorganization, and they can, if they will, make contributions of information that are invaluable because they are not obtainable from any other source. If their voice is to be heard, as it has not been heard in the past, and if their opinions are to carry weight, they must present a united front, having clearly formulated their aims, and speak with singleness of mind to a definite and agreed purpose.

§ 3

Inasmuch as the legal aid organizations are rendering an essential public service, it is likely that ultimately their work will pass under public control. This fact should never be forgotten by those who are, or may become, responsible for *Legal Aid under Judicial Control* the future of organized legal aid, and they will do well to shape their plans with this end in view. There is no need to hasten this process of transferring the responsibility to the state, the ideas which must precede it are imperceptibly but steadily taking possession of men's minds, and the change will come about in its own good time. It is always difficult, particularly for those in the midst of a movement, to gauge progress by present indications, but a glance backward over the road traveled gives a clue as to what is taking place. When the attorney for the first public legal aid bureau, in 1911, predicted that in ten years there would be a dozen public organizations,[1] his hearers, who were the best informed persons in the United States on legal aid work, were unable to give full credence to the statement. Yet within five years eight such bureaus were established.

[1] *Report of Proceedings of the First Conference of Legal Aid Societies,* page 41.

What will be the situation at the end of another ten years no one can foretell, but the tendency is none the less perfectly clear.

The task of the private organizations will be to bring legal aid work up to the highest possible point of efficiency, so that when the time comes they may surrender into public hands a definite undertaking which has passed beyond the experimental stage, with its guiding principles well established, and with a well-developed technique for the conduct of its work. They must also bring their experience to bear in order that this tendency toward public control may not go forward blindly, but may be given intelligent direction.

Their experience makes it perfectly clear that legal aid work is of a piece with the administration of justice, and that it has no logical connection with municipal government. Primarily for this reason, and also because they know that there is danger in entrusting this service to city officials, the legal aid societies will do well to consider if their work may not most properly, and most safely, be placed under judicial control. It is entirely possible that into the comprehensive plans for the reshaping of our judicial organization, which are now going forward, there might be incorporated a definite scheme for judicial control of legal aid work.[1] The accepted principle underlying the present proposals for reorganization of courts and simplification of procedure is that the judges must be our experts in justice; they must be charged with the responsibility and given the power to make the machinery of justice operate smoothly, and efficiently, and economically. It is just as important that they be made responsible and entrusted with power so that they may see to it that the administration of justice is accessible to all and operates equally. It involves nothing more than an extension of the work done by clerks of small claims courts under judicial direction, or by probation officers who are amenable to judicial control, or by the administrative departments of the industrial accident commissions. The author of the Chicago Municipal Court Act, which was the first law to put the theory of judicial responsibility for the administration of justice into practice, contemplated a "Bureau of Justice," under judicial control, which should give to poor persons the services of attorneys in both civil and criminal cases.[2] This is precisely what has been effected in England by the Supreme Court rules of 1913. It is akin to the method by which legal aid work has for years been carried on in France, Scotland, and Belgium.

The rules in France, which regulate "L'Assistance Judiciare Gratuite," prescribe

---

[1] Cf. Resolution introduced in 1917 before the Massachusetts Constitutional Convention (Convention, No. 8), which read:

"To the end that Article XI of Part I of the constitution may be given full force and effect throughout the commonwealth, the justices of the supreme judicial court may, in their discretion, make rules of court or take any other action designed to guarantee that no subject of the commonwealth shall, because of poverty, be denied certain access to the courts, or proper representation therein, in any proceeding, whether civil or criminal.

"It is hereby expressly declared that the above conferred power extends to provisions concerning the payment of court costs, the assignment of counsel, the creation, control and supervision of organizations or bureaus to render legal aid and assistance to poor persons, and to the expenditure of such sums of money as may be appropriated by the legislature for these purposes.

"The authority hereby entrusted to the justices of the supreme judicial court may, by them, be delegated in whole or part to the justices of any other court."

[2] Hiram T. Gilbert: *Practice in the Municipal Court of Chicago* (1906), pages 546 *et seq.*

that there be attached to each court of justice a quasi-tribunal of representatives of the legal corporations who pass on the poverty of all applicants for free judicial legal aid and also on the merits of the cases which they present. If the applicant is found to be a poor person with a meritorious claim, he is thereupon entitled to free legal assistance. The law corporations designate from among their membership lawyers who are to be called upon by the court for this purpose. Students share in the work, and it is a condition of their admission to the bar that during the last period of their training they shall have served in connection with the Bureau that regulates this judicial assistance. Expenses of litigation, such as witness fees and cost of printing, are borne by the public treasury. The system in Belgium and other continental countries is analogous, and by a Convention on Civil Procedure concluded at The Hague it was provided that the citizens of each country should be entitled to receive in each other country the benefits of this judicial legal assistance.[1]

The Scottish system, which traces its history back to an Act of 1424,[2] operates as follows: A number of solicitors are each year selected by their associations to act as agents for the poor. An applicant for legal assistance presents to such an agent certificates from his parish as to the fact of his poverty. The agent draws and presents a petition for leave to sue in forma pauperis to a tribunal of four attorneys, who pass upon the applicant's right to sue in that manner. If admitted to the Poor Rolls and given permission to sue without payment of costs, the person's case is entered, and the judge assigns as his representative a counsel from the list appointed by the Faculty of Advocates.[3]

The method which now obtains in England is an adaptation of these French and Scottish systems, which have much in common, worked out by judges of the Supreme Court after conferences with the bar, and promulgated by rules dated April 28, 1913, which took effect June 9, 1914.[4] Persons apply or write to the prescribed officers who are attached to each division of the High Court and receive the proper form of application. Before permission to sue without payment of costs or attorney's fees is granted, the court must be satisfied that the applicant has a reasonable cause of action or defence, and that his means, exclusive of wearing apparel, household goods, tools of trade, and the subject-matter of the action,[5] do not exceed the sum of £50, or in special circumstances £100. To ascertain these facts, the case is sent to a solicitor for his examination and report. Lists of solicitors who have volunteered to accept assignments are kept, and in addition the court may assign any solicitor it

---

[1] Norman Bentwick: *Legal Aid for the Poor*, 105 Contemporary Review (1914), 559, 562; Théry: *French Legal Assistance for the Poor*, 1 International Law Notes (1916), No. 1, p. 12.

[2] 135 Law Times (1913), 247.

[3] An excellent description of this system in Scotland is contained in 47 Law Journal, 49.

[4] All rules, together with forms, which set out this system in full are contained in the 1914 *Rule Book*, and are listed as Order 16, IV, §§ 22–31d. The best account of what has been done under these rules is to be found in the statement by W. F. A. Archibald, Chairman of the London Prescribed Officers, published in full in the *Law Times* for March 18, 1916, and in part in 1 International Law Notes, No. 4 (1916), p. 56.

[5] It is to be noted that no person is denied relief by the court, as the legal aid societies in the United States have denied their assistance, on any theory that the person can secure his own attorney by arranging for a contingent fee.

may wish. If the report is favorable, the judge then assigns a solicitor and barrister to prepare and present the case before the court for trial. There are lists of counsel who have volunteered their services, but the court is free to assign the case to any member of the bar. Persons admitted to sue or defend under these rules are not required to pay court costs and are not liable for the fees of the opposing party. They are prohibited from paying fees to solicitors and counsel for their services, and if members of the bar seek to obtain remuneration from such clients, they are punishable for contempt of court. Poor persons, if successful, may be awarded costs, and the court may fix an attorney's fee out of such costs, or out of the recovery if it is substantial. The rules contemplated a Treasury grant to defray the incidental expenses of such litigation, but the grant was not made owing to the immediate advent of war.

None of these systems is complete. Legal aid work, as it is organized in America, possesses many points of superiority. These other systems do, however, serve as excellent precedents, and they add to the fund of information from which sound plans may be formulated for placing legal aid work under judicial control and thereby making it an integral part of the administration of justice.

§ 4

These suggested future developments are all practical and capable of achievement. Once these matters are given proper presentation, the loyal support of the bar, the assistance of the courts, and the sustaining interest of the public may be *Conclusion* confidently expected. The ends which they seek to attain are of direct concern not only to the fair administration of justice, but to the well-being of the nation. It is of high importance that such developments be encouraged and supported, not for the sake of the legal aid organizations themselves, — they of themselves are nothing, — but because in them, with all their faults and weaknesses, is contained our best immediate hope for a realization of our ideal of such an equal administration of the laws that denial of justice on account of poverty shall forever be made impossible in America.

APPENDIX

NOTE TO STATISTICAL TABLES

IN the following three tables are contained the basic statistical records of legal aid work—the number of cases received by each organization, the sums of money collected for their clients by each organization, and the amounts expended by each organization in the conduct of its work. No table showing the income of the organizations is necessary for, as legal aid work is now financed, the organizations each year spend all that they receive, so that the income and expense figures are practically identical.

Not all of the desired information is available. In order to show to what extent the tables are incomplete, there are placed at the right hand side of each table two columns in which are noted the total number of organizations in existence each year and the number of organizations whose records are known and are contained within the table for that year. As the figures which are unavailable are those of the smaller societies, they would, if they were known and included, serve to increase the totals presented in the tables only in a slight degree.

These figures may be regarded as minimum figures. All "estimates," so far as they could be detected, have been excluded. The tables substantially underestimate the work in two particulars. The collection figures represent little more than cash sums secured and paid over to clients. There are many cases in which the debtor, after being called to account or sued by the legal aid society, pays the client directly. In most instances these recoveries, although properly to be credited to the society as the result of its work, cannot be known. Further, many cases result not in a cash payment, but in an order for weekly payments, as in husband and wife, support of children, illegitimacy, and workmen's compensation cases. The exact amounts paid under such orders, which have been secured by the efforts of the society, are not known and so do not appear in statements of sums collected for clients. The case figures represent only cases undertaken for poor persons. They do not include the advice and other work done for lawyers or social workers. Further, a few organizations list as cases only matters in which some action is taken, so that these figures do not include cases of poor persons where advice only was given.

The tables are arranged in cross columns, so that in each instance they show:

1. The work of each organization in each year.
2. The work of all organizations in each year.
3. The total work of each organization.
4. The grand total of all organizations from 1876 to 1916 inclusive.

The fiscal year of a number of the organizations does not conform to the calendar year. In such instances the work has been listed as of the year which included the greater number of months of the particular fiscal year. Thus the work done during a fiscal year running from November 1, 1915, to October 31, 1916, has been placed in the column of the year 1916. Although this is arbitrary in a way, such an arrangement was necessary to make possible any orderly and definite presentation.

TABLE I :

(a) ANNUAL NUMBER OF CASES OF EACH LEGAL AID ORGANIZA
(b) ANNUAL TOTAL CASES OF ALL ORGANIZATIONS.

Year	Akron	Baltimore	Boston	Buffalo	Cambridge	Chicago Legal Aid Bureau of Justice	Chicago Legal Aid Protective Agency	Chicago Bureau of Personal Service	Cincinnati	Cleveland	Columbus	Dallas	Dayton	Detroit	Duluth	Hartford	Jersey City	Kansas City	Los Angeles	Louisville	Milwaukee	Minneapolis
1876																						
1877																						
1878																						
1879																						
1880																						
1881																						
1882																						
1883																						
1884																						
1885																						
1886							156															
1887							385															
1888						1,164	1,145															
1889						2,497	1,614															
1890						3,783	1,455															
1891						3,523	1,347															
1892						4,020	1,095															
1893						4,881	—															
1894						5,096	2,496															
1895						5,217	3,284															
1896						4,564	2,980															
1897						4,087	2,678															
1898						4,507	2,290															
1899						4,618	2,135															
1900						3,755	2,776															
1901			198			3,760	3,085															
1902			305			3,421	2,861	294														
1903			334			3,625	3,269	508														
1904			568			4,158	4,290	669														
1905			664				2,929	823														
1906			707				4,955	811		456												
1907			1,085				4,990	1,358		606												
1908			996				6,169	1,478		908												
1909			1,107				5,102	1,666		1,208												
1910			1,175				6,282	2,888		1,158				73				2,313				
1911			1,114				8,442	3,124		1,382				70				5,406				
1912	11	287	1,041	630	83		13,904	3,515	885	1,533				117				5,354				
1913	22	499	1,154	966	191		15,409	4,167	1,179	2,435				148	607			6,573	3,199			1,039
1914	17	687	1,352	1,384	153		16,121	4,747	1,509	3,925			727	206	2,294	78		6,262	10,391			1,905
1915	14	504	2,229	1,257	147		10,674	2,537	1,688	5,805		914	768	292	4,564	86	149	6,202	10,277	113		1,965
1916	20	376	2,608	1,516	104		10,697	4,685	1,698	4,946	300	1,480	922	410	5,629	134	447	5,270	8,848	78	1,174	3,029
TOTAL	84	2,355	16,637	5,753	678		211,691	33,270	6,959	24,362	300	2,394	2,417	1,316	13,094	298	596	37,380	32,715	191	1,174	7,938

TION.　(c) Total Cases of Each Organization.

(d) Total Cases of All Organizations for 41 Years.

Nashville	Newark	New Haven	New Orleans	New York			Omaha	Philadelphia	Pittsburgh	Plainfield	Portland	Richmond	Rochester	St. Louis	St. Paul	San Diego	San Francisco	Washington	Total by Years	Year	Total Number of Organizations	No. Organizations Statistics Known
				Legal Aid Society	Educational Alliance	National Desertion Bureau																
				212															212	1876	1	1
				750															750	1877	1	1
				856															856	1878	1	1
				1,903															1,903	1879	1	1
				2,122															2,122	1880	1	1
				2,832															2,832	1881	1	1
				3,413															3,413	1882	1	1
				3,400															3,400	1883	1	1
				3,640															3,640	1884	1	1
				3,802															3,802	1885	1	1
				3,306															3,462	1886	2	2
				3,485															3,870	1887	2	2
				3,313															5,624	1888	3	3
				3,500															7,611	1889	3	3
				4,078															9,316	1890	3	3
				5,412															10,282	1891	3	3
				5,541															10,656	1892	3	3
				6,285															11,166	1893	3	2
				7,835															15,427	1894	4	3
				7,627															16,128	1895	4	3
				7,473															15,017	1896	4	3
				5,350															12,115	1897	4	3
				5,602															12,399	1898	4	3
				9,436															16,189	1899	4	3
				14,365															20,896	1900	5	3
	443			15,880															23,366	1901	6	5
				15,257	1,406														23,544	1902	10	6
				18,469	1,980			173											28,358	1903	10	7
				20,277	3,801			393											34,156	1904	13	7
	492			21,372	6,371			701											33,352	1905	12	7
	790			23,175	5,431			1,278											37,603	1906	12	8
				26,399	6,993			1,165											42,596	1907	13	7
	1,001			31,036	7,737			1,422	197										50,944	1908	13	9
				30,105	7,445			1,333	246										48,212	1909	14	8
				32,449	4,324			1,477	348				157						52,644	1910	15	11
				33,809	4,402	852		1,816	375				158						60,950	1911	16	12
				37,796	7,687	1,091		2,514	378				229	723					77,778	1912	21	18
				39,189	2,584	1,097		3,476	506		130		250	2,057	264				87,141	1913	28	23
			50	40,430	7,997	1,098		3,874	649				320	1,859	930			83	109,048	1914	32	26
260	2,140		150	42,000	6,715	1,101		4,290	771	173	1,998		353	1,905	1,551	30		97	113,719	1915	38	34
—	2,155	18	74	41,646	5,788	957	1,318	4,845	684	150	1,363	121	382	1,235	1,749	28	242	75	117,201	1916	41	39
260	7,021	18	274	584,827	80,661	6,196	1,318	28,757	4,154	323	3,491	121	1,849	7,779	4,494	58	242	255	1,133,700	Total All Organizations 41 Years		

TABLE II :

(a) ANNUAL AMOUNT COLLECTED FOR CLIENTS BY EACH LEGAL AID ORGANIZATION IN EVEN DOLLARS.
(b) ANNUAL TOTAL COLLECTIONS BY ALL ORGANIZATIONS IN EVEN DOLLARS.

YEAR	Boston	Buffalo	Cambridge	Chicago Bureau of Justice / Legal Aid	Chicago Protective Agency	Chicago Bureau of Personal Service	Cincinnati	Dallas	Dayton	Detroit	Duluth	Hartford	Kansas City	Los Angeles	Louisville	Milwaukee	Minneapolis	Nashville
1876																		
1877																		
1878																		
1879																		
1880																		
1881																		
1882																		
1883																		
1884																		
1885																		
1886					$277													
1887					885													
1888				$2,475	3,753													
1889				9,065	3,599													
1890				10,658	1,923													
1891				9,877	864													
1892				9,983	1,991													
1893				6,648	—													
1894				2,969	3,079													
1895				4,271	1,785													
1896				3,639	1,799													
1897				4,000	1,601													
1898				2,762	2,287													
1899				4,325	1,454													
1900				2,704	2,562													
1901	$585			2,715	2,266													
1902	1,231			4,338	2,313													
1903	2,000			3,890	2,885													
1904	4,600			2,741	3,515													
1905	5,917			3,857			$6,548											
1906	8,100			7,206			9,794											
1907	8,888			7,009			19,198											
1908	5,760			9,503			23,354											
1909	7,748			5,954			21,006											
1910	6,686			7,845			28,516				$610			$6,046				
1911	6,686			9,048			22,192				820			8,904				
1912	6,131			17,200			19,740				1,151			10,962				
1913	3,989			22,861			26,679	$1,175			2,751	$5,230		10,140			$3,530	
1914	4,005		$1,159	29,066			30,623	1,659		$746	1,202	8,086	$218	7,705			5,707	
1915	25,195	$948	1,647	18,528			29,269	2,036	$949	669	1,776	8,927	390	6,914	$26,273		5,450	
1916	22,808	2,881	410	21,529			32,787	2,271	3,889	1,209	2,586	10,787	323	5,143	23,183	$73	$1,892	7,401	$1,049
TOTAL	$120,329	$3,829	$3,216	$285,504			$269,706	$7,141	$4,838	$2,624	$10,896	$33,030	$931	$55,814	$49,456	$73	$1,892	$22,088	$1,049

(c) Total Collections by Each Organization in even Dollars.

(d) Total Collections by All Organizations for 41 Years in even Dollars.

Newark	New Haven	New York — Legal Aid Society	New York — Educational Alliance	New York — National Desertion Bureau	Omaha	Philadelphia	Pittsburgh	Rochester	St. Louis	St. Paul	San Diego	San Francisco	TOTAL BY YEARS	YEARS	Total Number of Organizations	No. Organizations Statistics Known
		$1,000											$1,000	1876	1	1
		5,019											5,019	1877	1	1
		8,089											8,089	1878	1	1
		7,514											7,514	1879	1	1
		8,680											8,680	1880	1	1
		9,149											9,149	1881	1	1
		12,460											12,460	1882	1	1
		17,040											17,040	1883	1	1
		19,062											19,062	1884	1	1
		17,711											17,711	1885	1	1
		19,080											19,357	1886	2	2
		16,870											17,755	1887	2	2
		14,624											20,852	1888	3	3
		20,104											32,768	1889	3	3
		34,999											47,580	1890	3	3
		55,077											65,818	1891	3	3
		74,232											86,206	1892	3	3
		30,955											37,603	1893	ʻ3	2
		62,624											68,672	1894	4	3
		60,285											66,341	1895	4	3
		71,257											76,695	1896	4	3
		72,819											78,420	1897	4	3
		67,811											72,860	1898	4	3
		66,796											72,575	1899	4	3
		96,704											101,970	1900	5	3
		78,173											83,739	1901	6	4
$15,770		54,855											78,507	1902	10	5
		59,646				$310							68,731	1903	10	5
		58,665	$1,070			414							71,005	1904	13	6
		61,140	1,649			909							80,020	1905	12	6
827		72,633				489							99,049	1906	12	6
		90,286				1,134							126,515	1907	13	5
1,908		86,063	2,000			974							129,562	1908	13	7
		100,074				1,323							136,105	1909	14	5
		101,724	13,348			2,076							166,851	1910	15	8
		122,838	10,822	$1,000		3,257							185,567	1911	16	9
		142,429	12,164	857		5,046			$1,852				217,532	1912	21	10
		138,046	7,125	6,191		3,987	$2,572		8,457	$1,429			244,162	1913	28	15
		134,895	14,413	6,330		6,676	5,648	$812	4,893	5,006			268,849	1914	32	19
3,589		139,327	14,566	10,894		7,073	4,191	900	7,390	5,781	$410		323,092	1915	38	24
6,704	$112	128,005	16,537	12,511	$5,063	11,286	6,800	689	5,109	6,477	—	$685	340,199	1916	41	29
$28,798	$112	$2,438,760	$93,694	$37,783	$5,063	$44,954	$19,211	$2,401	$27,701	$18,693	$410	$685	$3,590,681	TOTAL ALL ORGANIZATIONS 41 YEARS		

TABLE III

(a) ANNUAL EXPENSE OF EACH LEGAL AID ORGANIZATION IN EVEN DOLLARS.
(b) ANNUAL TOTAL EXPENSE OF ALL ORGANIZATIONS IN EVEN DOLLARS.

YEAR	Baltimore	Boston	Buffalo	Chicago Bureau of Justice	Chicago Protective Agency	Chicago Bureau of Personal Service	Cincinnati	Cleveland	Dallas	Dayton	Detroit	Duluth	Hartford	Jersey City	Kansas City	Los Angeles	Milwaukee
1876																	
1877																	
1878																	
1879																	
1880																	
1881																	
1882																	
1883																	
1884																	
1885																	
1886					$850												
1887					1,953												
1888				$2,966	2,783												
1889				3,771	3,382												
1890				5,371	3,086												
1891				3,958	3,651												
1892				6,598	3,634												
1893				6,124	—												
1894				5,407	3,094												
1895				5,132	2,871												
1896				3,956	2,554												
1897				3,424	3,357												
1898				3,439	2,539												
1899				3,551	2,349												
1900				3,499	2,551	$1,095											
1901		$1,263		3,886	3,873	2,883											
1902		1,648		4,187	3,194	2,750											
1903		1,438		4,710	2,988	3,000											
1904		1,400		5,460	2,749	3,450											
1905		1,500		4,224		3,900											
1906		1,788		7,457		4,600	$1,064										
1907		2,704		8,080		6,666	1,523										
1908		2,469		8,253		7,679	1,409										
1909		2,560		8,361		10,020	1,864										
1910		2,899		8,991		12,175	2,362				$500				$1,338		
1911		3,741		12,851		14,518	2,362				500				5,394		
1912	$1,107	4,567	$1,742	19,180		19,859	$492	2,298			500				5,107		
1913	809	5,030	2,015	24,826		19,075	1,220	2,603			500				5,283	$4,641	
1914	2,025	5,331	2,158	26,853		22,300	1,238	1,841		$552	500	$2,391			5,609	18,831	
1915	1,020	5,396	2,336	17,593		23,800	1,209	3,774	$2,430	1,222	500	3,032	$135	$22	5,144	21,613	
1916	1,020	6,498	2,372	18,318		25,297	1,359	3,210	2,415	1,315	500	4,280	114	364	4,226	21,199	$2,038
TOTAL	$5,981	$50,232	$10,623	$292,884		$183,067	$5,518	$24,310	$4,845	$3,089	$3,500	$9,703	$249	$386	$32,101	$66,284	$2,038

Table III

(c) TOTAL EXPENSE OF EACH ORGANIZATION IN EVEN DOLLARS.
(d) TOTAL EXPENSE OF ALL ORGANIZATIONS FOR 41 YEARS IN EVEN DOLLARS.

Minneapolis	Newark	New York Legal Aid Society	New York Educational Alliance	New York National Desertion Bureau	Omaha	Philadelphia	Pittsburgh	Richmond	Rochester	St. Louis	St. Paul	San Diego	San Francisco	TOTAL BY YEARS	YEAR	Total Number of Organizations	No. Organizations Statistics Known
		$1,060												$1,060	1876	1	1
		1,519												1,519	1877	1	1
		1,570												1,570	1878	1	1
		1,816												1,816	1879	1	1
		2,248												2,248	1880	1	1
		2,622												2,622	1881	1	1
		2,715												2,715	1882	1	1
		2,838												2,838	1883	1	1
		2,817												2,817	1884	1	1
		2,870												2,870	1885	1	1
		2,970												3,820	1886	2	2
		3,052												5,005	1887	2	2
		2,990												8,739	1888	3	3
		3,272												10,425	1889	3	3
		3,496												11,953	1890	3	3
		5,172												12,781	1891	3	3
		4,890												15,122	1892	3	3
		5,241												11,365	1893	3	2
		6,096												14,597	1894	4	3
		6,309												14,312	1895	4	3
		6,940												13,450	1896	4	3
		7,953												14,734	1897	4	3
		7,643	$33											13,654	1898	4	4
		10,130												16,030	1899	4	3
		14,524												21,669	1900	5	4
		17,980												29,885	1901	6	5
		17,307												29,086	1902	10	5
		20,808				$389								33,333	1903	10	6
		22,702				2,068								38,829	1904	13	6
		28,553	2,903			1,654								42,734	1905	12	6
		32,116	3,960			2,362								53,347	1906	12	7
		38,682	3,061			1,904								62,620	1907	13	7
		41,485	3,102			2,137								66,534	1908	13	7
		41,641	5,381			1,685	$658							72,170	1909	14	8
		39,409	6,169			1,713	1,046							76,602	1910	15	9
		43,114	6,740	$5,000		1,846	933		$251					97,250	1911	16	11
		46,194	7,053	7,516		2,295	1,176		619					119,705	1912	21	14
$1,324		45,200	3,765	8,973		2,510	1,024		833	$2,803	$1,175			133,609	1913	28	19
2,940		44,140	7,388	9,381		3,344	1,295		688		1,384			160,189	1914	32	20
2,231	$1,440	45,609	6,870	10,446		4,316	1,615		989	2,381	1,562	$16		166,701	1915	38	26
3,435	3,132	44,648	6,959	11,699	$650	4,437	1,882	$37	1,313	5,857	1,839	2	$993	181,408	1916	41	30
$9,930	$4,572	$682,341	$63,384	$53,015	$650	$32,660	$9,629	$37	$4,693	$11,041	$5,960	$18	$993	$1,573,733	TOTAL ALL ORGANIZATIONS 41 YEARS		

INDEX

INDEX

Could double work, 190.
Work limited by finances, 193.
Legislative work, 200.
Litigation avoided, 164.
Reference of cases, plan, 163.
Small loans, work in, 260.
Support from bar, 238.
CHICAGO MUNICIPAL COURT
Provision for arbitration, 71.
Small claims session of, *see* Small Claims
Courts : Chicago.
CHICAGO WOMEN'S CLUB, starts legal aid, 135.
CHILDREN, *see also* Domestic Relations.
Protective legislation secured, 201.
CHILDREN'S AID SOCIETY, THE BOSTON, coöpera-
tion with legal aid, 223.
CHOATE, JOSEPH H., quoted on contingent fees,
86.
CHURCHES, on legal aid directorate, 245.
CINCINNATI DOMESTIC RELATIONS COURT
Wide jurisdiction, 75.
Use of conciliation, 81.
CINCINNATI LEGAL AID SOCIETY, 33, 144, 168,
176, 191, 202.
Started in 1907, 144.
Extent of work, 191.
Fees charged by, 168.
Legislative work, 202.
CINCINNATI MUNICIPAL COURT, provision for ar-
bitration, 71.
CITIES
Growth of, cause of judicial breakdown,
xxxiii, xxxvii, 7.
Need for legal aid, 133.
Denial of justice in large, 187.
Extent of legal aid measured by, 187.
CITIZENSHIP, *see also* Immigrants, Americaniza-
tion.
Good, promoted by legal aid, 217.
Small claims court effect on, 53.
CLASS, no dominating, causes injustice, 15.
CLASS DISTINCTIONS
Foreign to Anglo-Saxon law, 3.
Result of, in law, 12.
Caused by court costs, 29.
Substantive law free from, 13.
Employer's liability law, 15.
CLASS LEGISLATION, public legal aid is not, 182.
CLERKS OF COURT
Assistance of, to parties, 48, 78.
Need for, 56.
CLEVELAND LEGAL AID SOCIETY, 116, 125, 129,
143, 146, 154, 159, 164, 166–168, 176, 177,
191, 201, 216.
Begun in 1904, 143.
Cases
Classified, 154.
Sources of, 159.

Defender urged by, 116.
Extent of work, 191.
Fees
Believes in, 167.
Charged, 168.
Legislative work, 201.
Litigation avoided, 164.
CLEVELAND MUNICIPAL COURT
Arbitration rule, 71.
Costs, report on, 20, 23.
Economy of, 26.
Conciliation branch, *see* Small Claims Courts :
Cleveland.
COLLECTION AGENCIES
Fraudulent in Missouri, 203.
Profit from defects in law, 42.
Small claims courts and, 54.
Watched by legal aid, 227.
COLONIES, AMERICAN
Lawyers in, 31.
Laws after Revolution, 6.
Were denied justice, 6.
COLORADO SPRINGS LEGAL AID SOCIETY, started
in 1912, 145.
COLUMBUS LEGAL AID COMMITTEE
Extent of work, 191.
Slow growth of, 174.
COLUMBUS MUNICIPAL COURT, power of, as court
trustee, 58.
COMMON LAW
Appeals by poor needed, 27.
Legal aid work and
In general, 206.
In test cases, 208.
Opportunity for, 206.
No costs in, 20.
Not scientific development, 214.
COMMUNITY AND LEGAL AID WORK, *see also* Citi-
zenship, Preventive Law.
Legal aid service to, 150, 210.
Prosecution of lawyers, 155.
Loan shark work, 210.
Benefited by legal aid and charities coöpera-
tion, 225.
COMPLAINTS AGAINST LAWYERS
Legal aid work in, 226.
Legal aid rule to reject, 153.
Criticism of, 154.
COMPROMISE OF CASES
Forced by delay, 17.
Forced by unfair law, 87.
CONCILIATION
Advantages, 65, 66.
Definition of, 60.
Nature and history, 60, 61.
Codes of ethics sanction, 60.
Court rules for, in New York, 55, 63.
Future of, 66, 67.

Small claims courts, 55.
Failure of legal aid to end, 194.
DENMARK
Conciliation courts in, 61.
Their success, 62.
Counsel for accused provided, 115.
DENVER LEGAL AID DISPENSARY, 143-145.
Started in 1904, 143.
Plan to use law students, 143.
DESERTION CASES
Failure of legal aid to handle, 170.
Special organization in New York for, 145.
DETROIT DOMESTIC RELATIONS COURT
Wide jurisdiction of, 75.
Conciliation employed, 81.
Held unconstitutional, 75.
DETROIT LEGAL AID BUREAU, 144, 160, 166, 174,
191, 236, 239.
Started by bar in 1909, 144.
Disposition of cases, 160.
Donations by clients to, 166.
Extent of work, 191.
Bar's failure to extend, 174.
DIFFICULTIES IN ADMINISTRATION OF JUSTICE, see
Administration of Justice, Court Costs, De-
lays, Expense of Lawyers' Services.
DISBARMENT PROCEEDINGS, cost of, borne by
state, 28.
DISPOSITION OF CASES, see Legal Aid Work : Dis-
position of cases.
DISSATISFACTION WITH LAW
Causes of, 15.
Led to administrative tribunals, 83.
DISTRICT ATTORNEY
Defender and, 121.
Duties in criminal cases, 108-110.
Powerful position of, 113.
Partiality, 110.
Shyster lawyer and, 114.
DISTRICT OF COLUMBIA MUNICIPAL COURT, econ-
omy of, 26.
DIVORCE CASES, see also Domestic Relations.
Assignment of counsel in, 102.
Conciliation in, 64.
Costs, 23.
Legal aid rule to reject, 155.
DIVORCE PROCTORS, in England and United
States, 102.
DOMESTIC RELATIONS, CASES OF
Many among the poor, 73.
Important in legal aid work, 135, 152.
Abuses in, investigated, 162.
Conciliation in, 64.
State control of, in Los Angeles, 181.
DOMESTIC RELATIONS COURTS
Conciliation used in, 64, 80.
Criminal process used, 75.
Future extension of, 81.

General work of, 80.
Needs of
Wider jurisdiction, 74.
Unification, 74.
Lawyers' services, 79.
Success of
In general, 77, 242.
Effect on delay and costs, 76, 77.
Effect on expense of lawyers, 78.
Use of probation staffs, 78.
DOMESTIC RELATIONS LAW
Civil and criminal remedies contrasted, 76.
Growth of criminal remedies, 74, 75.
Inadequacy of civil remedies, 75.
Contempt proceedings, 77, 79.
Interest of state in, 73.
Difficult field for law, 73.
DULUTH FREE LEGAL AID BUREAU, 28, 101, 145,
148, 176, 185, 190.
Started in 1913, 145.
Work taken over by city, 148.
Extent of work, 190.
Pays costs for clients, 28.

EDISON ELECTRIC ILLUMINATING COMPANY OF
BOSTON, plans legal aid for employees, 173.
EDUCATION, LEGAL
Legal aid organizations and, 226.
Clinical training, 165, 235.
Clinical work in Denver, 143.
Legal aid work done by law students, 145,
148.
Significance of, 174.
Plan in France, 248.
EJECTMENT PROCEEDINGS, see also Landlord and
Tenant Law.
Use of fictitious leases, 14.
EMBREE, WILLIAM DEAN, report of, quoted, 121.
EMPLOYEES, see Interstate Commerce Em-
ployees, Wage-Earners, Workmen's Compen-
sation Acts, Workmen, Injured.
EMPLOYERS
Legal aid furnished by, 171, 172, 236.
On legal aid directorate, 245.   [89,
Reports to industrial accident commissions,
Unscrupulous, aided by inadequate adminis-
tration of justice, 9.
ENDOWMENTS, legal aid organizations lack, 195.
ENGLAND, fraudulent legal aid societies in, 199.
ENGLISH COUNTY COURTS
Provision for small cases, 42.
Act as court trustee, 58.
Control over ejectment, 59.
Use of instalment judgments, 57.
ENGLISH LAW
Arbitration developed, 68.
Assignment of counsel, 102, 231.
Rules for, 232.

* new material added

PATTERSON SMITH REPRINT SERIES IN
CRIMINOLOGY, LAW ENFORCEMENT, AND SOCIAL PROBLEMS

* new material added   † new edition, revised or enlarged

PATTERSON SMITH REPRINT SERIES IN
CRIMINOLOGY, LAW ENFORCEMENT, AND SOCIAL PROBLEMS

* new material added   † new edition, revised or enlarged